Models in the Policy Process

MODELS IN THE POLICY PROCESS

Public Decision Making in the Computer Era

MARTIN GREENBERGER
MATTHEW A. CRENSON
BRIAN L. CRISSEY

Russell Sage Foundation   New York

PUBLICATIONS OF RUSSELL SAGE FOUNDATION

Russell Sage Foundation was established in 1907 by Mrs. Russell Sage for the improvement of social and living conditions in the United States. In carrying out its purpose the Foundation conducts research under the direction of members of the staff or in close collaboration with other institutions, and supports programs designed to develop and demonstrate productive working relations between social scientists and other professional groups. As an integral part of its operation, the Foundation from time to time publishes books or pamphlets resulting from these activities. Publication under the imprint of the Foundation does not necessarily imply agreement by the Foundation, its Trustees, or its staff with the interpretations or conclusions of the authors.

Russell Sage Foundation
230 Park Avenue, New York, N.Y. 10017

© 1976 by Russell Sage Foundation. All rights reserved. Printed in the United States of America. No part of this publication may be reproduced, stored in a retrieval system, or transmitted, in any form or by any means, electronic, mechanical, photocopying, recording or otherwise, without the prior written permission of the publisher.

Library of Congress Catalog Card Number: 76-1815
Standard Book Number: 87154-369-6

Dedicated to

David and Kari,
Ethan and Matthew,
and Robin—

Children who will come of age in a world shaped by today's policy decisions.

Contents

Preface   xiii
Acknowledgments   xix

1: MODELING IN THE PUBLIC EYE   1

Model of the World, 1
Debut, 1
Backstage, 3
Response, 6

Modeling the National Economy, 7
Forecasts of GNP, 8
Political Factors, 9
A Simple Calculation, 10
Hearings, 12
The LR Model, 14

Lessons, 19

2: MODELING AS A FORM OF POLICY RESEARCH   23

Appearances, 23
When Is a Model Used? 24
Disappointments, 26

Decision Making and the Domain of Knowledge, 27
Forms of Policy Research, 28
Some Historical Antecedents, 31
The PPBS Movement, 32
PPBS Inside and Outside the Pentagon, 33
Social Experimentation, 37
Incremental Decision Making, 39
Big Decisions, 40

The Political Context, 42
Attracting Public Notice, 43
Effect on Models and their Usability, 44
Political Uses of Models, 45

3: MODELING IN CROSS SECTION — 47

The Model—What Is It? 47
Schematic Models, 49
Physical Models, 51
Symbolic Models, 51
Role-Playing Models, 59
Purposes of Models, 59
Uses of Models, 62

The Modeling Process: Theory, Data, and Methodology, 63
Theory, 64
Data and Validation, 70
Methodology, 74

The Modeler: Horse, Cart, or Driver? 76
The Role of the Modeler, 76
Jan Leendertse and the Jamaica Bay Simulation, 79

4: METHODOLOGIES FOR POLICY MODELING — 85

Nine Methodologies, 85
Input-Output Analysis, 87
Linear Programming, 93
Two-Person Zero-Sum Games, 96
Probabilistic Methods of Operations Research, 98
Algebraic Methods of Operations Research, 102
Econometric Modeling, 104
Microanalysis, 107
Land-Use Analysis, 115
System Dynamics, 120
Recapitulation, 127

A Housing Example, 127
A Microanalytic Model of Housing, 128
A System Dynamics Model of Housing, 132
An Econometric Model of Housing, 136

5: SYSTEM DYNAMICS—A CONTROVERSIAL NEWCOMER — 141

Legacy of Controversy, 141

Urban Dynamics, 146
Conclusions of the Urban Dynamics Model, 146

Response to Urban Dynamics, 146
Applications of Urban Dynamics, 153
Nature of the Responses, 157

The World Models, 158
Simulation of World2, 159
Simulation of World3, 160
Response to World2, 161
The Limits to Growth, 164
Classifying the Responses, 166
Counter Modeling of the World Models, 170
Another Club of Rome Project, 177

A View of the Bridge, 179

6: ECONOMETRIC MODELING—A FAMILIAR OLDTIMER 183

Development and Recent Progress, 183
Role of the Computer, 184
The Nature of the Method, 186

Models of the American Economy, 195
Early Models and Genealogy, 195
The Klein Line, 201
SSRC-Brookings Model, 207
Federal Reserve Modeling, 210
Commercial Models and Auxiliary Services, 216
Two Small Models, 224
Recapitulation, 228

7: AN INSTITUTE FOR POLICY MODELING: THE NEW YORK CITY-RAND INSTITUTE 231

Mediating Institutions, 231
The Need for More Institutional Bridges, 232
Forging Appropriate Connecting Links, 234

The Rand Institute, 235
The Stated Plans and Objectives, 236
Unstated Objectives, 238
The Beginning, 240
The Problem of Constituencies, 242
The New Mayor and the Demise of the Institute, 246

8: PUTTING OUT FIRES IN THE FIRE DEPARTMENT 249

Client Meets Consultant, 249
The Department and Its Difficulties, 249
Rand's Fire Project, 252
Animosities and Alliances, 253

A Preliminary Use of Models, 257
Redefining the Problem, 257
Models and Intuitions, 259
The Findings and the Fire Dispatchers, 261

Modeling in a Labor Dispute: Rand's "Supreme Achievement," 263
The Unions on the Offensive, 263
The Department Calls on Rand, 265
Rand's Simulation Model, 267
Testing Proposed Policies, 270
The Unions, the Negotiations, and the Settlement, 274

The Aftermath and Some Conclusions, 276
The Impact of Rand's Research, 276
The Impact of the Research Setting, 280

9: HEALTH, HOSPITALS, AND HOSTILITIES 287

Conflicting Perspectives, 287
Rand and the Health Services Administration, 287
Rand and the Health and Hospitals Corporation, 288

Prelude to Disappointment: 1968–1970, 289
Instability in Rand's Research Staff, 289
Poorly Defined Research Tasks, 290
Health Research and Administrative Hostilities, 291
Obstacles to Comprehensiveness in Research, 293

Administrative Changes and a New Beginning, 294
Organizational Renovation in HSA, 294
Organizational Turmoil in the Hospitals Department, 296

The Rand Hospital Bed Utilizaton Model: 1970–1972, 297
The Political Setting, 297
An Inauspicious Beginning, 299
Conducting the Study, 301
Problems of Implementation, 304

Aftermath and Implications, 308
　Organizational Differences, 309
　Research Problems, 312
　Differentiated Roles, 314
　Mediating Institutions, 316

10: MODELING AND THE POLITICAL PROCESS　　　319

Nature of the Problem, 320
　Some Simplistic Answers, 321
　The Policymaker—An Unknowing Culprit, 322
　Responsibilities of the Policymaker, 324
　Institutionalizing the Modeling Process, 326

Apposition or Opposition, 328
　Politics in Modeling, 329
　The Tension Between Modeling and Politics, 330
　Explicitness and Conflict, 332
　Modeling in Debate, 333
　Entrée of the Expert, 335

Concluding Remarks, 337

Index　　　343

Preface

As this book was being written, the United States was reeling from the worst postwar recession coupled with the most serious inflationary spiral in modern history. Prices had soared while production sagged. Tens of thousands of people lost their jobs weekly. Energy was said to be the nation's major problem. One year the lines in front of gasoline stations seemed interminable. The next year unemployment lines were even longer. The country wanted to curb inflation, but corrective measures threatened to aggravate recession, and steps to treat recession threatened to worsen inflation. To stimulate the economy and reduce unemployment, the government risked pushing prices even higher.

On the energy front, price-regulated natural gas was in short supply and the nation became more and more dependent upon an unreliable part of the world for an increasing amount of its petroleum imports. The country, understandably, wanted to expand its domestic sources of energy. But its efforts to do so through an accelerated program of strip mining and offshore drilling were met with alarmed resistance by environmentalists. Anxiety about increased exploitation of nuclear energy ran even deeper.

The poor and the elderly were most concerned about the price of food and housing. But the price of food was directly affected by the cost of energy through agriculture's need for fertilizers, pesticides, irrigation, and diesel fuel. And the price of housing was influenced by high-interest rates, high costs of construction, and a depressed housing industry—all symptoms of the ailing economy.

Victims of a dysfunctional economy—many quite helpless—include people from all segments of society. They cry out for the government to do something. But government action for the sake of government action is no help. Government can (and does) make matters worse rather than better if it takes steps without understanding, or acts more from political than from therapeutic motives. Too often, efforts to partition the overall problem into separate parts so as to isolate the sources of difficulty and identify the so-called culprits serve more as grand displays of political demagoguery than sincere attempts at elucidation.

The United States economy is complex and interdependent with other economies of the world. The social and economic problems affecting our economy are strongly interlocked and are themselves increasingly complex and interdependent. To cope with these problems, one needs to comprehend enough of the socioeconomic systems from which they originate to be able to distinguish and represent the important modes of behavior that are characteristic of these systems. In order to make diagnoses and examine the implications of alternative actions, one needs a way of thinking about and portraying the systems that give rise to the problems.

To the reasonable person, it might seem that large, intricately interwoven problems would call for methods of attack that go beyond the ordinary and everyday. It might seem that government officials should be looking to science and mathematics, for example, for formal tools useful in analyzing available information and in understanding socioeconomic systems well enough to obtain guidance for decision making. In addition, conditioned as we are to appealing to technology for help, it might seem that the computer, the machine that thoroughly captures the hopes and imaginations of many of us (when we are not busy cursing it), could also lend policymakers a hand.

So we are led to look at computer models of socioeconomic systems—mathematical formulations of system interactions put in a form in which they can be probed and projected by machine in a process called "policy modeling." We ask, where does policy modeling stand? How is it being used in government decision making? Is it providing the needed guidance? When it is not, why not? What is its future? How can it be made more useful for policy purposes?

To address these questions, we investigated a multitude of different types of models being applied or developed in a wide variety of policy areas. We examined models of municipal operations, models of the national economy, and models of the world. We studied nine different styles of modeling used in creating these models that seemed to us particularly suitable for policy application. Practitioners of two of the most widely used (or quoted) of these methodologies are in sharp philosophical disagreement with one another. We studied these two modeling methodologies with special care, and with an eye to their complementarities and similarities as well as their differences. Trying hard to be neutral and objective ourselves, we weighed the points at issue and searched for ways in which the cause of policy modeling might be better served through greater mutual understanding and a rapprochement between the contesting parties.

Early in our project we reached the conclusion that the scope of our subject extends well beyond models and modeling methodologies. As we examined numerous case studies of the use of models in the policy process, we became more and more aware of just how critical the political setting is for policy modeling. Taking an historical perspective, we reviewed the contours of the political terrain that has influenced the conduct of policy research over the years. We view policy modeling as one of the latest forms of policy research.

The political context in which policy modeling is conducted makes it a strikingly different activity from the traditional modeling fundamental to scientific research.

A second early conclusion, closely related to the first, was that the organizational framework in which policy models are developed and applied is also of key importance. We looked for institutional arrangements that might facilitate and improve the use of policy models. The fairly new Rand Institute appeared intriguing. We studied its founding and activities (up until the time of its demise in 1975) in some detail. The equally new econometric modeling firms illustrate a different organizational approach to filling another kind of policy need. These companies are prospering, and we studied their operations as well.

We came out of our study with some strong impressions. On the development side, we find that those involved in modeling are for the most part building or working with their own models and paying relatively little attention to the models developed by others. On the applications side, we find that the modeler and especially the spokesmen for the model are often far more important than the model itself in determining how and whether the model gets used. We find that there is often a considerable gulf between the policymaker and the policy modeler, a reflection, we believe, of the different constraints under which the respective parties work and the dissimilar value systems to which they respond. We find that modelers, especially those who are at a distance from the actual workings of the policy process, tend to overestimate the real relevance and usefulness of models for practical decision making.

This is not to say that models have not been making any impact on policy. We find that policymakers commit a mistake opposite of that committed by policy modelers. They tend to underestimate the influence of models on their thinking and ideas. There is convincing evidence that the background effects of policy models have been significant and are growing. These indirect effects are exerted through the support that models lend to arguments in policy papers and expert testimony, and in the impact that models have on policy studies and public editorials—to say nothing of their routine use in forecasting services and agency operations.

We find that policy modeling is becoming more widespread and more patently political in character. It has been catching the public's eye more often and making the politician take greater notice than in times past. This trend has both salutary and troubling aspects; at the very least, it means that complacency about models is no longer tolerable. The citizenry can no longer be satisfied with leaving modeling to the experts. The experts, for their part, must now look at models under a more intense and critical light. They cannot afford to duck such tough questions as what makes models behave the way they do, and which properties of the models are important and true to the facts—and which are not.

Chapter 1 is an overture to the book, introducing a number of central themes about policy modeling: its political significance, its breadth of application, its tendency to be misused or misinterpreted, the different ways it is practiced, and the means by which it is introduced into the political process. We develop these themes more fully in subsequent chapters. They make their appearance in Chapter 1 in brief sketches of two very different models of the world and nation that have attracted much public attention.

Chapter 2 moves the discussion from the outward appearance of policy modeling to the internal reasons for its use and the political realities and constraints affecting its policy application. We view modeling in relation to the development of policy research in general, as one of several approaches to the design and testing of public programs and policy decisions.

Chapter 3 focuses on the characteristics of models themselves, examining the forms they take, their general nature, and their technical aspects. We define some basic terms and give consideration to the important roles played by theory, data, and methodology in determining both the structure and substance of models. We illustrate the critical importance of the modeler with a case study in hydrology.

Chapter 4 provides a survey of some of the specific methodologies with which models have been created for use in the policy process, including brief historical sketches of the development of these methodologies and some illustrations of their use. Chapter 5 looks at one of the newest and most controversial of these methodologies, system dynamics, and reviews at length its application to the modeling of cities and the world. Chapter 6 examines one of the older and more traditional methodologies, econometric modeling, and presents a genealogy of some of the major econometric models of the American economy. We discuss trends that are significantly affecting the way econometric models are used, as in the rise of the econometric modeling services. Thus, we begin our treatment of possible ways for more effectively linking the modeling process with the political process.

Chapters 7 through 9 consider in detail one particular institutional mechanism that had sought to place modeling within closer reach of public policymakers. We examine some of the policy modeling efforts of the late New York City-Rand Institute in order to identify the difficulties and opportunities facing an innovative organization that attempts to bring modeling directly to bear on the problems of government.

Chapter 10, the final chapter, offers a summary of earlier points and some suggestions for how policy models can be made more useful in decision making. We base our conclusions on the case studies and on our assessment of the responsibilities and performance not only of policy modelers, but of policymakers as well. We believe the tension that exists between policy modeling and policymaking can be a constructive force in the political process, but only if significant changes take place in attitudes, roles, and institutional arrangements. We indicate what some of these changes might be.

Acknowledgments

This study was undertaken as an outgrowth of an informal, broad-ranging discussion that was held in New York City during the summer of 1971. Orville G. Brim, Jr. of Russell Sage Foundation, Henry Chauncey of Educom, and Martin Greenberger of the Johns Hopkins University, had come together to talk about certain projects on which they were working, and to discuss areas of common interest. One result of the meeting was the realization that Greenberger and Hugh F. Cline of Russell Sage Foundation were both interested in exploring the ramifications, significance, and probable future impact of computers in the social sciences. Possibilities were explored for Greenberger's initiating an Educom project within this general subject area under the Foundation's sponsorship.

Over a series of subsequent letters and meetings, Greenberger, Cline, and Chauncey drew up the outlines of a study of the computer modeling of socioeconomic systems for policy purposes. It was agreed that Greenberger, an applied mathematician and computer scientist interested in economics and decision making, should pair with someone schooled in the methods of social science research. The search led to Matthew A. Crenson, a political scientist who had research interests in American government, sociology, and municipal politics. Also invited to join the study team was Greenberger's Ph.D. student Brian L. Crissey, who was doing dissertation research on simulation models.

The Russell Sage Foundation-Educom study ran for more than three years, despite the fact that it was budgeted as a one-year study. Often, a seemingly small question would lead to two larger ones, and thus expand the scope of research. We, the authors, thank members of Russel Sage Foundation and Educom for their patience in accepting repeated delays. We also thank the Center for Metropolitan Planning and Research at Johns Hopkins, where the study was conducted, for many services in aiding the project along its way. Jay Rockstroh and Dolores Sullivan of the Center staff were very helpful. Our greatest debt is to Joy Hall, our secretary at the Center, for the tireless and efficient assistance she rendered in her remarkably quiet and unassuming way.

Several hundred persons were interviewed in person and by telephone during the course of the study, some many times. We thank them all for the valuable information they provided and for their toleration of our inquisitive, often uninformed, and sometimes ungraceful questions. Also, without inflicting upon them any responsibility for the outcome, we express appreciation to our advisers on the study, Alfred D. Chandler, Jr., James S. Coleman, and Arthur M. Okun; to the project monitors, Hugh F. Cline and Arnold Shore; and to the many others who read parts or all of our preliminary drafts of the manuscript. We are indebted to them for their wise counsel and criticism, and for the generous way they offered it.

This has been a collaboration in the fullest sense of the word. We brought together our ideas and different points of view, helped each other, and learned from one another. The collaboration and the learning are what made the study rewarding and enjoyable for us. In writing this book, we hope to have conveyed to the reader some measure of the knowledge and understanding we have ourselves gained during the course of the study.

Martin Greenberger
Matthew A. Crenson
Brian L. Crissey

Baltimore, Maryland
August 1976

Models in the Policy Process

1

Modeling in the Public Eye

At the request of an international body of concerned persons seeking to make an imprint on public thinking and influence the leadership of nations, a computer model of the world is developed by a university group with a ready-made modeling methodology (system dynamics). The model succeeds in attracting widespread notice and stimulates deep and continuing controversy in the process.

A second model, a model of the United States economy arising from a sharply different modeling tradition (econometric modeling) becomes the center of attention in a political skirmish between Congress and the Nixon administration.

In this chapter we will discuss what these two dissimilar examples have in common, what they demonstrate about the ability of models to gain the public spotlight, and what they suggest about the difficulties that modeling has in meshing gears with the political process.

MODEL OF THE WORLD

Debut

There was standing room only in the imposing Great Hall of the stately Smithsonian Institution in Washington, D.C., on the morning of Thursday, March 2, 1972. Several hundred prominent members of the government, business, and academic communities, the military establishment, and the diplomatic corps gathered to hear some bright young people from M.I.T. report on their eighteen-month modeling study of the future of mankind.

The widespread interest that preceded, attended, and followed this event is uncommon in the world of project reports and scholarly presentations. One reason for the public attention was a popularly written paperback on the study made available ahead of time by an enterprising policy research and publishing organization.[1] The paperback, released simultaneously in a clothbound

---
[1] The publisher was Potomac Associates, an organization headed by William Watts that was on the White House's "enemies list." (Potomac was targeted for a break-in by the Watergate conspirators.) Before founding his new public interest policy research

edition, drew strong and unsettling conclusions on the calamity that mankind's lust for growth was inviting. It forecast societal collapse unless nations could bring themselves to curtail population and economic growth in the near future. The thesis struck a responsive chord in a world keyed up about environmental abuse. Coming four months before the Russian wheat deal and twenty months before the Mideast oil embargo, the prophecies foreshadowed the impending swells of concern about international shortages of food and energy.

The book, controversial from the first, was *The Limits to Growth*.[2] Its sales worldwide in its first two years ran into the millions of copies, over 350,000 in the Netherlands alone, where Queen Juliana presided over its public presentation, attended by cabinet members and prominent intellectuals. In Japan it became one of the best selling publications in the country. The authors of the book included Dennis Meadows, 29-year-old leader of the research team, and his wife Donella Meadows, whose talent for clear exposition is credited for the polemical volume's simple and lucid prose.

Publicity was energetic. With the Smithsonian meeting set for March 2 and publication scheduled for March 6, the publisher sent out a generous supply of press releases in February 1972. A flood of phone calls by notables wanting to come to the invitational meeting left the sponsors agape and short of seating space.[3] The privilege of standing in the rear of Smithsonian's Great Hall was gratefully accepted by many who usually make a practice of respectfully declining invitations to academic events. Elliot Richardson, Nixon's secretary of health, education and welfare at the time, gave the keynote address, calling the study too thoughtful, thorough, and significant to ignore.[4] Secretary of Commerce Peter G. Peterson, who later became chairman of Lehman Brothers, said he stayed up "well into the night" reading the book. Edward David, Nixon's science adviser, was asked to report to the president on the study, and discussion of it was placed on the agenda of the President's illustrious Science Advisory Committee.

The Malthusian conclusions cannot by themselves explain the extraordinary

---

enterprise, Watts was staff secretary of the National Security Council under Henry Kissinger. He hired the firm of Calvin Kytle Associates to handle public relations for the M.I.T. study and, together with its sponsors, distributed 10,000 complimentary copies of the book after its public release to chiefs of state, heads of government, American ambassadors, and top planning officers in every country of the world.

[2] Donella H. Meadows et al., *The Limits to Growth* (New York: Universe Books, 1972).

[3] The Smithsonian meeting had no less than four sponsors: the Smithsonian Institution, the Woodrow Wilson International Center for Scholars (whose offices are at the Smithsonian), Potomac Associates, and the Club of Rome. Head of the Woodrow Wilson Center at the time was Benjamin Read, who first saw the *Limits to Growth* study in his capacity as an informal reader for Potomac Associates. Watts says that he and Read conceived the idea for the Smithsonian symposium. The Xerox Corporation provided financial support. Smithsonian recorded the meeting and transcribed the proceedings.

[4] Elliot Richardson was a member of the board of the Woodrow Wilson Center.

Modeling in the Public Eye

interest evoked by the book. This was, after all, not the first study with an awaken-or-be-doomed message. As Rudolf Klein observed, no originality can be claimed for any of the predictions in *The Limits to Growth*, but only for its manner of justifying them. What makes the study distinctive, according to Klein, is its claims to have found a "scientific basis for its social prophecies."[5] The "scientific basis" was a computer model, a formal representation on a computer of selected aspects of the real world in a manner that allows future scenarios to be run and alternative policies examined. The model was developed under the auspices of the prestigious Club of Rome.

Backstage

The Club of Rome is a loosely knit international organization of businessmen, scientists, humanists, civil servants, and educators acting as private citizens. The members are alarmed at what they consider to be mankind's self-destructive tendencies. They call the subject of their concern the "world problematique" or the "predicament of mankind." Newscaster Howard K. Smith somewhat disdainfully described the club, in a critical television evening news editorial on the *Limits to Growth* study, as a "well-heeled group of intellectuals." By that description, one of the best-heeled members of the club would have to be its impressively able and dynamic leader, Italian businessman Aurelio Peccei, described by his admirers as a thoughtful, perceptive, sincere, thoroughly dedicated human being.

Peccei wanted a means for dramatizing the world problematique that would induce nations into a broad rethinking of goals. "For two years club members had plodded quietly from Moscow to Rio, from Stockholm to Washington, seeking out political leaders and apprising them of the dangers ahead." Says Peccei, "Our message was received with sympathy and understanding, but no action followed. What we needed was a stronger tool of communication to move men on the planet out of their ingrained habits. This is the reason for the M.I.T. study and the book."[6]

The Club of Rome commissioned the study with funds contributed by the Volkswagen Foundation (Stiftung Volkswagenwerk) in Germany. The fact that the study would center around a computer model came as no surprise. Indeed, although not part of the initial plans for the study, that turned out to be what the Club of Rome requested. The request was made to Jay W. Forrester, professor of management at M.I.T.

Forrester had attended a Club of Rome meeting in Bern, Switzerland, on June 29, 1970. On the agenda was discussion of a study plan for a project

---

[5] Rudolf Klein in "Growth and Its Enemies," *Commentary*, June 1972, p. 39.
[6] *Science* 175 (1972): 1088. For an indication of the thinking of the Club of Rome officials prior to their contacts with M.I.T., see Aurelio Peccei, *The Chasm Ahead* (London: Macmillan, 1969).

on the predicament of mankind. Forrester is the originator of a particular methodology for computer modeling called "system dynamics." He developed the methodology in the middle 1950s in an effort to use computers and the methods of science and engineering to explain the behavior of companies and help managers better understand their problems.[7] More recently, in the late 1960s, he had applied his methodology to the analysis of the problems of the city in a widely cited and very controversial book that faulted city fathers for building low-cost housing when they should have been tearing it down.[8] The book alleges that municipal officials have tended, in general, to adopt measures that make matters worse rather than better.

Forrester's criticism of public officials does not take the form of contempt. On the contrary, he claims empathy for their problems based on his own extensive management background.[9] He reserves his disapproval for some of his academic colleagues in social science (they reciprocate in kind) whom he considers to have their heads in the sand about the real behavior of the socioeconomic systems they are purportedly studying. Forrester considers social systems too complex for the unaided human mind. He attributes "counterintuitive behavior" to these systems, behavior that the models of system dynamics can help one to understand.

As he flew to the meeting in Bern, Forrester read the document that had been distributed in advance. It defined the preliminary goals for the planned project, surveyed the methodologies that might be used, and presented a statement of the "problematique." As Forrester saw it, the objective of the project was

> ... to understand the options available to mankind as societies enter the transition from growth to equilibrium. Man throughout history has focused on growth —growth in population, standard of living, and geographical boundaries. But in the fixed space of the world, growth must in time give way to equilibrium.

---

[7] Forrester's first published volume setting forth his goals, methods, and some company models was *Industrial Dynamics* (Cambridge: The M.I.T. Press, 1961). Industrial Dynamics, now called "system dynamics" in its more general application, was developed by Forrester beginning in the mid-1950s when he was invited to join the faculty of the newly formed Alfred P. Sloan School of Management (then called the M.I.T. School of Industrial Management). Forrester was looking for something M.I.T. might do in the field of industrial management that would give it M.I.T.'s own distinctive stamp.

[8] *Urban Dynamics* (Cambridge: The M.I.T. Press, 1969).

[9] Forrester's present work with system dynamics is his fifth career, having come after: cattle ranching (his family's business in Nebraska); servomechanisms (he was second in command at the M.I.T. Servomechanism Laboratory at M.I.T. in the early 1940s); computers (he was head of the M.I.T. Digital Computer Laboratory that built the Whirlwind Computer and he holds the basic patents on magnetic cores, the primary storage device of computers); military systems (he was head of the division at M.I.T.'s Lincoln Laboratory that had responsibility for development of the SAGE system for continental air defense). Forrester had become accustomed to dealing with officers of major corporations as a young research assistant at M.I.T. in the 1940s.

Little is known about the social and economic forces that will accompany entry into world equilibrium.[10]

While Forrester supported the goals as he read the plans for the project, he felt that they suffered from the lack of a means with which to interrelate the separate component processes of the world problematique. But he did not wish to be critical or outspoken at the meeting. He resolved to himself to listen politely and learn. He must have had more than an inkling of how difficult it was going to be to keep that resolution.

By 6 P.M. of the first day's discussion, according to Forrester, the meeting bogged down with a general sense of the need for a unifying methodology. Forrester spoke up. He talked about system dynamics and expressed his belief that it would suit the club's purpose well. He invited the club members to visit with his group at M.I.T. for ten days to experience the use of his methodology firsthand. Not everyone present knew what system dynamics was. To explain his approach, Forrester briefed the club in an impromptu seminar scheduled for after dinner. The seminar started at 10 P.M. and ran to midnight. The upshot was an agreement by the club to accept Forrester's invitation and come to M.I.T. on July 20, just three weeks away.[11]

With little time for preparation, Forrester got busy making arrangements. He placed some calls to M.I.T. from Bern to get things started. On the plane home he worked diligently to create a model of the world which he could use to demonstrate the system dynamics methodology to his visitors. He felt it was crucial to have a fresh example that would relate the methodology directly to the club's concern. By the time his flight arrived in Boston, the model was formulated. Forrester ran, revised, and refined it on two successive Saturdays, working at home from his teletypewriter terminal to the time-shared computer at M.I.T. The model was essentially the product of a few days of intensive effort, says Forrester, with all of the key runs made by the time of the club's visit. Forrester published the model, including the results of these runs, in his book *World Dynamics*.[12] Although presented in a tentative way, the results underscored the views of the Club of Rome. The model showed unrestrained

---

[10] Jay W. Forrester, *World Dynamics* (Cambridge, Mass.: Wright-Allen Press, 1971), p. viii.

[11] Eduard Pestel is a member of the Club of Rome and president of the Technische Universität, Hannover, Germany. Pestel had been intending to come to study urban dynamics with Forrester. His support may have been decisive. Forrester holds Pestel in high regard and considers him to be one of the most competent people he has ever met. Pestel was director of the Volkswagen Foundation, the source of the support for the *Limits to Growth* project.

[12] Forrester, *World Dynamics*. Forrester credits the time-sharing system at M.I.T., to which he had access from his home terminal, with making it possible for him to get so much done in such a short period of time. He is proud of the accomplishment, and understandably so, although critics may view the brevity of the effort in a different light.

growth leading to an almost unavoidable deterioration of life unless steps were taken to reorient national and international goals toward world equilibrium.

Peccei and his associates saw in Forrester's world model the potential for the stronger tool of communication they sought. On the basis of the M.I.T. meeting, they asked Forrester to take over the Volkswagen-sponsored project, originally slated to be based in Geneva. They wanted an in-depth study of the world model that would examine its assumptions, rethink its components, and determine whether its predicted effects were real. But Forrester was committed to another undertaking at the time.[13] He invited his young colleague and former Ph.D. student Dennis Meadows to assume responsibility for the project.[14]

Meadows had just come back from a year abroad with his wife, Donella, who holds a Ph.D. degree in biophysics. The two Meadowses had traveled from London to Ceylon where, according to Donella, they saw and shared a life of low consumption, painstaking frugality, and great cultural and social richness. The dismay they felt at the contrast with the American lifestyle upon their return, combined with the devastation of ecological systems apparent to them in all parts of the world, put them to thinking about how they might join forces to work toward bettering the human condition. The Club of Rome's project seemed like just such an opportunity. Dennis Meadows accepted leadership of the project, and it was moved to Cambridge, Massachusetts, with husband and wife both on the team.

Response

A former government official who finds Forrester arrogant and abrasive calls Dennis Meadows a sincere and unassuming human being. But Meadows is not timorous. He openly acknowledges that he disagrees with important aspects of Forrester's work. Meadows organized the Club of Rome project, hired the research team, and did little to involve Forrester in the conduct of the study. Yet the team's methodology was unabashedly system dynamics, and its findings, when ready, closely paralleled those of *World Dynamics*.

One chapter of *World Dynamics* (Chapter 4) is entitled "Limits to Growth." The Meadows' project was an elaboration and refinement of the simulation runs outlined in that chapter, so it is not surprising to find that the project's

---

[13] Forrester had a grant from the Independence Foundation to extend the work he had been doing in urban dynamics.

[14] Meadows' doctoral dissertation was an application of system dynamics to explain the persistent, regular production cycles in several key commodities. Dennis Meadows, *Dynamics of Commodity Production Cycles* (Cambridge, Mass.: Wright-Allen Press, 1970).

first report (originally intended as a position statement for internal distribution to the Club of Rome) carries the same title.[15] With *World Dynamics* having been distributed nine months before the time of the Smithsonian meeting, Forrester did not expect *The Limits to Growth* to receive much press response. He thought the press would be tired of the issues already covered in the numerous articles on *World Dynamics* and that the Smithsonian meeting would receive little additional attention.

On the error of that assessment and the magnitude of the acclaim accorded the Meadows' book, we have said enough earlier. On the mounting debate that the study has occasioned in hundreds of critical reviews and meetings involving the top levels of government and some of this country's and others' most distinguished intellectuals, we shall have more to say later. Our purpose for the moment is not to get into the substance of the debate, but rather to comment on its nature and political meaning.

At the heart of the debate is a computer model known as the World3 model. It produces curves that are said to represent future levels of population, natural resources, pollution, and the like, subject to parameter settings designed to reflect governmental policies and actions. At the Smithsonian meeting the curves were displayed to the assemblage by means of large multicolored charts. They were blown-up printouts taken directly from the computer at M.I.T., and they made an impact on many in attendance.

Curves and numbers generated by a computer give the appearance of objectivity and authenticity, especially when presented by a soft-spoken young man who receives criticism graciously and quickly acknowledges the tentativeness and tenuousness of the results. The Club of Rome had a message to impart. The World3 model served its purpose admirably, at least for the short term. What its effect will be after the critical crescendo dies down, we cannot know for certain, but of this we can be sure: computer modeling has been shown to be a potentially powerful political instrument; it has arrived with force in the policy arena; and it warrants close scrutiny. The next example makes the point in another context.

MODELING THE NATIONAL ECONOMY

In January of each year since the late 1940s, the White House has produced an "Economic Report of the President" including a companion "Annual Report of the Council of Economic Advisers." This report is read with great interest by economists, businessmen, journalists, and other active observers

---

[15] The position paper was sent to Peccei in August 1971. Watts saw it at about the same time. Both men played major roles in bringing the piece to publication.

of the national economy. That it is largely political in nature is no secret.[16] In January 1971, on the eve of the much discussed Nixon reelection campaign of 1972, the report seemed to many even more political than usual.

Forecasts of GNP

Each year since 1962, a formal forecast of gross national product (GNP) for the coming year has been included in the President's Economic Report. At the beginning of 1971, the country was about to emerge from a recession, with GNP slated to cross over the one-trillion-dollar mark for the first time. It is not surprising that a great deal of attention would be paid to the GNP forecast that year.

Despite the special interest accorded it, the White House's forecast is only one among a multitude. Like the celebrity who arrives late to the party with much flourish, this forecast makes its entrance well after the arrival of forecasts produced by banks, companies, research groups, financial houses, economic forecasting firms, and government agencies. In producing its forecast, the White House would seem to have the advantage of being able to see the other forecasts first, and of having available to it performance information on the previous year's fourth quarter, information not yet compiled at the time the other forecasts are made.

So the scene was set in January 1971, when it came time for the White House to publish the 1971 official forecast. As noted by *Business Week* in its December 1970 issue the month before, the other forecasts had all "come up with about the same number... a gross national product of $1,046 billion."[17] The magazine observed that "such unanimity is, to put it mildly, unusual in the forecasting fraternity." Only five of the thirty forecasts recorded came in at higher than $1,050 billion. A figure of between $1,046 and $1,050 billion became known as the "standard" forecast.

Announcement in January of an official White House forecast of $1,065 billion stunned the nation's economists and economy watchers. The prior year's GNP had been $977 billion. Thus, the White House was predicting a gain in GNP of $88 billion or 9 percent, in contrast to the $69 billion or 7 percent increase foreseen by a majority of the country's leading economic soothsayers.

Reaction all through 1971 to the White House's forecasting effort ranged

---

[16] One observer, for example, calls the Economic Report of the President of necessity "schizophrenic" in that it attempts at one and the same time to be both a "professional economic report on the American economy... prepared by three leading professional economists" and an apology or promoter for the president's economic program. See Carl F. Christ, "The 1973 Report of the President's Council of Economic Advisers: A Review," *The American Economic Review* 63, no. 4 (1973): 515. See also, "Politics and the CEA," *Challenge*, May-June 1974, pp. 70–72.

[17] "Consensus for 1971," *Business Week*, December 12, 1970, p. 66.

Modeling in the Public Eye 9

from reserved skepticism to indignant denunciation. Paul Samuelson called it a farce.[18] Publication the following January in the *Survey of Current Business* of a preliminary GNP for 1971 of $1,046.8 billion did little to quiet the outcry. Just the month before, *Business Week,* in an annual postmortem, labeled the White House figure "about the worst professional forecast made last year,"[19] although later revisions of 1971 GNP demonstrated that the forecast was not as far off as it appeared. But the point is, at the time, the White House seemed to have flunked according to any objective, apolitical measure of forecasting performance one might devise. Almost every private forecaster could claim to have done better. So could economists in the Commerce Department, Treasury Department, Federal Reserve Board, and other government agencies.

Political Factors

The nation does not bring its least qualified economists to Washington, so attributing the White House's extravagantly bullish forecast to a lack of good judgment or to inexperience was not convincing. A political explanation seemed more plausible. Although the Nixon administration largely dismissed the charge at the time, the political advantages of projecting a smart recovery from the recession were clear. For one thing, it would permit accelerated fiscal spending without enlarging the prospective budgetary deficit. Thus, many suspected influence or pressure from above. Senator Proxmire, chairman of the Joint Economic Committee of the Congress, echoed the views of a number of his colleagues when he remarked that "it is obviously in the interests of the president, in the interests of his reelection, to have this kind of an estimate."[20]

In fact, the administration did acknowledge some political motive. It was well known that Nixon was working for a return to "full employment" by

---

[18] Samuelson said in testimony to the Joint Economic Committee of Congress "the economic welfare of our great nation is too serious a business for this comic opera operation of forecasting." "No Sale on the President's Bullish Forecast," *Business Week,* March 6, 1971, p. 70.

[19] "Second Guesses on '71 Forecasts," *Business Week,* December 11, 1971, p. 74. *Business Week's* estimate of actual 1971 GNP at the time of its article was $1,052 billion. The preliminary GNP figure of $1,046.8 billion was revised in July 1972 to $1,050.4 billion and further revised in July 1973 to $1,055.5 billion, about midway between the standard forecast and the White House figure, with half of the 8 percent gain attributable to inflation. The final estimate of 1971 GNP of just under $1,055 billion came out in July 1974. Defenders of the White House forecast point to the latest estimate as partial vindication, although they concede they were "off the mark" and "turned too early in an expansionist direction." Bruce Winters quoting Herbert Stein in "Stein forecasts economic gains," *Baltimore Sun* (morning), July 20, 1974, p. A12.

[20] Hearings before the Joint Economic Committee, 92nd Congress, 1st sess., P. 1, February 1971, p. 11 (hereafter cited as Hearings).

mid-1972, a goal that traditionally is viewed as a level of about 4 percent unemployment. At the end of 1970, unemployment stood at 6.2 percent, having risen steadily during the year from a beginning level of 3.9 percent, an increase of almost two million people on the unemployment rolls since January 1970. Nixon was anxious not to carry that economic burden into the 1972 election campaign.

According to Harvard professor of economics Hendrik Houthakker, at the time a member of the Council of Economic Advisers, the council saw the full-employment goal as "its duty under the Employment Act of 1946,"—the act that set up the council to maintain a high level of employment in the economy. Houthakker and his colleagues on the council felt that an activist approach was "needed to bring the economy closer to its potential." More precisely, this meant that the council should see to it that the economy did outperform the "standard" forecast in 1971. The council believed that "acquiescence in the standard forecast would probably not be consistent with any reduction of unemployment."[21] Houthakker's own calculations reassured him that $1,065 billion was not implausible.

Herbert Stein, another member of the council at the time and later its chairman, argued that the government could not afford to "look at the future of the economy as an exercise in forecasting. For the government, the future is something to be determined or at least influenced by policy, not something to be forecast passively. The government's intentions are a critical element in any forecast of the future of the economy."[22]

Stein contends that the White House's estimate was not comparable in nature to the other forecasts. It was not an expression of what the economy *would* do, but rather of what it *had* to do for the administration to realize its goal of full employment—and what it *could* do given suitable government policy. Stein saw $1,065 billion as lying on a two-year optimum feasible path that a task force he led had constructed for Nixon in July 1970. His task force's initial projection for a GNP on this path was $1,075 billion, but that figure was dismissed as unreasonable and was revised downward in the light of the experience in the second half of 1970, which included a ten-week strike against General Motors. Stein considered the $1,065 billion figure more a target than a forecast—a target he regarded as achievable.

A Simple Calculation

A "simple calculation," according to Stein, could be used to infer a $1,065 billion GNP from the requirement that there be full employment within two years.

---

[21] Hendrik S. Houthakker, "Econometrics and Public Policy," Remarks made at the University of Wisconsin, February 10, 1971, p. 3.

[22] Herbert Stein, Remarks at the Financial Times and Investor Chronicle Conference on the Future of the United States Economy, London, October 28, 1970, pp. 10–12.

Modeling in the Public Eye

"We estimated that in the second quarter of 1970 the actual gross national product was about four percent below what would have been produced at full employment. We also estimated that the potential, full employment output grows by about 4.25 percent a year." Over a two-year period the amount by which actual GNP would fall below full-employment GNP if output did not grow at all would be 4 percent + 4.25 percent + 4.25 percent = 12.5 percent. "Therefore, to get the economy up to its potential in two years would require an increase of real output of about 12.5 percent or a little over 6 percent a year. Even with reasonable success in reducing the inflation rate, one might perhaps count on average price increases of 3 percent a year during this period —more at first and less at the end." Since the percentage rise in the money value of GNP is the sum of the percentage increases in prices and real output, "this would mean average increases in the money value of gross national product of 9 percent a year." A 9 percent gain in the $977 billion GNP of 1970 is $1,065 billion.

This "simple calculation" contains in fact the elements of a model—a very approximate model and very different from the World3 model. It does not require a computer to produce its results; paper and pencil are adequate, but it is a model nonetheless. It is a conceptualization—admittedly highly simplified—of how the economy works. It is made up of implicit relationships and assumptions, such as the relationship that a fully employed economy will grow at 4.25 percent in real terms and the assumption that the economy can be brought to full employment by an additional 4 percent real growth without aggravating inflation. Assumptions, relationships, and simplifications are the hallmarks of a model.

This model does not possess the simultaneous and secondary effects found in more sophisticated models. In fact, it is such a gross simplification that one might feel assured that no one would take it seriously. And maybe no one did. On the other hand, there is reason to believe that within the inner circles this calculation (or something like it) may have been used to obtain or justify the $1,065 billion figure. It derives from the concept of a full-employment budget, a concept used as a fiscal guide by the Nixon administration under Stein's tutelage. In 1974, in the face of spiraling inflation, and shortly before Stein left the government, the concept of the full-employment budget was abandoned. (See the discussion in Chapter 3.)

According to the Stein calculation, a GNP of $1,065 billion would put the economy on the road to full employment. It is interesting to note that by replacing the assumed 3 percent per year price increase by 4 percent, which would have been closer to what the administration might realistically have hoped to achieve in 1971, the calculation requires an annual growth in GNP of 10 percent; in other words, a 1971 GNP of $1,075 billion. And $1,075 billion was indeed the figure set early in 1970 for a 1971 GNP on the "optimum feasible path" toward full employment.

Hearings

Like the $1,075 billion projection, the highly optimistic assumption that prices would not increase more than 3 percent was dropped by the end of the year. On February 5, 1971, after publication of the $1,065 billion forecast and the resulting outcries, the Joint Economic Committee of the Congress held hearings. Paul W. McCracken, then chairman of the Council of Economic Advisers, was the first to testify. He allowed that half of the 9 percent projected increase in GNP, or about 4.5 percent, would come from inflation. The 4.5 percent estimate was close to being right, as things turned out. Substituting it into the Stein calculation suggests that even a $1,065 billion GNP in 1971 would not have sufficed to put the economy on Stein's optimum feasible path toward full employment.

In his defense of the $1,065 billion number before the committee, McCracken suggested a relationship between GNP and money supply, a relationship that goes well beyond the assumptions of the Stein calculation.

> From 1952 through 1970 the annual rate of increase of GNP was about three percentage points higher on the average than the annual increase of the money stock. If this relationship continued, a 6 percent increase of the money stock between 1970 and 1971 would produce the desired 9 percent increase of GNP.[23]

McCracken acknowledged that in certain periods the relationship has been very different. But note how by the words "would produce" he attributes a direct causal effect to money supply. The assumed role of money as a prime determinant of GNP is a keynote of the so-called monetarist doctrine that helped shape government policy during the Nixon administration. This doctrine forms the theoretical base for a number of small monetarist models, of which McCracken's quoted statement is a very simple example.

The central importance of money supply has long been propounded by economist Milton Friedman of the University of Chicago. In recent years Friedman's ideas have gained increasing favor in general economic circles, although most economists (namely those of Keynesian persuasion) do not accept the proposition that only money (monetary policy) really matters over the long run, and that fiscal policy *per se* has essentially no predictable effect of any significance on prices and employment.

McCracken, known as an eclectic economist, did not rest his case with the simplified monetarist model. He went on to point out that more sophisticated models yield similar results. He noted a 6.1 percent rate of increase of money in the first nine months of 1970, and the fact that the government was proposing to increase fiscal expenditures by about 8.2 percent and reduce taxes by about 1 percent during the coming year, thus stimulating the economy

---

[23] Hearings, p. 7.

still further.[24] The fact that a GNP of $1,065 billion would keep the 1971 federal deficit from exceeding its 1970 value was also germane. The deficit and the full-employment surplus would be unchanged if $1,065 billion were realized.

The committee was not entirely persuaded by McCracken's testimony. It pursued the same line of questioning a few days later when George Shultz, head of the Office of Management and Budget, appeared before it.[25] Shultz, arguing that economists almost always tend to underestimate the rate of recovery of the economy on the upswing, implied that they had repeated their mistake with the "standard" forecast for 1971 GNP. But Shultz did not want the committee to think that the White House obtained its $1,065 billion estimate simply by adding a typical error to the standard forecast. Committee Chairman William Proxmire had already remarked that both Shultz and McCracken "primarily defended the administration's forecast by pointing historically [to] how poor the forecasts of other people have been," yet these errors were due to an underestimation of inflation, not growth. Proxmire objected to the fact that the White House had not constructed its forecast by what he considered to be the correct procedure: a "sector-by-sector analysis."

---

[24] There is reason to believe that McCracken and some of his staff were uneasy about the $1,065 billion forecast. In one of numerous drafts of the economic report distributed only to government agencies, the council hedged the $1,065 billion figure with a range prediction of $1,045-$1,065 billion that upset both Stein and OMB for different reasons. Stein felt the $1,045 and $1,065 billion figures had different derivations and therefore should not be coupled. He also viewed a range prediction as implying more (not less) accuracy than a single-point prediction, since to him it made no allowance for a result outside the range. OMB, for its part, was loathe to revise the extensive calculations it had made based on $1,065 billion.

[25] Shultz, a prominent labor economist, had come to Washington with the Nixon administration in January 1969 as secretary of labor. He quickly gained Nixon's confidence and favor, and was appointed director of the newly formed Office of Management and Budget in June 1971. In that post he became, according to *Business Week* ("Architect of Nixon's New Economics," March 20, 1971, p. 72), "chief architect of the administration's program for economic recovery" and "first among equals" on the policy troika that included McCracken and (then) Treasury Secretary John B. Connally. Shultz took over the Treasury helm in June 1972 and became head cabinet officer for economic affairs in 1973, remaining in those positions until May 1974 when, at a time of impeachment hearings and a spiraling inflationary problem, he decided to return to private life. Although Nixon is said to have threatened to fire Shultz if he interfered as secretary of the treasury with the president's use of the Internal Revenue Service against his political enemies (*New York Times,* July 27, 1974, p. 11), Shultz outlasted any other member of Nixon's original cabinet, a measure both of his political dexterity and the influence he wielded. Shultz will be remembered as a monetary expansionist and activist who favored adoption of the full-employment concept and who was critical of the Federal Reserve Board for not increasing the money supply faster. As might be expected of a labor economist, he gave greatest weight to the reduction of unemployment in what many economists see as a continuing and unavoidable seesaw with inflation. He opposed the adoption of price and wage controls, but relented without losing influence or authority when controls were instituted over his objections, to the administration's later regret.

As far as Proxmire was concerned, whatever crystal ball Shultz was using, it had not been made clear to the committee.[26]

Shultz was now up against the ropes. He parried by referring, for the second time in his testimony, to a "different method" that his staff used and elaborated "to quite an extensive degree." This different method involved a "characterization or model of the economy."

The LR Model

The model to which Shultz alluded was developed by Arthur B. Laffer and R. David Ranson, new staff members at OMB. Laffer, 30 years old at the time, had joined Shultz at OMB as staff economist five months before. He came from the business school faculty at the University of Chicago that Shultz earlier had served as dean. Ranson was Laffer's student. Shultz, a labor economist by training, believed firmly in the causative effect of money stock as a determinant of GNP. Laffer and Ranson said they were not monetarists, although on the basis of how their model was used, most people believed they were. Clearly, they were influenced by Friedman, whom they knew well.

What Laffer and Ranson did was relate statistically the continuously compounded growth rates of GNP, prices, and unemployment to certain lead indicators such as the Treasury-bill interest rate and the continuously compounded growth rates of money supply, government purchases, stock prices, and time lost due to strikes. The relations they derived took the form of a few simple equations whose parameters they estimated from historical postwar data covering the period 1948 to 1969. They used the familiar procedures of regression analysis and ordinary least squares in deriving the equations and estimating the parameters. Their equations constitute a very simple example of an econometric model,[27] a type of model that we will have more to say about later. It is monetarist in appearance if not intent. Ranson said that if they had been working for someone other than Shultz—if he had not been the boss—they would not have placed the emphasis they did on money supply in the use of the model.

Despite their basically straightforward approach, on at least one count Laffer and Ranson departed from conventional practice in macroeconomic

---

[26] Hearings, p. 92.

[27] The LR model is not a full "structural" model, as that term is used in econometrics, and not typical of most econometric models. Generally, Keynesian models are structural in form, whereas monetarist models are in "reduced form." The LR model is not, strictly speaking, in reduced form, although it is close to it. A description of the LR model appears as an appendix to the Hearings, pp. 279-300. A somewhat revised version of the paper was published as Arthur B. Laffer and R. David Ranson, "A Formal Model of the Economy," *The Journal of Business* (The University of Chicago) 44, no. 3 (1971).

forecasting. They did not use seasonally preadjusted data. They did not, for example, smooth out, as is customary in the compilation of aggregate economic indicators, Christmas bulges and other seasonal influences in GNP and money stock. They argued that doing so might result in a loss of information and a distortion or "smearing" of the data. Instead, they took account of seasonal effects by introducing dummy variables into their regression analysis.

Because its data were not seasonally adjusted (and for other reasons as well), the Laffer-Ranson model, which we will refer to as the LR model, has a very curious property. It has an increase in the growth rate of money stock associated with an equal and almost instantaneous effect in the growth rate of GNP. The standard monetarist models, including ones used by the Council of Economic Advisers,[28] allow for a significant lag factor, a period of several months or longer, before changes in the money supply lead to changes in the level of business activity. Even Milton Friedman could not swallow the idea that changes in money stock might influence GNP immediately.

According to the LR model, however, changes in money supply do have "an immediate and permanent impact on the level of GNP."[29] For every 1 percent increase in money stock, there will be a 1 percent increase in GNP, not next year, but in the same quarter. Thus, a 6 percent increase in money stock during 1971 would by itself account for two-thirds of the 9 percent growth in GNP forecast by the White House. And 6 percent was not an unreasonable expectation, since that rate had already been exceeded on an annual basis during the first nine months of 1970. As it turned out, during the first half of 1971 money stock (seasonally adjusted) expanded by an average annual rate of more than 11 percent, according to the January 15, 1971, *Monetary Trends* prepared by the Federal Reserve Bank of St. Louis. But the economic recovery was disappointing. By the middle of 1971 the Federal Reserve put the brake on further monetary expansion.[30] Money growth during

---

[28] Hearings, p. 30.

[29] Hearings, p. 287.

[30] Monetary restraint was part of the president's new economic policy announced by the Nixon administration in August 1971. The administration's economic actions seemed to many like reed grass in the wind. Despite the failure of its expansionary policy in the first half of 1971, the Federal Reserve pressed down the monetary accelerator again in 1972 during the vigorous Nixon reelection campaign, apparently to buoy the economy. The monetary expansions of 1971 and 1972, along with price and wage controls, were considered culprits in the nation's severe inflationary spiral of 1973 and 1974. This view was held both inside and outside the administration, although the administration stoutly denied accusations that the Federal Reserve was politically motivated and subjected to illegal pressure from the White House. See, for example, Herbert Stein's remarks quoted in "Stein forecasts economic gains." Milton Friedman in an interview with *Challenge* (November–December 1973, p. 31) says, "I think it was a great mistake for the Fed to have gone in for rapid monetary expansion in 1970 and to an even greater extent in 1971." Friedman adds, "we offset the recession, but at the cost of inserting an inflationary stimulus that's now set us off on a still higher level of inflation."

the second half of 1971 was negligible, resulting in a growth rate for the year of slightly over 6 percent.

No sooner had the LR model been publicized than it was roundly criticized and rejected by just about everyone outside of the Office of Management and Budget, including Paul Samuelson of M.I.T., Arthur Okun of the Brookings Institution, economists at the Commerce Department, the Treasury Department, the Federal Reserve System, and even the Council of Economic Advisers (the one other government group officially allied with the Office of Management and Budget on the $1,065 billion forecast). The press had a heyday. More than one witness following Shultz, upon being prodded about the model by the chairman or a member of the Joint Economic Committee, expressed disagreement or skepticism. Harold Passer, assistant secretary of commerce for economic policy at the time, testified that his department's economic forecasts for 1971, generated by (what the *New York Times* referred to as) traditional estimating methods, conflicted sharply with the product of the White House's "new method of forecasting."[31]

Arthur F. Burns, chairman of the Federal Reserve Board, was another such witness.[32] He was reported to have called the model "probably simplistic" and he asked a member of his research staff to analyze it. The analysis, prepared by James L. Pierce, later associate research director for the Federal Reserve, found that when the model was based on data taken from 1952 to 1969 instead of from 1948 to 1969, the effect on GNP of increases in money supply was considerably less pronounced and less immediate. The model-generated GNP for 1971, based on a money growth of 6 percent and a growth in stock prices of 10 percent, was no longer $1,065 billion, according to Pierce, it was $1,049 billion. Use of seasonally preadjusted data (from 1948 to 1969) in estimating coefficients reduced even further the effect of increases in money supply on GNP.[33]

Pierce charged that in deducing GNP from money supply, the LR model failed to recognize that GNP can influence money supply. The increased business activity at Christmastime, for example, requires that more money be put into circulation for transactions in order to keep interest rates from temporarily rising. By its misrepresenting the causality, Pierce maintained that the LR

---

[31] *New York Times*, February 18, 1971, pp. 47–49.

[32] In his testimony (Hearings, p. 244), Burns alleged that rates of increase of money supply "above the 5 to 6 percent range—if continued for a long period of time—have typically intensified inflationary pressures." He declared that the "Federal Reserve will not become the architects of a new wave of inflation" and that it is "well aware that an excessive rate of monetary expansion now could destroy our Nation's chances of bringing about a gradual but lasting control over inflationary forces." Burns' words were unfortunately prophetic.

[33] The text of Pierce's critique follows the Laffer-Ranson paper as an appendix to the Hearings, pp. 300–312; also included is a rejoinder to the critique by G. Feketekuty and R. D. Ranson, pp. 313–319.

Modeling in the Public Eye

model awarded a greater weight and immediacy to the effect of money than is warranted.

In their paper, Laffer and Ranson deny the ability or intent of their model to identify causal relations. They declare that "the results can only show statistical correlations [not] cause and effect." Yet that is not how their results were received. In their findings they state that "fiscal policy, as represented by federal purchases of goods and services (assumed exogenous), provides a powerful temporary stimulus to GNP. Over a year, the cumulative effect is near zero. Changes in the conventionally defined money supply (for expositional purposes assumed exogenous) have an immediate and permanent impact on the level of GNP. Additional search yields no evidence of lags."[34]

Laffer and Ranson emphasize that they were only doing a statistical analysis of data. Their purpose, they say, was not to develop a model to forecast GNP from a *single* predicted money growth, but rather to examine the plausible outcome deriving from several possible values of money growth. They declare the model is clearly not a forecasting model and by its very nature could not be used as one. Yet their findings state that: "Movements in the stock market provide reliable *forecasts* of future changes in GNP. The market rate of interest provides a reliable *forecast* of the future rate of inflation.... The nominal GNP equation possesses greater precision than the St. Louis model, and is most likely a better conditional *forecaster* than the well-known large-scale models." Also, "We can see little evidence of any underestimation bias in our *forecasts*."[35] The authors dropped these references to *forecasts* (the italics are ours) from the final published version of their paper, suggesting that they thought better of their use of the term in the face of swelling criticism.

Laffer charges that the press exaggerated the importance of his model and chose to concentrate on it despite the fact that Shultz cited several other reasons for the $1,065 billion forecast. We know, in fact, that Laffer's model was not the basis for the original White House forecast. The president's economic advisers rejected the model; they had their own means of rationalizing the number, as we have seen. But the truth is that Shultz did pointedly draw attention to the model when his other justifications were dismissed or disputed by members of the committee. Shultz used the model as a lightning rod—and it caught fire.

Shultz took Laffer with him to the hearings. The press got most of its information on the model not from Shultz's testimony, but from off-the-cuff discussion with Laffer afterwards. Laffer admits to having been naive to the ways of Washington and the media. He says he hardly ever picked up a newspaper before joining the government. He also appears to have been less than

---
[34] Hearings, p. 292.
[35] Hearings, pp. 292–293.

moderate in his claims and was his own worst enemy when it came to explaining his work to the layman. *Time* magazine quoted him as having boasted that his model was "most likely better than any of the well-known larger models" of the economy,[36] and the *Wall Street Journal* reported him as having exulted that his was "the best equation of any in the country by far," and that although he was not "certain that sole reliance was placed on his work," his results were very consistent with the GNP forecast of the Council of Economic Advisers.[37]

The impression given by the press is one of overstatement and excessive faith in a model. The first principle of modeling is that "models are to be used but not to be believed."[38] In other words, the modeler who believes literally in his model, when he should be questioning it, is driving recklessly with his head in the clouds.

This danger was not unknown to Laffer and Ranson. It is alluded to, curiously enough, by a quote at the head of their paper.

> Persecution is used in theology, not in arithmetic, because in arithmetic there is knowledge, but in theology there is only opinion. So whenever you find yourself getting angry about a difference of opinion, be on your guard; you will probably find, on examination, that your belief is getting beyond what the evidence warrants (Bertrand Russell, *Unpopular Essays*).

Ranson says they included the quote in an attempt to remove themselves and their paper from the raging (theological) dispute between monetarists and nonmonetarists. They did not succeed.

Laffer feels it was a mistake for him to have been present at the hearings and to have faced the reporters. He also regrets having prepared and distributed the paper explicating the LR model. He reasons that the explicitness of the paper and model is what made a target of his work. Ranson attributes the critical outpouring primarily to Democratic economists looking for an opportunity to malign the Republican administration. The more positive way of looking at what happened, of course, is that the paper and the model focused the disagreement and provided a basis and structure for analysis and rational dialogue. A model facilitates reasoned debate, and this is a plus for models in policy.

Many would counter and maintain that the political process depends on the lubricants of ambiguity and imprecision in reconciling the positions of different interest groups. The dry definitiveness intrinsic to a model grinds against the gear wheels of political machinery. This raises a vital question. Assuming models do indeed have something beneficial to add to traditional political

---

[36] "1065 and All That," *Time*, February 22, 1971, p. 83.
[37] *Wall Street Journal*, February 10, 1971, p. 8.
[38] Henri Theil, *Principles of Econometrics* (New York: Wiley, 1971), p. vi.

apparatus, how then can they engage its workings? If they are so foreign to the way in which politicians are accustomed to operate, how can they be used constructively in the making of public policy?

LESSONS

Some readers may conclude prematurely from the examples of the *Limits to Growth* study and the Shultz-Laffer incident that models are out of place in policymaking. At best, they will say, models have nothing to offer. At worst, they are a menace, a snare, a delusion.

This hasty oversimplification is itself a trap. It makes the mistake of selling models short on at least two counts. First, it overlooks the large number of policy-oriented models being used routinely and effectively behind the scenes, feeding results and insights into the policymaking process via staff reports, analysis, and expert testimony. Second, it misses a main lesson of the two examples. It fails to recognize the political significance of the ability that some models have (or more accurately, their promoters and defamers have) to attract public notice and hold national interest.

Like the World3 model in the *Limits to Growth* study, the LR model received sustained public attention—and for some of the same reasons. In both cases there were highly charged political issues at stake. Both models produced tentative, qualified results bearing on the issues. Despite the disclaimers of their authors, both sets of results were taken as strong and provocative conclusions. The LR model defended a more optimistic return to economic prosperity than anyone but the administration was willing to accept and based its conclusions on statistical results that attributed an importance to money supply that even most monetarists could not buy. The World3 model foresaw dire consequences from the course the world was taking, just what the Club of Rome wanted to dramatize; but many considered the warnings overdone and rejected them as alarmist. Both models drew on the mystique of quantification and systems analysis, but with different methodological slants: LR emphasized data and statistical relationships, while World3 stressed computers and feedback flows.

The World3 model was created by academicians outside government and attracted worldwide attention through the publication and wide distribution of a provocative, clearly written paperback. The LR model, also produced by academicians, was developed within government and became widely known through the defensive remarks of a public official under interrogation by a congressional committee and his overzealous staff economist in speaking with the press. The numerous critics of both models faulted the modelers for their naiveté and the excessive simplicity of their creations.

Criticism of the LR model came directly on the heels of its release. Since repudiation of the $1,065 billion forecast was already widespread before the release, the opposition was well mobilized. Many of the adversaries were economists who understood basic economic theory and the methodology of econometric modeling. They were fast to spot which assumptions were crucial and which practices unorthodox. They knew immediately where the study was vulnerable. The model that Shultz had intended as armor for his position quickly became an Achilles heel.

The World3 model, in contrast, was generally lauded and well received at first. Most of those in attendance at the Smithsonian debut were greatly impressed by it. Antagonists to its conclusions were not well mobilized; the modeling methodology was not widely known; and the premises were not clearly understood. Because of the unfamiliarity of the methodology (and also because the technical description of the model was not yet generally available[39]), it took time for serious critics to fully comprehend the workings of the model and the import of its assumptions. The Club of Rome's call to action via the World3 model sounded loudly and resonantly. Only later, and gradually, did critics identify and draw attention to some sour notes and weaknesses in tone. Some say the Club of Rome's use of the World3 model backfired (as did Shultz's use of the LR model). Others insist that the use and presentation of the World3 model performed a great and lasting service whose imprint on policy will be noted in future decisions.

Thus, there are differences as well as similarities in the political meaning of the two modeling examples. Much of the difference has to do with the dissimilar political environments in which the models were introduced to public view. This suggests a second principle of policy modeling (to add to the first principle cited earlier). It is that the political setting in which a model is presented may be decisive in how the model is received by policymakers. This seems self-evident, but is easily overlooked. A related principle, not as apparent from the two examples treated here but of major significance in behind-the-scenes modeling, is that the organizational framework in which a model is developed can also be a crucial determinant of its usefulness.

Given the apparent ingredients necessary for a model to come to wide public attention, as illustrated by the World3 and LR examples, it is no wonder that there is a popular misconception of models and their use in decision making. Most of the models routinely used in policy matters, and there are many, never surface, get public exposure, or reach public consciousness. There are a variety of models being applied to energy problems, environmental control, and government regulation of natural resources. There are numerous

---

[39] The World3 model is not described in the *Limits to Growth* (Meadows et al.) paperback. The volume that does describe it is entitled *The Dynamics of Growth in a Finite World* (Cambridge, Mass.: Wright-Allen Press, 1974).

large-scale econometric models being updated continuously to provide regular quarter-by-quarter forecasts of the nation's business and industrial activity. There are countless operations research models being used by government agencies and their advisers to monitor and improve the performance of ongoing operations at federal, state, and municipal levels. The department of defense may have more models than missiles: it has been building them longer.

The models discussed in the following pages are just a minuscule sampling of the large number of models in active use. These behind-the-scenes models are being developed and applied in a wide variety of organizational and political settings, and many would be as susceptible to controversy, were they open to inspection, as the two models of this chapter. The fact of their being closeted needs more attention than it gets, as does the bureaucratic environment of modeling. Organizational and political factors can determine more than technical factors whether a model is used well, badly, or at all.

The application of models to policy is not of recent origin but is growing due to the spread of computers and the increasing number of analytically trained people in government. Recent surveys[40] offer a better indication of this expanding application than the conspicuous publicity attracted by the World3 and LR models, yet this publicity constitutes a phenomenon of considerable significance in its own right. It illustrates the early and potentially powerful use of models as political instruments.

Models are capable of exciting widespread interest. They can be used not only as research tools but also as image makers to bolster points of view. In June 1972, for example, President Nixon was warned that the *Limits to Growth* study was being used to buttress the sociopolitical positions and proposals of those who believe in a managed society.[41] Both the World3 and LR models were developed within a framework of established political persuasion. Both models became proponents of the persuasion; neither model can be said to have been objective or apolitical in the way it was used. This is an observation, not a criticism. A model cannot be objective and apolitical when used to recommend policy.

As objective constructs in scientific research, models have long been taken for granted. They are commonplace in the field of economics and in many

---

[40] See, for example, Gary Fromm, William L. Hamilton, and Diane E. Hamilton, *Federally Supported Mathematical Models: Survey and Analysis* (Washington, D.C.: National Science Foundation, June 1975), study performed by Data Resources, Inc., and Abt Associates, Inc., under contract with the Division of Social Systems and Human Resources, Research Applied to National Needs, of the National Science Foundation; also Janet R. Pack et al., *The Use of Urban Models in Urban Policy Making*, 2 vols. (Philadelphia: The Fels Center of Government, University of Pennsylvania, 1974).

[41] The warning to Nixon came from Edward E. David, science adviser to the president at the time.

other areas of intellectual endeavor. In the physical sciences, their primary purpose is to advance or integrate knowledge. In the social sciences, models may be used to defend or put forward a theoretical position.

As political instruments, computer models are just starting to gain notice. In this role they assume a different character, offer new opportunities, pose new problems and dangers. It is no longer enough for only technicians and specialists to understand and appreciate the value and limitations of computer modeling. The subject of modeling is becoming generally relevant to everyone concerned with or about the functioning of government and the making of policy.

2

Modeling as a Form of Policy Research

Modeling as a modern-day form of policy research is another phase in the continuing attempt by quantitative researchers to apply systematic analysis and scientific procedures to the understanding of policy problems and the making of public decisions. It suffers from all of the difficulties and tensions that over the years have complicated and impaired the uneasy partnership between knowledge and political power.

The nature of the partnership has been changing in recent years as policy research has tended to shift toward the systematic testing of policies as opposed to the identification of policy problems and the invention of policy options. Models have been playing a significant part in policy testing, and their numbers are growing despite considerable disappointment shown in their performance.

Reasons for the disappointment are rooted in the characteristics of the political environment. Although the domain of knowledge in the policy process seems to have been expanding, the expansion may be more apparent than real. There is no evidence that the domain of politics has really contracted.

APPEARANCES

Model celebrities like World3 that enter the policy arena with a fanfare of publicity are only the most visible members of a much larger company. In and around government, modeling has become a rather commonplace activity. But neither the widespread public attention received by a few models nor the large and growing population of more obscure models at the lower and middle levels of public agencies is a reliable gauge of the influence that models now exert upon the functioning of government. To bring models within the orbit of policymaking institutions is one thing. Putting them to use in the policy process is another, and several studies hint that a large fraction of the models that have accumulated in policymaking institutions are never put to use. A survey of models, simulations, and games in the Department of Defense, for example, reports that almost half of these research ventures never generated information that was transmitted to departmental officials in briefings.[1] A study of nondefense modeling efforts in the federal government estimates that "at least one-third and perhaps as many as two-thirds of the models failed to achieve their avowed purposes in the form of direct application to policy problems."[2]

When Is a Model Used?

One difficulty in interpreting such findings is the uncertainty about what it means to "use" a model in the policy process. Neither of the two studies just cited could be said to have employed an overly demanding test of use. A "used" model was not necessarily one whose influence could be detected in specific policy decisions. It was enough that a model had generated information of certain kinds, which the modelers had communicated to others. General discussions of model use are often framed in similar terms. The "uses" enumerated refer to the kinds of information-producing tasks for which models can be employed; considerably less attention is given to the kinds of things that policymakers actually do with this information.

The information-producing uses are of several types.[3] One of the most frequently mentioned is unconditional forecasting. Modeling is put forward as a technique for arriving at predictions about the circumstances that policymakers are likely to face at some time in the future—the unemployment and interest rates that they can expect, the travel patterns that they can anticipate, or the amount of energy likely to be produced. Such forecasts do not tell policymakers how they should prepare for the future, but they could forewarn public officials about emerging problems that require attention or inform them about the resources likely to be available in the future for the treatment of problems already recognized. Today, econometric models are routinely employed for unconditional forecasting.

Conditional forecasting is another of the tasks for which modeling is used. A forecast is conditional if it is contingent on the actions that policymakers take

---

[1] Martin Shubik and Garry D. Brewer, *Models, Simulations, and Games: A Survey* (The Rand Corporation, R-1060-ARPA/RC, May 1972), pp. 40–41.

[2] Gary Fromm, William L. Hamilton, and Diane E. Hamilton, *Federally Supported Mathematical Models: Survey and Analysis* (Washington, D.C.: National Science Foundation, 1974), p. 4.

[3] The following discussion of model use draws on several sources. In particular, Garry D. Brewer, *Politicians, Bureaucrats, and the Consultant* (New York: Basic Books, 1973), chapter 6; Janet R. Pack et al., *The Use of Urban Models in Urban Policy Making*, 2 vols. (Philadelphia: The Fels Center of Government, University of Pennsylvania, 1974), I: chapter 1; Fromm, Hamilton, and Hamilton, chapter 7; Britton Harris, "Quantitative Models of Urban Development: Their Role in Metropolitan Decision Making," in Harvey S. Perloff and Lowdon Wingo, Jr., (eds.), *Issues in Urban Economics* (Baltimore: The Johns Hopkins Press, 1968), pp. 363–410.

—the adoption or rejection of a particular program, for example. Conditional forecasts, therefore, deal with the likely consequences of policy decisions; they provide some of the information necessary for testing proposed programs. The effects of several program alternatives might be estimated, for example, by modeling them and the environment in which they are to operate and by simulating their consequences. Through such a process, modeling might conceivably contribute not only to the testing, but also to the design and fine tuning of proposed policies.

Like unconditional forecasts, conditional forecasts do not prescribe a course of action for policymakers. They can suggest how the consequences of various actions may differ, but they do not indicate whether one set of consequences is more desirable than another. By itself, no model can decide whether one policy is better than others, but the use of models for normative analysis or normative specification can still aid public officials in making decisions. Optimizing models in operations research are designed to identify the "best" procedures (from the standpoint of efficiency) for carrying a policy into effect. Models are also recommended for "the creation and examination of various desired end states"[4] in order to help specify public objectives and call attention to inconsistencies among them.

A more elusive and indirect use of models is in education—not to make forecasts or test specific policy proposals or identify optimum solutions, but to refine the intuitions of policymakers. Models are instruments for exploring reality as well as for portraying it, and modeling can be a useful device for stimulating the inventiveness and sharpening the perceptions of decision makers. Simulation gaming is a form of modeling designed specifically for these purposes, but other kinds of models can serve the same ends. A model used for what Garry Brewer has called "descriptive clarification"—the determination of the "present state and past trends" in a problem area—can, for example, extend a policymaker's understanding of the situation that he faces, without testing any policy proposals or offering any predictions of the future.[5]

Cataloging the ways in which models might serve policymakers provides a starting point, at least, for considering the place that the modeling process occupies in the policy process. But the catalogue as it now stands includes no suitable pigeonholes for some of the most common and perhaps most important purposes that models have served in policymaking. We have already seen some examples of them. The World3 model was not merely a research tool for producing forecasts concerning the future state of mankind, it was also a medium for the articulation of policy problems and a device for concentrating public attention upon them. In short, the model was a mechanism for framing

---

[4] Brewer, p. 59.
[5] Ibid., p. 58.

and raising political issues. The Laffer-Ranson model, in contrast, was put to use not for the purpose of raising an issue, but in the hope that it might help to settle one. Officials of the Nixon administration brought the model forward in an attempt to bolster a position which they had already taken and to overcome the reservations of their critics in congress and elsewhere. It is evident that the model was not used successfully for these ends. Nevertheless, the Laffer-Ranson episode provides an indication of one way in which policymakers may seek to use models: namely, to reinforce or justify decisions or predictions already made.

Some of the most significant uses of policy models may be obscured if we regard modeling simply as a means of producing information for the intellectual task of problem solving. Problem solving is certainly one function of policymaking, but another is developing a political warrant for authoritative decision making:[6] converting perceived problems into political issues, assembling support for proposed actions, resolving conflicts, legitimating decisions, and securing compliance. Meeting these tests of political validity is no less essential to the policy process than meeting the tests of intellectual or rational validity. In practice, of course, it is almost impossible to separate the processes of political validation from those of rational validation. The same research data used to ascertain the existence of a problem, for example, may also be brought to bear in the effort to transform that problem into a political issue. The use of models for the production and rational analysis of information cannot be divorced from their role in generating the forces that drive (or retard) the policy process.

Disappointments

What it means to "use" a model in the policy process remains an open question; there are not only different types of uses but different dimensions of use. To say that modeling is used a lot or a little does not do justice to the complexity of the situation, but the complexity of the situation cannot completely conceal a widespread disappointment with the performance of policy models. Both model designers and sponsors share a general impression that the actual uses of modeling in government have fallen short of expectations. The gap between expectation and achievement is widest in the policy applications of modeling.[7]

The explanations offered for these disappointments are numerous, but most tend to look for the sources of failure in models themselves or in the modeling

---

[6] A similar distinction between the various functions of policymaking has been made by Charles O. Jones, *Clean Air: The Policies and Politics of Pollution Control* (Pittsburgh: University of Pittsburgh Press, 1975), p. 41.

[7] Fromm, Hamilton, and Hamilton, pp. 29–30.

process. It is suggested, for example, that the application of models to policy problems may be hindered by the fact that models are seldom as "specialized and detailed" as the policy issues they are supposed to illuminate. The "absence or high cost of obtaining or processing 'fine grained,' specialized information" means that many policy models can produce only generalized results that hold only limited interest for policymakers confronted with the special intricacies of particular problems.[8] Closely related to this explanation for the failure of models to serve policymakers is the contention that policy variables are often inadequately or crudely represented in models. As a result, modelers may be incapable of distinguishing the likely consequences of one policy option from the consequences of others.[9]

In sharp contrast to these views are explanations that point not to a lack of detail, but to precisely the opposite failing—an excess of detail or complication. It is argued that large, complicated models are difficult to understand, and policymakers are not likely to place great faith in things they do not understand. Even the modeler may lose touch with the workings of the model when it grows too large. At the same time, the model may become costly or difficult to run and the mass of results produced may be too overwhelming to digest or trust.[10]

We have here no single, consistent diagnosis of what goes wrong with policy models, whether the trouble is too much detail or too little. In all likelihood, there *is* no single diagnosis; different things go wrong with different models. Moreover, it is worth considering whether the models themselves are indeed the only major source of trouble. Modeling, after all, is not the only form of policy research whose usefulness is seriously questioned, and it is quite possible that some of the faults attributed to model design or modeling techniques may in fact be symptoms of more general difficulties that are not peculiar to modeling, but inherent in the task of conducting research and applying its results in the context of the policy process. Modeling cannot be considered in isolation from policy research in general.

DECISION MAKING AND THE DOMAIN OF KNOWLEDGE

The migration of modeling from academic disciplines to policymaking institutions is one manifestation of a general upswing in almost all forms of policy research. In the conduct of government, says Robert Lane, the "domain of knowledge" is expanding while the "domain of politics" contracts. The decisions of policymakers, he argues, are shaped less and less by "calculations of

---

[8] Ibid., p. 4.
[9] Pack et al., p. 60.
[10] For a discussion along these lines, see Douglass B. Lee, "Requiem for Large-Scale Models," *Journal of the American Institute of Planners* 39 (1973): 163–178.

influence, power, or electoral advantage." Political leaders rely increasingly on the advice of experts who can presumably tell them "how to implement agreed upon values with rationality and efficiency."[11]

It is no easy matter to measure growth in the "domain of knowledge." Nor are simultaneous reductions in the "domain of politics" plainly evident. But it is apparent that political leaders at the highest levels have recently been attempting to cede large tracts of traditionally political territory to the custody of experts. One of the most ambitious of these attempts was made by President Johnson in 1965, when he issued a sweeping order to the members of his cabinet directing them to adapt the Defense Department's program-planning-budgeting system for use in their own agencies. Under the new system, according to Johnson, each department and agency was to establish "a very special staff of experts" who would seek to allocate the agency's funds among various programs so as to maximize the achievement of its aims at the minimum cost.[12] These experts soon required the assistance of other experts, who could provide the social and economic information essential for the measurement of program effectiveness. Still other experts were introduced into the policy process by the social programs of the 1960s. With almost every new piece of social legislation, congress required that the conduct of social research should run parallel to the implementation of social policy.[13]

The participation of experts in public policymaking was, of course, not new. The research efforts of natural scientists have for some time played a part in the formation of national defense policy. More recently, however, some of the largest additions to the domain of knowledge have occurred in the field of domestic social and economic policy, and social scientists have been called upon to serve as expert advisers to government officials. The extension of program-planning-budgeting to domestic agencies, the provisions that Congress has made in recent social legislation for research programs, rapidly increasing federal support for social science research during the 1960s, and the more recent need to unravel the complex interrelationships of energy and economics —all have contributed to an expanding role for social science expertise in the political process.

Forms of Policy Research

While it is difficult to state exactly what functions the social science experts are supposed to perform, researchers and policymakers have outlined two general conceptions of the part that producers of knowledge might play in

---

[11] Robert E. Lane, "The Decline of Politics and Ideology in a Knowledgeable Society," *American Journal of Sociology* 31 (1966): 657–658.

[12] Walter Williams, *Social Policy Research and Analysis: The Experience in the Federal Social Agencies* (New York: American Elsevier, 1971), pp. 5–6.

[13] James S. Coleman, *Policy Research in the Social Sciences* (Morristown, N.J.: General Learning Press, 1972), p. 3.

the business of policymaking. One of them calls for researchers to participate in the process of policy evaluation. It would be their responsibility to assess the effectiveness of existing programs, using established principles of research design to distinguish the influence of the program from the effects of environmental factors. An obvious prerequisite for such research efforts is a precise definition of the objectives that particular programs are supposed to achieve, and precise definitions of this kind are seldom provided by public agencies. As a result, policy evaluators would frequently be required to specify the goals of the programs that they are evaluating and to translate these aims into measures of output and criteria of effectiveness. Once they have done this, policy evaluators might be able to generate several kinds of information useful to policymakers. Information about the overall success or failure of public policies, for example, could assist budgetmakers in deciding how to allocate funds among various programs. More detailed information about the conditions for program success or about the types of activities most closely associated with success could be used by program administrators to modify their current operations.[14]

It is one thing to describe the functions that policy evaluators should perform, but it is quite another to explain exactly how to provide for their performance—what organizational arrangements to make for policy evaluation and how to assure that the results of research are actually brought to bear in policy decisions. Even if these questions could be resolved, however, it is unlikely that policy evaluation would be able to satisfy some of the most urgent information needs of policymakers. Policy evaluation, after all, would generate information about programs that are already in operation. It would provide little guidance in the creation of new programs, and it is in the design of new programs that the demand for information has been both most intense and least adequately satisfied. The Community Action Program came to grief, says Daniel Patrick Moynihan, because of a failure of social and political intelligence in its design,[15] and such failures have not been limited to the War on Poverty. In 1973, an outgoing secretary of health, education, and welfare left his office with a warning that the unthinking creation of new social programs was producing a "crisis of performance" in the nation's "human resource system."[16] Policymakers require information, not only about the effectiveness of existing programs, but about the kinds of programs that ought to be brought into existence, and policy evaluation leaves this need largely unmet.

To fulfill it, policy researchers would have to undertake the more ambitious task of policy analysis. Like policy evaluation, the job of policy analysis includes a specification of program objectives and criteria of effectiveness. But

---

[14] See Joseph S. Wholey et al., *Federal Evaluation Policy: Analyzing the Effects of Public Programs* (Washington, D.C.: The Urban Institute, 1970), pp. 23–24.

[15] Daniel Patrick Moynihan, *Maximum Feasible Misunderstanding* (New York: Free Press, 1969), pp. 167–70.

[16] *Baltimore Sun,* January 19, 1973.

the investigations of the policy analyst extend beyond the assessment of existing programs to a consideration of alternative policies and programs and an attempt to measure the prospective costs and benefits of these hypothetical alternatives. Ideally, policy analysis would enable public decision makers to select from among a wide range of alternative programs the one with the highest benefit/cost ratio.[17] Stated crudely, the difference between policy evaluation and policy analysis is this: policy evaluators organize their research efforts around an existing program and ask how well it is achieving its intended objectives; policy analysts tend to organize their investigations around a set of policy objectives, and they inquire whether there is any conceivable program or combination of programs that might achieve the desired ends more efficiently than others.

Once again, it is easier to describe the functions to be performed than to arrange for their performance, but in the case of policy analysis, there are special difficulties that could prevent researchers from performing the tasks expected of them under any arrangements. As policy analysts, social scientists would be expected to test the consequences of programs that have not yet been put into operation. The problem here is not simply that program data are nonexistent—a rather common difficulty—but that there appears to be no obvious technique for generating such information short of implementing a hypothetical program and observing its effects. This can be an extremely expensive way in which to satisfy one's curiosity, and it defeats the purpose of policy analysis, whose aim, after all, is to determine which programs should be implemented in the first place.

There may be more sensible ways to proceed. Small-scale social experiments, for example, have been used in several recent policy research efforts to test the consequences of programs before they are put into full-scale operation. Another approach to policy analysis is provided by computer-aided modeling and simulation. Through simulation, policy analysts might produce the conditional forecasts essential for estimating the effects of alternative policy proposals; the use of models for normative analysis might play a part in comparing and evaluating the predicted consequences of these policy options; and modeling as an instrument for unconditional forecasting might supply information about the circumstances that are likely to confront any new policy in the future. Although modeling can have its uses in policy evaluation as well, its greatest opportunities appear to lie in the field of policy analysis. Its use for this purpose also seems to constitute one of its chief attractions for policymakers—promising to provide them with information about the likely effects of untried ideas, policies, or administrative arrangements.[18]

---

[17] Williams, p. 12.
[18] See for example Pack et al., p. 39.

Some Historical Antecedents

Policy analysis and policy evaluation are not the only functions that researchers and professional experts may perform in the process of public decision making. They are only the functions that have recently become most prominent. In earlier times, the testing of policies seems to have taken a back seat to the identification of policy problems and the invention of policy options. Franklin Roosevelt's National Planning Board, later transformed into the National Resources Planning Board, epitomizes this early stage in the development of policy research. The board's members, a majority of whom were professional social scientists, hoped that their investigative efforts would "make it possible to apprehend more clearly and promptly the emerging trends and problems of the nation." The board envisioned itself as "a general staff gathering and analyzing facts, observing the interrelation and administration of broad policies, proposing from time to time alternative lines of national procedure, based on thorough inquiry and mature consideration."[19]

During the 1930s, the board's conception of the policy researcher's role seems to have been reflected in the work of economists for the New Deal farm programs, of anthropologists for the Bureau of Indian Affairs, of political scientists in the administrative reorganization of the executive branch, and of a variety of other social scientists scattered throughout the government. Their function was to identify emerging problems and "to propose from time to time alternative lines of national procedure." Systematically testing the effects of alternative lines of procedure seems to have been a secondary activity. The principal purpose was to focus or expand the attentions of the policymaker by giving definition to particular problems or by extending the range of policy alternatives under consideration.[20]

Just how research might perform these functions, it is difficult to say. In some cases, the research enterprise seems to have consisted simply of having some social scientists on hand to be consulted. In others, the collection of information was confined to a survey of past research efforts, few of which could be expected to address themselves directly to the problem at hand. The National Planning Board was persuaded that the proposal of new policy options should be based upon thorough inquiry and mature consideration. But often, inquiry and consideration were not the same as research. They might amount to nothing more than an expert drawing on the collected wisdom of his profession and his own ingenuity to make an educated guess about the likely solution to some national problem. This was policy research after the fashion

---

[19] Quoted in Gene Lyons, *The Uneasy Partnership: Social Science and the Federal Government in the Twentieth Century* (New York: Russell Sage Foundation, 1969), p. 65.

[20] Ibid., chapter 3.

of the celebrated Rooseveltian brain trust. And while such efforts could produce important results, they were clearly different from research enterprises designed specifically to test the consequences of particular policy alternatives.[21]

Until recently, research of this kind had not been common. One reason, perhaps, is that until World War II, social scientists tended to flow in and out of government in response to the rise and decline of national crises—two wars and a national economic depression. Their *ad hoc* role in policymaking may have made it difficult to launch extended investigations of particular programs and their consequences. After 1945, the tidal flow of social science expertise subsided. Long-term positions were created within the government for social scientists, and federal agencies established relatively stable connections with social scientists outside the government, in universities and research centers.

One manifestation of this postwar effort to institutionalize the role of social science expertise in policymaking is the president's Council of Economic Advisers. But even the council is not primarily a research organization. Its research activities have been subordinated to the invention and advocacy of policy options, and it has tended to restrict its advice-giving business to matters of general economic policy, leaving to others the assessment of particular programs and program proposals.[22] What was institutionalized in the council were the problem-defining and policy-inventing roles of the social scientist, not the function of testing specific policies.

The PPBS Movement

The testing of policies has never been entirely ignored by social scientists in government, but it did not come into its own as a major function of policy research until the 1960s. A watershed in this development was the adoption in the 1960s of the program-planning-budgeting system (PPBS) by the Department of Defense and its subsequent diffusion to other federal agencies. PPBS was a decision making tool contrived by economists and operations researchers working under Charles Hitch at the Rand Corporation during the 1950s. The concern of Hitch and his associates was to discover how the country could "purchase" national security in the most efficient manner—how much of the national wealth should be devoted to defense, how the funds allocated to defense should be distributed among different military functions, and how to assure the most effective use of these funds.[23]

Probably the most controversial part of PPBS was the planning stage,

---

[21] Ibid., pp. 59–60.
[22] Ibid., p. 232; Edward S. Flash, *Economic Advice and Presidential Leadership* (New York: Columbia University Press, 1965), p. 317.
[23] See Bruce L. R. Smith, *The Rand Corporation: A Case Study of a Nonprofit Advisory Corporation* (Cambridge: Harvard University Press, 1966), pp. 33–38; Lyons, p. 163.

over which systems analysts presided. Systems analysis was the heart (or the brain) of PPBS, and it was also chiefly responsible for whatever impact PPBS had upon the conduct of policy research by government agencies. The process begins with the specification of the objectives to be achieved and the alternative "systems" that might be used to achieve them. A cost is attached to the use of each alternative, and the analyst employs a model of reality in order to trace the relationship between the expenditures made on a particular option and the outcome which can be expected to result. The model may be a formal mathematical one, a physical model, or merely a mental representation of reality that the analyst uses to forecast the consequences of different alternatives. These policy outcomes are then ranked in order of preference according to specified decision making criteria.[24]

The activities of the systems analyst are one expression of what we have described in more general terms as policy analysis. Although PPBS itself enjoyed only a passing fashionableness among government officials, it did help to implant policy analysis in the decision-making processes of some public agencies. By so doing, it produced changes in the character of policy research which proved to be more durable than PPBS itself. At the same time, it helped to engender a demand for policy models which has become increasingly evident during the past ten years. Perhaps just as important, the trials and tribulations of PPBS reveal the outlines of several problems likely to be encountered by the practitioners of policy analysis in the course of their work, whether they use models or not.

While some critics argued that PPBS dealt in decision making platitudes and everyday common sense, it did not blend easily with conventional decision making practices in most policy areas. For convinced partisans of PPBS, these regions of public policy were fruitful ground for missionary endeavor. Skeptical observers were less sanguine. If systems analysis was a way of looking at problems to which any reasonable person could subscribe, why were not more reasonable people using it? Perhaps they had good reasons. Perhaps PPBS was workable only in special circumstances.

PPBS Inside and Outside the Pentagon

PPBS seems to have encountered those circumstances in the Department of Defense. It was here, shortly after Charles Hitch became assistant secretary and comptroller of the department in 1961, that systems analysis and PPBS first established themselves in the federal government as official decision making

---

[24] Charles J. Hitch and Roland N. McKean, *The Economics of Defense in the Nuclear Age* (Cambridge: Harvard University Press, 1960), pp. 118–120; see also Charles J. Hitch, *Decision Making for Defense* (Berkeley: University of California Press, 1965).

strategies. Two factors in particular seem to have facilitated their acceptance in the Defense establishment. First, although PPBS and systems analysis were costly, the expenditure of millions on analysis could be justified because it contributed to military decisions that dealt in billions.[25] In addition, these were decisions that posed questions of national survival and destruction. The stakes could not be measured in money alone, and because they were so weighty, the tolerance for uncertainty in these decisions was relatively low. Systems analysis could be justified as a means for reducing uncertainty to acceptable levels. It is not surprising, as Kathleen Archibald points out, that systems analysis first made a name for itself in the field of nuclear strategy.[26] It was a decision making aid that tended to flourish in an atmosphere of big risks and big money. The Defense establishment provided both.

The Defense Department also represented a field of policymaking that was somewhat insulated from its political environment—less vulnerable than most government agencies to importuning constituent groups and their representatives. The secrecy of many defense decisions and the association between national defense policy and patriotism has given the department a degree of immunity from external political pressure.[27] It has also meant that cost-effectiveness could sometimes prevail over political effectiveness as a criterion for decision making. When PPBS was extended to the civilian agencies of the federal government by President Johnson's 1965 directive, it was removed from a politically sheltered environment and exposed to a new and less congenial set of conditions.

The differences were noticed almost immediately. The goals of national social policy seemed more difficult to specify than the goals of national security policy, and there was more disagreement about them. Even when policy objectives could be satisfactorily defined, there frequently was no reliable information concerning the extent to which existing policies had been achieving those objectives. It was therefore difficult, if not impossible, for analysts to trace the relationship between the money spent on a particular program and the public benefits that would result. These obstacles to analysis were probably aggravated, in many cases, by the inexperience of the analysts themselves. The application of systems analysis to defense policy had been preceded by at least five years of preparatory studies at the Rand Corporation, and by 1961, when the Rand analysts carried PPBS to the Pentagon, they had not only mastered

---

[25] Aaron Wildavsky, "Rescuing Policy Analysis from PPBS," in U.S. Congress, Joint Economic Committee, *The Analysis and Evaluation of Public Expenditures: The PPB System,* 3 vols. (Washington: U.S. Government Printing Office, 1969), 3:838–39 (hereafter cited as Joint Economic Committee).

[26] Kathleen Archibald, "Three Views of the Expert's Role in Policy Making: Systems Analysis, Incrementalism, and the Clinical Approach," *Policy Sciences* 1 (1970): 77.

[27] Wildavsky, p. 840; Ida R. Hoos, *Systems Analysis in Public Policy: A Critique* (Berkeley: University of California Press, 1972), p. 48.

the techniques of analysis, but acquired a familiarity with the substantive issues of national security policy. The analysts who were hurried into the civilian agencies of the federal government after 1965 did not always have the same opportunity to become conversant with the intricacies of national health, conservation, education, or manpower policies. Some observers have also suggested that they may not have been as talented as the team of analysts that brought PPBS to the Defense Department.[28]

Aside from the problems that beset the work of the systems analysts themselves, additional difficulties were encountered in translating the work of the analysts into budget decisions and legislative proposals. In the Department of Health, Education, and Welfare, for example, policymakers were seldom likely to have the same degree of political autonomy that was enjoyed by their counterparts in the Department of Defense, and their decisions were more likely to be tempered by considerations other than cost-effectiveness. Each of the department's several hundred programs had to be adapted to its own unique political environment.

> It has a legislative history and an authorization level. It is handled by a particular committee or subcommittee whose chairman may have definite views. It may have a strong lobby supporting it or gunning for it. It may be administered by states or localities or other non-federal institutions. All of these particular characteristics [of] programs are relevant to a decision to translate a program budget decision into budgetary or legislative terms.... No matter how useful a program budget proves, as a way of organizing information and as a planning tool, the final decisions on the budget must be made in appropriations terms and in the light of all these complicated considerations which, though they may not be desirable, are facts of life for a secretary of Health, Education and Welfare.[29]

The facts of life for the policymakers in the civilian agencies were clearly different from those facing the Pentagon executives, and not surprisingly, PPBS as it was practiced in the civilian agencies did not always conform to the Pentagon model. The civilian agencies adapted it to their own circumstances. In some cases, for example, PPBS became not the comprehensive budgeting tool that it was intended to be, but a device to be used in special situations. "We have tried," reported an Interior Department official, "to more heavily relate our PPBS work and our analytical work to the new program thrusts, and major issues, not because it is easier to talk about new programs, but rather, there is a good question of judgment on how much time one should spend on ongoing programs that are pretty well set."[30] Those

---

[28] Wildavsky, p. 838.

[29] Alice M. Rivlin, "The Planning, Programming, and Budgeting System in the Department of Health, Education, and Welfare: Some Lessons from Experience," in Joint Economic Committee, 3:912.

[30] Quoted in Wildavsky, p. 848.

programs that are pretty well set, of course, are also likely to be ones about which congressional committee chairmen have developed definite views and to which strong lobbying groups may have become attached. The decision of agency analysts to steer clear of these ongoing programs may have been a good way to avoid trouble. It may also have represented a very sensible assessment of the costs and benefits of systems analysis. To the extent that established programs are subject to change, those changes are likely to be marginal ones, involving relatively small stakes. In these circumstances, expensive efforts at research and analysis are seldom likely to be justified by the resulting modification in policy. It makes far better sense for a bureaucratic agency to concentrate its scarce research resources in areas of "new program thrusts and major issues." This is precisely how some federal agencies chose to use the skills of systems analysts and program budgeters.

While they were adapting PPBS to their own tastes and circumstances, the civilian agencies of the federal government were also finding it necessary to adapt their own activities to the demands of PPBS. In particular, they found that the program budgeting system had an enormous appetite for information, and it was often information of a kind that program administrators had never before bothered to collect. PPBS served to focus attention on the consequences of public programs and on the relationship between the money spent and the benefits produced. In many instances, federal administrators discovered that they lacked even the most elementary information about the benefits that resulted from public policies. Although the federal government was spending substantial sums of money on child health programs, for example, there was no evidence to show that children who saw doctors regularly were healthier than those who did not. Nor was there substantial evidence to show that there was any relationship between the amount of money spent on public education and the educational results. Federal officials had long proceeded on the simple maxim "that spending money makes good things happen, and spending more money makes better things happen."[31] PPBS demanded a more rigorous justification for program and budgetary decisions, and since the Bureau of the Budget had made such justifications a prerequisite for the allocation of funds, federal agencies had a strong incentive to provide them. The exigencies of program budgeting prompted many agencies to launch evaluation studies—some serious, and some not so serious—in order to document the presumably beneficial effects of their programs.[32]

But perhaps more notable than the encouragement given to policy evaluation was the stimulus that PPBS provided for policy analysis. Under program

---

[31] Elizabeth Drew, "HEW Grapples with PPBS," *The Public Interest* 8 (1967): 29.
[32] See, for example, Rivlin, "The Planning, Programming, and Budgeting System," in Joint Economic Committee, vol. 3, pp. 505–510.

budgeting, there was a tendency, as we have already noted, for agencies to divert their scarce research resources from the examination of existing policies to a consideration of new programs that might be undertaken. In these largely uncharted areas of decision making, policy evaluation would be almost useless. There was little or nothing to evaluate. Instead, the task of the investigator was to specify hypothetical policy options and to estimate their consequences.

Social Experimentation

It was a problem of precisely this kind that confronted policy analysts in the Office of Economic Opportunity when they attempted to assess the consequences of a guaranteed annual income program. Although the federal government had more than thirty years of experience with income maintenance policies, its public welfare programs had almost always been directed at the nonworking poor and yielded little information about how the working poor would respond to the availability of income subsidies. In particular, there was no way to determine whether and to what extent the payment of such subsidies to working people might reduce their incentive to work. If a general program of income subsidies were ever to be proposed—and most of the OEO analysts were partial to such proposals—its effect on the work incentive would surely become a major factor in its acceptance. In order to resolve the uncertainty surrounding this issue, the staff of OEO's Office of Research, Plans, Programs and Evaluation (which also presided over the agency's program budgeting system) proposed a novel experiment in public policy formation. Under the experimental design that was eventually developed, samples of low-income families in New Jersey were to receive supplements according to several different formulas. Their behavior as consumers and workers was to be compared over a period of three years with the behavior of a control group consisting of families that received no income supplements. The experiment, which got underway in 1968, generated previously unavailable information about the impact of income maintenance upon the work efforts of low-income families, and about its effect upon family stability and consumption patterns. Some of this information figured in the debate over President Nixon's Family Assistance Plan (FAP) during 1969 and 1970.[33]

The New Jersey Guaranteed Annual Income Experiment seems to have triggered a more general outbreak of policy experiments in the federal government. Many of these subsequent experiments were initiated by OEO's analytical office and then farmed out to other federal agencies. The Depart-

---

[33] Margaret Boeckmann, *The Politics of the New Jersey Income Maintenance Experiment* (Baltimore: Center for Metropolitan Planning and Research, The Johns Hopkins University, 1973).

ment of Health, Education, and Welfare, for example, assumed the responsibility for the conduct of several income maintenance experiments designed to supplement the results of the New Jersey inquiry. Other experiments have been launched to test the effects of performance contracting in public education, housing allowances, educational vouchers, and new health insurance programs. Under the influence of PPBS, policy research was employed increasingly to test the outcomes of policy options and not just to stimulate the invention of options.

But this change in the character of policy research did not necessarily mean that policymaking itself had been transformed. In the "domain of politics," PPBS and its progeny made scant headway. Behind the facade of program budgeting, many agencies carried on business as usual. And policy experimenters sometimes found that the influence of their work tended to evaporate in the course of political debate. In 1970, for example, the New Jersey income maintenance experimenters were induced by government officials to release some of their study's preliminary results—not yet fully substantiated—in the hope that this experimental evidence might help to strengthen legislative support for the President's Family Assistance Program. In response, Senate opponents of FAP turned their hostile attentions from the welfare proposal itself to the experiment and its results. Their challenge of the preliminary findings quickly became an effort to discredit the experiment and the experimenters, and possibly even to sabotage the conduct of the research.[34] In the end, the experiment survived to run its course, but FAP was defeated.

The experience of the income maintenance researchers was not an unusual one. The use of policy analysis and policy evaluation to shape public decisions has often been similarly frustrated,[35] and occasionally the research that does influence decisions turns out to have been unsound or incomplete. Such disappointments became more numerous as the volume of policy research grew during the 1960s. By the end of the decade, politicians and experts alike had begun to express serious doubts about the value and efficiency of the extensive analyses and evaluations that had been undertaken. Most observers acknowledged that the great promise of program-planning-budgeting had never been fulfilled, and the Office of Management and Budget finally authorized its abandonment. To some, it seemed that the social programs of the decade had been thoughtlessly throwing good money after bad, in spite of sizable research and planning efforts. Daniel Patrick Moynihan surveyed the contributions that social scientists had made to the anti-poverty programs and concluded that, for all the expert advice it had received, "the government did not know what it was doing."[36]

---

[34] Ibid., pp. 31–34.
[35] See for example Williams, chapter 7.
[36] Moynihan, p. 170.

Incremental Decision Making

If the "domain of knowledge" had indeed grown larger, as Robert Lane suggests, it was evident to many that knowledge had not expanded sufficiently to take full possession of its new domain. Many explanations might be offered for this apparent shortfall in the production of applied intelligence. It is not difficult, after all, to identify many potential points of incompatibility between the research and policy processes. Researchers and policymakers are usually representatives of different subcultures with different and sometimes contradictory interests. The mismatch between their respective outlooks may check the development of the mutual trust and understanding that would be necessary for a fruitful partnership between them.[37] Also, the pace of research work is likely to be different from the tempo of policymaking. Timing, therefore, becomes a critical problem for policy research. Inopportune timing may nullify the impact of research findings upon the policy process.

These much-discussed problems of "interface" undoubtedly hinder the mutual adaptation of the policymaker's questions and the researcher's answers. Another set of problems arises not from the inherent differences between research activities and decision making activities, but as a by-product of the attempt to combine them in a single enterprise. The outlines of such problems are evident in the experience of PPBS and its offspring.

Many agencies, for example, tended to take PPBS seriously only when they had embarked on "new program thrusts" involving "major issues." When public officials were proceeding along lines of policy already well established, the analytic demands of program-budgeting were more likely to be ignored or evaded. Proceeding in established directions, of course, is what policymakers do most of the time. Public policy usually develops, not by dramatic leaps and bounds, but by the making of marginal changes in existing programs. The mode of decision making employed is likely to be the "incremental" one explicated by Charles Lindblom, and incremental decision making tends to impose restrictions on the policymaker's demand for the services of researchers and analysts.

Incrementalism is a way of shaping policy that takes its bearings from the status quo. It begins with the recognition of some deficiency in an existing policy or program, and the search for remedies extends only to those alternative policies that are marginally different from the one already in operation. By restricting his attention to this relatively narrow array of policy options, the decision maker limits the burdens that are imposed on his knowledge and comprehension and minimizes the uncertainties that he must reckon with. When the policy changes being considered represent only small departures

---

[37] For some explanations along these lines, see Yehezkel Dror, *Public Policymaking Reexamined* (San Francisco: Chandler, 1968), pp. 3–6; Williams, pp. 62–63.

from what has come before, past experience may provide a firm basis for predicting the consequences that can be expected to result from each of the proposed modifications, and in any case a mistaken prediction about the results of a small policy alteration is not likely to have disastrous consequences.[38]

For policymakers, the chief value of research is that it can help to reduce the uncertainties attendant on decision making by clarifying the consequences that lie at the end of a proposed course of action. For incremental decision makers, however, those uncertainties have already been reduced substantially by the fact that no course of action is considered that diverges very far from the familiar ones that have already been tried and whose results seem fairly well-known. Incrementalism is also a strategy that tends to minimize the value of the stakes that ride on individual decisions. When policies are made and remade in small steps, it is unlikely that the bestowal of huge public benefits or the imposition of great public deprivations will hinge on any particular decision. Since the prospective costs and benefits of incremental decisions will tend to be relatively small, it makes little sense to invest large amounts of time, energy, and money in the collection and analysis of information to illuminate them. For this reason, too, incremental decision making offers few footholds for policy research.

Policy research seldom emerges as a distinct function to be performed by distinct specialists because, in incremental systems, policymaking itself serves the purpose of policy research. The decision maker behaves like an experimenter who makes limited and tentative adjustments in policy so that he can observe their effects and refine hypotheses about the likely consequences of future adjustments. Under these circumstances, the task of policy research tends to remain undifferentiated from policymaking itself, and there is little demand for formal policy evaluation or policy analysis conducted by professional experts with the aid of computer models, sample surveys, or controlled experiments.

Big Decisions

When they are embarking on nonincremental decisions, policymakers are more likely to seek the assistance of professional researchers. As the stakes involved in a decision grow larger and the uncertainties become greater, the call goes out for more information. National crises, for example, tend to bring out a demand for social science expertise. In the past, the number of social scientists employed by the federal government has tended to increase sharply in periods of national emergency, when public officials, faced with a need to make extraordinary departures from business-as-usual, have sought to supplement the wisdom acquired from administrative experience with the products

---

[38] David Braybrooke and Charles Lindblom, *A Strategy of Decision: Policy Evaluation as a Social Process* (New York: Free Press, 1963), chapter 5.

of systematic investigation.[39] America's wars and depressions have been good times for policy research. For similar reasons, policymakers in the 1960s tended to resort to systems analysis when they were making decisions about major policy innovations. And the work of OEO's income maintenance experimenters was associated with the proposal of a nonincremental change in welfare policy.[40]

Not surprisingly, the demand for policy research varies with the nature of the policy process. Under the regime of incrementalism the demand is likely to remain modest. By itself, of course, this disinclination to conduct policy research should not diminish the usefulness of the research that *is* conducted. But it is necessary to consider the political setting in which these research efforts are most likely to be undertaken—an atmosphere of big decisions involving major changes, large stakes, and great uncertainty. Such circumstances can usually be expected to draw large numbers of intensely interested parties into the area of decision making. Some of them—such as the Senate critics of the Family Assistance Plan—may be inclined to attack research and researchers whose conclusions conflict with their own deeply held policy preferences. Others may simply not regard research findings as an appropriate basis for political decision making, preferring to be guided by public opinion or political precedent.

The pressures of the situation may affect conduct of research itself, as well as the reception of the results. Investigators may be led to release their findings prematurely, as in the case of the income maintenance experiment, or they may feel constrained in presenting unwelcome findings. The political conditions most likely to engender a demand for policy research are also conditions that tend to impede the use of research findings for the rational validation of policy decisions.

Harold Wilensky's observations concerning the intelligence function in large organizations lead to approximately the same conclusion.

> The greater the costs and risks or uncertainty and the more significant the changes in method and goals involved, the more intense is the search for information. But the stronger, too, is the weight of established policy and vested interests. Decisions involving many people, much money, great uncertainty or vast risks, and major innovations evoke action and advice from every specialized unit at every level of the hierarchy, thereby increasing the dangers of overload, distortion, or blockage of communication and of paralyzing delays.[41]

---

[39] See, for example, John McDiarmid, "The Mobilization of Social Scientists," in Leonard White (ed.), *Civil Service in Wartime* (Chicago: University of Chicago Press, 1945), pp. 76–80.

[40] Daniel Patrick Moynihan, *The Politics of a Guaranteed Annual Income: The Nixon Administration and the Family Assistance Plan* (New York: Random House, 1973), pp. 10–11.

[41] Harold Wilensky, *Organizational Intelligence: Knowledge and Policy in Government and Industry* (New York: Basic Books, 1967), p. 78.

In one situation after another, a critical dilemma of policy research becomes evident: the greater the demand for policy research, the dimmer the prospects that its results will actually be heeded and understood by decision makers, or that its results will be worth heeding.

The dilemma is not inescapable. It is more or less acute depending on the organizational arrangements made for policy research, the structural characteristics of the client organization, or the political peculiarities of the policy area in question. We will examine the possibilities more fully later.[42] In any case, it is not likely that the central dilemma will be overcome soon or easily. It is a long-standing problem whose effects are as evident in the painful experiences of Department of Agriculture economists during the 1930s and 1940s[43] as they are in the troubled adventures of the Coleman Report during the 1960s and 1970s.[44]

THE POLITICAL CONTEXT

Policy research, like policy itself, is burdened with a political history. The partnership between social science and government is not simply a product of contemporary governmental sophistication, on the one hand, and a recent academic longing for "relevance" on the other. It is a relationship that has had its ups and downs for more than fifty years. Yet our perspective on this relationship often seems to disregard the fact that it has a history. Extravagant hopes for the rationalization of government decision making through social science expertise might not be so inflated if they took account of the fact that government has already enjoyed the benefits of social science expertise for more than half a century. Likewise, those who catch a glimpse of 1984 in the policymaking activities of social scientists might take some comfort from the fact that those activities probably reflect as much of 1934 as of 1984. Nevertheless, it cannot be denied that the role of experts and their research efforts in the policy process has become noticeably more prominent, especially since the 1960s, and the functions performed by policy researchers today are not what they were thirty or forty years ago. The systematic testing of policies now receives more attention than it did in the past.

The movement toward policy research is unlikely to be reversed. It results from fundamental trends in American politics and does not depend simply on the increasing assertiveness or recent accomplishments of researchers. Robert

---

[42] See, in this volume, chapters 7–9.

[43] See Richard S. Kirkendall, *Social Scientists and Farm Politics in the Age of Roosevelt* (Columbia: University of Missouri Press, 1966).

[44] Frederick Mosteller and Daniel Patrick Moynihan, "A Pathbreaking Report," in Mosteller and Moynihan (eds.), *On Equality of Educational Opportunity* (New York: Random House, 1972), pp. 28–34.

Lane suggests that the expanding role of experts in government may reflect a growing independence of political decision makers from their traditional constituencies.

> [T]he dominant scholarly interpretation of policy making processes has changed in the direction of emphasizing the greater autonomy of political leaders and legislators with respect to the role of pressure groups, the power elite, and the electorate. If legislators and other leaders are less bound by the domain of pure politics than we had thought, then they are freer to be guided by the promptings of scientists and findings from the domain of knowledge.[45]

The new prominence of scientific experience in the policy process has been described in similar terms by Don K. Price, who argues that "the development of public policy and the methods of its administration owe less in the long run to processes of conflict among political parties and social and economic pressure groups than to the more objective processes of research and discussion among professional groups."[46]

Political decision makers may have become more attentive to expert advice because of their increasing ability to disregard pressure groups and citizens. But no one seriously predicts that the domain of pure politics will wither away to be replaced by the domain of knowledge. The era of scientific policy-making is not at hand, and political criteria will continue to play a leading role in public decisions. Democracy is not in danger on that account. The elevation of the domain of knowledge may signify not an abandonment of political criteria and traditional constituencies, but an emphasis on political criteria of certain kinds.

Attracting Public Notice

If growing autonomy has liberated political leaders from some of the inconveniences of political opposition and interference, it may also have aggravated the difficulties of cultivating political support. Pressure groups that are not on hand to harass the makers of public policy may also not be available to mobilize support for the policies that are made. In gaining support for their decisions, therefore, political leaders may be thrown back on their own resources. The substance of policy itself is one especially valuable resource. To the extent that a policy can be made to appear exciting, unprecedented, grand in scope, and dramatic in conception, it may also be able to capture the attentions and support of the public at large. Modest enterprises, on the other hand, are not so likely to be viable ones politically.

To justify dramatic policies, of course, it is usually necessary to assume the

---

[45] Lane, p. 658.
[46] Don K. Price, quoted in Daniel Bell, *The Coming of Post-Industrial Society: A Venture in Social Forecasting* (New York: Basic Books, 1973).

existence of some major crisis in the society for which a drastic remedy is urgently needed. Perceived crises, as Anthony Downs points out, have lately become a staple of the American political diet. "Public perceptions of most 'crises' in American life," says Downs, "do not reflect changes in real conditions as much as they reflect the operation of a definite and systematic cycle of heightening public interest and then boredom with major issues." In order to survive in the struggle for public attention, an issue must have strong dramatic appeal, and to the extent that an issue is not inherently dramatic, the drama must be supplied artificially. As the real dimensions of the problem become evident, the drama evaporates and so does public interest. Hence, a cycle emerges that "causes certain individual problems to leap into sudden prominence and then gradually fade from public attention...."[47]

Changed political circumstances may force policymakers to travel the roller-coaster tracks of the "issue-attention cycle." If decision makers have become somewhat detached from their traditional constituencies, as Lane implies, resorting to attention-getting devices, dramatic gestures, and imaginary crises may be increasingly necessary in order to cultivate public support for public decisions. Today, perhaps, the key to successful political leadership is to do nothing small.

To do nothing small is also to depart from the traditional, incremental mode of decision making that Lindblom has described, and some observers of the policy process have in fact detected signs of just such a development—a tendency to forsake the humdrum pace of incrementalism for more adventurous decision making practices.[48] It is these tendencies that may underlie the recent expansion of policy research in government. Departures from incrementalism, as we have already noted, are apt to be accompanied by enlarged demands for policy research and expert advice—but not necessarily by a stronger inclination to use the products of policy research. An increasing demand for expert advice is one thing; an increasing readiness to translate advice into policy is another; and the two things do not necessarily go together. The very conditions that help to create the demand may also reduce the likelihood that research results will be put to use in the policy process.

Effect on Models and their Usability

Much depends, of course, on what is meant by "use." The uncertainty of its meaning has already been noted in the case of policy models. But

---

[47] Anthony Downs, "Up and Down with Ecology: The 'Issue-Attention Cycle'," *The Public Interest* 28 (1972): 38–50.

[48] Jones, p. 155; John F. Manley, "The Family Assistance Plan: An Essay on Incremental and Nonincremental Policymaking," Paper presented at the annual meeting of the American Political Science Association, 1970.

Modeling as a Form of Policy Research

it is clear, at least, that the uses of models, as well as their usability, can be influenced by the political environment in which policy research is conducted. For example, the tendency of policy research to emerge in connection with "big" (nonincremental) decisions may be reflected in an urge to construct complicated policy models for comprehensive, far-reaching decision making. The inclination toward large-scale modeling has been most fully discussed in the field of urban land-use policy,[49] but it is evident in other policy areas as well. Complicated, large-scale models may contain much that is not fully understood or substantiated. The very magnitude of these models may diminish their helpfulness to policymakers.[50] Ironically, at the same time that they suffer from an excess of detail, they may also fail to capture important aspects of the large, complex problems to which they are addressed. The mass of data they require in attempting to represent complex situations is seldom readily available. In its absence, modelers may adopt crude shortcuts or questionable simplifying assumptions. Such technical flaws appear as understandable consequences of the influences of the political setting, and are not simply "technical" in nature.

But modeling need not be restricted to big decisions. Many models, once designed and constructed, can be periodically updated and reused. The time, effort, and money necessary to keep a model up-to-date may be considerable, but they are certainly not so great as the cost of building it anew each time there is a need for the kind of information it provides. By amortizing development costs of a model over numerous repeated uses, the model may become accessible for routine decisions of an incremental kind. Much of the econometric modeling conducted for government agencies is linked to decision making processes of precisely this sort.

Political Uses of Models

Other kinds of modeling remain more dependent on and sensitive to the ups and downs of the issue-attention cycle. The political setting in which policy research occurs is likely to have a pronounced influence upon the way these models are used. The big issues that foster a demand for policy research are also likely to arouse many claimants for the attention of policymakers and, as we have argued, diminish the impact of the research results on public decisions. Certain types of model uses will tend to become more prominent than others. The use of models in analysis, guidance, and problem solving (that is, in the rational validation of policy decisions) will give way to their use in providing political validity.[51] When big issues requiring unusual deci-

---
[49] Lee, pp. 163–178.
[50] Brewer, pp. 77–78, 143–144, 163.
[51] See p. 26.

sions are under consideration, and the audience of interested parties is large, the need for political validation is likely to become especially significant, and fulfilling this need is likely to become a more conspicuous function of models.

One political hurdle confronting almost any policymaking enterprise is the problem of earning a recognized place on the agenda of the political system—creating a political issue, in other words. Models can do political service here because they are devices for focusing attention. Their capacity for clarifying, defining, and simplifying complex situations makes them useful political instruments for converting dimly perceived problems into distinct political issues. These political functions are not much different from those performed by earlier generations of policy researchers in defining emergent problems or "proposing from time to time alternative lines of national procedure."

Apart from promoting political issues, models can also be useful for submerging or defusing issues—another political function to which past generations of policy researchers have contributed. The big, attention-getting issues that create a demand for policy research may also cause public officials to become wary of making decisions. Referring such politically difficult subjects to modelers for extensive study is one way to evade the pressures for immediate action. When the modeling efforts are completed, the need to make a decision may have receded.

Models may also be used as instruments of political advocacy, devices for marshaling support behind particular policy positions. A model can lend the dignity of science to a policy proposal and thereby seek to earn for it the respect of the undecided. But the scientific aura provided by modeling can also backfire.

Modeling can provide political opponents with ammunition to attack a proposed policy. Precisely because modeling is so useful for clarification and specification, it also compels its users to be explicit about the assumptions and hypotheses on which their policy proposals are based. Some of the ambiguity so helpful to political actors would therefore have to be sacrificed, exposing the intellectual substructure of a policy to scrutiny and criticism. Models employed to corroborate policy proposals may be used as political instruments not only by their sponsors, but also by antagonists.

These few examples of the political uses of models make it clear that the domain of knowledge need not be an entirely independent sovereignty, but a mere dependency of the domain of politics. While this should occasion no surprise among modelers and other policy researchers, neither is it a state of affairs from which they will draw great satisfaction. Yet, it is probably unavoidable. The demands of politics are likely to be as inescapable in policy research as they are in policymaking itself. In fact, they become all the more significant because the conditions under which much policy research is conducted are precisely the ones under which the demands of politics are likely to become most intrusive.

3

Modeling in Cross Section

Having discussed the setting for policy modeling in the last chapter, we will now proceed to consider the modeling process itself. Here the model is the thing. Taking a tutorial approach, we will inspect the model on a most basic level, beginning with the fundamental question, "What is it?" In attempting to answer this question, we will review a wide variety of different kinds of models.

A model is like a tripod. The three legs on which it depends for its support, balance, and soundness are theory, data and methodology. We will examine the vital roles played by each of these three elements in determining how models are conceived and put together.

Last in our consideration of the modeling process, yet first in importance, is the modeler and his relationship to the model. The modeler not only builds and runs the model, he affects the way it is received by emphasizing its strengths and points of interest and by compensating for its weaknesses and vulnerabilities.

We will conclude this chapter by telling the story of one modeler who had a marked impact on policy in New York City. We will look into the part that his model did and did not play in policy decisions. We find that a major factor in the effect it had on policy was the contribution of the model—its construction and running—to the modeler's expertise. This effect, although indirect, was decided.

THE MODEL—WHAT IS IT?

To this point, models have been defined only by example. "Model" is a general term that may be applied to many different things, from a toy car to a full-scale prototype of a supersonic aircraft, from the game of Monopoly to a set of mathematical equations that represent the behavior of the national economy, and from an engineering curve to a complex procedure for making long-range projections of future energy resources. A model need not be quantitative or even explicit. One's subjective perceptions of his surroundings form a mental model composed of images of meaningful features and important relationships, such as "I react to poison ivy" or "I vote Republican." The rules that govern the mental model need be neither scientifically precise nor mutually consistent, as with a nurse we know who believes that colds are caused by germs but puts onions in her shoes at night.

Mental models are not the main subject of this book, yet it is true that for the most part decisions are made almost entirely on the basis of mental models (despite their limitations). Perhaps they always will be, since mental models are relatively flexible and adaptable to changing political circumstances. But their strength is also their weakness. Mental models as philosophical constructions and schemes of ideas dominate thought and guide the imagination, said Alfred North Whitehead, yet they exist largely unacknowledged with an importance that is rarely questioned. Implicit, they are elusive to criticism and just as elusive to modification or correction.

The reverse is true of explicit models; they invite examination and revision but in so doing they provoke debate and disagreement. The LR model discussed in Chapter 1 illustrates the furor that a precise, explicit form of model can create in a charged political setting. Still, with the wide availability of high-speed, mass storage computers, we are seeing the growing use of precise, unambiguous, consistent models. Computer models, belonging to a class of models called "formal models," are at the opposite end of the spectrum from implicit mental models. Formal models are our main concern in this book.

Typical dictionary definitions of the word "model" are, "a small replica of an existing object," "a standard of excellence," "a particular style or design," or "a person who displays clothes by wearing them." In *Webster's Seventh New Collegiate Dictionary* (1969) two additional definitions appear.

1. a description or analogy used to help visualize something (as an atom) that cannot be directly observed;
2. a system of postulates, data, and inferences presented as a mathematical description of an entity or state of affairs.

Although these newer definitions come closer than their predecessors to describing what we mean by a formal model, even they are not completely satisfactory. The first is deficient because observable systems can also be modeled, and the second because not every formal model need be mathematical nor have data or postulates. We now proceed to build our own definition.

A model must refer to some object, system, or process which is of interest to the modeler, or else the model has no meaning and is not a model *of* anything. For clarity we will refer to the entity being modeled as the "reference system." Thus, the reference system for Monopoly is the real estate business in Atlantic City; the reference system for the LR model of Chapter 1 is the United States economy. A model with no reference system is no model at all.

The essence of a model is that it represents selected features of the reference system so that one can learn about the reference system by working with the model. The fact that children's toys have traditionally been models of objects in the adult world indicates that we have long been aware of the didactic potential that derives from the selective representation through models of important features of the environment.

By "analysis" we mean the resolution or separation of the reference system into its parts to illuminate their nature and interrelationships and to determine general principles of behavior. By "synthesis," on the other hand, we mean the putting together of expressions of these general principles with representations of parts of the reference system so as to form a replica that exhibits behavior similar to that of the reference system. Theory is the product of analysis, whereas a model is the product of synthesis, using theory. A theory is a general abstraction of important behavioral relationships from the reference system obtained by observing and analyzing the system. A formal model is not a theory, although it may represent or embody theory in its construction. It is synthesized from available tools, constructs, and possibly other smaller models. A single theory may be used by many different kinds of models.

Formal models have need of a language for expression. A linguistic system, whether it be English, mathematics, or a computer programming language, provides building blocks which the model-builder synthesizes into a model, building it piece by piece until its operation or structure parallels to some accepted degree that of the observed reference system.

We are now ready to define what we mean by a formal model: A formal model of a given reference system is another system expressed in a formal language and synthesized from representations of selected elements of the reference system and their assumed interrelationships. More concisely, a model is a simplified representation of the interrelationships among elements of a given reference system. (Notice that the concise definition omits certain features of the fuller definition for purposes of clarity, just as models themselves omit the less relevant details of the reference system.)

Formal models vary in the mode of their expression. Four forms are distinguished in Figure 3–1: schematic, physical, symbolic, and role-playing. Each will be treated in turn.

Schematic Models

"Schematic" or "iconic" models represent the reference system through the language of pictures (icons), points, lines, curves, graphs, or schemata. The earliest models were schematic representations or drawings of animals and other features of the environment. The familiar blueprint is a schematic model of a building to be constructed. It is essential to the construction process. Schematic models also can be instrumental in the development of other forms of models. An example of a schematic model is shown in Figure 3-2.[1] Geometric models are an important type of schematic model.

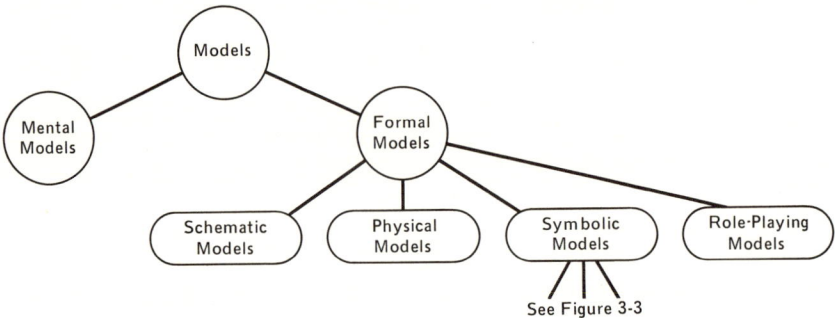

Figure 3-1: Classes of Models

Models can be imprecise, piecemeal and informal (mental models) or formally explicit (formal models). Formal models vary in the form they take: schematic, physical, symbolic, and role-playing.

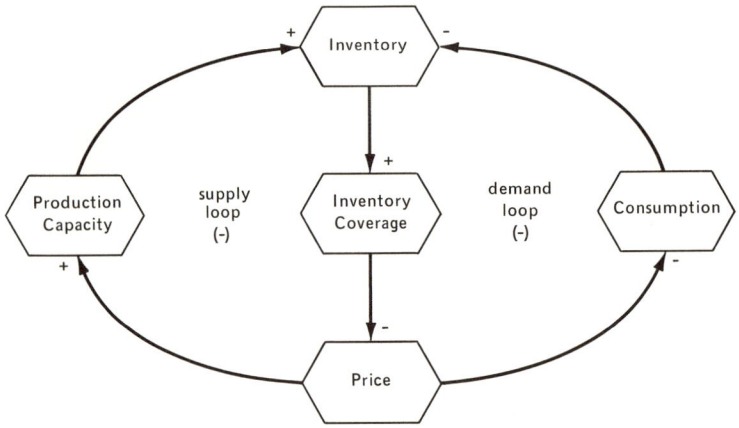

Figure 3-2

Schematic model of a commodity production model. Arrows indicate causal relationships. A plus (+) sign denotes a positive effect, e.g., if price increases, production capacity will increase also. A minus (−) sign signifies negative effect, e.g., if price increases, consumption will decrease. Price is itself affected by changes in inventory coverage so that when inventory coverage increases, price will decrease.

---

[1] This schematic model was used to develop a model of the United States hog industry. See Roger F. Naill et al., "Dynamic Modeling As a Tool for Managerial Planning: A Case Study of the U.S. Hog Industry," *Proceedings of the 1973 Summer Computer Simulation Conference,* Montreal, Canada, July 17–19, 1973 (La Jolla, Calif.: Simulation Councils, Inc., pp. 1043–1051.

Physical Models

A "physical" or "analog" model represents selected features of the reference system by means of the language of physical analogies. A toy airplane is a physical model of a real aircraft. A child's erector set is a physical model of construction materials. In hydrology, the breaking of a dam can be reproduced in miniature through experimentation on a physical model of a river basin built from plaster or concrete according to topographical maps of the region, with all dimensions considerably scaled down. By sprinkling appropriate amounts of water on the model, one can observe the drainage flow through the watershed. Sudden removal of a dam from the model simulates the consequences of the breaking of the real dam.[2]

Physical models are one of the oldest forms of models. Pottery models of Mayan temples, predating Columbus by several hundred years, have survived largely intact. They are thought to have been used to guide construction of the temples. Small models of the human figure made as early as 300 B.C. have been found in West Mexico.[3] Miniature physical models of ancient Egyptian palaces and grounds placed in tombs thousands of years ago were intended to provide amenities and services in the lives of the pharoahs after death.

In electrical analog models, relationships are represented by interconnected networks of electrical devices. Flows of people, material, and information are physically modeled by flows of electricity. An electrical analog model, when including a digital computer as a component, is called a "hybrid system." Hybrid systems are hardly ever used in policy research, but are used in operational fields, such as urban traffic control where they may be used to direct a network of vehicle-responsive traffic signals at intersections of the city. A hybrid system directing traffic through the city of Tokyo reportedly has resulted in a 25 percent decrease in average travel time from one side of the city to the other.

Symbolic Models

"Symbolic" models use symbols as linguistic constructs that stand for selected elements of the reference system. School children learn a type of symbolic modeling when they learn to count. The abstract symbols 0, 1, and 2 stand for properties of real objects, while the relational symbols +, −, and = stand for relationships among the objects. Depending upon the type of symbols

---

[2] There is some discussion later in this chapter concerning a physical hydraulic model of Jamaica Bay, New York. This model was built by and for the use of the U.S. Army Corps of Engineers which uses such models frequently.

[3] Clement W. Meighan, "Prehistory of West Mexico," *Science* 184 (1974): 1254–1261.

and language used, a symbolic model may be classified as either a verbal, mathematical, or computer model, as portrayed in Figure 3–3.

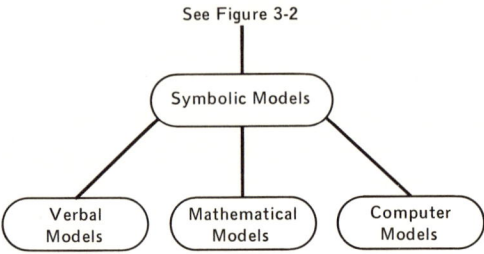

Figure 3–3: Symbolic Models

Symbolic models come in three varieties: verbal models, mathematical models, and computer models. Verbal models are expressed in spoken or written languages, mathematical models are expressed in formal mathematics, and computer models, which depend upon computers to calculate values or manipulate symbols, can be thought of as being expressed as computer programs and computer-stored data.

"Verbal" models are symbolic models which use the symbols of a formal language such as English or French, to express relationships. The following is a verbal model of the operation of a thermometer.

> A thermometer is a glass tube containing a quantity of mercury that expands in volume when heated, thus registering an increase in temperature.

Chapter 1 contains a number of examples of verbal models of the operation of the national economy. Stein's simple calculation verbally modeled the hypothetical functioning of a full-employment economy, while McCracken's comments on the possible relationship between money supply and GNP constituted a simple verbal model of the effect of money on aggregate economic activity.

Verbal models play a crucial part in the policy process. As expressions or presentations of other forms of models, whether mental or formal, they provide the means for conveying the policy import of these models to policymakers. By impinging upon the mental model of the policymaker, verbal models become the avenue for influencing decisions. Thus, when President Nixon sent his first "full-employment" budget to Congress in January 1971, he said, "The full-employment idea is in the nature of a self-fulfilling prophecy. By operating as if we were at full employment, we will help to bring about that full employment." This verbal model was a reflection of Nixon's mental model, which had been influenced by the verbal models of Shultz and Stein. After Shultz left office as secretary of the treasury in 1974, his successor, William Simon, dismissed the full-employment model. "I never did believe in it," Simon said. Simon set out to balance the real budget, not the "mythical" full-employment accounts.[4] Simon's mental model of the economy differed significantly from those of Shultz and Stein, and his verbal expressions of it led to a shift in policy. Verbal models are the primary means of influencing a person's mental model, and since decisions are made via the policymaker's mental model, verbal models are critical to the policymaking process. See Figure 3–4.

The most concise and potent form of symbolic model is the "mathematical" or "analytical" model, of which the representation of Einstein's theory of general relativity as a set of mathematical equations is a celebrated example. An analytical or closed-form solution of a mathematical model is a logical rear-

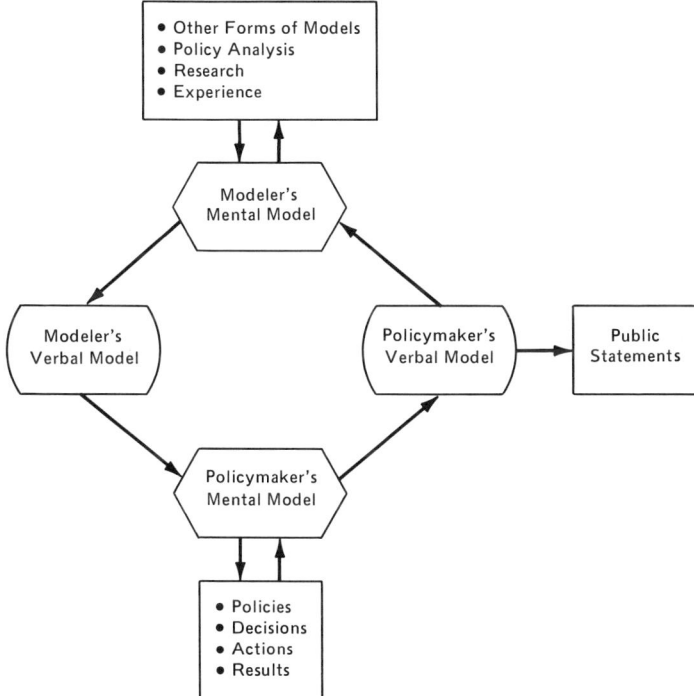

Figure 3–4: Mental Models and Verbal Models in the Policy Process

The modeler's mental model is formed by his modeling, experience, and research. He verbally communicates the relevance of his work to the policymaker, who either incorporates the information into his own mental model or responds verbally, giving feedback to the modeler who may then alter his work. It is through the policymaker's mental model that decisions are made.

---

[4] Joseph R. Slevin, "Simon Shuns Shultz Idea," *Baltimore Sun* (morning), July 9, 1974, p. A15.

rangement of the equation or equations to express symbolically one or more items of the model in terms of the others. Consider the following equation from Newtonian physics that may be used to represent the dropping of a coin. It calculates the height (F) of a coin over time during its fall from an initial height (h)

$$F = h - \tfrac{1}{2} g (S - t)^2$$

Here h is the initial height of the coin at time t; F is its height in feet at time S in seconds; and g is the gravitational constant equal to 32 feet per second.[2] The analytical solution of this equation for S in terms of the other elements is

$$S = t + (2(h - F)/g)^{1/2}$$

This solution gives the time required for the coin to drop to a height F. It holds for any value of F between 0 and h, and is thus a general solution. When an equation cannot be solved analytically, it may still be possible to derive a specific numerical solution for a given set of values. Let us make believe, for example, that the equation for F can be expanded to include a (fictitious) statistical measure of air resistance, a, as follows.

$$F = h - \tfrac{1}{2} g(S - t)^2 + a(S - t)^5$$

One cannot solve for S generally or analytically, but a value of S can be derived numerically for given values of F between 0 and h. For equations that do not have analytical solutions there are standard computing procedures for calculating particular numerical solutions.

In the coin-falling model, the quantities F and S are called "variables," since their values vary during the course of the process being modeled. The quantities a, g, h, and t, on the other hand, are "constants" whose values are unchanging during a given fall of the coin. Since h and t can be varied between falls, they are not the same kinds of constants as a and g. We call them "parameters" of the model. They must be set before the model is calculated or run. The constant g is assumed known and fixed for all time. It is a "universal" constant. Unlike g, the constant a is not known either precisely or with certainty. Nor can we be assured that it will not change under different meteorological conditions. We call it a "coefficient" of the model. Many authors use the terms "parameter" and "coefficient" interchangeably, but we make a distinction between the two. Parameters are *set*, whereas coefficients are *estimated* either statistically (when relevant data on the reference system are ample), numerically, as by simple averaging (when data are limited), or intuitively (when data are nonexistent or unusable). In the two models of Chapter 1, coefficients were obtained largely by nonstatistical, intuitive means for the

World3 model and by statistical regression methods for the LR model. In the World3 model, different possible policy actions on such issues as population control and economic growth were represented by parameters. The assumed future growth rate in money supply was a parameter of the LR model. Parameters were varied between successive runnings of each model; coefficients, in general, were not.

Variables that represent the different configurations or states of the reference system (such as F and S in the coin example) are known as "status" or "state" variables. Some status variables may be supplied or determined externally to the model and are treated as known. They are called "exogenous." If the coin-falling model were used to calculate coin heights at certain times specified by externally determined values of S, S would be an exogenous variable. Variables determined within (or by) the model (F, for example) are considered as unknown. They are called "endogenous." Which variables are endogenous and which exogenous depends on how a system is modeled and how the model is used. This, in turn, is a function of what is known about the system and what the modeler chooses to assume rather than to incorporate into the model.

Computer models are symbolic models which use a computer to carry out calculations or manipulations, as do the LR and World3 models of Chapter 1. The LR model uses the computer to estimate statistically the coefficients of each equation and to calculate future values of the endogenous variables, such as GNP. The World3 model uses the computer to project forward the assumed influences of the size of the population on the amount of natural resources and of capital investment on birth rate. Most of the models discussed in this book are computer models.

A computer model of the falling coin could be built as follows: Instruct the computer to accept (or "READ" from punched cards or typed input, for example) the initial height (H) of the coin, its release time (T) and the time (S) at which we want to know the coin's height. Then, using the simple mathematical formula described earlier, the height (F) of the coin at time (S) can be computed. Finally print (or "WRITE") the answer on the output device (punched cards, paper, magnetic tape, etc.). An abbreviated computer model for this problem might look like the following:[5]

```
READ H, T, S
G = 32
F = H - 0.5 * G * (S - T) * (S - T)
WRITE "HEIGHT IS", F, "FEET AT TIME", S, "SECONDS."
```

---

[5] This computer model is stylized for the lay reader in that the syntax used does not belong to any specific established computer programming language. Also, the model needs additional statements to prevent negative heights.

In this brief model the symbol * indicates multiplication. The third line of the "program" is not a mathematical equality; rather it signifies that the right-hand side is to be calculated using available information (the input), and that this value is to be assigned to the left-hand side (F). If the following input values for H, T, and S were given to the model,

1000, 0, 5

the output would return as:

HEIGHT IS 600 FEET AT TIME 5 SECONDS.

This run of the model corresponds to a coin dropped from 1,000 feet and observed after five seconds. As in mathematical models, computer models have variables and constants: F is an endogenous status variable, S is an exogenous status variable, G is a (universal) constant, and H and T are parameters. There are no coefficients in this model.

Models can be classified as "static" or "dynamic" according to the treatment of time in the model. A static model either carries no explicit reference to time, as when it purports to represent an equilibrium state, or produces results for only one instant of time. A painting or snapshot is a static schematic model, a molded tin soldier is a static physical model, and the equations for a supply and demand curve in economics form a static mathematical model.

Dynamic models include time as a variable or critical dimension. They are by nature time-oriented and typically produce results for a sequence of successive time instants. The falling coin model can be seen as dynamic by having it display the position of the object as a function of time. The model is asked by the program shown in Figure 3–5 to compute the height of the coin once

```
         READ H, T
         TIME = T
TOP:     F = H - 0.5 * G * (TIME - T) * (TIME - T)
         IF (F. LT. 0) THEN STOP
                   ELSE PLOT (F, TIME)
         TIME = TIME + 1
         GO TO TOP
```

Figure 3–5: A Dynamic Computer Model of a Falling Coin

The height F of the coin is calculated at one-second intervals of time until it becomes negative. Each calculated position is expressed as an asterisk on a two-dimensional graph, as in Figure 3–6. The fourth line of the program tests whether F is less than (.LT.) zero. If so, the program stops.

for every second of time that has elapsed following release of the object. A display of the results is given in the form of a graph in Figure 3–6. A policy model that is concerned with the effects of policies over time is most likely to be dynamic.

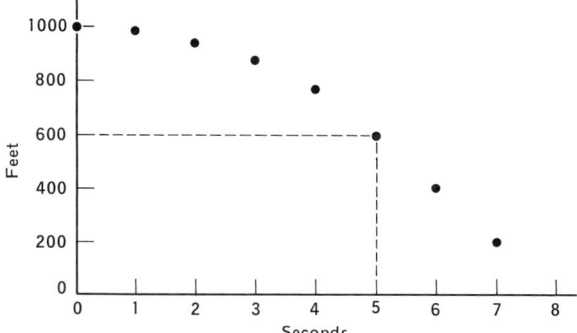

Figure 3–6: Dynamic Display of the Height of a Falling Coin as a Function of Time

Dynamic models are normally either periodic or event-oriented. A periodic dynamic model produces results at regularly spaced intervals of reference time (i.e., time in the reference system). The length of these intervals is known as the "time interval" of the model. The time interval is a parameter of the model if it can be varied from one run to the next. For example, the dynamic model of the falling coin produces one output (or one point on the graph) for every second of reference time. The time interval we chose for it was one second, but, clearly, it might just as easily have been two seconds or half a second. Event-oriented models, on the other hand, do not move evenly in reference time, but rather produce a result only when an event occurs in the model. A dynamic event-oriented model of persons arriving at a waiting line (or queue) at a hospital check-in desk can be created by scheduling arrivals and departures of patients by means of random samplings[6] from known probability distributions.[7] Whereas a periodic model would compute the total number of arrivals and departures during each time interval (0, 1, 2, ...),

---

[6] Actually, internally generated "random" numbers are not random at all, but only appear to be random. The same sequence of numbers will always be generated unless the user instructs the random number generator to begin with a different starting value. It is imperative to be able to reproduce a given sequence of these numbers for purposes of verifying the internal structure of computer-based models; hence these not-so-random numbers are called "pseudo-random" numbers.

[7] A probability distribution is one means of specifying the relative frequencies with which events occur. A probability distribution for an unbiased coin toss would indicate that the probability of heads is one-half and of tails is one-half.

an event-oriented model moves directly from one such event to the next. Periodic models are more efficient when events occur frequently and are closely spaced. Event-oriented models are more efficient when events are infrequent or widely spaced.

The falling coin model, the World3 model, and the LR model are all deterministic in that they give the same response whenever run with the same assumptions about the reference system. A probabilistic or stochastic model, on the other hand, uses computer-generated random numbers to affect the model's outcome according to probabilistic effects built into the model. In stochastic models, different results follow from the use of different sets of random numbers without any change to the model. In a recent survey of over 650 federally supported modeling projects, about half of the models surveyed were stochastic.[8]

Suppose that in the model of the falling coin we were interested in determining whether the hypothetical coin lands heads or tails. We could simulate the action of the coin by introducing a random number between zero and one, calling the coin heads if that number is less than one-half and calling it tails otherwise. This is accomplished by the following additional programming:

```
R = RANDOM (0, 1)
IF (R .LT. ½) THEN WRITE "HEADS"
              ELSE WRITE "TAILS"
```

The first line assigns to R an internally generated random number between zero and one. The last two lines cause the words HEADS or TAILS to be written, depending upon the size of the random number.

The many outcomes possible with stochastic models call for repeated running of the model to produce a distribution of outcomes, the so-called "Monte Carlo" approach. Monte Carlo is a common method for examining the behavior of large, complex systems. The fact that uncertainty is simulated by a Monte Carlo procedure does not make the model any less explicit. The model is completely specified even though some of its elements are probability distributions. The outcome is determined once the random numbers are selected.

A model is called "micro" or "macro" depending upon its level of disaggregation or detail. Micro models deal with small units of the reference system and often use behavioral theory to represent the behavior of the individual components of the system. Macro models, by using trends and patterns, directly represent the aggregate or overall behavior of the system without referring to individuals.

---

[8] Gary Fromm, William L. Hamilton, and Diane E. Hamilton, *Federally Supported Mathematical Models: Survey and Analysis* (Washington, D.C.: National Science Foundation, 1975).

Role-Playing Models

Role-playing or gaming models represent a reference system with the help of roles enacted by human players. Role-playing models may use a computer[9] as an automatic score keeper, participant, referee, or oracle, or they may not use a computer at all.

The game of Pit is a good example of a computerless role-playing model. All it requires is a deck of "commodity share" cards. Each player takes the role of a trader in grain futures in the "pit" at the Chicago Board of Trade and trades facsimiles of commodity shares until someone corners the market. Many popular social games incorporate role-playing models.

A child who takes the role of a general while playing with physical models of soldiers is engaged in a role-playing model of an army. An interactive multi-region model of the world,[10] built in a second Club of Rome study, has the user playing the role of policymaker within an environment produced by a computer model. The user decides on priorities, sets policies, and periodically revises his decisions as he receives updated information about the probable effects of his choices.

Establishing roles is a way of introducing an element of uncertainty into a model, but, unlike a probability distribution, it is an implicit, not an explicit representation of uncertainty. The outcome is subject to the vagaries of human behavior. The role-playing model provides a means for incorporating aspects of the player's *non*formal mental model into a formal framework.

Purposes of Models

Formal models can be classified according to purpose. "Descriptive" models characterize important features of the reference system to allow for experimentation and help in understanding. "Prescriptive" models prescribe a solution to a problem or find the best answer in a given situation. "Normative" models identify feasible and desirable configurations of the reference system to serve as goals, norms, or standards. Descriptive models often display the expected behavior of the reference system given restrictions on its internal behav-

---

[9] A good example of a computer-based role-playing model is Peter House's CITY model which has evolved through several versions in recent years. See, for example, Peter House and Phillip Patterson, *An Environmental Laboratory for the Social Sciences* (Washington, D.C.: U.S. Environmental Protection Agency, 1973). The River Basin Model reported on in this book is CITY IV, the fourth version of House's CITY model.

[10] See Mihajlo Mesarovic, "An Interactive Decision Stratum for the Multilevel World Model," *Futures,* August 1973, pp. 357–369, for an example of an interactive world model. Also Mihajlo Mesarovic and Eduard Pestel, *Mankind at the Turning Point: Organic or Cancerous Growth Path?* Second Report to the Club of Rome (New York: E. P. Dutton, 1974).

ior specified by setting parameters. Prescriptive models indicate the behavior that the reference system *should* follow in order to meet given constraints on its external behavior (supply sufficient to meet demand, for example). But such distinctions can be overdone. The same model can almost always be used for more than one purpose.

The falling-coin model is a descriptive model in that it describes the position of the coin at any given time following its release from a specified height. To use the same model prescriptively, we ask at what initial height should the coin be released in order to hit the ground in exactly ten seconds? By analytically solving the basic equation for h, we have

$$h = F + \tfrac{1}{2} g (S - t)^2.$$

Since F is zero when the coin hits the ground, and $(S - t)^2$, the square of the elapsed time, is 100, we find that $h = 50g = 1{,}600$ feet. The model "prescribes" that the coin be dropped from a height of 1,600 feet in order to touch down in ten seconds.

In this case, there is only one possible solution. In other cases, there may be many feasible solutions, but again there may be only one solution that is best or optimum. An example is the mixing of ingredients in the manufacture of dog food. There may be several mixtures (feasible solutions) that satisfy the minimum daily nutritional requirements for dogs, but only one of these (the optimum solution) that satisfies the requirements at least cost. A model that lends itself to calculation of the optimum solution is called an "optimization" model. It is clearly prescriptive. Optimization models are solved to derive the optimum solution. The solution procedure is sometimes called an "algorithm."[11] For example, the simplex method (or simplex algorithm) is used to solve the class of optimization models called linear programming models.

Simulation models, in contrast, are descriptive models which use the computer to update the values of variables so as to mimic the behavior of the reference system. Typically, simulation models are *run* instead of *solved*. See Figure 3-7 for a comparison of simulation and optimization models. The dichotomy is not absolute. The same model can sometimes be used for simulation and optimization, and a simulation model may use solution procedures to update the values of its variables. The equations of some econometric models must be solved, for example, to take account of simultaneous effects.

---

[11]An algorithm is an explicit procedure designed to produce an answer to a given type of problem. Algorithms are guaranteed to stop at some point and produce an answer, whereas nonalgorithmic procedures may in some cases never terminate. For example, square root finding methods taught in high school are algorithms, but methods for finding the largest prime number are only procedures, as there is no guarantee that such a number can be found.

Modeling in Cross Section 61

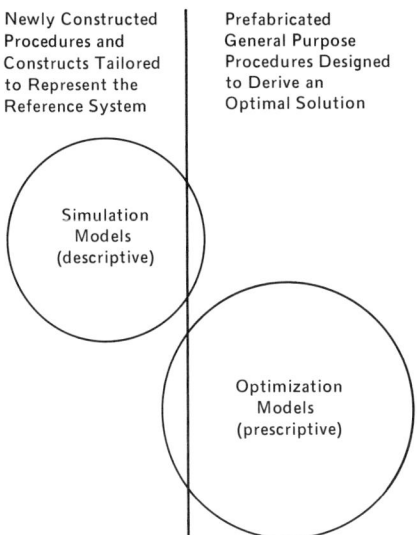

Figure 3–7: Simulation vs. Optimization

Simulation models use special constructs and computational procedures designed to represent processes in the reference system. Some use is also made of general purpose procedures. Optimization models use prefabricated general purpose procedures to calculate optimal solutions.

This is an indispensable part of the process of simulating such econometric models and advancing them in time.

When the possibility of using simulation was first broached to the Pittsburgh City Council in 1962, one prominent member reportedly asked, "Is that anything like artificial insemination?"[12] How does one explain simulation? It is a way of studying the properties of a reference system.[13] It explores the system's behavior through experimentation with a formal model of the system. A simulation model must reproduce behavioral aspects of the reference system in areas where policy options are expected to have impact. Take, for example, the simulation of patients arriving at each of two hospitals. Assume that one hospital usually has a longer waiting line or queue than the other hospital. A health department interested in policies that would keep all hospital entrance lines of similar length might use a simulation model to experiment with different allocations of services and scheduling procedures.

---

[12] Garry D. Brewer, *Politicians, Bureaucrats and the Consultant* (New York: Basic Books, 1973), p. 171.

[13] Some modelers use the term "simuland" instead of "reference system" in a context specific to simulation models. The more general term "reference system" applies to all models.

If, however, the model incorporates the disparity in queue lengths as part of its internal structure, no amount of experimentation with the model would help the health department decide what policies to favor to reduce this disparity.

Uses of Models

Many models are used in forecasting. A conditional forecast is a projection of a model's assumptions about the reference system. For example, the World3 model can be used to project world population to the year 2100 assuming a reduction in natural resource utilization or a change in birth rates. A recent survey[14] found that of 335 urban models, about 80 percent were being used for projection purposes.

An unconditional forecast is a prediction whose assumptions are considered to be the best possible. A prediction suggests a level of confidence that a projection does not. One can predict the occurrence of a lunar eclipse because the underlying assumptions are accepted and established, and because the model has been highly accurate in its past predictions.

Projections and predictions obtained from periodic models are made at fixed intervals of reference time. The practice of single-interval projection produces one set of results. Multiple-interval projection, a more common procedure, produces interim projections as well as a final set. Projections are obtained by running the model forward one period at a time. The modeler can sometimes alter parameters and the structure of the model between periods. Such changes were made in the second study for the Club of Rome (see note 10).

Feasibility targeting is a use of models related to projection. Here, one selects an *a priori* goal for the reference system—next year's desired GNP, for example—and uses the model to examine whether there are any feasible policies that might achieve the goal. The LR model of Chapter 1 was used to determine the feasibility of the target level for 1971 GNP of $1,065 billion.

Two other functions related to projection that a model can perform are allocation and derivation. An example of allocation is the distribution of a projected population into census tracts or income classes. Allocation is a central function of transportation models which use projected travel demand to infer traffic loads on particular streets in the future. Examples of derivation are the deduction of travel demand from land use patterns or tax revenues from projected distributions of population by income class. A model may be

---

[14] Janet R. Pack et al., *The Use of Urban Models in Urban Policy Making*, 2 vols. (Philadelphia: The Fels Center of Government, University of Pennsylvania, 1974), I–iii.

executed or run to perform projection, allocation, and derivation iteratively. A land-use model, for example, may project next year's population, allocate it to land areas, derive taxes and densities from the allocation, then project the following year's population, and so on.

We distinguish between routine and policy models. A routine model is one whose reference system is well-defined and noncontroversial. Policy models, on the other hand, tend to be subject to dispute. It is in their nature to reflect uncertainty, ambiguity, and disagreement. Usually, no one knows for sure what processes and relationships govern a policy area. Since formal models must be explicit, guesses and assumptions fill in where knowledge is lacking. When the modeler personally supplies the missing information, the policy model reflects his worldview and biases.

Policy models differ most from routine models in the nature of the problem area they address and in the degree to which the controversiality of the policy area causes the model itself to become controversial. Routine models are less prone to question regarding their structure and internal relationships. Disagreements generally can be settled by consulting available data or observing the reference system. But routine models may still be germane to policy decisions. For example, a problem concerning the size and shape of police patrol zones in a major city may be routine, with known constraints and effectiveness criteria, yet it may also be a central issue in a police department labor dispute. The personal desires and vested interests that enter into such a dispute transcend modeling considerations and can quickly immerse the most routine model in heated political controversy.

THE MODELING PROCESS: THEORY, DATA, AND METHODOLOGY

In creating a formal model, the modeler draws upon theory, data, and methodology. A balance among these three aspects is healthy. A model that is deficient in one or more of them may be supported by the clever or forceful intervention of the modeler, but like a tripod with a short leg, the model is likely to be shaky despite the best efforts of the modeler to compensate for the deficiency.

Theory, data, and methodology are not independent of one another. One theory may require less data than another; the lack of data may preclude the use of a methodology that depends on data; and a particular methodology may make difficult the expression of a certain theory. Figure 3–8 illustrates this interdependence among the three factors and the influence of each on the model.

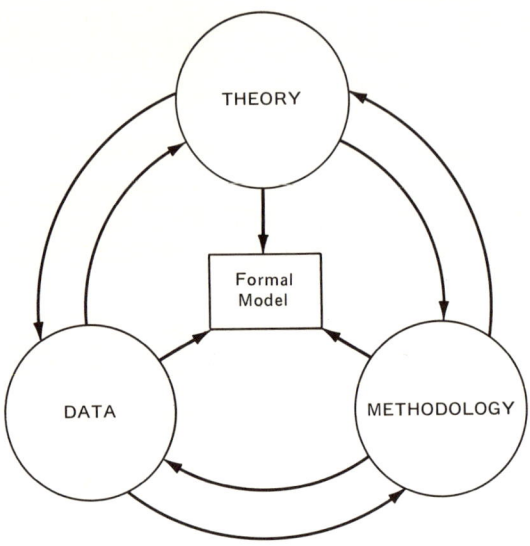

Figure 3-8

A formal model is determined by its choice of theory, data, and methodology. These three factors are interdependent so that the choice of one impinges both upon the other two and upon the formal model itself.

Theory

Underlying every formal model is the modeler's mental conception of it, its interrelationships, and its elements. The conception of a model is a reflection of the reference system as perceived by the modeler and is the product of the modeler's analysis of the reference system through a glass colored by his methodology. The conception is the blueprint for synthesis of the formal model. See Figure 3-9.

Laws, principles, and hypotheses form the theoretical substance of a model's conception. A law is an exact formulation of general relationships or processes that are universally observed to occur with regularity under the same conditions. The law of gravity used in the model of the falling coin is a good example. By a principle, on the other hand, we mean a formulation of general relationships underlying a wide class of observed phenomena which have been only partially confirmed. The principles of evolution offer an example. Although great amounts of evidence support these principles, they are not proven or universally accepted as law.

Hypotheses are tentative formulations that are not supported by evidence to the same extent as are principles. Hypotheses constitute the major portion of

Modeling in Cross Section 65

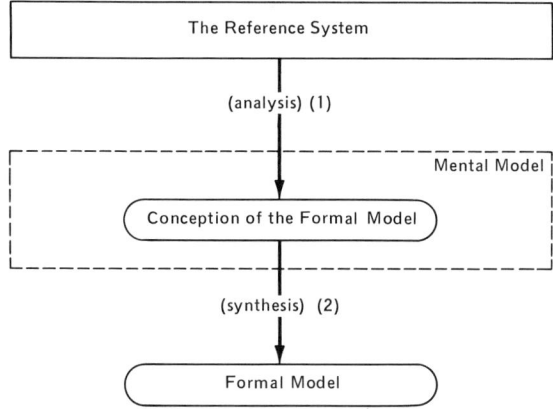

Figure 3–9: Hierarchy of the Modeling Process

A conception is created by analysis (1) of the reference system and then transformed into a formal model by synthesis (2) from the available tools and "building blocks" of the modeling methodology.

the conceptions of most formal policy models. The *Limits to Growth* model, for example, hypothesizes that the aggregate generation of persistent pollutants—from suspended particulates and fertilizers to heavy metals and radioactive wastes—is a precisely specified function of resource use and total world population.[15] Although the modelers cite historical evidence to support their hypothesis,[16] the evidence is not strong enough or widely enough accepted at the present time to warrant calling the pollution hypothesis a principle.

If the evidence suggests that a hypothesis is incorrect and it is dropped from the model or replaced, it becomes a discredited hypothesis. Occasionally an incorrect hypothesis is deliberately incorporated into a model in order to explore its consequences, as, for example, in an animated movie of a world in which gravitational force varies inversely with the cube, rather than the square, of the distance between bodies. Verbal models, when used to confuse or mislead, often employ fallacious hypotheses.

Formal models play an integral role in the process of developing knowledge (see Figure 3–10). A hypothesis expressed in a formal model can be tested against reference data and the opinions of experts. As Britton Harris puts it, "A model is an experimental means of putting the theory into contact with

---

[15] Dennis L. Meadows et al., *The Dynamics of Growth in a Finite World* (Cambridge, Mass.: Wright-Allen Press, 1974), p. 429.
[16] Ibid., pp. 431–432.

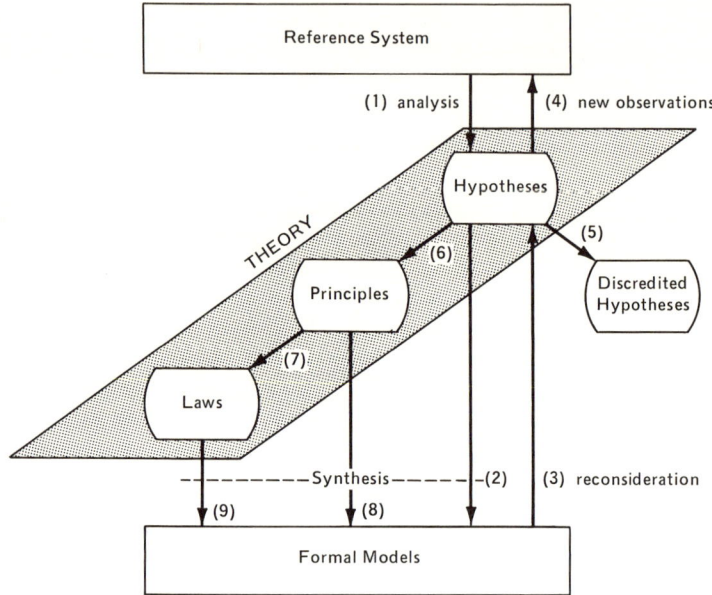

Figure 3–10: Schematic Model of the Role of Modeling in the Testing and Development of Principles and Laws

The modeler analyzes (1) the reference system and creates hypotheses which he represents by a synthetic (2) formal model. Deficiencies, faults, and inconsistencies cause the hypotheses to be reconsidered (3), possibly requiring new observations (4) of the reference system. Hypotheses which fail tests of plausibility, accuracy, significance, etc., become discredited (5). Those that survive all tests achieve the status of principles (6) or even laws (7). Formal models can be based on established principles (8) or laws (9), as well as hypotheses (2).

the real world."[17] Many hypotheses fall short and are discredited. Some that survive the rigorous tests of significance, relevance, plausibility, and consistency may become widely accepted as principles or even laws, although in policy modeling, laws rarely if ever exist. Policy problems are not understood well enough to acquire the universal support and respect that a law commands.

Absolute proof of a hypothesis is unattainable; only continued *lack of disproof* is possible. The hypotheses, principles, and laws used in building a formal model together constitute the theory on which the model is based. Since this theory refers back to the reference system being modeled, we call it "referential" theory to distinguish it from the methodological theory that

---

[17] Britton Harris, "Quantitative Models of Urban Development: Their Role in Metropolitan Decision Making," in Harvey S. Perloff and Lowdon Wingo (eds.), *Issues in Urban Economics* (Baltimore: The Johns Hopkins University Press, 1968), p. 116.

underlies the techniques and constructs of the modeling methodology. The body of theory used in the LR model of Chapter 1, for example, refers to the presumed behavior of the American economy and is thus referential. The duality theory of linear programming, on the other hand, is methodological. Referential theory for policy models is typically drawn from the behavioral or social sciences, whereas methodological theory customarily comes from the mathematical sciences.

Referential theory provides a general foundation of relationships and entities that gives the model structure. It is often the best guide as to what items should be included in the model, and it also helps those previously familiar with the theory to identify with and understand the model. A model soundly rooted in theory has a better chance of being accepted and used, other things being equal, than a model weak in theory. But the use of theory is not a guarantee of acceptance. The LR model drew on three well-known theories of economics—Keynesian theory, quantity theory, and efficient-markets theory[18]—yet the model was bitterly attacked and widely rejected. Nor does theory offer any more than a specious sense of authority when its assumptions do not hold. The world changes, and theories based on past trends may soon be outdated.

Model forecasts of automobile sales, for example, were excessively high in the midst of the 1974 fuel crisis. The possibility of petroleum shortages had not been included in the theory used by the models. All the major econometric models of the United States economy, to take a second example, were far off the mark in their 1974 forecasts of real growth and prices.[19] The economic theory of many of these models assumes that the United States economy is unaffected by the problems of other nations and that supplies will always be available at an appropriate price. The models do not account for stubbornly persistent inflation, serious shortages of basic materials, cartels of oil producers, effects of international money flows, floating of currencies, and dollar devaluations. The economic theory used by the models, though sound, is incomplete. It lags the developments it attempts to explain. Theory as a basis for a formal model is of greatest value when it refers to reference systems that change only slowly. Unfortunately, policy areas are among the most volatile fields of application for models. Economist Robert M. Solow of M.I.T. puts it this way: "One advantage the physicist has over the economist is that the velocity of light has not changed over the past thousands of years, while what was in the 1950s and 1960s a good wage and price equation is no longer so."[20]

Theories that change only slowly over time may not keep up with policy

---
[18] Hearings, Joint Economic Committee, U.S. Congress, February 5, 1971, p. 281.
[19] "Theory Deserts the Forecasters," *Business Week*, June 29, 1974, pp. 50–59.
[20] Ibid., p. 53.

areas that change rapidly and constantly. Recognizing this shortcoming in theory, a modeler may personally adjust the projections of his model to reflect an impending strike, war, bankruptcy, or other events and trends not covered by the theory. In a model of the national economy, "add factors" may be applied to the model's projections to incorporate the modeler's judgment and intuition about economic trends. The practice is widespread. Many well-known econometric models use some form of judgmental adjustment.

In 1971 Victor Zarnowitz investigated the performance of the Wharton model of the United States economy.[21] He compared over a three-year period the accuracy of *ex ante* forecasts with *ex post* forecasts. *Ex ante* forecasts take the modeler's estimates of future exogenous data as input, whereas *ex post* forecasts are made *after* the fact using the actual recorded data as input. Zarnowitz's surprising finding was that the errors in the *ex post* forecasts were as much as one and one-half times *larger* than the errors in the *ex ante* forecasts. Zarnowitz's explanation was that the modeler could compensate for misspecifications in the model when estimating future data, an opportunity that the use of real data does not afford. To illustrate his point, Zarnowitz cited the use of underestimated values for future governmental spending in an econometric model whose fiscal multipliers were too high. This is one way that a computer modeler can directly affect the performance of his model.

A model that uses theory where it does not pertain may be worse than no model at all. As Lewis Mumford has observed, computer models can acquire a "godlike authority,"[22] and their results can be taken as gospel. A model, masquerading as an oracle, may be nothing more than an advocate in technological guise. An urban model that assumes perfect equilibrium may be used by local officials to legitimize previously planned slum clearance programs despite the fact that its assumptions do not apply to their city. Policymakers and their staffs generally do not have the technical sophistication or interest to discern whether the underlying theory of a model faithfully captures the essence of the problem being modeled.

When theory is lacking, for whatever reason, the modeler may resort to intuitive guesses. He may then try to convince others that his guesses are correct, thus propping up the theory leg of the modeling tripod. Another approach is to identify a representative spectrum of opinions on the policy

---

[21] Victor Zarnowitz, "New Plans and Results of Research in Economic Forecasting," Center for Mathematical Studies in Business and Economics Reprint Series, No. 278 (Chicago: University of Chicago, Department of Economics, September 1971), p. 57.

[22] Interview with Lewis Mumford, p. 89 in Willem Oltmans (ed.), *On Growth: The Crisis of Exploding Population and Resource Depletion* (New York: G. P. Putnam's Sons, 1974).

area in question and express them in a set of models that permit the relevant policy options to be compared.[23] We call this approach "multimodeling."

More generally, multimodeling is the use of a collection of models differing from one another in the choice of theory, data, or methodology to examine a given policy area. Multimodeling can occur without premeditation, as when different modelers come together to defend their respective positions in a hearing or policy dispute. Or it can be consciously preplanned, as when two or more modelers work separately but cooperatively from the start of a policy study to take account of different points of view or different aspects of the area under investigation. A set of models incorporating a variety of assumptions and theories is a more solid basis for policymaking than a single model, as a general rule. In addition, a single model is usually an easier target for critics than a set of models. Whereas a single model is subject to being countermodeled or modified to produce conclusions countering those of the original version, a set of models that agree on policy conclusions despite dissimilar approaches and assumptions can provide convincing support for policy action. If the conclusions of the different models do not agree, they may still provide a very useful basis for decision making by giving the policymaker the implications of a range of assumptions and points of view.

One of the hazards of multimodeling, especially when it is part of an adversary proceeding, is that the process may become a competitive contest in which the positions become polarized. Even when the models agree on the essential conclusions, the modelers may still battle over technical matters, theory, or approach. A case in point occurred in Maryland in 1972 when the Brandon Shores Power Plant proposed by the Baltimore Gas and Electric Company (BG&E) became the subject of the first hearing under the 1971 Maryland Power Plant Siting Law. To determine the final engineering design for a new 1,200-megawatt, fossil-fueled plant that would not seriously harm the environment, BG&E asked the NUS Corporation to create an air pollution computer model of the plant. NUS, using the models and experience of the Tennessee Valley Authority, presented their modeling results before the Public Service Commission to show that the new plant, together with an older adjacent plant, would exceed 33 percent of a particular sulphur dioxide (SO_2) standard a total of only three hours per year.[24] The state of Maryland hired its own modelers, the Applied Physics Laboratory (APL) of the Johns

---

[23] See, for example, Brian L. Crissey, "A Rational Framework for the Use of Computer Simulation Models In a Policy Context," Ph.D. Dissertation, The Johns Hopkins University, 1975.

[24] T. C. Koss, "The Air Quality Impact of the Brandon Shores-Wagner Generating Complex: A Summary Report," Prepared for the Baltimore Gas and Electric Company by NUS Corporation, November 1972, p. 11.

Hopkins University, and a division of Martin-Marietta Laboratories, then called the Research Institute for Advanced Study. Still another model was exhibited by the Maryland Bureau of Air Quality Control (BAQC) which was concerned about the fact that Brandon Shores constituted a new SO_2 source within seven miles of downtown Baltimore.

The BAQC model, the least specific of the models, was the most pessimistic in estimating the injurious effects of the new plant. The state-sponsored models, using different data, concluded that the combined plants would exceed 50 percent of the SO_2 standard twenty-six hours per year.[25] After several rounds of sharp debate among the modelers, it was discovered that except for the dispute over data and the issue of whether Brandon Shores should be considered on its merits separately or as an expansion of the older plant, the most fundamental disagreement related to NUS's position that two of the five major types of air instability occurred so infrequently that they were not of consequence in the assessment of the plant's air pollution impact. APL contended that those two classes occurred at least 5 percent of the time and caused the worst air pollution at ground level. On May 16, 1974, the Public Service Commission endorsed the NUS results and granted BG&E permission to build the plant.

Data and Validation

Data provide a tangible link between a model and its reference system, and a means for gaining confidence in the model and its results. A model that closely reproduces data on observed past behavior of the reference system gains credibility and wins the acceptance and trust of potential users. One needs to distinguish between verification and validation. Verification is a test of whether the model has been synthesized exactly as intended. Verification of a model indicates that it has been faithful to its conception, irrespective of whether or not it and its conception are valid. Validation, in contrast, is a test of whether the model is an adequate representation of the elements and relationships of the reference system that are important to experiments planned with the model. Validation is not a general seal of approval; it is an indication of a level of confidence in the model's behavior under limited conditions and for specific purposes—a check on its operational agreement with the reference system.

There is no uniform procedure for validation. No model has ever been or ever will be thoroughly validated. Since, by design, models are all simplifications of the reference system, they are never entirely valid in the sense of being

---

[25] "Addendum to PPSE 1–2 Power Plant Site Evaluation Brandon Shores Site," Prepared by The Johns Hopkins University for the Maryland Power Plant Siting Program, January 18, 1973, p. 14.

Modeling in Cross Section

fully supported by objective truth. "Useful," "illuminating," "convincing," or "inspiring confidence" are more apt descriptors applying to models than "valid." One can bolster one's confidence in a model by having it reproduce past behavior of the reference system, exploring its response to perturbations, critically examining the premises and theories on which it is based, and finally, putting it to use. In fact, such tests are aimed more at invalidating than validating the model. They can only reveal the presence (not the total absence) of errors. However convincing a model, there is always a chance that its next test or use will turn up a serious shortcoming.

Jay Forrester has been criticized, especially by econometricians, for accepting a model as valid or reasonable on the basis of whether its behavior agrees with the policymaker's common sense knowledge about the behavior of the reference system. Forrester, in turn, charges that the comparison of a statistical time history with the output of a model, the test that econometric model builders use, "cannot be met. And it is not necessary to meet it to have tremendously useful results."[26]

One might add that even if a model passes such a statistical test, there is still no guarantee that the model's projections are accurate. Any attempt to validate a model by seeing if it reproduces past system behavior is fraught with problems.[27] Since historical data are normally used to estimate a model's coefficients, the fact that the model traces past behavior reflects more on its ability to interpolate than extrapolate. Partitioning the data period into two consecutive sets of points, one for estimating coefficients and the other for validating the model, is a way around this particular difficulty, but questions remain on which data to use, how to partition them, how to adjust or correct them, what years to begin and end with, and what level of significance to adopt. There are many ways, primarily unintentional, in which a modeler can affect the outcome of a statistical validation test.

Yet econometricians consider statistical validation to be indispensable. Thus, Gary Fromm declares that:

> properly constructed and validated models ... should improve decisions ... [but] such improvements can only be brought about if the premises on which

---

[26] Martin Greenberger, *Computers and the World of the Future* (Cambridge: The M.I.T. Press, 1962), pp. 85 and 89. Forrester has probably modified his views on validation in the years since the discussion recorded here. He also appears now to have less trust in the common sense perceptions of the policymaker, at least in the government setting. See Jay W. Forrester, "The Counterintuitive Behavior of Social Systems," in D. L. Meadows and D. H. Meadows (eds.), *Toward Global Equilibrium: Collected Papers* (Cambridge, Mass.: Wright-Allen Press, 1973).

[27] An example is Roger Naill's system dynamics model which matched past data very well and forecast a decline in hog prices the following year. In fact, hog prices increased markedly. Naill explains his model's poor performance as an error of omission rather than extrapolation, since the model left out many factors affecting hog prices, such as beef price effects on hog consumption. See Naill et al., "Dynamic Modeling."

models are constructed are made explicit and the systems are subjected to a battery of validation tests. The importance of doing this cannot be stressed too highly. All too frequently what purports to be a model based on theory and evidence is nothing more than a scholar's preconception and prejudices cloaked in the guise of scientific rigor and embellished with extensive computer simulations. Without empirical verification there is little assurance that the results of such exercises are reliable, or that they should be applied for normative policy purposes. This has been one of the most troublesome aspects of the work of Jay Forrester and his associates, whose deductive model simulations (with assumed parameters) of population and urban growth have been widely publicized notwithstanding that their accuracy or validity has never been determined.[28]

Some models require a great deal of accurate and relevant data that may be difficult or impossible to obtain. Data may be unavailable, misreported, altered to fit circumstances, or self-contradictory. Furthermore, the accuracy of data may decline as their detail increases. Reliable statements are often easier to make about total populations and overall trends than about subpopulations and detailed effects, although the latter may be of greater interest. In David Birch's work on the "New Haven model,"[29] a large, data-rich model of urban change, he found that the relative data error was as much as five times greater for census tract data than for data relating to the entire metropolitan area. "The more detail the better" is often not true in modeling, especially if the greater detail entails additional calculation that compounds or aggravates the errors in the data.[30]

A simple model may have better performance characteristics over the long run than a more complicated model, even though it provides less information.[31] As more detail is added, a model can become more opaque to the user, harder to understand, and more expensive to operate. Even models of simple systems can be complicated if they include unnecessary items or attempt to be overly precise. Garry Brewer makes a useful distinction between complexity and complication.

> Complexity refers to substantive logico-mathematical interrelations and difficulties; *complication* can arise in almost any arrangement of facts, concepts, or thoughts. Complication is an undesirable characteristic of any construct; com-

---

[28] Gary Fromm, "Policy Decisions and Econometric Models," paper presented at an NSF seminar, April 1973.

[29] David Birch, et al., *Patterns of Urban Change* (Lexington, Mass.: Lexington Books, 1974), p. 51.

[30] William Alonso, "Predicting Best With Imperfect Data," *Journal of the AIP,* July 1968, pp. 248–255.

[31] Brian L. Crissey, "A Conceptualized Framework for Selecting Quality and Level of Aggregation for Dynamic Computer Simulation Runs," *1974 Summer Simulation Conference Proceedings,* July 9–11, Houston, Texas, p. 68.

plexity may be an inherent feature. Complication often expresses lack of effort to give the construct its appropriate form.[32]

Complication is to be avoided, but complexity may be unavoidable (if the reference system is complex).

One of the most important advantages of a model is its ability to illuminate causal relationships that are obscured by complexity in the reference system. A modeler who feels that his simple but understandable model is not "rich" enough in behavior may fall victim to the tendency to add layer upon layer of detail to the model in an attempt to make it more realistic. Walter Carlson coined the phrase "the artichoke effect" for this process when he observed a similar procedure occurring in the design of complex computer systems.

> We have a proclivity to add features, add functions, and add interfaces—layer upon layer—onto existing systems. Each succeeding layer has less and less useful or tasty substance on it, until the outside layers merely add weight, complexity, and a prickly hindrance to reaching the core of the problem.[33]

Carried to the extreme, the model:

> produces output resembling those observed in the real world, and inspires confidence that the real causal process has been accurately represented. However, because the assumptions incorporated in the model are complex and their mutual interdependencies are obscure, the simulation program is no easier to understand than the real process was.[34]

John Dutton and William Starbuck have named this phenomenon "Bonini's paradox" after C. P. Bonini whose 1963 model of decision systems in the firm duplicated the complexities of the firm to such a degree that he was unable to "pinpoint the explicit causal mechanism in the model."[35]

A model created without using "formal data" may be difficult to evaluate.[36] Whatever its true value, the model may seem little more than an embodiment of the opinions of the modeler, who must then convince others that the model is a reliable and useful representation of the reference system. The modeler must prop up the data leg of the modeling tripod, as Forrester does in his

---

[32] Brewer, p. 4.

[33] Walter M. Carlson, "A Decade for Dialogue," *Communications of the Association for Computing Machinery* 13, no. 12 (1970): 713.

[34] John M. Dutton and W. H. Starbuck, *Computer Simulation of Human Behavior* (New York: John Wiley & Sons, 1971), p. 4.

[35] C. P. Bonini, *Simulation of Information and Decision Systems in the Firm* (Englewood Cliffs, N.J.: Prentice-Hall, 1963), p. 136.

[36] "Formal data" includes time series data, cross-sectional data, and other numerical information that is systematically collected and tabulated. It does not include the nonquantifiable or nonsystematic information of an institutional nature that is used in some models, notably those of system dynamics. For the most part, when we refer to "data" throughout the book, our meaning is "formal data."

urban and world dynamic models, by calling upon persuasive argumentation and verbal models appealing to common sense.

Methodology

A formal model is created as a synthetic representation of the modeler's mental conception. A modeling methodology is the means by which that conception is transformed into the formal model, much as a painter's style and technique is the methodology by which he synthesizes paints into a formal schematic model—the painting. Several methodologies for the construction of computer models are described at length in Chapters 4, 5, and 6.

Some computer modeling methodologies include special programming languages. Examples are DYNAMO (for the system dynamics methodology)[37] and GPSS (for the discrete systems simulation methodology of operations research).[38] Other methodologies use general programming languages together with special computer routines for specific tasks, such as statistical estimation in econometrics. TROLL is a general system for econometric modeling.[39] In some modeling methodologies, such as microanalysis, there is little need for custom tools, although even here special systems have been built to make the construction and running of models more convenient.[40]

The nature of the problem addressed should guide the selection of methodology. For example, an analysis of the changes in individual tax revenues and transfer payments caused by a modification of the tax code is better done with a microanalytic model, where the simulated impact on representative microunits can be observed, than with an aggregate system dynamics or econometric model. But the effect on national employment of a proposed tax reduction is better determined with a macroeconometric model.

Methodologies provide the modeler with ready-made tools and constructs with which to create a model and they allow the modeler to use the work of others instead of creating tools *ab initio*, a tedious and time-consuming process fraught with error. Whereas use of an accepted methodology makes it easier for those familiar with that methodology to perceive the structure and rationale of a new model, it also may prompt one to make idiosyncratic or

---

[37] Alexander L. Pugh III, *Dynamo II User's Manual* (Cambridge: M.I.T. Press, 1973).

[38] Geoffrey Gordon, *The Application of GPSS V to Discrete System Simulation* (Englewood Cliffs, N.J.: Prentice-Hall, 1975).

[39] John Kirsch, *Troll Primer* (Cambridge: Computer Research Center for Economics and Management Science, National Bureau of Economic Research, 1972).

[40] George Sadowsky, *MASH: A Computer System for Microanalytic Simulation for Policy Exploration*, Working Paper 5096 (Washington, D.C.: Urban Institute, 1975, in press).

Modeling in Cross Section

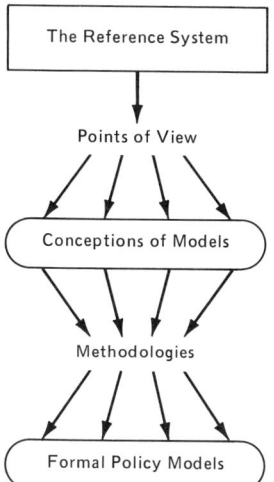

Figure 3-11: Points of View and Methodologies

In policy modeling, the modeler's point of view affects a model's conception. To create a formal model, a methodology is chosen. The methodologies are not independent of the points of view. Some methodologies favor one position over another, while others cannot represent certain views because of conflicts between the underlying assumptions of the viewpoint and the limitations of the methodology.

restrictive assumptions about the reference system. (See Figure 3-11.) A methodology that makes it awkward to accommodate nonlinearities, for example, may discourage the use of nonlinear representations. Or a methodology based on deterministic flows may lead one to neglect probabilistic effects. The choice of methodology does influence the way the reference system is modeled. The nature of the application should be more of a factor in choosing a methodology than is typically the case.

A methodology usually develops from repeated model-building efforts in a given field for a particular type of problem and tends to be favored by modelers in that field. Their special constructs, procedures, devices, and assumptions may or may not be applicable to other fields and situations. The methodology of system dynamics, for example, evolved from the concepts of servomechanisms and electrical circuits, where a central assumption is that the reference system is completely encompassed within a closed boundary. All characteristic behavior is generated within the boundary. "Outside occurrences can be viewed as random happenings that impinge on the system and do not themselves give the system its intrinsic growth and stability characteristics."[41]

---

[41] Jay W. Forrester, *Urban Dynamics* (Cambridge: M.I.T. Press, 1969), p. 12.

When Forrester used system dynamics to model a single city, he assumed that outside forces such as suburban growth and programs by other cities to train people and clear houses would not affect inner city behavior. Leo P. Kadanoff[42] disputed this assumption, but he did not discard the methodology. By differentiating between inner city and suburb, and adding other metropolitan areas, he expanded Forrester's model and came to a different set of policy conclusions.

Care must be taken in the application of a methodology to ensure that its underlying assumptions hold. Econometric modeling, for example, assumes that the internal structure of the reference system is relatively constant in time, so that a model's coefficients can be estimated reliably using historical data. Jay Rockstroh[43] has demonstrated that the estimated values of the coefficients in the LR model are not reliable. Rockstroh produced substantial deviations in projected GNP by making only small changes in the starting date of the historical data used in estimation of the coefficients. Figure 3-12 shows the estimated values of a coefficient in one equation of the LR model as a function of the period of time over which the coefficient was estimated. The effect of the variation in estimates was to raise the projected 1971 GNP by over $11 billion merely by estimating the coefficients from data beginning in 1958 instead of 1959.

THE MODELER: HORSE, CART OR DRIVER?

The Role of the Modeler

Just as a modeler must support his model where it is weak, he may also have to come to its assistance to avoid misunderstanding and to defend it against those antagonistic to its use. Computer modeling is still foreign to most people and frightening to many. As a new policy tool, it faces opposition on two fronts: from those affected by its possible recommendations and from those whose jobs or status may seem threatened by its use. Models that bear on the economic welfare of people, as many policy models do, and models that are introduced into established organizations, are especially liable to be resisted.

Janet Pack, in a survey of urban models, analyzed the use of models by three regional planning organizations. The Bay Area Transportation Study Commission and the Washington, D.C., Council of Governments "both were substantially new organizations, unhampered by existing ways of doing things

---

[42] Leo P. Kadanoff, "From Simulation Model to Public Policy," *American Scientist* 60, no. 1 (1972): 74–79.

[43] Jay Rockstroh, unpublished report, The Johns Hopkins University Department of Mathematical Sciences, Baltimore, Md., 1974.

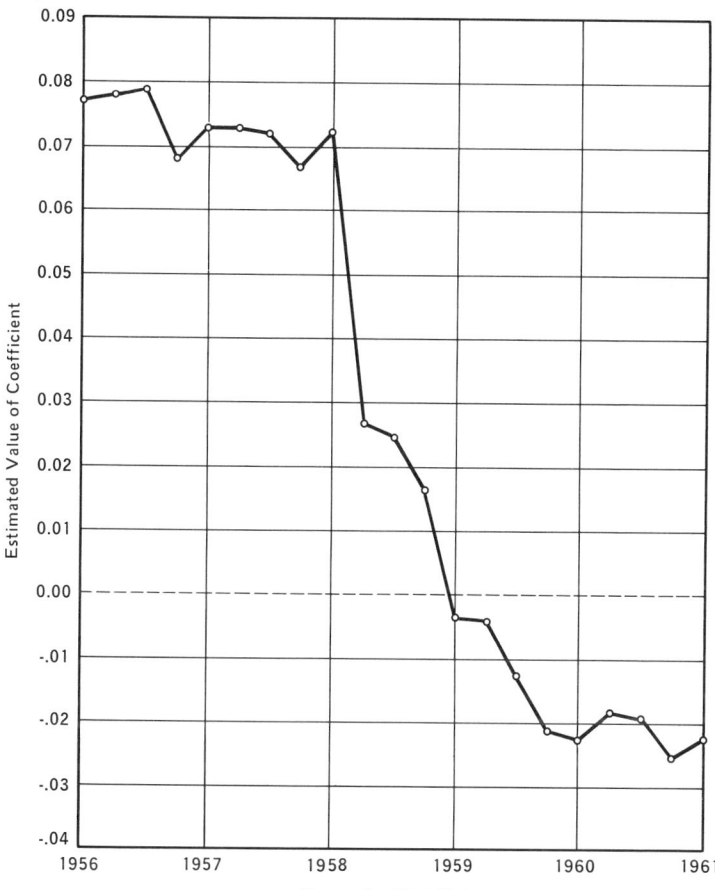

Figure 3-12: Change in Econometric Coefficient as Function of Regression Start Date

In the Laffer-Ranson model of the economy, the stock variable is represented by lagging the Standard and Poor's Composite Stock Index. The coefficient of this variable is shown here to be sensitive to the period of time over which it is estimated. Each point on the graph represents an estimation of this coefficient by ordinary least squares regression, using data from the date on the abscissa up to and including the fourth quarter of 1969.

or entrenched staff allegiances and coalitions."[44] The Minneapolis-St. Paul Metro Council, however, was an established organization, so that modeling would "have to compete with the existing way of doing things."[45] When modeling was introduced into these organizations, the first two newer groups

---
[44] Pack, p. III-5.
[45] Ibid., p. III-11.

eagerly adopted the technique, while in the older, more established body, there was more resistance.

A strong-willed, convincing modeler may be able to win favor for his work by using persuasiveness and articulateness to compensate for the model's deficiencies. It is scarcely an exaggeration to say that behind almost every well-known model there has been a forceful modeler with a strong grasp of the model's properties. Jay Forrester, with the urban and world models (see Chapter 5), and Dennis Meadows, with the World3 model (Chapter 1), are controversial examples.

The mature policy model deals with variables, phenomena, and policies of direct interest to the decision maker, presents its results in terms meaningful to him, is economical and easy to use, and has been streamlined and tempered by repeated application. It needs comparatively little support or defense from the modeler, except insofar as it requires his personal attention for documentation and presentation. A model that is poorly documented or too complicated to understand cannot be easily transferred to other users and altered to reflect different situations.

Modelers take various positions about the need for model transfer, its desirability, and how it is best accomplished. Pugh-Roberts Associates, a successful builder of system dynamics models, constructs models specific to the requirements of its clients. Data Resources, Inc., (see Chapter 6) provides advice, methodological tools, and model-based economic forecasts as fee-paid services. Ira Lowry (see Land-Use Modeling, Chapter 4) used the published literature to distribute information on his model of urban housing and employment (so effectively, in fact, that use of the model, which spread widely in the mid-1960s, did not require Lowry's personal participation—the first major implementation of the model in Pittsburgh's Community Renewal Program went ahead without Lowry's assistance).

In striking contrast to the Lowry example is the case of the Rand Corporation's Jan J. Leendertse. Leendertse has been deeply and personally involved in extensions and applications of his innovative water quality model.[46] The model is less widely known than Lowry's and is not as simple in concept or as transferable. The Leendertse story illustrates the powerful role the modeler can play as an interface between the model and the policy process and shows, as is frequently the case in policy modeling, how the modeler may dominate the model.

---

[46] There have been, however, applications of Leendertse's tidal water flow model that were carried out without his assistance. See, for example, K. W. Hess and F. M. White, "A Numerical Tidal Model of Narragansett Bay," University of Rhode Island Marine Technical Report no. 20, 1974, and M. D. Palmer, D. J. Poulton, and J. B. Izatt, *Hamilton Harbour Study* (Toronto: Water Quality Branch, Ontario Ministry of the Environment, May 1974).

Jan Leendertse and the Jamaica Bay Simulation

Jan J. Leendertse, a Dutch hydraulic engineer, joined the Rand Corporation in Santa Monica, California, to work on underwater missile basing and the wave propagation effects of nuclear blasts. Leendertse had developed new computational methods for predicting the tidal flow patterns of coastal seas and estuaries, techniques that were later to appear in his simulation of Jamaica Bay,[47] a large tidal estuary in New York bordering Brooklyn and Queens. Leendertse was convinced that computer simulation models of water flow could be made more dependable, efficient, and flexible than the traditional physical models, and when Rand opened a branch office in New York City (later to become the New York City Rand Institute),[48] he saw an opportunity to apply computer techniques to Jamaica Bay. The New York City Rand group put Leendertse in touch with the Director of Water Pollution Control, Martin Lang, who encouraged Leendertse to proceed with computer modeling of the bay. Leendertse chose Jamaica Bay rather than a site closer to his home in Santa Monica since the Rand Corporation had a presence in New York, and the necessary data for the kind of simulation he planned were already available, having been processed by a consulting firm working for the Department of Water Resources under an earlier contract.

Martin Lang, an old-line Democrat from the borough of Queens, entered the city government during the Depression and worked his way to the top. A receptivity to new ideas set him apart from the stereotypical career civil servant, as was evident in his attempts to initiate an ambitious system study of the entire New York "bight" area, including the continental shelf around New York, all coastal seas and estuaries, and each river up to the point of intake of potable water. Lang had been seeking federal funding for this purpose for three years before he met Leendertse. Lang welcomed the Rand engineer, although with some caution, but Leendertse soon gained his confidence and strong support for the modeling effort.

Lang arranged for Leendertse to work alongside a consulting firm under contract to his agency since 1966 to study the water quality in Jamaica Bay. Leendertse received all the sampling and laboratory material he needed, plus data from the U.S. Geological Survey and the U.S. Army Corps of Engineers. Both the consulting firm and the city agency seemed to benefit from the association with the Rand engineer. Said Lang, "If Rand didn't exist, I'd have to

---

[47] J. J. Leendertse and E. C. Gritton, *A Water-Quality Simulation Model for Well-Mixed Estuaries and Coastal Seas,* 6 vols. (New York: The New York City Rand Institute, February 1970–September 1974).

[48] Chapters 7, 8, and 9 present a detailed discussion of the Rand Institute's work in the areas of health and fire, and give an analysis of its ability to apply policy research to the problems of New York City.

invent them. Traditionally ... in New York City, decisions have been made viscerally. Rand helped bring rationality into it."[49]

Leendertse and his model were involved in at least five policy problems facing New York. The first was to estimate the environmental impact on Jamaica Bay of the newly constructed Spring Creek Water Pollution Control Facility.[50] During periods of rainfall, when loads from combined sanitary and storm sewers increase, this auxiliary treatment facility handles overflows from the 26th Ward treatment plant. The Leendertse model was used to assess the seriousness of sewage outfalls into the bay. Many New York City officials who know of the Leendertse model mistakenly believe it was used to determine either the location of the new treatment facility or the priority order in which such facilities should be built. In fact, the Spring Creek facility was under construction before the model was applied and the order of construction of future treatment plants in the area was set in the 1950s. The real value of Leendertse's simulation of the Spring Creek facility and its impact on Jamaica Bay was to help assess the worth of such plants and the new treatment processes they incorporated.

The second policy issue in which Leendertse was involved concerned a controversial proposal by the U.S. Army Corps of Engineers to construct a large hurricane barrier along the Rockaway Peninsula (which separates Jamaica Bay from the Atlantic) and across the mouth of the bay at Rockaway Inlet. The purpose of the proposed barrier was to prevent the flooding of basements in private homes in Howard Beach and other low-lying communities in the vicinity of John F. Kennedy Airport on those occasions when winds caused by tropical storms raise the level of the bay to the point of flooding. Such storms occur infrequently (about three times in a century), raising the question of whether the barrier's estimated total construction cost of $53 million and annual maintenance costs of $400,000[51] might be better spent in reimbursing property owners. The Corps of Engineers did not address this question. Instead, it sought to give protection against "any anticipated storm, except one so large that it could be expected only 'once in a thousand years'."[52] The proposed breakwater would constrict the mouth of Jamaica Bay from 4,530 to 600 feet. A flood gate across the remaining gap could be opened or closed as necessary. Along the beaches, an eight-foot-high barrier would be constructed of sand dunes and steel pilings. In subsequent public controversy, it was charged that the proposed barrier would separate the oceanfront from

---

[49] When Lang says "Rand" he may mean "Leendertse." Leendertse had no support staff in New York.

[50] Leendertse and Gritton, Vol. 5.

[51] National Academy of Sciences and the National Academy of Engineering, *Jamaica Bay and Kennedy Airport: A Multidisciplinary Environmental Study*, 2 vols. (Washington, D.C., 1971), 2:87–89.

[52] Ibid., p. 87.

the houses, impair the view of the ocean, restrict accessibility to the beaches, and force elderly retirees on Rockaway Peninsula to climb ramps and stairways to get to the beach.

Disagreement also arose concerning the hydraulic model of Jamaica Bay that the Corps of Engineers operated in Vicksburg, Mississippi. This physical model predicted that a particular secondary current in Jamaica Bay would flow in a clockwise direction. Leendertse's computer model showed it flowing counterclockwise, and he explained the disparity by showing that the corps had constructed its model using faulty data, which had probably originated in malfunctioning measurement instruments. Commissioner Lang agreed. But there was little hope of recasting the inflexible hydraulic model.[53]

Leendertse did not alter his model to reflect the hurricane barrier, but offered the opinion that such a device would curtail the circulation necessary to "flush" the bay of its daily accumulation of treated and untreated sewage. The Corps of Engineers did simulate the barrier and its ability to withstand large storms. It reported that there would be "no interference with the ebb and flow of the tides through the bay."[54] Another study, done in 1963 by the Division of Water Supply and Pollution Control of the U.S. Public Health Service,[55] using a mathematical model and admittedly inadequate data, also concluded that the proposed hurricane barrier would not seriously harm the water quality of the bay. Nevertheless, Commissioner Martin Lang, whose approval was necessary, chose to follow Leendertse's advice and halted the project.

It is significant that Leendertse's opinion prevailed over the simulation results of the Corps of Engineers.[56] His expertise and authority, acquired with the help of his computer model, carried as much influence as the model itself. William Pressman, project engineer for research and development for the

---

[53] The corps' model is a physical analogue of the Bay, built to reproduce the flow patterns and dimensions on a miniature scale, both dimensionwise and timewise. It is distorted a hundredfold, however, in the vertical dimension, in order to create turbulent flow which would not result if everything were taken to the same scale. For an analysis of the corps' model, see Jan J. Leendertse and Shiao-Kung Liu, "Comparison of Observed Estuarine Tide Data with Hydraulic Model Data by Use of Cross-Spectral Density Functions," The New York City Rand Institute, R-1612-NYC, September 1974. Leendertse's original model also tampers with the vertical dimension in that it assumes that the bay is "well-mixed," meaning that there is no significant difference in water velocities, salinities, or pollutant concentrations between any two points taken on the same vertical line anywhere in the Bay. Leendertse has, however, corrected this defect by expanding his model into three dimensions. Jan J. Leendertse et al., *A Three-Dimensional Model for Estuaries and Coastal Seas*. Vol. 1, *Principles of Computation*, R-1417-OWRR (Santa Monica, Calif.: The Rand Corporation, December 1973).

[54] *Jamaica Bay and Kennedy Airport*, 2:87.

[55] Ibid.

[56] It must be noted that the U.S. Public Health Service study noted above carried no weight in this choice, as it was not seen by the Department of Water Resources.

Water Resources Administration, asserts that Leendertse was "the only source of real knowledge that we had."

A third issue in which Leendertse exerted influence concerned the environmental impact of the state's construction of a mental hospital on Jamaica Bay along the border of Brooklyn and Queens. Part of the operation involved dredging the floor of the bay and filling in low-lying areas. Leendertse, again without actually running his model, charged that the dredging operations being carried out would adversely affect water quality by creating stagnant areas near the rear of the bay where the flushing effect of the tides was at a minimum. It would be better, he stated, to have the dredging operations nearer the mouth of the bay. Convinced, the state moved its dredging operations to Nova Scotia Bar, nearer the Rockaway Inlet. Again, the expert modeler rather than the model itself provided the policy guidance.

A fourth policy area concerns Commissioner Lang's lengthy efforts to have Jamaica Bay included in federal plans for the Gateway Recreation Area in New York Harbor. Leendertse's computer model predicted that if all treatment plants were constructed as planned, the water of the bay would be of bathing quality by 1980. Many believe that Jamaica Bay's eventual inclusion in the Gateway Recreation Area and its development by the National Park Service as a natural park with bathing beaches, nature centers, and hiking trails was due in part to this prediction.

A final area in which Leendertse may have had an impact was in connection with a proposal by the Port of New York Authority (PONYA) to extend the runways of John F. Kennedy International Airport into Jamaica Bay. At the behest of PONYA, the Environmental Studies Board of the National Academy of Sciences (NAS) and the National Academy of Engineering formed a study group in early 1970 to inquire into the impact of the proposal[57] and to address the question, "Should additional portions of Jamaica Bay be filled in to provide more runway capacity for Kennedy Airport?"[58]

The study group devoted its first five days to testimony from all concerned parties, including Martin Lang and, at his request, Jan Leendertse. Without running the model to simulate the runways in the bay, Leendertse testified that the runway extension would probably cause irreparable harm to the water quality of the bay by altering the flow patterns, thereby creating stag-

---

[57] In a letter to Gordon F. MacDonald, chairman of the Environmental Studies Board, dated January 26, 1970, Austin Tobin, the executive director of PONYA, stated that "The question Port Authority representatives have posed is *not* whether airport extension into a portion of Jamaica Bay would affect the bay. It is, on the contrary, whether through carefully employing the resources involved in an extension of the airport, a program could be developed that would result in a complete redevelopment of the entire bay to achieve distinct environmental benefits for mankind and wildlife and sustain the region's economy." *Jamaica Bay and Kennedy Airport,* 1:xi.

[58] Ibid., p. 1.

nant pools with little or no tidal flushing. The study group went on to examine many other facets of the problem, such as jet noise, disturbances of waterfowl, and operational aspects of the airport. Leendertse feels that his testimony was a major influence on the group's decision to recommend against extension of the runway, an opinion that Steven Ebbin, the Jamaica Bay Environmental Study Group director, does not fully share. Ebbin claims that Leendertse's simulation model was still being developed at the time of the NAS effort, and that it, as well as the Corps of Engineers' hydraulic model, was incorrect on the currents in the immediate vicinity of JFK Airport,[59] and was therefore unusable to the NAS group.[60] Whatever Leendertse's influence on the decision not to extend the runways, it is a fact that his name surfaces frequently among New York City officials, many of whom seem to assume erroneously that his model was the primary factor in the decision. His work in general has earned widespread acclaim and has continually expanded in scope.[61]

There are many factors in Leendertse's success. His ties with the city were never constricting. He had excellent rapport with his client, the Department of Water Resources. His modeling work was of high professional calibre and his model was very sophisticated. It was clear that no one else could easily take his place. The goal of bettering the water quality of Jamaica Bay was widely supported. By working out of Santa Monica, Leendertse was largely insulated from the political upheavals of New York City and, to some extent, from the Rand Institute as well, which became a target for critics of former Mayor John Lindsay. When the Rand Institute terminated operations in 1975, Leendertse's work continued unimpeded. Finally, the necessary data were available and had only to be processed to be useful to Leendertse. No ex-

---

[59] Both models used 1966 PONYA runway extension plans for JFK Airport, calling for construction of circulation conduits under the land fill for runway 4L-22R. The conduits were to accommodate existing currents in that part of the bay but were not actually built when the runway was extended into Jamaica Bay in 1968.

[60] It has been reported to us that PONYA, although it had in its possession around thirty different possible configurations for the new runway extension, refused for some time to release the plans to anyone. PONYA probably did not want the public to think that it was further along in its planning than it was. It is doubtful that Leendertse could have gained access to the plans.

[61] Compared to other contracts with the Rand Institute, the water resources work was one of the lowest in total cost to New York City, yet it was also one of the better-received projects—it is difficult to find a bad opinion of it. The water resources contract was not planned in the original work schedule for the institute. Its initiation was due in large part to the personal efforts of Jan Leendertse. After a public controversy in New York led to consulting contracts of $10,000 or more having to be approved by the New York City Board of Estimates (Council of the City of New York, *Report on Consultant Contracts,* December 21, 1970, Edward L. Sadowsky, chairman), the Rand contracts for health and housing were delayed by heated arguments. The Water Resources contract, in contrast, was quickly approved during the first round of board review.

pensive data gathering was necessary, and there was no footdragging by the Department of Water Resources. The data were harmless. No one had much to gain from withholding information, misrepresenting facts, or hindering the work. Unlike the data for the Rand Institute's studies in health, housing, and police (see Chapters 7, 8, and 9), the data collected were physical rather than social or administrative in nature and threatened no one's bureaucratic position.

In summary, Leendertse devised an innovative methodology for modeling pollutant transport in tidal waters based on extensive data and the traditional theories of his discipline. Blessed with a relatively hospitable political environment, he became known as an expert on Jamaica Bay, and his opinion outweighed physical simulations done by the Corps of Engineers. Although his model was often assumed to have directly affected numerous water resource policy decisions, in reality it was little used for direct decision making. Much of the discernible impact on policy was due to Leendertse and only indirectly to his model, which was unable to answer fast-changing policy questions. But the model did help Leendertse expand his understanding of the bay and develop his more adaptable mental model.

Leendertse's computer model was strong in theory, data, and methodology, but without his personal interposition between the volatile political process and the not fully developed model, many of the requests for technical advice could not have been answered and the project might have been dropped. The lesson for the would-be policy modeler is not to expect the model by itself to carry the day with the policymaker. The corresponding lesson for the policymaker, is to take at least as careful a reading of the modeler as of the model.

We are reminded of an observation by Arthur M. Okun, chairman of the Council of Economic Advisers under Lyndon Johnson, concerning economic models. The model, said Okun, "is not an alternative to judgment. It is not a product in and of itself. It is a tool in the hands of a trained economist."[62] Like any tool, its effectiveness is governed by the skill and expertise of its user. Conversely, its use and development can help build skill and expertise.

---

[62] Arthur M. Okun, "Uses of Models for Policy Formulation," in Gary Fromm and Lawrence R. Klein (eds.), *The Brookings Model: Perspective and Recent Developments* (Amsterdam: North-Holland, 1975), p. 362.

4

Methodologies for Policy Modeling

Model builders are creative carpenters, artful designers and synthesizers who select their instruments of construction from any of several toolboxes we call modeling methodologies. A modeler typically has his own favorite methodology. This chapter sketches the history of the development and application of nine modeling methodologies that seem to us particularly or potentially relevant to policymaking. With each methodology we will identify one or more key innovators or expositors closely associated with the development of that methodology.

Outlining the development of methodologies for policy modeling is of more than historical interest. It serves to illustrate the very different traditions and backgrounds from which the methodologies have sprung. In so doing, it suggests the different biases and outlooks often implicit or subtly embedded in the articulation and application of the methodologies.

A housing example at the conclusion of the chapter pinpoints a few of the differences that bear on the application (partly hypothetical) to the housing field of three methodologies for policy modeling: microanalysis, system dynamics, and econometric modeling.

NINE METHODOLOGIES

Policy modeling has an intriguing history. In documentary form, it could be told as a story of a number of individuals of imagination, initiative, and perseverance from different backgrounds, each of whom succeeded in his own formal way in expressing the complexities and interdependencies of systems of people, activities, and institutions. These individuals helped in understanding the inner workings of the systems they modeled.

Most started by trying to solve a certain kind of problem or build a model of a particular reference system. What sets these individuals apart from the average model builder are the innovativeness or insightfulness of their approach and their ability to perceive its generality. They are also distinguished by the enterprise they displayed in putting their methods in a form that others could appreciate and use, and the missionary zeal they showed in the teaching of their ideas, despite discouragements and even severe criticism and verbal attack.

Almost all of the twelve modeling innovators mentioned were still alive when this book was written. Six were economists by training, three were mathematicians, two were physicists, one was an engineer. All but three of the innovators did their major work in the United States, although only half of them were born and reared here. The majority were still working with the modeling methodology with which we credit them. By "methodology" we mean the general approach and set of techniques deriving from the innovator's concepts, constructs, style, theories, and philosophy. It is the means by which he created his models and gave expression to his theories. But more important, it is the instrument by which others have been able to form their own models of their own reference systems, systems that may differ markedly from the original subject studied by the innovator.

In creating their methodologies, the modeling innovators were not working in isolation. They were influenced by the ideas of others, they were directly assisted by others, they collaborated with others, often in different fields. Nor were their inventions fortuitous or serendipitous. The methodologies met a recognized need or deficiency. Some filled gaps in the analytical arsenal of an established discipline, such as economics. One gave a quantitative approach to the profession of urban planning and helped satisfy the research requirements of a national program in highway development. Several were developed to serve the country in World War II. In almost every case, the digital computer played a key role either in the development or later implementation of the methodology.

We cite nine modeling methodologies produced by the dozen innovators, falling into five fields of study according to the origins and general nature of the methodologies. The fields are those either from which the methodologies came or to which they contributed. The innovators are noted alongside their methodologies.

    A. Linear Economics
        (1) Input-Output Analysis: Leontief
        (2) Linear Programming: Dantzig, Kantorovich, Koopmans
        (3) Two-Person Zero-Sum Games: von Neumann
    B. Operations Research
        (4) Probabilistic Methods: Morse, Blackett
        (5) Algebraic Methods: see (2)
    C. Statistical Economics
        (6) Econometric Modeling: Tinbergen, Klein
        (7) Microanalysis: Orcutt
    D. Urban and Regional Development

(8) Land-Use Analysis: Lowry
E. Engineering
(9) System Dynamics: Forrester

The nine methodologies listed are the ones that seem to us particularly germane to policy problems. We make no attempt to be either all-inclusive or nonoverlapping in selecting them and in naming the innovators.

Linear economics is a branch of economic theory useful in the static analysis of a variety of economic problems. Its keynote is the heroically simplifying assumption of linearity in expressing relationships. Two units of a variable have just twice the effect of one unit of the variable. Thus, in a paradigmatical linear equation of linear economics,

$$y = a_0 + a_1 x_1 + a_2 x_2$$

a doubling of the input variable x_1 doubles x_1's contribution to the output variable y, from $a_1 x_1$ to $2(a_1 x_1)$, irrespective of x_2. (It does not, in general, double y. Doubling both input variables, x_1 and x_2, in fact, doubles y only if $a_0 = 0$.) The same linearity property for x_1 does not hold in the equation

$$y = b_0 + b_1 x_1^2 + b_2 x_2$$

where doubling x_1 quadruples its effect on y, nor does it hold in the equation

$$y = c_0 + c_1 x_1 x_2$$

where the effect of x_1 on y interacts with the effect of x_2 on y. Such nonlinear relationships violate the restrictions of linear economics.

The limitations of linear economics are also its strength. By admitting only linear relationships, linear economics is able to make advantageous use of the elegant mathematics of linear algebra and the powerful solution methods of linear equalities and inequalities. The methodologies of linear economics include *input-output analysis, linear programming,* and *two-person zero-sum games.* These three methodologies, although linked theoretically, have quite separate histories. We will discuss each in turn.[1]

Input-Output Analysis

In early 1974, when the Middle Eastern oil-producing countries placed an embargo on their oil exports, thermostats in the United States had to be set

---

[1] For a classic treatment and full account of linear economics and its three methodologies, see Robert Dorfman, Paul A. Samuelson, and Robert M. Solow, *Linear Programming and Economic Analysis* (New York: McGraw-Hill, 1958).

down and the lines at gasoline stations seemed interminable. The so-called energy crisis was the hottest political issue in Washington. The stock market took a deep plunge, and businessmen began to worry about the secondary effects of the oil shortage. They wondered if the shift in revenue to the Arab states and the rapid rise in oil prices would permanently disrupt the world economy. The nation turned to its economists for an answer.

The economics profession has three things to call upon at such a time. It has theory; it has studies—ongoing and completed; and it has tools with which to perform analyses pointed specifically at the questions being raised. Economists tried to find an answer in roughly that order.

Economic theory was less than fully illuminating on the implications of the oil shortage. There were some relevant studies, both by industry and academic economists, but the results were mixed and uncertain. So economists looked to their tools. The tool that seemed most promising to many of them was a modeling methodology depicted as "unequaled in its ability to describe the structure of the economy."[2] This comprehensive methodology has a wide range of application. It has been called upon in the past to help with such problems of broad national importance as the impact on employment of conversion to a peacetime economy in anticipation, during the 1960s, of the ending of the Indochina war.[3] It is being used today to track industrial waste and to determine the resources required for pollution control and recycling.[4] During the 1950s it was applied to assess the effects of increases in the price of steel on inflation.[5] It has also been applied in recent years to the problems of metropolitan and regional growth.

The methodology is input-output analysis. Its advocates consider it the "only technique we currently have or are likely to have in the near future for comprehensively probing the intricate interdependencies of the joint economic-ecologic system."[6] There is similar hopefulness about its application to the energy problem, especially when it is combined with certain other modeling methodologies.

---

[2] Walter Isard and Phyllis Kaniss, "The 1973 Nobel Prize for Economic Science," *Science* 182, no. 4112 (1973): 571.

[3] The application of input-output analysis to the problem of disarmament is discussed in W. Leontief and M. Hoffenberg, "The Economic Effects of Disarmament," *Scientific American* 204, no. 34 (1961).

[4] Discussion of the application of input-output analysis to environmental management is found in Wassily Leontief, "Environmental repercussions and the economic structure: An Input-Output Approach," *Review of Economics and Statistics* 52, no. 3 (1970). Also, Wassily Leontief and Daniel Ford, "Air Pollution and the Economic Structure: Empirical Results of Input-Output Computations," in A. Brody and A. P. Carter (eds.), *Input-Output Techniques* (Amsterdam: North-Holland, 1972). For a current application, see U.S. Environmental Protection Agency, "Strategic Environmental Assessment System: (SEAS)" (Washington, D.C., 1974).

[5] Paul A. Samuelson, "Nobel Laureate Leontief," *Newsweek*, November 5, 1973, p. 94.

[6] Isard and Kaniss, p. 571.

Methodologies for Policy Modeling

Input-output analysis pictures the economy as a set of interdependent industries and activities, each of which requires the productive output of the others as input to its productive process. The steel industry uses coal and the coal industry uses steel. Both industries use some of their own output, as well as labor (the output of households), and the output of many other industries, such as power and services. The simplifying (and debatable) assumption of input-output analysis is that the ratios of one industry's inputs to its output are fixed. These ratios go by a variety of names: input-output numbers, production coefficients, technical coefficients of production, and so on. They are assumed constant in the absence of technological progress and other effects whose influence on the coefficients is considered recognizable and predictable.

As an example, suppose that it requires 40,000 tons of steel, 134,000 tons of coal, and 20,000 man-hours of labor to produce 200,000 tons of steel. The production coefficients for steel (ratios of inputs to output) are then .20 (steel), .67 (coal), and .10 (labor). Since the coefficients are assumed fixed, twice as much input, namely 80,000 tons of steel, 268,000 tons of coal, and 40,000 man-hours of labor, will product twice as much output, namely 400,000 tons of steel.

The fixed production coefficients, when arranged in a square tableau or input-output matrix (call it a; see Table 4–1), provide a structural representation of the interaction between components of the economy. If the reader will excuse a brief lapse into the jargon of linear algebra, the set of final demands or net product (column vector Y) is related to the set of total outputs required of all industries to meet those demands (column vector X) by the matrix equation $Y = X - aX$. This equation can be written in terms of the identity matrix, I, as $Y = (I - a) X$. One now defines an inverted matrix $A = (I - a)^{-1}$, so that $X = AY$, which provides a way of working back from the set of final demands to the set of total required outputs.

Table 4–1: Hypothetical Input-Output Coefficients for the Steel and Coal Industries and for Labor (Households), Arrayed in the Form of an Input-Output or Leontief Matrix, Designated a. The Input-Output Coefficients for the Coal Industry and for Labor are Expressed Symbolically.

	Steel	*Coal*	*Labor*
Steel	.20	a_{12}	a_{13}
Coal	.67	a_{22}	a_{23}
Labor	.10	a_{32}	a_{33}

Suppose in the example that the final demand for steel increases.

> Aside from the direct requirement for more steel which requires an expansion of the steel industry, the inverse matrix A captures the numerous indirect effects. All industries which supply inputs directly to steel must also expand as

steel expands, thus yielding a first round of indirect effects. But the expansions of these industries mean more inputs into their operations, producing a second round of indirect effects. And so forth. After a number of rounds, these indirect effects on each industry, for a properly constructed a matrix, converge to zero. The summation of the direct effect and all the round-by-round indirect effects is what is embodied in the use of the inverse matrix A.[7]

The results of changes in technology, the labor force, government spending, and so on, are inferred by estimating their effects on the production coefficients and reworking the matrix calculations. Thus, the method is quite general. It can be made even more general—even dynamic—by the introduction of capital stock and inventories. One is also able to introduce capacity-building activities to take account of industries operating at capacity, and other extensions are possible.

The number of coefficients required for input-output analysis goes up with the square of the number of industries considered; the number of multiplications required to invert $(I-a)$ goes up with the cube. With several hundred industries (not unusual) the number of coefficients runs into the hundreds of thousands and the number of multiplications runs into the millions. Such prodigious computational requirements are not out of the ordinary in the business of modeling. They make the automatic computer a must. The inventor of input-output analysis, Wassily W. Leontief, was one of the earliest computer customers.

In 1935, according to one account, "Leontief swallowed his parochial pride and drove over to Massachusetts Institute of Technology to use the simultaneous equation solver that mathematician John Wilbur had just pieced together. That, Harvard science historian Bernard Cohen notes, was the first time an economist was introduced to something that could be called a computer." As rudimentary and awkward as the computer was in those early years, it "contributed significantly" to Leontief's invention of input-output analysis.[8]

It was a fortunate coincidence for Leontief to be teaching at Harvard, which he joined as a member of the economics faculty in 1931. Neighboring institutions Harvard and M.I.T. are where much of the early work on computers took place. The first automatic computer was built at Harvard. Harvard professor Howard H. Aiken, a close friend of Leontief, conceived the Mark I Automatic Sequence Controlled Calculator in 1939, and under Navy aegis had it operational within five years. It was not long before Leontief was a major user. Some of Aiken's bright Ph.D. students worked with Leontief. Herbert Mitchell inverted the Leontief matrices and Kenneth E. Iverson,

---

[7] Ibid., p. 569.
[8] "Economists Play the Number Game," *Business Week,* June 5, 1971, p. 125.

who years later developed the APL computer language, did his doctoral dissertation on the use of the Mark IV computer to investigate an extension of Leontief's basic model.

Leontief, born in Leningrad in 1906, started to form his ideas on the circular flows of economies in the context of the Soviet economy.[9] He has spent a lifetime developing the input-output methodology, and was awarded the Nobel Prize for Economics in 1973 for this pioneering work and landmark achievement. The honor to Leontief was widely anticipated,[10] and there was little doubt that he was deserving.

It was not always so; input-output analysis was a long time in gaining recognition. Leontief had brought his ideas together into a rigorous formulation of the input-output methodology by 1936, and into a full exposition in 1941,[11] but the concept was resisted for many years. During World War II and afterwards Leontief cooperated with the Bureau of Labor Statistics to develop detailed input-output tables for the United States. This helped gain acceptance for the approach, but considerably more resistance had to be faced before its widespread adoption was secured.

By 1949 the U.S. Air Force was funding Leontief to do research on defense material requirements. The Air Force support for input-output studies became important, both at Harvard and in several agencies in Washington. In the latter part of 1953, the aid was cut off, purportedly as an economy measure, but it was widely rumored at the time that the recently installed Eisenhower administration was responding to the fears of businessmen that input-output analysis would be "an entering wedge for national economic planning—something possibly useful in wartime, but dangerous in peace."[12]

Because of the businessmen's complaints, the Eisenhower administration cancelled plans in 1953 to continue publication of the official input-output tables initiated by the Bureau of Labor Statistics the year before. Subsequently, the Commerce Department convinced businessmen that input-

---

[9] W. W. Leontief, "The Balance of the Economy of the USSR" in N. Spulber (ed.), *Foundations of Soviet Strategy for Economic Growth, Selected Short Soviet Essays 1924–1930* (Bloomington: Indiana University Press, 1964), pp. 88–94.

[10] See, for example, "A Revolutionary Idea Catches Fire," *Business Week,* November 22, 1969, p. 126. At the time this article was written, the Nobel Prize for Economics had just been awarded for the first time; it went to two Europeans, Ragnar Frisch and Jan Tinbergen. The article predicted that Leontief was "almost certain to be in front sometime within the next few years." He had already been elected president of the American Economic Association.

[11] See W. W. Leontief, "Quantitative Input and Output Relations in the Economic System of the United States," *Review of Economic Statistics* 18 (1936): 105–125; also, W. W. Leontief, *The Structure of the American Economy, 1919–1929,* 2nd ed. (Cambridge: Oxford University Press, 1951).

[12] "Discovering How U.S. Economy Fits Together and Grows," *Business Week,* March 31, 1956, pp. 180–181.

output analysis was a useful tool in business as well as in government. "Now," Leontief is quoted as having observed, "the demand for... input-output numbers comes more from businessmen than bureaucrats."[13]

This is not the only time that models have been associated adversely and undeservedly in people's minds with central planning and state control. This particular image of models has been one of the recurrent factors retarding their acceptance by policymakers. The theme appears in a warning to President Nixon in June 1972 that the *Limits to Growth* study was being used to support the views of those favoring a managed society.[14] There are many more important and valid reasons for resistance to models, not the least of which is their spotty record and (like their human users) their acknowledged inadequacies. But the use of models need not be synonymous with central control. Models that illuminate economic behavior may be used both by industry and governments to *improve* (not repress) the functioning of the free enterprise system. Nevertheless, equating models with state planning and federal regulation has been a factor impeding their use. The image of models, especially their false image, has been as important as their technical characteristics and performance record in determining their role in policy.

Not surprisingly, the acceptance of input-output methods has been faster and greater outside the United States than within. As Paul Samuelson observed, "a prophet is with even greater honor outside his own country. The United Nations, the World Bank, government agencies in Scandinavia and Western Europe, the five-year plans of the developing countries—all have taken up input-output budgeting."[15] Even the Soviet Union employs input-output analysis. By officially sanctioning its use and promoting it as a Russian invention, Russia seems to have forgiven Leontief for emigrating to the United States.

We have Leontief first on the list of modeling innovators, but there is no meaning attached to the order. One final point about him bears note. He has little use for abstract economic theory of no practical relevance. He eschews modeling for the sake of modeling, that is, modeling solely as an academic exercise. To Leontief, economic theory is of value only insofar as it helps in understanding the workings of the economy. Given relevant theory, a model is the means for formally expressing the theory, allowing it to be examined and tested. Leontief has always emphasized the need for data, exhaustive observation, and careful measurement to support theory. Much of his effort

---

[13] *Business Week,* November 22, 1969, p. 126.

[14] Nixon was counseled by Edward E. David that although the *Limits to Growth* study was not a sound basis for policymaking, models could provide helpful insights in government decision making. David was concerned that negative reactions to the *Limits to Growth* study might cause policymakers to reject modeling altogether.

[15] *Newsweek,* November 5, 1973, p. 94.

and that of his disciples has gone into painstaking industry-by-industry studies and estimation of production coefficients. Even critics consider this empirical work invaluable.[16] Not all model builders have such a strong appetite for data.

Linear Programming

The history of science and intellectual endeavor is filled with examples of the same discovery made by different people separated geographically, each innocent of the other's work. That such unknown coincidences occurred frequently a century ago when communication times across the Atlantic were measured in months instead of seconds is not much of a surprise. That they are still happening today is a greater wonder. What may seem truly astonishing at first glance is that a major intellectual breakthrough in Russia as recently as 1939 went unnoticed in the United States until well after it was rediscovered here eight years later. That is what took place in the case of the very important modeling methodology known as linear programming. The Iron Curtain had not yet been erected; there were other reasons for this failure of communication.

Leningrad, Leontief's birthplace, was the site of the breakthrough, but Leontief was not in this instance the innovator involved. Nor was it another economist. On May 13, 1939, Leonid V. Kantorovich, a distinguished Russian mathematician, presented a report to a meeting of the Mathematics Section of the Institute of Mathematics and Mechanics, attended by representatives of industrial research institutes in Russia. Kantorovich had discovered that "a whole range of problems of the most diverse character relating to the scientific organization of production (questions of the optimum distribution of the work of machines and mechanisms, the minimization of scrap, the best utilization of raw materials and local materials, fuel, transportation, and so on) led to the formulation of a single group of mathematical problems." Kantorovich called them "extremal problems," which is mathematical parlance for problems having to do with values at the boundary or outer limits of a region. The extraordinary insight that Kantorovich had was that this whole class of problems could be treated mathematically as a unit in theory and also in finding numerical solutions.

Kantorovich viewed an increase in the efficiency of Soviet production as

---

[16] Milton Friedman was said in 1956 to be highly skeptical about the overall Leontief approach. But he also was quoted as having predicted that "the understanding of particular industries, of the process of technological change, and like matters, which at this stage seem like unimportant by-products, will turn out to be the lasting and important contributions of the Leontief program to economic knowledge." (*Business Week,* March 31, 1956, p. 181.)

the motivation and expected result of his work. One way to increase efficiency, he observed, was by improvements in the organization of planning and production: "The immense task laid down in the plan for the third Five Year Plan period required that we achieve the highest possible production on the basis of the optimum utilization of the existing reserves of industry: materials, labor, and equipment." Although he regarded his work as providing a means for boosting production, Kantorovich saw little reason for the United States or any other capitalist country to be interested, partly explaining why scientists in this country were not informed.

> I want to emphasize again that the greater part of the problems of which I shall speak, relating to the organization and planning of production, are connected specifically with the Soviet system of economy and in the majority of cases do not arise in the economy of a capitalist society. There the choice of output is determined not by the plan but by the interests and profits of individual capitalists.[17]

It is curious to see a modeling innovator himself downplaying the appropriateness of his methodology for use in another country. It may very well reflect a cultural difference between socialistically-minded Russians and entrepreneurially-minded Americans. It is hard to imagine a modeling innovator born in the United States (like Forrester) or even emigrating here (like Leontief) disclaiming the applicability of his methodology to the analysis of problems in the Soviet Union; quite the contrary.

In the last analysis, Kantorovich was wrong about the applicability of linear programming in the capitalist society, although his remarks show insight into the bias that exists in the United States against central planning. Linear programming was, in fact, warmly received on this side of the Atlantic, especially by businessmen and industrial executives for use in streamlining production in their companies. Its application to the control of refinery operations in the petroleum field is only one of many success stories that could be cited. But its development here does not trace back to Kantorovich's report; the fact that it came almost a decade later is significant. It starts with George B. Dantzig, an American mathematician who was working with Leontief in the Pentagon on the Air Force's Project SCOOP in the 1940s, completely unaware of Kantorovich's earlier findings.

Dantzig, the son of Tobias Dantzig, also a well-known American mathematician, formulated the linear programming approach, a generalization of the Leontief model, as a means for planning or *programming* Air Force recruit-

---

[17] L. V. Kantorovich, "Mathematical Methods of Organizing and Planning Production," *Management Science* 6, no. 4 (1960): 366–422.

Methodologies for Policy Modeling 95

ment, maintenance, training, and other programs.[18] He assumed that the degree to which each of the programmed activities consumes and produces various commodities could be expressed in a linear relation. The coefficients of these linear relations could be arrayed as a matrix of fixed numbers, similar but not identical to the Leontief matrix of production coefficients.

This comparison highlights the fundamental connection between input-output analysis and linear programming. The major difference between the two is that whereas input-output analysis postulates a single set of industry outputs (i.e., one feasible solution) as being uniquely determined by a specified set of final demands, linear programming generally allows for any of a number of feasible solutions or combinations of activity levels to produce enough commodities to meet or surpass an indicated set of final demands (i.e., satisfy a set of constraints). To help choose among the possible alternatives, linear programming provides a linear *criterion* or *objective* function, typically a cost or benefit function, expressed in terms of the activity levels. The statement of the standard linear programming problem is to find that nonnegative set of activity levels that optimizes (maximizes or minimizes) the linear objective function subject to the linear constraints. The statement of the problem can take any of numerous other analogous forms, depending on the application.

There is more than one way to solve a linear programming problem. It is not as simple conceptually as inverting a matrix, the technique employed by Leontief for doing input-output analysis. One of the best-known procedures is the simplex method, an iterative scheme invented by Dantzig. Like matrix inversion, the simplex method requires a huge number of calculations for a linear programming problem of significant size. Once again, the computer has been indispensable. The perfection of highly efficient computer programs for solving linear programming problems by William Orchard-Hays and others has greatly facilitated the acceptance and usefulness of the linear programming methodology.

Strictly speaking, the purpose of linear programming is to optimize; that is, to find the best solution available from among a number of alternatives under certain, often severely restrictive, assumptions. Were that its only use, its value to decision makers would be considerably more limited than it actually is. Linear programming can be used to examine the influence on the

---

[18] Dantzig's first written account of his method, circulated privately in 1947, was not published until several years afterward. Entitled "Maximization of a Linear Function of Variables Subject to Linear Inequalities," it appears in T. C. Koopmans (ed.), *Activity Analysis of Production and Allocation* (New York: John Wiley & Sons, 1951), pp. 339–347. Koopmans' edited volume contains the first attempts to apply linear programming to economic theory.

objective function of different feasible solutions. It can be used to explore the effects of changes in coefficients and constraints. Rather than considering coefficients as given and fixed, they can be treated as parameters and varied to test their significance. A fruitful field of inquiry known as parametric programming has grown up around this idea. Such extensions of linear programming make it into more than a tool for optimization. Like input-output analysis and other modeling methodologies, it becomes a means for representing, exploring, and understanding a complex system of interdependent processes. It becomes useful in policy and strategic decision making as well as in operations. For such reasons as these, it is now widely accepted.

Many other people besides Dantzig were instrumental in developing and promoting linear programming in the United States. We note especially the catalytic efforts of Tjalling C. Koopmans in bringing linear programming to the attention of economists, and in illuminating its relevance to economic theory.[19] Koopmans, who took his Ph.D. in economics in the Netherlands and was a student there of Jan Tinbergen (see the later account of econometric modeling), came to the United States in 1940. He has been with the Cowles Foundation for Research in Economics since 1944, first at the University of Chicago, then at Yale, where the foundation later moved. Along with David Gale, H. W. Kuhn, A. W. Tucker, A. Charnes, A. Wald, and others, Koopmans is responsible for important conceptual advances in the theory of linear programming. His work on the transportation problem, a special kind of linear programming problem, is referred to in Dantzig's original paper. We associate Koopmans with Kantorovich and Dantzig as a key developer of linear programming for the breadth of his contribution and for the central role he played in clarifying, interpreting, and organizing the ideas of this methodology.

Two-Person Zero-Sum Games

When John von Neumann died in 1957 at the age of 53, the world was deprived of one of the most fertile and prodigious minds of the twentieth century. A mathematician, von Neumann (like Leontief) received his Ph.D. at the age of 22. Born in Budapest, he emigrated to the United States in 1930 and accepted an appointment at Princeton in 1931, about the same time that Leontief joined the Harvard faculty. His achievements, spanning several fields, run the gamut from the physical to the biological and social sciences. His discovery of the theory of two-person zero-sum (TPZS) games was hailed as a landmark in the history of ideas.

---

[19] Koopmans' *Activity Analysis* volume is a good example of the role Koopmans played.

Von Neumann proved the central minimax theorem of TPZS games in 1928,[20] but it was not until 1944, in collaboration with Princeton economist Oskar Morgenstern, that he made available a full exposition of the theory.[21]

> Briefly stated, the theory of games rests on the notion that there is a close analogy between parlor games of skill, ... and conflict situations in economic, political, and military life ... [T]here are a number of participants with incompatible objectives, and the extent to which each participant attains his objective depends upon what all the participants do. The problem faced by each participant is to lay his plans so as to take account of the actions of his opponents ... [by surmising what they] will expect him to do and how [they] will react to these expectations.
>
> It was von Neumann's remarkable achievement to demonstrate that something definite can be said about such a welter of cross-purposes and psychological interactions. He showed that under certain assumptions ... each participant can act so as to be guaranteed at least a certain minimum gain [thus preventing] his opponents from attaining any more than their minimum guaranteeable gains. Thus the minimum gains become the actual gains, and the actions and returns for all participants are determinate.[22]

The ideas of von Neumann and Morgenstern were received with great enthusiasm and hopefulness by economists, statisticians, and military strategists alike. Rand Corporation, the Air Force's think tank, took a special interest, and a modeling methodology based on the theory emerged. No other methodology had approached the problems of conflicting objectives and choice under risk so boldly and directly. But what Morgenstern clearly foresaw from the start, others did not recognize in the early optimism. The TPZS assumptions needed to make the game-theoretic model mathematically and computationally palatable were too restrictive for the model to be generally applicable. Attempts to relax various assumptions have by now occupied the attention of mathematicians and economists for over three decades and have dominated the literature on game theory. The results have been intellectually stimulating but have not led to any major increase in the applicability of the methodology to policy areas.

Although game theory has left a distinct mark on the subject of statistics (Bayesian analysis) and has enriched the theory of utility in economics, its imprint on the practical side has been less than originally expected. Yet it has

---

[20] John von Neumann, "Zur Theorie der Gesellschaftsspiele," *Mathematische Annalen* 100 (1928): 295–320.

[21] John von Neumann and Oskar Morgenstern, *Theory of Games and Economic Behavior*, 3rd ed. (Princeton, N.J.: Princeton University Press, 1953).

[22] Dorfman, Samuelson and Solow, p. 2. A zero-sum game between two persons requires that what one wins the other loses. Thus, the sum of the winnings and losses (negative winnings) is zero.

been applied by the military to duels, games of pursuit, search, and weapons evaluation, and it has, in general, provided a disciplined way of thinking about situations of conflict and choice. The importance of such a contribution is easy to overlook.

A problem phrased in a simplified TPZS game framework can be rephrased as a linear programming problem. The connection between these two methodologies is subtle. The minimax theorem provides the connecting link. It allows one to use the mathematical notation and numerical procedures of linear programming for expressing and solving TPZS game problems. This is the justification for including TPZS games (but not their extensions) under the heading of linear economics. The formulation of the minimax theory in 1928, and its use by von Neumann in 1937 to model a uniformly expanding closed economy with production relations expressed as linear inequalities, place von Neumann's work as one of the forerunners of linear programming. In his original account of linear programming, Dantzig acknowledged his debt to von Neumann as well as to Leontief.[23]

Probabilistic Methods of Operations Research

Operations research (O/R) was the product of the World War II mobilization of scientists in England, the United States, Canada, and France. Between the two world wars there had been twenty years of peace, during which there was no occasion to use or test new military technologies, such as radar, in combat. Scientists were needed by the military services to help determine (by means of the scientific method) the best way to use these technologies. The scientists, working in teams assigned to operational commanders, developed radar countermeasures, strategies for antisubmarine warfare, tactics for maneuvering a ship to dodge an incoming suicide plane or avoid a torpedo attack, and procedures for evaluating weapon systems. In England their work and methods became known as "operational research." In the United States the activity was known by a variety of names: operations analysis, operations evaluation, systems analysis, systems evaluation, management science, or, most frequently, operations research.

Because of the national emergency and strong sense of commitment at the time, scientists of the highest calibre made themselves available to the wartime effort. The U.S. Navy's O/R group was headed by Philip M. Morse, a professor of physics at M.I.T., assisted by other scientists, such as chemist George E. Kimball and mathematician B. O. Koopman.

By virtue of his own research experience, Morse sought scientists with

---

[23] Marshall K. Wood and George B. Dantzig, "The Programming of Interdependent Activities: General Discussion," in T. C. Koopmans, p. 15.

mathematical training and an experimental orientation for his O/R group. He felt that research in the natural sciences invested one with a healthy tendency to view a system as a whole. Morse was put off by theoreticians wedded to their theories and gadgeteers whose solution to any problem was more equipment rather than more analysis.

Of the 30 to 40 people who worked in England for the Operational Research Section, Coastal Command, of the Royal Air Force, five became fellows of the Royal Society and two received Nobel prizes. One of these two was physicist P. M. S. Blackett, later Lord Blackett, who served as president of the Royal Society.[24]

Both Morse and Blackett played key roles in helping to define the new field of O/R and in explaining the methods that shaped it. Both of them have made several original contributions to the development of the field, contributions that helped give the field its character. Both men returned to physics after the war. Until his retirement from the M.I.T. faculty, Morse served as director of the Operations Research Center that he founded at M.I.T. following his return there from wartime service.

England cut back drastically on its defense expenditures after the war and concentrated on rebuilding its damaged industry. Military O/R quickly became industrial O/R. In the United States, where postwar defense budgets remained high, most O/R continued to be conducted in a military context. It took another decade for American business and industry, encouraged by the growing application of the computer, to see how O/R could be profitably applied to their operations. By the middle 1960s, after another ten years, state and local governments started trying to use O/R, too. It is interesting to speculate on the reasons for the delay in their interest. Later in this book we will analyze the history of one such attempt by New York City. It is a revealing account of the efforts of an energetic mayor and a prestigious research organization to make O/R work in the feverish political climate of a busy metropolis.

Getting O/R to work in a military environment in the 1940s was not the same as it is in a city today, since military problems had more to do with technology than with people. Also, the crisis of war may have reduced normal resistance to change and innovation. Nevertheless, no matter what the time or context, it is people who do the analysis and it is people who do or do not pay

---

[24] The history of operations research in England was outlined in a letter to *Science* by C. H. Waddington, Blackett's colleague in operations research during the war. Waddington was contesting a reference to "some low-level operations researcher" made by Aaron Wildavsky in a *Science* book review of Garry D. Brewer, *Politicians, Bureaucrats, and the Consultant: A Critique of Urban Problem Solving* (New York: Basic Books, 1973). Wildavsky's review appeared in *Science* 182 (1973): 1335–1337. Waddington's letter appeared in *Science* 183 (1974): 1141. Waddington had recently published a book on British O/R during the war: C. H. Waddington, *O. R. in World War 2, Operations Research against the U-Boat* (London: Elk Books, 1973).

attention to the results of the analysis. Morse and Kimball recognized that the relationship between the decision maker (or executive) and the operations researcher is essential.

> The task of the operations research worker is to present the quantitative aspects in intelligible form and to point out, if possible, some of the nonquantitative aspects that may need consideration by the executive before he reaches his decisions. But the operations research worker does not and should not make the decision.... This separation of the duties and activities of the operations research worker and the executive officer is important.... The requirement that the executive reach a decision concerning an operation is to some extent antagonistic to the requirement that he look at it scientifically and impersonally, as would be required in operations research. The proper use of an operations research group by an executive department implies a sort of symbiosis, requiring, on the part of each, trust in the other's activities and respect of the other's prerogatives.[25]

> The reaching of a working understanding on "terms of reference" between the operations research worker and the administrative head to whom he is assigned is one of the most important organizational problems encountered in entering a new field of operations research. Scientist and administrator perform different functions and often must take opposite points of view. The scientist must always be skeptical and is often impatient at arbitrary decisions; the administrator must eventually make decisions which are in part arbitrary and is often impatient at skepticism. It takes a great deal of understanding and mutual trust for the two to work closely enough together to realize to the fullest the potentialities of the partnership.[26]

These observations apply with equal force today. The difficulties of the relationship between modeler and decision maker, understood by Morse and Kimball, become even more troublesome when the partnership must be established in the complex political setting of contemporary national and urban policymaking, rather than in the much less politicized military environment.

In 1950, when Morse and Kimball produced their accounting of O/R in World War II, it was still possible to write without dispute that the theory of probability was the branch of mathematics most useful in operations research. Today, although probability is still of central importance in O/R—especially in queueing theory, stochastic processes, Bayesian analysis, portfolio analysis, and parts of inventory theory, search theory, and scheduling—other mathe-

---

[25] Philip M. Morse and George E. Kimball, *Methods of Operations Research*, 1st ed. rev. (Cambridge: M.I.T. Press, 1951), pp. 1–2. The Morse-Kimball book reviews the use of O/R by the United States during World War II, as the Waddington book does for England. Morse also has a chapter on the history of O/R in Grace Kelleher (ed.), *The Challenge to Systems Analysis* (New York: John Wiley & Sons, 1970). The same book contains the recollections of E. C. Williams on the start of O/R in England.

[26] Morse and Kimball, p. 10a.

matical approaches have ascended in significance. Probability theory has trouble representing structural interdependencies by itself without getting mired in prodigious mathematical complexity. As O/R moved into the civilian sector, its scope of application expanded beyond the primarily technological to organized systems of people, activities, and institutions. New, more encompassing research tools were needed.

One avenue taken was Monte Carlo simulation, a probability sampling technique originally suggested by John von Neumann and Stanislaw M. Ulam (in connection with their work on atomic weapons at Los Alamos in the 1940s) as a means for solving problems of mathematical physics.[27] Operations researchers further developed the Monte Carlo method and applied it to the simulation of nonphysical processes, including industrial operations and social systems. Monte Carlo simulation uses probability distributions to characterize the elements of a system and random sampling rather than analytical deduction to infer interactions. Random sampling (also called model sampling) was not a new technique. It had been employed by statisticians since early in the century, but prior to the suggestions of von Neumann and Ulam, it had never before been used to solve, by a process of analogy, deterministic problems in mathematical physics; never before had it been used in the simulation of large, complex systems.

One of the most ambitious attempts to apply Monte Carlo simulation to socioeconomic systems was "microanalysis," a methodology we will discuss later under statistical economics. Equally ambitious was the Rand Corporation's use of simulation on a grand scale in the 1950s to study the operational characteristics of Air Force logistical systems. The Rand Corporation has been the site of more important methodological work on modeling of various kinds than any other institution in the United States. Rand's logistical studies in the 1950s were man-machine simulations, with real Air Force personnel playing their own parts as supply officers, etc., and a first-generation computer playing other roles and doing the bookkeeping and analysis. Although Rand's logistical simulations were phased out, the use of man-machine simulation has grown in scope and popularity over the years to include business, urban, and environmental games, and many other types of role playing models.

The Rand logistical studies served to illustrate that the generality and flexibility of the simulation approach present dangers as well as advantages.[28] It is easy to overmodel with simulation (whether of the Monte Carlo or another

---

[27] For an account of the origins of the Monte Carlo method, see A. W. Marshall, "An Introductory Note," in Herbert A. Meyer (ed.), *Symposium on Monte Carlo Methods* (New York: John Wiley & Sons, 1956), pp. 1–14.

[28] There have been many criticisms of the misuse and overuse of the simulation technique. See for example Douglass B. Lee, Jr., "Requiem for Large-Scale Models," *Journal of the American Institute of Planners* 34 (1968): 251.

variety), that is, build the model so large and complex that its properties become as baffling as those of the reference system being modeled. This temptation is great for a modeler armed with a fast, versatile computer. Another danger is the Pygmalion-like temptation to become enamored of the simulation model and lose touch with reality. Morse cautioned that it is a "fact, often forgotten nowadays, that successful operations research keeps close to actual happenings and does not lose itself in esoteric theories or computer simulations."[29] Blackett emphasized the importance of "collecting the actual data" and "the necessity of obtaining a clear definition of the problem which the data are expected to elucidate."[30] Morse and Blackett would agree that modeling is at best a *means* in O/R, never an *end* unto itself.

A simple hypothetical example of a Monte Carlo simulation is the flipping of a coin to simulate an event with two possible outcomes, say "war" and "peace." Let us make believe that the probability of a head turning up is known to be exactly equal to the probability of war. Clearly, a single flip of the coin would not provide a very reliable reading on whether or not war will occur. One would have to flip the coin ten, a hundred, or a thousand or more times, depending on the accuracy desired, to estimate the chance of war. The same principle applies to more seriously intentioned Monte Carlo simulations where each simulation run (instead of being the flip of coin) may involve millions of calculations. Monte Carlo simulation can be a very useful and flexible means for exploring the properties of a probabilistic model, but it can also be inefficient and costly. Investigators confronted with this problem have developed a variety of methods for reducing the variance, and thereby increasing the efficiency, of Monte Carlo simulations. These techniques take on names like "importance sampling" and "Russian roulette." An early account can be found in an article by Herman Kahn, the provocative futurist, written in the days when he worked as a physicist with the nuclear energy division of the Rand Corporation.[31]

Algebraic Methods of Operations Research

Many of the methods that operations researchers use in their attempts to represent problems of ever greater complexity tend to relegate probability to a back seat. For want of a better name, we call these methods "algebraic methods" to distinguish them from the probabilistic methods of O/R that continue to occupy a major role in the field. They include what often are referred to as methods of "mathematical programming."

---

[29] Philip M. Morse, review of Waddington, *O. R. in World War 2*, in *Science* 184 (1974): 1365.

[30] Waddington, letter, p. 1141.

[31] Herman Kahn, "Use of Different Monte Carlo Sampling Techniques," in Meyer, pp. 146–190.

Linear programming, whose development we described under linear economics, has been the leader among the algebraic methods of O/R. Mathematician Abraham Charnes and economist William W. Cooper, working as a team, have been instrumental in adapting linear programming to a wide variety of management problems in the petroleum, lumber, transportation, power, and manufacturing industries.[32] For the past decade, linear programming has been standard fare in the curriculum of most business schools, especially in courses on production management.

It is possible to relax the linearity requirement of linear programming in certain ways. Philip Wolfe of Rand developed a technique for quadratic programming, where the constraint and objective relations take on a general quadratic form as in the following expression.[33]

$$a_o + a_1 x_1 + a_2 x_2 + a_{11} x_1^2 + a_{12} x_1 x_2 + a_{22} x_2^2.$$

While at Princeton in 1958, Ralph A. Gomory discovered an algorithm for solving a linear programming problem whose variables are restricted to be integers,[34] as they are, for example, when they designate the number of airplanes of each of several types purchased by an airline. Gomory's algorithm and its refinements opened up a fertile field of application called "discrete" or "integer" programming, another important extension of linear programming.

Dynamic programming, developed by mathematician Richard Bellman,[35] and network or graph theory, developed by the mathematical team of L. R. Ford, Jr. and D. R. Fulkerson,[36] are other significant algebraic methods in O/R, but they are not directly related to linear programming. Both developments took place at the Rand Corporation in the 1950s, further evidence of the central position Rand held in modeling research at that time.

Many other O/R tools (and their developers) could be cited. Of all the algebraic methods, linear programming has so far been the most useful for policy questions. Since we have already listed Kantorovich, Dantzig, and

---

[32] A. Charnes and W. W. Cooper, *Management Models and Industrial Applications of Linear Programming*, 2 vols. (New York: John Wiley & Sons, 1961).

[33] See Philip Wolfe, "The Simplex Method for Quadratic Programming," *Econometrica* 27, no. 3 (1959). Algorithms that apply to the solution of quadratic programming problems depend upon the character of the quadratic forms; that is, upon whether they are "convex" or "concave," properties that relate to the behavior of their derivatives.

[34] Ralph A. Gomory, "Outline of an Algorithm for Integer Solutions to Linear Programs," *Bulletin of the American Mathematical Society* 64, no. 5 (1958).

[35] Richard Bellman, *Dynamic Programming*, A Rand Corporation Research Study (Princeton, N.J.: Princeton University Press, 1957).

[36] L. R. Ford, Jr. and D. R. Fulkerson, "A Simple Algorithm for Finding Maximal Network Flows and Application to the Hitchcock Problem," *Canadian Journal of Mathematics* 9 (1957): 210–218.

Koopmans as modeling innovators for their work on linear programming, we will avoid altogether the dilemma of who else to include as innovators for algebraic methods by settling for this threesome.

Econometric Modeling

Statistics is the mathematics of data analysis. It receives significant use by those modeling methodologies that rely heavily on empirical data. Some methodologies do more than others. Morse and Blackett stressed the importance of data in wartime applications of the O/R methodology. Statistical theory was a key part of their analytical approach.

Statistics is also used a great deal in economics. Quantitative measurement and data collection have become major activities of economic research in the past half century, thanks in large part to the influence of the careful work on national accounts performed by economist Simon Kuznets and others. An entire new field within economics has developed around the analysis and use of economic data; we call it "statistical" economics. Others might refer to the field as quantitative economics or, more narrowly and specifically, econometrics. "Econometrics," writes econometrician Lawrence Klein, "is measurement in economics, where that measurement is applied to the mathematical formulation of economic theory and carried out according to the principles of mathematical statistics."[37] Econometricians are big users and also extenders of statistical theory. Some econometricians work with empirical data and economic theory to build models of the economy and its components. The main methodology they use is econometric modeling.

An econometric model is, in practice, usually a set of simultaneous difference equations. Take a simple example: suppose for each of an indefinite number of time periods from some starting time into the future

$$Y = C + I$$

and

$$C = a + bY + cC_{-1} + \mu$$

These two equations form a very gross model of an economy. The first equation expresses national income (Y) in terms of total consumption (C) and total investment (I). The second equation expresses C in terms of Y, C in the last time period (C_{-1}), and a random disturbance (μ). The first equation is "definitional." It is exact. The second equation is "behavioral" and "stochastic." It is probabilistic and approximate, and represents presumed behavior only. Its coefficients, a, b, and c, must be estimated statistically from the data.

---

[37] Lawrence R. Klein, "Nobel Laureates in Economics," *Science* 166 (1969): 715.

These equations are "difference" equations in that they state how variables such as Y and C change from one discrete time period to the next. The equations are "simultaneous" in that a variable is not (normally) defined completely by just one of them. Both equations are needed to give a full picture of the behavior of Y and C.

The equations may be rewritten in a reduced form by replacing $C + I$ for Y in the second equation, solving for C, substituting the result in the first equation, and solving for Y. This gives

$$Y = a/1-b + (1/1-b)I + (c/1-b)C_{-1} + (1/1-b)\mu$$
$$C = a/1-b + (b/1-b)I + (c/1-b)C_{-1} + (1/1-b)\mu$$

In the reduced form, it is much easier to see how the equations can generate C and Y each period, since these variables now appear only on the left-hand side. Suppose that through a process of statistical estimation based on historical data on Y and C in past years, the coefficients are assigned the following values: $a = .3$, $b = .1$, $c = .8$. The equations, then, neglecting disturbances, are

$$Y = .33 + 1.11I + .89C_{-1}$$
$$C = .33 + .11I + .89C_{-1}$$

Suppose, further, that C last year was measured at $3.0 billion, I at $1.0 billion, and I is expected to increase 10 percent a year for the next several years. This is all the information needed to produce expected values of Y and C for the next several years. Using subscripts on the variables to designate the time period, with $C_0 = 3.00$, $I_0 = 1.00$, and $(I_1, I_2, \ldots) = (1.10, 1.21, \ldots)$, the calculation (or simulation) proceeds as follows.

$$Y_1 = .33 + 1.11 \times 1.10 + .89 \times 3.00 = 4.22$$
$$C_1 = .33 + .11 \times 1.10 + .89 \times 3.00 = 3.12$$
$$Y_2 = .33 + 1.11 \times 1.21 + .89 \times 3.12 = 4.45$$
$$C_2 = .33 + .11 \times 1.21 + .89 \times 3.12 = 3.24$$

and so on.

Inputs for the simulation of this simple econometric model were a starting value for C and values for I over the entire span of the period being simulated. As discussed in Chapter 3, variables like I, whose projected values need to be assumed or entered from *outside* the econometric model, are called "exogenous" variables. Variables like Y and C, whose projected values are generated *inside* the model, are called "endogenous" variables. Statistical estimation of the coefficient requires historical data on both the endogenous and exogenous variables. The data are arranged in an exceedingly simple format, known as a "time series," namely, one value for each successive period. The simplicity of the data format is of great advantage in the computerization of econometric modeling.

The first econometric business cycle model was produced by economist Jan Tinbergen of the Netherlands in the 1930s. Tinbergen undertook his study to examine the question of whether a recovery in the domestic economic situation of his country, by which he primarily meant an expansion of employment, was possible with or without action on the part of the government, even without an improvement in its export position.[38] The problem of economic recovery was of utmost concern in the 1930s at a time of worldwide depression. Tinbergen recognized that he was "dealing with a complicated subject."

> Complicated in two respects. In the first place, with respect to time. The relationships between present variables and variables four months hence work along numerous different channels. All sorts of differing lag phenomena play a part in these relationships. Secondly, the subject is complicated even if we leave time out of the picture, because many different variables in the economic mechanism are interconnected.[39]

Tinbergen was convinced of the necessity for building "an apparatus for systematizing" his thoughts. The apparatus he developed was the econometric model. He quaintly referred to what he was doing as "quantitatively stylizing" the economic process, contrasting his approach to the "qualitative stylizing" in vogue at the time. These phrases may have suffered in translation, but the distinction Tinbergen seems to have intended (put in the language of Chapter 3) is reasoning with a formal quantitative model as opposed to reasoning with a mental qualitative model. Tinbergen wanted to replace the "literary description of economic processes" with "mathematical precision."[40] Tinbergen argued: "Only a systematizing of the relations ... can ... lead to fertile discussion. It is hardly conceivable that mutual understanding and further progress are possible without an accurate localisation of the sources of differences in opinion."[41]

Tinbergen's model had twenty-nine variables and twenty-four equations. Although he recognized its shortcomings and cautioned the reader not to place

---

[38] L. H. Klaasen, L. M. Koyck, and H. J. Witteveen (eds.), *Jan Tinbergen, Selected Papers* (Amsterdam: North-Holland, 1959), pp. 36–84.
[39] Ibid., p. 41.
[40] "The Nobel: Reward for Econometricians," *Business Week*, November 1, 1969, p. 42.
[41] Klaasen, Koyck, and Witteveen, p. 82.

Methodologies for Policy Modeling 107

too much faith in the results, the model led him to conclude that a devaluation of Dutch currency could lead to a fairly considerable domestic revival of employment, at the cost of some deterioration in the Netherlands' balance of payments.

Tinbergen went on to model the United States economy in 1939 in a landmark study conducted under the auspices of the League of Nations. The objective was to understand the nature of business cycles and the causes of the Great Depression. The study produced the first large-scale formal model of the American economy.[42]

Tinbergen has made important contributions to international trade and finance, economic growth, economic development and planning, income distribution, and economic cycles, as well as to econometric modeling. For his seminal work, Tinbergen shared the Nobel prize with Ragnar Frisch of Norway in 1969, the first year the honor was awarded in the field of economics.[43] Tinbergen's pioneering work in the development of econometric models of the economy is now an integral part of the eminently practical business of running or forecasting the national economy, especially in the Netherlands, and in most other industrial countries of the world as well, including the United States.[44]

Tinbergen's work on econometric models was taken up in the United States by Lawrence R. Klein. Proceeding from Tinbergen's League of Nations model, Klein fathered a family of econometric models of the American economy that are used routinely today in government and business for forecasting and analysis. We will take up the story of econometric modeling with Klein in Chapter 6. Tinbergen and Klein were founders of a modeling activity that is now of great importance in applied economics.

Microanalysis

Econometric models of the national economy, as introduced by Tinbergen and carried forward by Klein and others, take major sectors of the economy, such as the business and household sectors, as their basic components. They

---

[42] Jan Tinbergen, *Statistical Testing of Business Cycle Theories;* Vol. 1, *A Method and Its Application to Investment Activity;* Vol. 2, *Business Cycles in the United States of America, 1919–1932* (Geneva: League of Nations, 1939).
[43] "Models Bring Nobel Prize," *Science News,* November 1, 1969, p. 397; also, Klein, p. 715.
[44] There are several interesting parallels between Jan Tinbergen and his younger brother Nikolaas, a distinguished ethologist. Nikolaas received the Nobel Prize for Physiology or Medicine in 1973, four years after Jan, who is older than Nikolaas by exactly four years. Nikolaas is an "animal watcher" whose *scientia amabilis* is acknowledged as an integral part of medicine. Nikolaas Tinbergen, "Ethology and Stress Diseases," *Science* 185 (1974): 20. Jan, of course, is an "economy watcher" (as every good applied economist must be) whose modeling inventions are fundamental to the forecasting of economies.

are "aggregative" or "macro" models. That is, they are not concerned with the separate behavior of individual households and firms in the economy, only with the sums of individual behavior aggregated over all units of a sector. The equations of the aggregative models express macroeconomic relations in time among the sector totals, using probabilistic elements. That is, they are dynamic and stochastic, as well as aggregative. The variables of the equations—aggregate consumption, total disposable income, annual automobile production, and the like—correspond to items tabulated in the national income and product accounts. Time-series data from these accounts are used to test the models and estimate their coefficients. Because they are aggregative, the models are not attuned to such distributional effects as the disposable income paid to automobile workers in California or the welfare received by unskilled female heads of households, information that can be very important to an analysis of the effects of various social programs. The aggregative models cannot deal with these effects for the simple reason that they are not constructed at a sufficiently fine level of detail.

Leontief's input-output analysis, like econometric modeling, is a methodology developed to model the national economy. Industries are the basic components. Standard input-output models are nonstochastic (deterministic) and nondynamic (static), unlike their econometric cousins, although they can be made dynamic by the introduction of inventories. They are aggregative at the industry level. The models concentrate on capturing the interindustry cross-sectional structure of the economy, not its dynamic behavior in time. They do not use probabilistic elements in their relationships. Input-output models do not separately represent firms within industries or workers and their families within the labor population. They do not (and cannot) attend to distributional effects at the microunit level or, for that matter, at any level beneath the industry level represented by the model. In recent years, input-output interindustry relations have been incorporated into some of the largest of the econometric models of the national economy—making them much larger still—to allow them to produce forecasts pertaining to specific industries.

There is a third methodology for modeling the national economy that does operate at a micro-unit level and does lend itself to analysis of distributional effects. Called "microanalysis" (or, by some, "microeconometrics" in contrast to "macroeconometrics"), its primary components are the "decision units" of which the economy is composed: individuals, families, households, manufacturing firms, retailers, banks, insurance companies, labor unions, local, state, and federal governments, and the like. Microanalysis represents decision units by microeconomic relations called "operating characteristics" that update status variables and transform input variables into output variables. Decision units interact with each other either directly or through markets whose function is to distribute the outputs of one set of decision units as inputs to another set of decision units. The operating characteristics are typically probability statements in the form of statistical regression equations that define the probability of a decision unit's taking some step, such as a married couple's deciding to get a divorce or a manufacturing firm's expanding production capacity.

A microanalytic model is run or moved forward in time by the process of Monte Carlo simulation. The probability of an action is calculated and the computer is made to draw a random sampling that is compared with the derived probability to determine whether or not the action is to take place and to what degree. Thus, the microanalytic model, like the econometric model to which it is closely related, is stochastic and dynamic. The major differences between these two types of models is in the levels of detail they represent in their methods of simulation. The microanalysis model works with a representative population of decision units and invokes each operating characteristic (regression equation) for each decision unit each time period. The econometric model, in contrast, invokes each of its equations only once per time period. It has no population of decision units. The disaggregation and Monte Carlo approach of microanalysis are advantages when it comes to producing detail and providing flexibility. But the benefits are not without cost. Microanalysis is time-consuming and expensive when compared to aggregative econometric modeling, even on the fastest computers, not only because of the multiplicity of decision units, but also because of the substantial variance inherent to Monte Carlo simulation. A run must often be repeated many times with different random numbers to generate a distribution of outcomes or an average that can be accepted with confidence. Macroeconometric modeling takes fewer calculations per forecast, while microanalysis has a wider range of possible applications and affords a finer level of detail, but at the cost of having much greater data and model specification requirements. Although it is easier to make certain kinds of changes to the model with microanalysis, it is harder to determine the real meaning of the changes; that is, it is harder to understand the nature and properties of the model.

Originator of the microanalytic technique for modeling economic systems was Guy H. Orcutt, who formulated the concepts of the microanalytic methodology in the middle 1950s while a colleague of Leontief's on the Harvard faculty. At Harvard, Orcutt taught courses in quantitative economics and economic statistics, which included discussions of econometric models of the economy. He had made some important research contributions himself to the development of econometrics, and was very likely influenced in his thinking by both input-output analysis and econometric modeling, especially the researches of Leontief, Tinbergen, and Klein. He was also much taken with the ambitious man-machine simulations being carried out by the Rand Corporation during the mid-1950s to study Air Force logistical systems. The electronic computer was then just a toddler and very primitive in operation compared to its present-day progeny, but the Rand work dramatized for Orcutt the flexibility and power that one might expect from computers as they further matured.

The strongest stimulus to Orcutt's thinking came from the ideas and data studies at the University of Michigan's Survey Research Center. Orcutt was discouraged with the very limited number of data observations available to econometricians in the national income and product accounts. He felt that much of the interesting informational content of the national income data was drained out in the process of aggregating it. The Survey Research Center, on the other hand, was collecting data on the behavior of the individual decision units of the economy, e.g., the spending of households on consumer nondurables as a function of type and composition of household. Orcutt reasoned that time-series (as opposed to cross-sectional) data collected on the behavior of selected decision units over a period of time would permit statistical estimation of regression equations characterizing the probable future behavior of such decision units. A model incorporating these equations, along with a statistical population of decision units chosen to be representative of the actual population across several key dimensions, could be used both to simulate the future behavior of decision units and to infer, by summation, the aggregate behavior of the economy as a whole. This new approach to modeling the economy is the methodology that within a few years became known as microanalysis.

Orcutt took a sabbatical leave from Harvard in 1955 to visit the University of Michigan, where he had once been a student. At the Survey Research Center there, he traded thoughts with James Morgan, Harvey Brazer, Martin David,[45] and others. Upon his return to Cambridge, Orcutt got busy forming a team to produce and run a model of the economy on the IBM 704 computer being installed at the newly established M.I.T. Computation Center, one of the more advanced computers of the day. Philip Morse, first director of the M.I.T. Computation Center, was interested in Orcutt's project and made time on the M.I.T. computer freely available to it. IBM, who shared operation of the M.I.T. Computation Center with M.I.T., was also generous with computer time as well as with programming assistance. The first runs of the model, a demographic simulation of the economy from 1950 through 1960, were made during 1958.[46]

---

[45] James N. Morgan, Harvey Brazer, and Martin David were associated with the Survey Research Center at the University of Michigan at the time of Orcutt's stay there. See James N. Morgan et al., *Income and Welfare in the United States* (New York: McGraw-Hill, 1962).

[46] Guy H. Orcutt et al., *Microanalysis of Socioeconomic Systems: A Simulation Study* (New York: Harper and Row, 1961).

The development and application of microanalysis since those early runs has taken several paths. The main line of development has been pursued by Orcutt, who left the Harvard faculty in 1958 for the University of Wisconsin to establish and direct the Social System Research Institute. At Wisconsin, Orcutt collaborated with others on a number of component studies of the economy using the microanalytic framework. He resumed full-scale modeling of the economy in the late 1960s after joining the Urban Institute in Washington, D.C. At the Urban Institute, microanalytic modeling became an activity of major proportions. Orcutt's own modeling project at the Urban Institute was funded initially from a Ford Foundation project grant ($350,000), later by the Office of Economic Opportunity (OEO) to assist in the design and evaluation of alternate strategies for the poverty program, and then by HEW, NSF, and the Office of Tax Analysis of the Treasury Department. Started in 1969, Orcutt's project reached a peak budget of $600,000 a year in the early 1970s, and ran subsequently at about half a million dollars a year. In September 1973, a ten-year simulation of a population of 4,000 persons cost approximately $400 to run on the PDP-10 computer, using a programming system by the name of MASH, constructed at the Urban Institute specifically for microanalytic modeling.[47]

A second line of development of the microanalytic technique came about through its adaptation and diffusion into a number of fields different from the one for which it was originally created. It lends itself well to such adaptation because of its conceptual simplicity, its generality, and (more than most other modeling methodologies) its high degree of flexibility and freedom from restrictive conventions. Ithiel de Sola Pool and Robert Abelson took a microanalytic approach to modeling the 1960 and 1964 presidential elections for the Democratic party.[48] Ford Motor Company and a number of other private firms have used microanalysis to model consumer behavior. The Arthur D. Little Company applied microanalysis to the simulation of housing development in San Francisco.[49] This last application is sketched later in the chapter under the housing examples.

A third line of development has been in the fields of tax and welfare reform, where the microanalytic model has been reduced to a static version that is used to explore the first-order implications of policy changes applied to a sample population. An example is the sample population of 100,000 1960

---

[47] George Sadowsky, *MASH: A Computer System for Microanalytic Simulation for Policy Exploration,* Urban Institute Working Paper #5096 (Washington, D.C.: Urban Institute, 1975).

[48] Ithiel de Sola Pool, Robert P. Abelson, and Samuel L. Popkin, *Candidates, Issues, and Strategies* (Cambridge: The M.I.T. Press, 1965).

[49] San Francisco Department of City Planning, "The San Francisco Community Renewal Simulation Model," in Ira M. Robinson (ed.), *Decision Making in Urban Planning* (Beverly Hills: Sage Publications, 1972), pp. 555–595.

United States income tax returns used in a revenue estimation study by Joseph A. Pechman of the Brookings Institution.[50]

Pechman and his Brookings colleague Benjamin A. Okner have used static microanalysis on repeated occasions to assess the revenue effects of proposed legislative modifications to tax rates and structural features of the tax code and to prepare the income tax estimates required in budget and tax planning. One of their studies was the simulation of a major tax code revision recommended by the Carter Commission of Canada as a way of broadening the individual tax base and reducing tax rates. The revision included the limiting of personal deductions, the elimination of separate corporation, estate, and gift taxes, and the inclusion of undistributed corporate profits, gifts, and inheritances in the individual tax base. The Pechman-Okner study simulated the tax liabilities under the Carter proposals for a large sample of 1966 federal individual income tax returns and compared them with actual United States tax liabilities by family status, source of income, and income class. The study found that at 1966 income levels, adoption of the Carter tax structure in the United States would raise the tax base by 29 percent and redistribute tax burdens "from single individuals to married couples, from low-income to high-income persons, and from shareholders in corporate enterprise (particularly those with low incomes) to other taxpayers."[51] The study cannot be considered more than an academic exercise because of the welter of political obstacles that would impede any serious attempt to adopt the Carter proposals, but it is richly suggestive of the kinds of policy questions that can be treated with the microanalytic approach.[52]

Okner has a basic reluctance to use the term "model" to describe the instrument he used with Pechman. His preference is to refer to it as a "data file," since it does not incorporate any operating characteristics or behavioral relations for aging the population and taking account of interactions and secondary effects. Yet it is not difficult or unnatural to make such additions to a static microanalytic model. The point is illustrated by the next application of microanalysis we shall consider.

---

[50] Joseph A. Pechman, "A New Tax Model for Revenue Estimating," in Alan T. Peacock and Gerald Hauser (eds.), *Government Finance and Economic Development* (Paris: Organisation for Economic Cooperation and Development; Brookings Reprint 102, 1965).

[51] Joseph A. Pechman and Benjamin A. Okner, "Simulation of the Carter Commission Tax Proposals for the United States," *National Tax Journal* 22 (Washington, D.C.: 1969): 11.

[52] Pechman and Okner published a more recent application of their approach in "Individual Income Tax Erosion by Income Classes," *The Economics of Federal Subsidy Programs,* Joint Economic Committee, Part I, General Study Papers, 92nd Congress, (Washington, D.C.: Brookings Reprint 230, May 1972), pp. 13–40. They also used a microanalytic approach for the computer analysis of tax distribution reported on in Joseph A. Pechman and Benjamin A. Okner, *Who Bears the Tax Burden?* (Washington, D.C.: Brookings Institution, 1974).

Methodologies for Policy Modeling

The Pechman-Okner simulation of the Carter tax reform highlights the ability of microanalysis to examine the distributional implications of simultaneous proposed changes in tax (and grant) programs. This feature was put to use in the late 1960s by the President's Commission on Income Maintenance Programs (chaired by Ben W. Heineman), a commission that considered and later recommended substituting a negative income tax for the welter of federal grant programs that make up the welfare system in the United States.

One of the senior government workers to join the commission staff was Nelson McClung from the Office of Tax Analysis of the Treasury Department. McClung proposed that the commission construct a model that would do for grant programs what the Pechman-Okner model and the Treasury Department's Personal Income Tax Model were doing for tax programs. McClung's proposal was readily accepted by staff director Robert Harris, a former HEW analyst who, intrigued by Orcutt's modeling efforts, had earlier tried (unsuccessfully) to generate funds for development of a microanalytic model for analyzing income transfer programs within HEW.

Harris and McClung put together a team that included economist Gail Wilensky, who developed the model,[53] and Herbert Miller, of the Hendrickson Corporation, who was principal programmer. Wilensky, like Okner, was a former student of Harvey Brazer at the University of Michigan. McClung persuaded her to adopt a microanalytic modeling approach similar to the one being used by Pechman and Okner, instead of the somewhat more aggregate approach that she had started with based on her earlier work with Brazer. The model was completed during the life of the commission and guided the commission in its recommendations to the president. Daniel P. Moynihan credits the modeling work and the full information made available to both sides with making possible a disciplined debate in the hearings on welfare reform.

Upon completion of his work at the commission, McClung went to the Urban Institute to head a new program of income maintenance studies and recruited a staff to analyze variations and alternatives of the Family Assistance Plan for HEW using a somewhat refined version of the Heineman Commission model known as RIM. At HEW was Michael Mahoney, the individual primarily responsible for obtaining cost and caseload estimates of alternative welfare plans. Mahoney was chief contact person for the Urban Institute group. Jodie T. Allen, a key staff member concerned with program planning and evaluation of the income maintenance experiments, was also at HEW at the time. She had contributed to the development of the RIM model.

The RIM model was not designed for continuing, fast-response policy use.

---

[53] Gail R. Wilensky, "An Income Transfer Computational Model," *The President's Commission on Income Maintenance Programs: Technical Studies* (Washington, D.C.: Government Printing Office, 1970), pp. 121–134.

It proved to be costly and time-consuming. With financial support from the Urban Institute's discretionary funds, supplemented by money from HEW and OEO, McClung initiated a thorough redesign of the model at the Urban Institute. His modeling group was under the direction of Jodie Allen, who by then had moved to the Institute from HEW. The revised model, called TRIM, was designed by John Moeller.[54]

Maintenance and application of the TRIM model later spread to government agencies and to a group at the Mathematica Corporation formed by Jodie Allen and others formerly associated with TRIM at the Urban Institute. Modelers tend to bring their models with them when they move. One of the Mathematica group's projects was building dynamic behavioral responses in family composition and labor supply into the TRIM model for HEW, an addition that would make TRIM somewhat closer in form to the original Orcutt model, a direction that the Urban Institute also pursued in its modifications to TRIM.

Although analysis of the Family Assistance Plan stopped when the plan was shelved by the Nixon administration, the TRIM model itself was not retired. HEW used TRIM to design a negative income tax replacement for the programs of aid to families with dependent children, food stamps, and supplemental security income. The Department of Agriculture used TRIM to evaluate changes in the food stamp program. And the Office of Tax Analysis in the Treasury Department adapted TRIM to run on a matched file of Current Population Survey and tax return records to make possible more accurate estimates of simultaneous changes in tax and grant programs.

A modeling effort parallel to the RIM-TRIM development blossomed under Dorothy Projector in the Office of Research and Statistics (ORS), within the Social Security Administration of HEW. At the time of the RIM model, the ORS group took up the model, made extensive changes to it, and did most of the estimating for the Family Assistance Plan and its alternatives. Since then the group pursued a model development effort that was largely independent of the TRIM work.

Mahoney and his associates recommended moving the RIM model "in-house" because they felt that it was inappropriate for HEW to be dependent upon a single contractor for cost and caseload analyses. In addition, they recognized that the model could be used by the Social Security Administration in studying the impacts of its programs on national income distribution. The Urban Institute, the Mathematica Corporation, the Social Security Administration, and HEW's assistant secretary for planning and evaluation all had working versions of the model.

[54] Harold Beebout and Peggy Bonina, "TRIM: A Microsimulation Model for Evaluating Transfer Income Policies," Urban Institute Working Paper 971-04 (Washington, D.C.: Urban Institute, January 1973).

Both the TRIM and ORS models were used in the design of national health insurance programs, but not always with comparable results. Some people in government, disturbed by the disparities, called for greater coordination of federal microanalytic policy modeling. But disagreement and competition between modelers is healthy. It can lead to a greater understanding of the problems, as we see in some of our other case studies.

Another policy model similar in design to the Orcutt model, though simpler, was one built by Murray Cohen and Mary Frances le Mat for the Railroad Retirement Commission to evaluate various financial rescue operations for preventing the Railroad Retirement Fund from becoming insolvent. Another was a more elementary pension actuarial model built by Nicholas Tideman and John Hancock, for the Treasury Department, to evaluate alternative vesting and funding requirements in connection with the 1974 pension reform legislation. James H. Schulz developed a microanalytic model for his Ph.D. dissertation at Yale that was adopted by the Social Security Administration and used to trace out the implications of existing and alternative social security laws. A group at the Research Triangle Institute built a series of POPSIM models designed for computer simulation of the principal demographic processes occurring in human population,[55] and numerous other examples of microanalytic models exist.

Orcutt's own work at the Urban Institute on family behavior was presented in a book: *Microanalytic Simulation of American Family Behavior: A Tool for Policy Analysis.*[56] Orcutt remains convinced of the ultimate usefulness of microanalytic modeling in the policy making process, although he believes the methodology is still in an early state of development and its real value remains to be demonstrated.

Land-Use Analysis[57]

The 1960s saw massive federal efforts to plan urban transportation systems and rationalize regional development. Federal grants were made to local governments to promote comprehensive urban renewal planning and to develop

---

[55] B. V. Shah, "A Demographic Microsimulation Model, POPSIM, and Its Applications" (Research Triangle Institute, North Carolina, 1975).

[56] Guy H. Orcutt et al., *Microanalytic Simulation of American Family Behavior: A Tool for Policy Analysis* (Washington, D.C.: Urban Institute, 1975).

[57] For a discussion of the application of land-use models to metropolitan planning, see David E. Boyce, Norman D. Day, and Chris McDonald, *Metropolitan Plan Making: An Analysis of Experience with the Preparation and Evaluation of Alternative Land-Use and Transportation Plans,* Series 4 (Philadelphia: Regional Science Institute, 1970). For a useful compilation of articles on land-use models, see Franklin J. James (ed.), *Models of Employment and Residence Location* (New Brunswick, N.J.: Center for Urban Policy Research, Rutgers University, 1974). For a comprehensive textbook on the creation and use of land-use models for regional planning, see A. G. Wilson, *Urban and Regional Models in Geography and Planning* (London: John Wiley & Sons, 1974).

master plans for the nation's cities. In February 1961, an initial two-year $200,000 grant was approved for the Pittsburgh Community Renewal Program (CRP). The resulting project led to the development and implementation of an imaginative computer model of urban housing and employment. That model, known as the "Lowry model" after its developer, Ira S. Lowry, was the prototype for the modeling methodology we call "land-use analysis." Land-use analysis has some similarities to microanalysis, by which it may have been influenced.

Lowry, while teaching economics at The Carnegie Institute of Technology in 1960, became a consultant to the Pittsburgh Regional Planning Association as it began an economic study of the Pittsburgh region under the sponsorship of the Ford Foundation. From 1960 to 1963, Lowry developed the basic structure of his experimental "first generation" model. As the three-year study drew to a close, the University of Pittsburgh created a Center for Regional Economic Studies (CRES) to continue the effort. The city of Pittsburgh had been receiving CRP funds for two years with little to show for them. It requested an additional $500,000 and a three-year extension to have CRES assist its Department of City Planning. It was by this circuitous route that Lowry's model was eventually applied. Ironically, Lowry did not himself participate in the Pittsburgh CRP project. He joined the Rand Corporation in Santa Monica in 1963, where he published the final documentation of his model.[58]

"The Lowry model constituted a breakthrough," according to urban modeler William Goldner in an article entitled, "The Lowry Model Heritage."[59] The strength of its conception was its simplicity. The model was simple enough to be made usefully operational in a short time, and it was easily understandable to laymen. Lowry separated employment into two types: "basic," in manufacturing for markets extending outside the city, and "retail," in commercial enterprises serving local markets. He disaggregated the land area of the city into separately treated zones, and devised an ingeniously simple iterative scheme to allocate employment and residential activities to the zones.

The user supplies the model with basic employment situations by zone. Then the model allocates basic employees and their families' residences in zones near their work, subject to population density limitations, using a so-called "gravity" hypothesis that sets the probability of a worker living a given distance from his place of work as inversely proportional to some power (square, cube, etc.) of that distance. Next, the model infers the amount of retail employment necessary to serve the resident population in each zone. Allocation of this employment is made in centralized clusters according to

---

[58] Ira S. Lowry, *A Model of Metropolis,* RM-4035-RC (Santa Monica, Calif.: Rand Corporation, 1964).

[59] William Goldner, "The Lowry Model Heritage," *Journal of the American Institute of Planners,* March 1971, pp. 100–110.

Methodologies for Policy Modeling 117

another inverse power hypothesis that assigns to each zone a retail "potential" based upon the population densities of the surrounding zones. This generates retail employees who need residences. The model also allocates them and their families, resulting in a demand for more retail employment, and the model is iterated until a steady-state equilibrium is attained.

Lowry never claimed that his model was anything but crude. His zones were arbitrarily chosen to be one-mile squares; his allocation functions were simple algebraic functions of the straight-line distance between points; and his model was static. It could produce a consistent equilibrium allocation of employment and residential activities, but could not reproduce past behavior nor explain how equilibrium was attained. So simple was the conception that almost anyone could quickly understand it and devise ways to expand and improve it. It is not surprising that the model produced many successors and extensions. Although it may have been too crude to be useful to policymakers, the model exhibited a clarity that none of its successors matched.

After Lowry moved to Rand in 1963, his ideas were adopted and further developed by the Consad Research Corporation under contract to the Pittsburgh City Planning Department. First to be altered was the model's static nature. The iteration procedure was given a time reference by Consad's John P. Crecine who produced a Time-Oriented Metropolitan Model (TOMM).[60] Crecine disaggregated households into five classes (high status, older couples, lower-middle class, transitional, and low status) and reduced zone size to the level of census tract. The resulting increase in the number of relationships, and the fact that the relationships were now dynamic in nature and required time series data for estimation of coefficients, created severe data problems. Four years after getting started, Crecine reported that the "incompleteness, incompatibility, and nonexistence" of needed data kept TOMM in the "development stage."[61]

By the mid-1960s, many Lowry-type land-use models were in production. William Goldner and R. S. Graybeal at the University of California at Berkeley developed a Bay Area Simulation Study (BASS) model that modified Lowry's basic-retail employment dichotomy, used census tracts, and disaggregated many of Lowry's system-wide coefficients into census tract-specific parameters.[62] Allen G. Feldt of Cornell developed a noncomputerized role-playing model, called the Cornell Land Use Game (CLUG),[63] that introduced

---

[60] John P. Crecine, "TOMM (Time-Oriented Metropolitan Model)," Technical Bulletin Number 6 (Pittsburgh: Pittsburgh Community Renewal Project, 1964).

[61] John P. Crecine, "A Dynamic Model of Urban Structure" (Santa Monica, Calif.: Rand Corporation, 1968).

[62] William Goldner and R. S. Graybeal, "The Bay Area Simulation Study: Pilot Model of Santa Clara County and Some Applications" (Berkeley: Center for Real Estate and Urban Economics, University of California, 1965).

[63] Allen G. Feldt, "The Cornell Land Use Game" (Ithaca, N.Y.: Center for Housing and Environmental Studies, Cornell University, 1966).

governmental revenues, money flows, and four densities of residential allocation. Feldt conducted experiments using information on city utilities, governmental services, and roadways to allocate residences. Crecine continued to elaborate TOMM, incorporating white-collar and blue-collar workers, zoning restrictions, rents, and locational inertia. In the latest version (TOMM IV), he has significantly restructured the housing supply adjustment relationships. Goldner brought out a Projective Land Use Model (PLUM)[64] featuring minimum time-paths between points (with free-flow and peak-hour versions), three types of trips (work-to-home, work-to-shop, and home-to-shop), and a highly refined allocation function. Peter House drew on CLUG to produce a set of computerized games called CITY. Other applications of Lowry-type land-use models appeared in England[65] and in Ljubljana, Yugoslavia.[66]

The successive extensions of the original Lowry model destroyed much of its clarity and simplicity. As the cost of the models rose without clear evidence of their usefulness, support for them began to fall off. Critics pointed to the high cost, long development period, exacting data demands, and dubious results of the models. Basing his comments on the experience with the Pittsburgh CRP model, Garry D. Brewer suggested that "the long-term prospects for the integration of the computer into the urban decision process are dismal indeed."[67] William Alonso considered land-use models "beyond the capacity of the data," in the sense that no matter how accurate their specification, the low quality of the data "results in a deterioration of prediction."[68] Douglass B. Lee expressed his disenchantment with a provocative article entitled "Requiem for Large-Scale Models" in which he encouraged "those who would apply quantitative methods to urban problems ... to redirect their talents into more valuable pursuits than repeating the mistakes of the last decade."[69]

The land-use model did not die. Lee saw a cycle like that of the 1960s about to begin again.[70] A survey of urban modeling in 782 governmental agencies at all levels reported a striking "difference between the types of models in use and the types in development.... While land use and transportation models make up 63 percent of the models in use, they comprise only 32 percent of the models in development."[71] Of the land-use models being used,

---

[64] William Goldner, "Projective Land Use Model (PLUM): A Model for the Spatial Allocation of Activities and Land Uses in a Metropolitan Region," BATSC Technical Report 219 (Berkeley: Bay Area Transportation Commission, 1968).

[65] Goldner, "Lowry."

[66] John W. Dyckman (ed.), *Summary Report of the Ljubljana Region Demonstration Study* (Detroit: Center for Urban Studies, Wayne State University, April 1972).

[67] Brewer, p. 215.

[68] William Alonso, "Predicting Best with Imperfect Data," *Journal of the American Institute of Planners* 34 (1968): 251.

[69] Lee, p. 175.

[70] Ibid., p. 170.

[71] Janet R. Pack, *The Use of Urban Models in Urban Policy Making: Report on*

most were in regional planning councils. City governments accounted for less than 20 percent of the land-use models in use, but over 40 percent of those in development. Regional planning councils have been modeling for years. City governments have not, but they appear to have become principal developers (or revisers) of land-use models.

Lee describes one of the new modeling efforts, the urban simulation model of the National Bureau of Economic Research,[72] as "representative of the best of current designs, but... nonetheless, simply larger doses of all the things that have failed to work in the past."[73] Goldner continued to develop PLUM, applying it to San Diego as the Urban Development Model (UDM).[74] Michael A. Goldberg, based on his experience with BASS, created a large land-use modeling system called the Vancouver Regional Inter-Institutional Policy Simulator (IIPS) that directly involved urban "problem solvers" with academicians in the design of the model.[75]

Another approach was that taken by David Birch of Harvard in New Haven.

> Our approach has been quite different from related past efforts. Most have started with theories; we started with facts. Several years were devoted to gathering information about what has actually happened in New Haven. As the data began to accumulate, we developed instruments to reveal patterns in the data and ultimately suggest explanations (or theories) of what was taking place. What emerged was an increasingly well-defined set of theories that explained how the "pieces" worked and how they fit together. As the theories took shape, they were "mounted" on a "frame" where they could be related easily to one another—the result being a computer simulation model of the region that can reproduce past history and make predictions for the future for each neighborhood in New Haven.[76]

Birch's work was not so much a model as a technique for creating models for

---

Research to Refine the Relevant Questions and to Provide an Appropriate Research Design, 2 vols. (Philadelphia: Government Study Center, The Fels Center of Government, University of Pennsylvania, January 1974), 2:13–14.

[72] Gregory K. Ingram, John F. Kain, and J. Royce Ginn, "The Detroit Prototype of the NBER Urban Simulation Model (New York: National Bureau of Economic Research, 1972).

[73] Lee, p. 175.

[74] William Goldner et al., *The Urban Development Model: A Regional Planning Tool*, 3 vols. (San Diego: San Diego Comprehensive Planning Organization, May 1973).

[75] Michael A. Goldberg and C. S. Holling, *The Vancouver Regional Inter-Institutional Policy Simulator* (Vancouver, British Columbia: University of British Columbia, 1971); and R. F. Kelly, *IIPS: Vancouver Regional Simulation Project: Third Year Report 1972–1973* (Vancouver, British Columbia: Resource Science Centre, The University of British Columbia, October 1973).

[76] David L. Birch et al., *Patterns of Urban Change* (Lexington, Mass.: Lexington Books, 1973), p. 2; see also David L. Birch and Cyrus F. Gibson, "Environmental Models for Planning and Policy Making," vol. 1, October 1974.

a given city. Results of the model were translated into terms meaningful for special users, e.g., growth of bank deposits, numbers of school children, and energy demand. Birch also worked with the Houston/Galveston Area Council, and the Department of Housing and Urban Development funded the application of his work to six additional cities. Federal funding played a major part in stimulating the land-use modeling of the 1960s, and became active again in the 1970s as Birch's success in obtaining federal support indicated. Lowry was not one of the players in the revival. He switched from modeling to social experimentation in order to generate the kind of data he believed to be essential for effective policy research.[77]

System Dynamics

Only in system dynamics (with the possible exception of input-output analysis) are the modeling innovator and the modeling methodology so closely identified. It is rare to come upon a description or review of a system dynamics model that does not mention M.I.T.'s Jay W. Forrester, father and principal advocate of the system dynamics methodology. Forrester set forth his methodology to deal with complex nonlinear feedback systems in *Industrial Dynamics*[78] in 1961. Originally applied to problems of industrial management, the system dynamics approach is very general. Forrester further expanded on it in *Principles of Systems* in 1968,[79] applied it to the problems of the city in *Urban Dynamics* in 1969,[80] and to the problems of world growth in *World Dynamics* in 1971.[81] He is currently developing a national model of the United States economy, with special attention to the problems of inflation and unemployment.[82] The choice of focus in Forrester's models suggests a sharp sense of political timing. The models tend to be long-term; the time frame of both the world model and the national model extends to the twenty-first century.

In Chapter 1, we reviewed Forrester's career and background. We also discussed the public debut of the *Limits to Growth*[83] model, a team effort led by Forrester's former Ph.D. student Dennis Meadows. This model received an

---

[77] See Ira S. Lowry, *Preliminary Design for the Housing Assistance Supply Experiment*, WN-7866-HUD (Santa Monica, Calif.: Rand Corporation, June 1972).

[78] Jay W. Forrester, *Industrial Dynamics* (Cambridge: The M.I.T. Press, 1961).

[79] Jay W. Forrester, *Principles of Systems* (Cambridge, Mass.: Wright-Allen Press, 1968). A very clear exposition of the fundamentals of system dynamics for teaching purposes is found in Michael R. Goodman, *Study Notes in System Dynamics* (Cambridge, Mass.: Wright-Allen Press, 1974).

[80] Jay W. Forrester, *Urban Dynamics* (Cambridge: The M.I.T. Press, 1969).

[81] Jay W. Forrester, *World Dynamics* (Cambridge, Mass.: Wright-Allen Press, 1971).

[82] Jay W. Forrester, "A National Model for Understanding Social and Economic Change," *Simulation* 24, nos. 4, 5 (1975).

[83] Donella H. Meadows et al., *The Limits to Growth* (New York: Universe Books, 1972).

Methodologies for Policy Modeling

extraordinary amount of public attention and much criticism. In Chapter 5, we will examine the responses to the world models and the urban dynamics model. For now, we present a brief explication of the system dynamics methodology. An example of a system dynamics model of housing from *Urban Dynamics* is given later in the chapter.[84]

System dynamics had its genesis in the field of engineering, although it is not the primary or sole approach taken by engineers in the analysis of systems and operational problems. System dynamics is not to be confused with (though it is related to) the less specific, more encompassing subjects of "systems analysis" and "systems engineering."

In a section of *Principles of Systems* entitled "The Ubiquity of Systems," Forrester defines a system to be "a grouping of parts that operate together for a common purpose."[85] By this definition, almost any collection of interacting items can be considered a system, especially if the phrase "common purpose" is interpreted broadly, as it is when the system is the world. What one chooses to model as a reference system varies with one's perspective, and whether it is useful to do so depends on the model's success in depicting the system. No matter how intriguing a model is in and of itself, if it correlates poorly with reality, it is of doubtful usefulness, at best. At worst, if believed, it can be dangerously misleading.

Caveats aside, the system dynamics approach provides a framework within which to view the internal operation of systems in a coherent and orderly manner. All systems are viewed in terms of two major types of constructs: "levels" and "rates." A level is a number which represents the state of some part of the system. Levels in Forrester's urban dynamics model include the number of underemployed persons, mature businesses, and premium housing units in the city. System dynamics models move forward in time by fixed intervals. A rate defines the amount by which a level will change during the next interval.

The idea of a closed boundary, within which all meaningful interaction is assumed to occur, is of basic importance. As Forrester describes it,

> The cause and effect relationships between environment and system are unidirectional, whereas the internal elements are structured into feedback loops that cause the internal elements to interact. The environment can affect the system, but the system does not significantly affect the environment.[86]

Forrester views the occurrences external to the system boundary as "random happenings that impinge on the system and do not themselves give the system

---

[84] For a comparison of the urban dynamics model with the Lowry model, see Nathaniel J. Mass (ed.), *Readings in Urban Dynamics,* 2 vols. (Cambridge, Mass.: Wright-Allen Press, 1974), 1:75–85 and 98–100.
[85] Forrester, *Principles of Systems,* p. I-1.
[86] Forrester, *Urban Dynamics,* p. 17.

its intrinsic growth and stability characteristics."[87] The fact that the behavior of the environment is considered to be unaffected by the system during any given system simulation has been criticized by reviewers of *Urban Dynamics* who believe that exclusion of suburbs and other cities from the urban system causes serious distortion.

Within the boundary of the system are "feedback loops" containing chains of alternating levels and rates. The simplest feedback loop is a single level whose state affects the rate at which the level "fills" or "drains." Figure 4–1 displays such a simple feedback using Forrester's schemata.

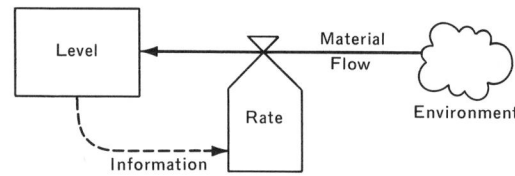

Figure 4–1: A Simple Feedback Loop

Material flows from the environment into the level at a rate that is controlled by the amount of accumulated material in the level.

Feedbacks in system dynamics models are of two types: the "goal-seeking" or "negative feedback," and the "divergent" or "positive feedback." The first type has a goal or "normal" value for the level. When the level departs from its normal value or goal, the rate is modified in an effort to approach the goal once more. For example, consider a self-filling water tank that has a normal water level. When water is removed, the tank refills itself at a rate proportional to the disparity between the current and normal water levels. As the water approaches the normal level and the goal is being reached, the rate of inflow drops towards zero. See Figure 4–2.

A positive feedback loop is unstable. The rate of inflow to the level (growth rate) is dependent upon the current state of that level. Most population growth systems contain positive feedback. If a constant fraction of the current population gives birth each year, then (if one neglects deaths and lag effects) the number of births per year will increase directly as the population increases. (See Figure 4–3.) This type of "exponential" growth occurs whenever a quantity grows by a constant fraction per unit time. Exponential growth is guaranteed to "overtake" eventually any fixed limit and any type of linear growth.

Forrester asserts that "feedback loops are the fundamental building blocks of systems."[88] Every system dynamics model is composed of positive and nega-

---
[87] Ibid., p. 12.
[88] Ibid., p. 13.

Methodologies for Policy Modeling 123

tive feedback loops of levels and rates, often combined in intricate and complicated ways. A level appearing in a single feedback loop must either seek a goal or grow exponentially, whereas the inclusion of a single level within two or more feedback loops of different types allows the opposing forces to check

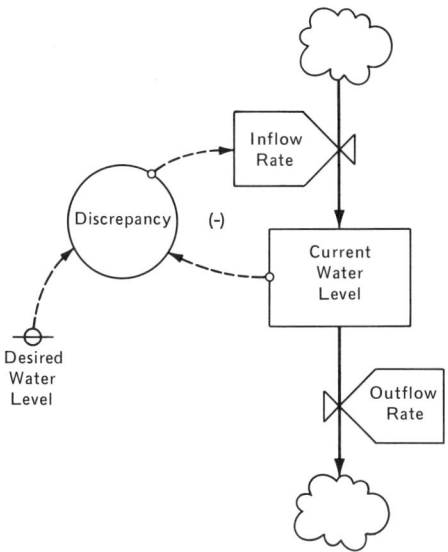

Figure 4–2: A Negative Feedback Loop (Goal-Seeking)

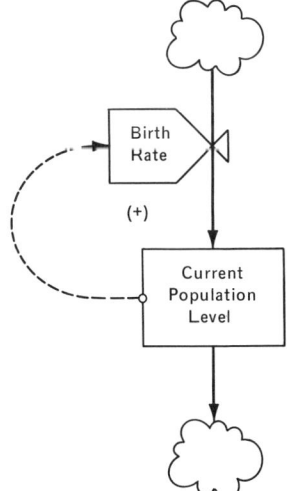

Figure 4–3: A Positive Feedback Loop (Divergent)

one another. In *World Dynamics,* for example, an increase in capital investment causes a higher standard of living which depresses the birth rate. At the same time, the increase in capital investment also enlarges the ratio of food to population which causes the birth rate to rise. These opposite influences tend to moderate the effect of capital investment on birth rate.

In system dynamics modeling, levels affect rates by means of constructs called "table functions." A table function is a set of points implicitly connected by straight lines representing the impact of a given system level on a specific internal variable occasionally called a "multiplier." Figure 4–4 shows the impact in *World Dynamics* of the material standard of living level on the birth-rate-from-material multiplier.

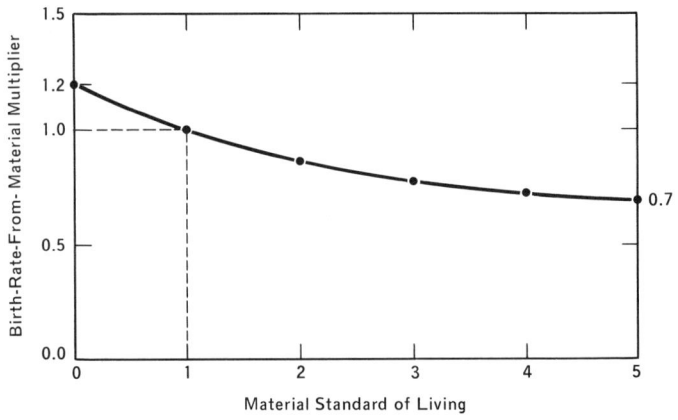

Figure 4–4: A Table Function Showing Impact of Material Standard of Living on the Birth-Rate-from-Material Multiplier

As the standard of living increases from 1.0 to 4.0, the multiplier decreases from 1.0 to 0.7. The multiplier, which has a "normal" value of 1.0, is multiplied by the product of the current population and the "normal" birth rate fraction to reduce the effective birth rate for the next time segment.

The delay is another construct used in the formulation of a system dynamics model. The methodology typically uses an averaged or distributed delay rather than a fixed-time delay. *Urban Dynamics,* for example, assumes that it requires an average of fifteen years for laborers from the outside environment to perceive the attractiveness of the city. This effect is represented by means of two level variables: the labor arrival multiplier and the labor arrival multiplier perceived. Each year the latter variable is reduced by 1/15 and then incremented by 1/15 of the new value of the former variable. This averaging process, termed a "first-order" delay, tends to smooth out as well as delay labor arrivals.

When several first-order delays are connected to each other in series, the result is a higher-order delay. Figure 4–5 shows the effects of delaying a level variable by means of several different types of delays, including the fixed-time or "pipeline" delay.

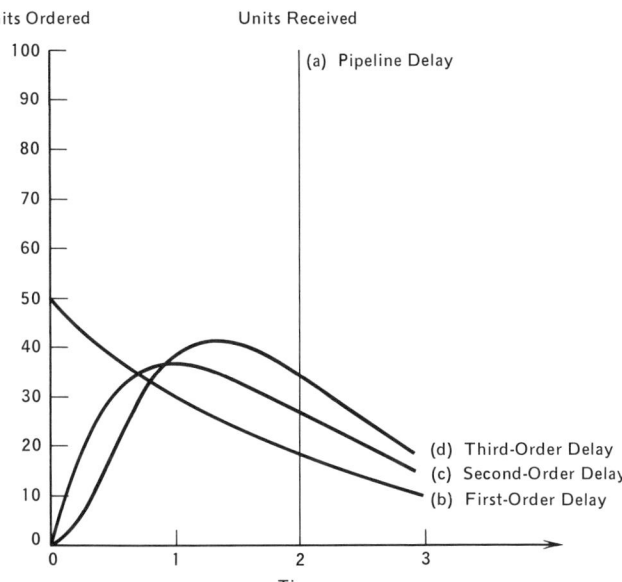

Figure 4–5: Four Types of Delays in System Dynamics Models

An order for 100 units is placed at time 0. (a) A *pipeline* delay of two time intervals has all of the order arriving at time 2. (b) A first-order delay distributes the arrival of the order in an exponentially decaying fashion, with a fixed percentage of what is still due arriving each period. (c) A second-order delay subjects the output of a first-order delay to another first-order delay. (d) A third-order delay subjects the output of a second-order delay to still another first-order delay. All four delays have an average time of arrival of two time periods.

The concept of "equilibrium" is central to system dynamics. Equilibrium exists whenever the system levels are unchanging through time.[89] Most system models will attain equilibrium if run with constant inputs for a sufficiently long time,[90] sometimes a very, very long time. O. Rademaker, in experimenting with Forrester's World2 model, reports that "the calculations would have to be extended by at least several hundred thousand years in order to arrive somewhat near the final equilibrium."[91]

---

[89] Dennis L. Meadows, *Dynamics of Commodity Production Cycles* (Cambridge, Mass.: Wright-Allen Press, 1970), p. 4.

[90] Joseph Talavage, "Control Theory Applied to Systems Dynamics Simulations," *Proceedings of the 1973 Summer Simulation Conference*, Montreal, July 17–19, p. 849.

[91] O. Rademaker, "Project Group Global Dynamics Progress Report No. 3" (Eindhoven, The Netherlands: Technische Hogeschool Eindhoven, March 31, 1974), p. 4.

In practice, slow changes in the level variables may indicate a sufficiently close approximation to equilibrium. The approximate equilibria may be compared for several simulation runs under alternative policies. Lowry calls the technique of comparing alternative equilibria the "method of comparative statics"[92] to distinguish it from "analytical dynamics, an approach which focuses attention on the processes of change rather than on the emergent state of the system at a specified future date."[93]

The users of system dynamics do not shy away from applying their models to complex social problems. They strive to compensate for the limited supply of reliable data by drawing on the opinions of experts and on their own intuitions. They seek to identify causal structures and set parameter values, not by traditional data analyses and correlation studies, but by what some consider "armchair speculation" and economist Lawrence Klein apprehensively refers to as "stylizing the facts." Whereas they will occasionally attempt a short-term prediction, system dynamicists typically do not try to project precise future values of variables. Instead, they concentrate on trying to formulate general patterns of interrelationships and structural properties for use in comparing and evaluating policy alternatives, an area where they believe accurate forecasting is unnecessary and generally impossible.

Forrester feels that "the techniques commonly used by social scientists to analyze statistical data can be inconclusive or misleading when applied to the kind of nonlinear dynamic systems found in real life."[94] He considers system dynamics models to belong to the same class of systems as the real world, and rejects the use of statistical tests of goodness of fit to validate his models. Forrester favors a qualitative test instead, namely that "the model generate output data that are 'essentially the same as' the data observed from the real world."[95] Referring to this criterion as the "mistaken-identity test," Forrester proposes that the model be left to run on its own without exogenous input. If the behavior it generates can fool a knowledgeable examiner, it passes the test. (In the artificial intelligence field, this criterion is known as the "Turing test" after A. M. Turing, a pioneer in computer science.)

Economist Jacob Marschak describes the approach of successively improving guessed parameter values by simulating their consequences and comparing the output with actual time-series data as a possible alternative to the econometrician's usual practice of statistical estimation. According to Marschak, it is a conceivably superior alternative if done responsibly and with a

---

[92] Ira S. Lowry, "A Short Course in Model Design," *Journal of the American Institute of Planners,* May 1965, p. 161.
[93] Ibid.
[94] Jay W. Forrester, "Educational Implications of Responses to System Dynamics Models," submitted to *Management Science,* May 30, 1974, p. 6 of mimeo.
[95] Ibid., p. 6.

high degree of expertise. This is an unusual and interesting point of view, especially for an economist.

The system dynamics methodology derives from engineering but has been applied to policy areas as disparate as water pollution, health care maintenance, narcotics addiction, and world growth. The ease with which the methodology has entered new fields reflects the generality and simplicity of its concepts as well as its unconventional attitude towards the thorny problems of data. It is one of the newest and fastest growing methodologies, as well as the most controversial.

Recapitulation

The nine methodologies we have outlined vary widely in age. Two had their major theoretical and conceptual development in the 1920s (input-output analysis and TPZS games), one in the 1930s (econometrics), one in the 1940s (linear programming), two in the 1950s (microanalysis and system dynamics), and one in the 1960s (land-use analysis). The ages of the other two are harder to pin down. In some cases, refinement of the methodology, experimentation with it, and its initial use in the United States began with or soon after its invention (e.g., input-output analysis and econometrics). Serious application of the methodology to decision making and planning came quickly in the case of O/R, while for TPZS games the use has not been as clear. At least three of the methodologies are today widely accepted and routinely used directly or indirectly by policymakers, their staffs, and their advisers. These are the methodologies of input-output analysis, linear programming, and econometric modeling. It is too soon to know which (if any) of the others may attain similar status in future years.

Microanalysis, land-use analysis, and system dynamics are the three newest of the methodologies and the least mature in their development. In Chapter 5 we will examine and review the newcomer, system dynamics, at some length. We will do a similar study of the oldtimer, econometric modeling, in Chapter 6, and we will compare these two methodologies along several dimensions. First, we will provide simple illustrations of the application of these methodologies and microanalysis to the policy area of housing.

A HOUSING EXAMPLE

Each modeling methodology has its own characteristic approach. To highlight some of the differences, we will present simplified examples of three approaches to modeling the same problem area: a microanalytic model, a system dynamics model, and an econometric model, all of urban housing.

Microanalysis infers the behavior of an entire system from the simulated behavior of its components or micro-units. The components may be persons, families, automobiles, or geographical subdivisions. System dynamics prefers to work with flows between aggregates or macro-units, such as the total number of houses in a city, the population of a region, or the volume of urban traffic. Econometric modeling also favors aggregates, but unlike system dynamics, it tends to use only variables that can be measured empirically and estimated statistically—variables for which there are ample time series or cross-sectional data.

A Microanalytic Model of Housing

A microanalytic model is composed of a population of individual items, each of which has a set of assumed attributes. A model of manpower, for example, can be simulated by predicting the behavior over time of each individual worker in a worker population. A traffic system can be simulated by monitoring the progress of each vehicle in the traffic flow at regular time intervals.[96] Future tax revenue can be estimated for some proposed change in the tax code by subjecting a sample of individual tax records to that change.[97] Even air and water pollution can be modeled microanalytically by dividing the area being examined into unit quantities of air or water.[98] We now review a microanalytic model of urban housing.[99]

Suppose a file of individual housing records is kept for a city. For each particular record in the file, one can predict changes in the record by analyzing and extrapolating past changes in similar records. By also allowing for the insertion of new records and deletion of old records, the entire file can be moved into the future.

To save computing time, one can pick a small, representative sample of records from the file and treat each record as if they were many. For a one in ten sample, for instance, each simulated record is counted tenfold in interpreting the results of the simulation. When one record of each distinct type is chosen, its impact is weighted by the number of such records in the complete file. If every record is unique, there is no saving unless minor differences be-

---

[96] Martin Wohl and Brian Martin, *Traffic System Analysis for Engineers and Planners* (New York: McGraw-Hill, 1967), chapter 15: "The Use of Simulation in Traffic Engineering Design."

[97] Pechman and Okner, "Simulation."

[98] Jan J. Leendertse et al., *A Three-Dimensional Model for Estuaries and Coastal Seas,* Vol. 1: *Principles of Computation,* R-1417-OWRR (Santa Monica, Calif.: Rand Corporation, December 1973).

[99] For a more recent microanalytic model of housing than the one described in the text, see Frank de Leeuw et al., *The Market Effects of Housing Policies* (Washington, D.C.: Urban Institute, November 1974). This urban housing model deals with ten-year changes in housing quality and household location.

Methodologies for Policy Modeling 129

tween records can be ignored. This was done for the San Francisco Community Renewal Program (CRP) model.[100]

The San Francisco CRP model was designed to simulate the changes in the housing stock of the city of San Francisco between the years 1960 and 1978. Starting with the 1960 Census, the housing stock of San Francisco was divided into 288 distinct types of housing for each of the 4,980 two-acre areas of the city. Each housing type was weighted according to the number of such housing units in that area in 1960. The housing was classified by the number of families per structure, number of rooms per family, condition of the structure, and dominant housing type and rental range of the location, as shown in Table 4–2.

Table 4–2: SF Housing Stock Characteristics*

Size	Condition	Location Area	Dominant Housing Type	Mo. Rental Range
1. Single Family, 1–4 rooms	1. Sound	1	Single Family	$0–140
2. Single Family, 5–6 rooms	2. Needs Minor Repair	2	Single Family	$140–275
3. Single Family, 7 or more rooms	3. Deteriorating	3	Single Family	$275+
4. 2–4 Families, 1–4 rooms/family	4. Dilapidated	4	2–4 Families	$0–75
5. 2–4 Families, 5 or more rooms/family		5	2–4 Families	$75+
6. 5 or more Families, 1 room/family		6	5 or More	$0–75
7. 5 or more Families, 2 rooms/family		7	5 or More	$75–150
8. 5 or more Families, 3–4 rooms/family		8	5 or More	$150+
9. 5 or more Families, 5 or more rooms/family				

* Based upon an early version of the CRP model. Later versions had even more categories. See reference in Robinson, footnote 43.

The CRP model updated the housing stock by predicting the yearly changes in each type of housing. The updated stock from one period was the input population for the next period. Nine two-year periods were simulated to cover the 1960–1978 time interval.

---
[100] San Francisco Department of City Planning in Ira M. Robinson (ed.), *Decision-Making*.

As a basis for simulating change in the housing stock, the CRP model needed information on population growth, government programs, zoning restrictions on new construction, and the real estate development market. For each of the nine periods, two major sets of data were entered into the model: (1) a prediction of the number of households in San Francisco broken into eighty-four categories by number of persons in the household, age of the head of the household, race, and household income; and (2) a list of planned government actions such as land clearance, redevelopment, and public housing.

The CRP model assumed that of all the possible changes that could occur over two years to the housing stock, only the one hundred most profitable would be implemented by private developers. To find these hundred, the model made use of data on costs of construction, minimum return on investment, and rental revenues collectable from given housing types. Except for the last item, which was derivable from census data, these data had been collected for the modeling team by special surveys and studies.

The operation of the model proceeded as follows (see Figure 4-6). The initial housing stock from the 1960 census was entered into the model, giving

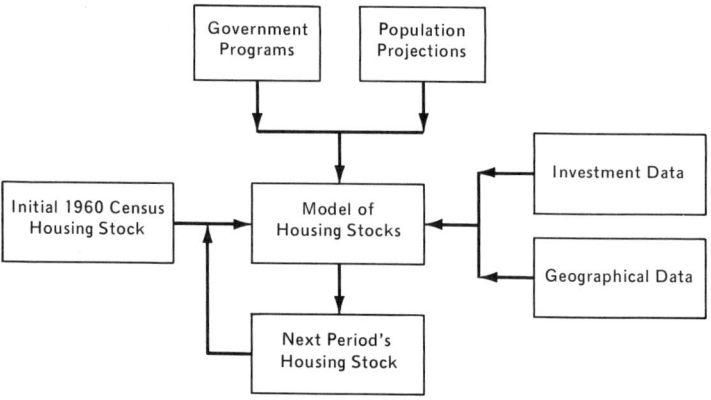

Figure 4-6: The SF Model

each of the 288 housing types in each of the 4,980 areas a weight indicating its representation in the total San Francisco housing stock. The 1960 population of households was entered similarly in a weighted partition of eighty-four types, and the households were assigned to housing units according to their ability to pay rent. Excess households created a demand for housing which caused rents to rise in the next period. Excess housing units created a buyer's market, driving down the next period's rents, and governmental programs were applied, changing the distribution of housing-unit types for the next period. A list of all possible changes to the housing stock was examined as to the return on investment and legality, and the hundred most profitable projects were implemented, causing further changes in the housing stock. The altered housing stock from the first period replaced the 1960 census data as the household input to the second period. New population projections and governmental actions were used for each of eight other two-year periods.

The San Francisco model could theoretically give estimates of the effects of government policies on the numbers and locations of housing units throughout the city of San Francisco. But the detailed data needed were not continuously available, and the model presented a false impression of accuracy and validity.

The CRP model was much criticized.[101] Its predictions were not within the limits of reasonable error (they were sometimes off by 1,600 percent), and its voluminous results were not readily understandable. As Brewer describes it,

> The quantity of information generated by the model is prodigious, and little effort was expended to distill the outputs into an intelligible form. Analyzing the output from a production run of the model requires *at least one week* of mind-numbing devotion. There are no summary statistics, graphic displays, or critical indicators.[102]

Only a few runs were ever made with the model—no wonder, considering the fact that a typical run produced nine hundred pages of numerical output, two inches thick.

There were other alleged shortcomings. The model did not allow for changes other than aging in the housing stock. It did not allow for a change in tenure or demolition of residences to create commercial sites. It arbitrarily drew a boundary around the city that ignored the Bay Area influence on the San Francisco housing stock. The two-year periodic reassignment of households to housing units was unrealistically short. Finally, the model depended upon external data for population predictions rather than incorporating an aging process for households as well as for housing units. Some of these flaws have been corrected in a model designed to simulate regional housing markets in New York State.[103]

The CRP model was designed at a very high level of disaggregation. A model of this detail might be useful for questions about the neighborhood impact of local policies such as zoning restrictions, clearance operations, and new developments, but not for questions about long-range trends in urban migration. Such questions are the focus of the next model we will examine.

---
[101] See, for example, Brewer.
[102] Ibid., p. 133.
[103] David W. Sears, "The New York State Regional Housing Model," *Simulation and Games,* June 1971, pp. 131–148.

A System Dynamics Model of Housing

In *Urban Dynamics,* discussed further in Chapter 5, Forrester displays a system dynamics model of an idealized city in which the important interactions occur between highly aggregated components.[104] Forrester posits three subpopulations in his urban dynamics model: an upper class, called the managerial-professional group, composed of all households in the city whose head is a "white collar" professional; a middle class, called the labor group, consisting of families headed by "blue collar," skilled laborers; and a lower class of unemployed, underemployed, and unskilled heads of households and their families. (Compare this with the version of the San Francisco model that had 84 household and 288 housing types.)

The urban dynamics model has three housing types, one for each of the three population components: managerial-professional housing; labor housing; and underemployed housing. There are level variables for the number of households in each classification and the number of housing units of each type. They change over time as the model is run. Another level variable represents the attractiveness of the city to potential newcomers. Information on individual members of the population is not included.

The interactions between components in a system dynamics model are controlled by rates which monitor the flows between levels. An upward mobility rate allows a limited number of lower class families to become middle class families during each time period. Other rates control the deterioration of upper-class housing into middle-class housing, the deterioration of middle-class housing into lower-class housing, the construction of new housing, and the birth and death processes that modify the sizes of subpopulations.

Figure 4–7 displays a simplified schematic diagram of the population and housing levels. Levels are represented by rectangles and rates by valves attached to the solid lines of flow between levels. Dotted arrows represent flows of information from levels to rates. The clouds represent the external environment, assumed to be able to supply or accept whatever numbers of units the controlling rates specify.

The first step in using the model is to determine initial values for all levels in the system. The model is run until the values of the levels and rates settle down to an approximate equilibrium, typically after about 250 simulated years. From the steady state, the model is run under a change in policy, and the effects of the policy are projected. To determine the long-range impact of a slum clearance program, for example, the rate at which lower-class housing disappears from the urban housing market is increased and the model is run until new patterns in housing and population become clear and remain relatively steady.

---

[104] Forrester, *Urban Dynamics.*

Methodologies for Policy Modeling

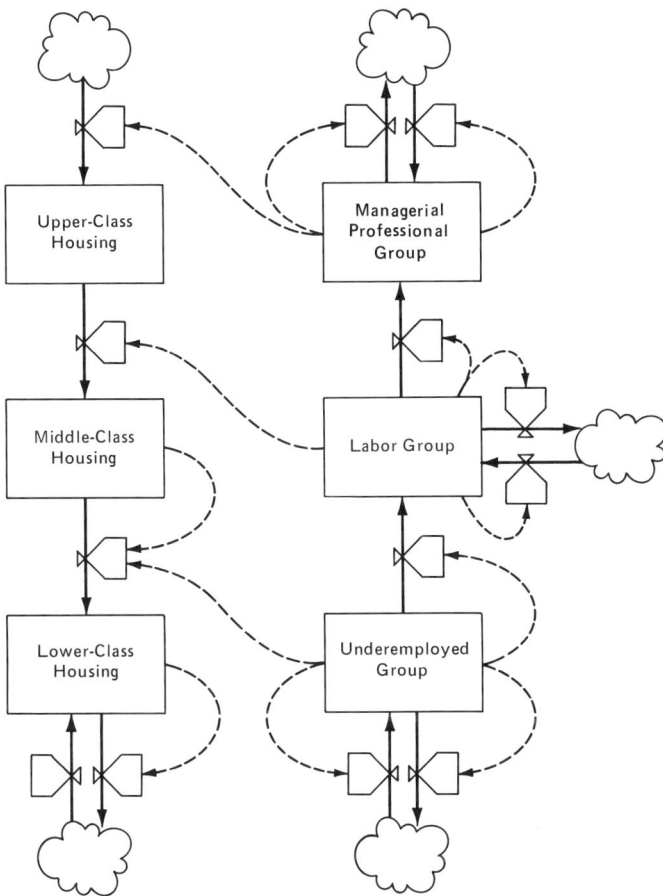

Figure 4–7: Housing and Population Components in the Urban Dynamics Model

Figure 4–8 shows the results of running the urban dynamics model with a slum clearance program, starting from steady-state conditions. The unmarked scales are different for each curve. After initial fluctuations die down, the values of the subpopulation levels and housing stock are compared with their initial steady state values to see whether the slum clearance program is likely to attain its goals.

In this example, the slum clearance program results in a net reduction of lower-class housing and a net increase in middle-class housing. The total size of the underemployed group falls slightly, then rises back to its initial level. Laborers are attracted to the city and their numbers increase.

To gain a better understanding of the operation of the model, let us ex-

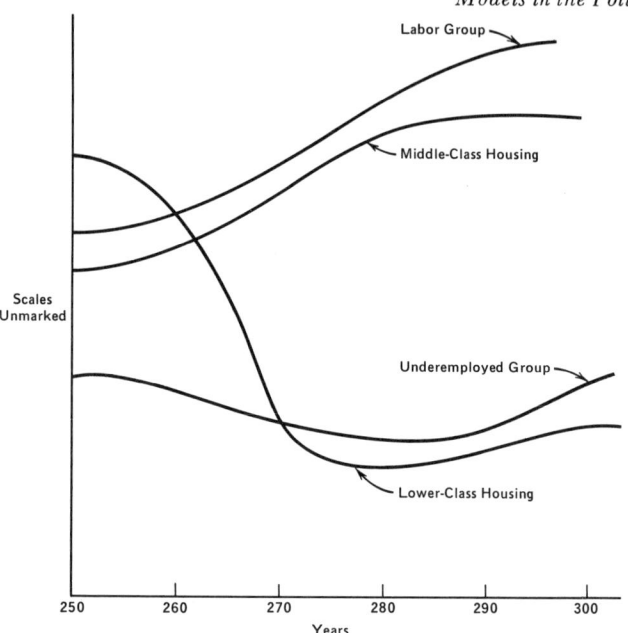

Figure 4–8: Effect on Labor and Underemployed Populations and Housing Stocks Due to Implementation of a Slum Clearance Program in the Urban Dynamics Model

amine how the simulation makes calculations in the housing sector. For simplicity, we assume that the simulation calculates one year's values from the previous year's values. The number of lower-class housing units in the city is increased during the year by the middle-class housing units that have deteriorated, and is decreased by the lower-class housing units that have been razed, destroyed, or abandoned as uninhabitable. The number is also increased as a direct result of low-cost housing programs. To be specific, the number of lower-class houses at the end of a year equals the number from the previous year, plus additions from obsolete middle-class houses, plus new lower-class houses, minus demolished lower-class houses. See Figure 4–9 for details.

Since the rates on the right hand side of the equation in Figure 4–9 are variables, the equation cannot be used independently of the rest of the model to predict yearly changes in the stock of lower-class housing. The number of middle-class housing units that become obsolete in a given year is dependent upon the total number of middle-class housing units, maintenance effectiveness, rental levels, and tax rates. Similarly, the amount of new low-cost housing is directly dependent upon governmental policy. These effects must also be modeled. Figure 4–10 shows some of the relationships.

The urban dynamics model became controversial as soon as it appeared in 1969. The model focuses on interactions within the fixed boundaries of the

Methodologies for Policy Modeling 135

The Equation for Underemployed Housing in Urban Dynamics

$$UH(n) = UH(n-1) + LHO(n) + LCHP(n) - UHD(n)$$

$UH(n)$ = Underemployed (lower class) Housing units at the end of year n.
$LHO(n)$ = Labor (middle class) Housing units which have become Obsolete over year n.
$LCHP(n)$ = number of lower class housing units provided by Low Cost Housing Programs in year n.
$UHD(n)$ = number of Underemployed Housing units Demolished by the city in year n.

Figure 4-9

The number of lower class housing units at the end of year n equals the number at the end of year n − 1, plus the number of middle-class housing units which have deteriorated during the year, plus the number of new low cost housing units, minus the number of lower-class housing units which were demolished during the year. (Abbreviations used are diffferent from those in *Urban Dynamics*.)

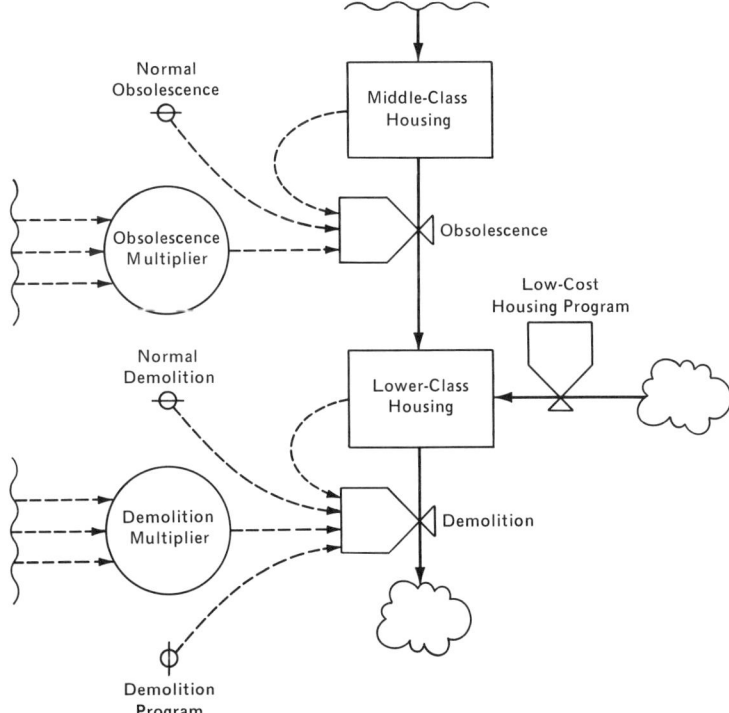

Figure 4-10: The Lower-Class Housing Sector of the Urban Dynamics Model

metropolitan area. It does not contain suburbs. The total land area is fixed and can never change, i.e., the city cannot annex land area to accommodate growth. Such influences on housing as rent control, rising prices, and interest rates are omitted. Many critics have discussed these and other alleged shortcomings of the model at length. Some have attempted to add suburbs and otherwise alter the model, its behavior, and its policy conclusions.[105]

The urban dynamics model is intended to identify causal structures and explore long-term behavioral modes in the housing market of the city. Now consider a shorter-range problem. A sudden drop in the city's per capita income due to an accelerated emigration of wealthy families to the suburbs causes increased deterioration of inner-city houses. Will lowering taxes or raising municipal spending be more effective in stemming the tide? The following (oversimplified) econometric model of housing addresses this question.

An Econometric Model of Housing

The econometric modeling methodology is based on statistically significant, theoretically justifiable relationships among measurable quantities. The relationships are established and calibrated by statistical analysis of historical data. Unfortunately, the available data may be irregular, inaccurate, misrepresented, incompatible, or just not sufficient. This is a problem with which the economist has learned to live. Milton Friedman is once said to have remarked that although he was not working as an economist during World War II, the government was glad to have his services because, as an economist, he was used to working with miserable data.

To construct the desired econometric model of housing, we look for a relationship between the condition of a city's housing stock and its economic health. Specifically, we seek to relate the fraction of the total stock deteriorated to average per capita income, which we take to be an indication of the funds available to maintain housing. As with the urban dynamics model, we project changes in variables in yearly time increments.[106]

Let Y_t be the average per capita income during year t, and let D_t be the fraction of the total housing stock considered to be deteriorated at the end of year t. Historically, as city housing deteriorates, more middle- and upper-income households depart for the surrounding suburbs. As households above

---

[105] Leo P. Kadanoff, "From Simulation Model to Public Policy," *American Scientist* 60, no. 1 (1972): 74–79. See chapter 5 for a survey of critical reactions to the urban dynamics model and to the World2 and World3 models.

[106] This example is based upon a model described in W. E. Oates, E. P. Howrey, and W. J. Baumol, "The Analysis of Public Policy in Dynamic Urban Models," *Journal of Political Economy* 79, no. 1 (1971): 142–153. It is, in the words of one of the authors, "a highly oversimplified illustration, not a sophisticated analysis of the sort we would want to work with in a full econometric analysis."

Methodologies for Policy Modeling

the median income level leave the city, the city's per capita income falls, all else constant. The following simple equation relates per capita income to the fraction of deteriorated housing.

$$Y_{t+1} = r - s\, D_t$$

where coefficients r and s are estimated statistically to fit the historical data. Figure 4-11 displays this linear relationship.

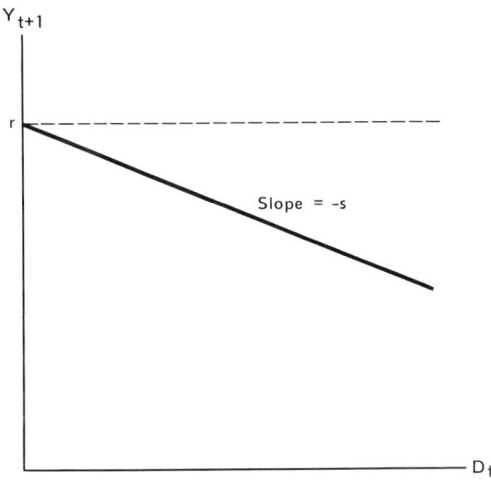

Figure 4-11: An Assumed Linear Relationship Between Deteriorated Housing Fraction in Year t and Per Capita Income in Year $t + 1$

While D_t affects Y_{t+1}, Y_t also affects D_t. If the city's per capita income falls during the year, there is less money in the city per housing unit. Less money will be used for maintenance and repair, causing more rapid deterioration and a larger fraction of housing in disrepair. The following equation expresses these observations.

$$D_t = u - v\, Y_t$$

Combining the last two equations and solving analytically for Y_t gives:

$$Y_{t+1} = r - s(u - v\, Y_t) = (sv)\, Y_t + (r - su)$$

A simpler way of writing this linear relationship between successive years' per capita income, defining $a = sv$ and $b = r - su$, is

$$Y_{t+1} = a\, Y_t + b$$

If a and b are constant, the city's per capita income might remain permanently at an equilibrium value (*if it exists*) of:

$$Y_E = a\,Y_E + b = b\,/\,(1-a) = (r - su)\,/\,(1 - sv)$$

Figures 4–12 and 4–13 show how Y_t might converge to Y_E over time starting from a value either larger or smaller than Y_E.

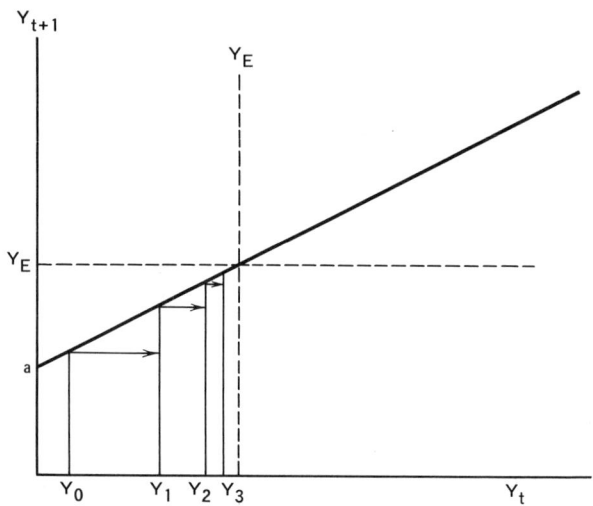

Figure 4–12: The Convergence of Y_t to Y_E for $Y_0 < Y_E$

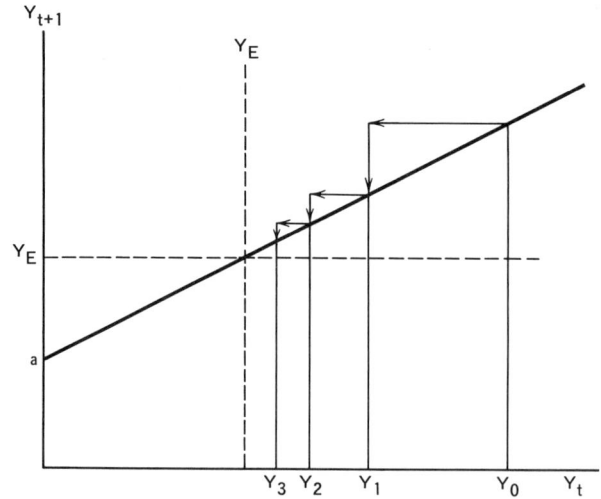

Figure 4–13: The Convergence of Y_t to Y_E for $Y_0 > Y_E$

Some conditional conclusions can be drawn. First, any clearance program intended to reduce the fraction of deteriorated housing in order to increase per capita income is at best a delaying tactic. According to Figure 4–13, the consequences of increasing per capita income in year 1 from Y_1 to Y_0 (its value the year before), is that the next year Y_t will again return to Y_1, where it will continue to converge toward Y_E. Further, any public program designed to alter the per capita income must be a continuing program. There can be no permanent change in Y_E from programs of limited duration.

To alter Y_E permanently requires affecting the factors that determine it. For example, Y_E can be raised either by reducing u or increasing v, such as might result from suitable changes in public expenditures or tax rates. An increase in rate of public expenditure may affect deteriorated housing through rent subsidies, maintenance programs, and new construction. Similarly, the tax rate may affect emigration from the city, especially among above-median income households. These effects can be incorporated into the model and the coefficients of the model estimated using cross-sectional data from many cities. The result is the following equation

$$Y_{t+1} = 682 + 12\,E_t + 0.9\,Y_t - 6\,T_t$$

where T_t is the tax rate and E_t is the level of public expenditure in year t. Since the coefficient of E_t has twice the numerical magnitude of the coefficient of T_t, each dollar spent in public expenditures has twice the impact upon per capita income as that of a dollar saved in reducing taxes according to this equation.

Econometric models generally do better at identifying and measuring historical relationships than at predicting the future. One hazard is the possibility of obtaining a statistically significant relationship between variables related only by chance. Another is inferring false causality between variables that are in actuality mutually influencing. A case in point is a study whose chief finding was that: "The more bedrooms per home, the larger the household and the more children of school age."[107] One should not conclude that a family that moves into a larger dwelling will then have more children. It is likelier that an increase in children motivated the move to more spacious accommodations.

---

[107] *Baltimore Sun*, May 19, 1974, p. F8.

5

System Dynamics—A Controversial Newcomer

The newest of the methodologies for policy modeling—and the most controversial—is system dynamics, an approach that has roots in electrical engineering and modern industrial management. From the vast range of attempted application of this methodology, one observes that its practitioners—collectively and in some cases, individually—consider the principles of system dynamics as almost universal in scope.

In this chapter, we will concentrate on two areas of application: urban and world problems. We will review the modeling work that has been done, how it has and has not been used, and the reactions it has occasioned. Many of the responses have themselves been modeling or "counter modeling" efforts.

In a charged field, it is difficult to stay constantly objective. We have tried to be neutral in our account of system dynamics, but at the cost of leaving the reader in doubt about where we stand. We will therefore attempt at the end of this chapter to clarify the nature of our position on some of the main issues that divide the disputants. We also will give our interpretation, throughout the chapter, of the factors going beyond substantive issues that seem to keep the parties at odds and raise the temperature of the debate.

LEGACY OF CONTROVERSY

Jay Wright Forrester, strong-minded originator of the young methodology of system dynamics, is used to generating controversy. As an iconoclast, he upsets traditional economists. As an outspoken critic of urban policy and technological growth, his views agitate government officials and social scientists of a different persuasion. His methodology, with which he is very closely identified personally, is (partly for this reason) subjected to continual attack, almost in the nature of a conditioned emotional response, by adversaries whose disagreements with Forrester color their attitudes about all system dynamics modeling, regardless of author. Forrester, more than any other modeling innovator, has created a legacy of controversy which has engulfed him, his followers, and their work.

All of the first four major system dynamics works, *Industrial Dynamics, Urban Dynamics, World Dynamics,* and *The Limits to Growth*,[1] have been vigorously challenged as to the structure of the models, the conclusions obtained, and the absence of supportive data. Many of the objections concern matters of technical substance, some have to do with the newness of the methodology, some with the seeming brashness with which it is applied to areas to which it is not indigenous.

A methodology applied within its native discipline is more likely to be accepted than one appearing from the outside. The stranger is always suspect, especially the stranger with messianic zeal. System dynamics came out of the fields of engineering and industrial management. Alien to most social scientists, it has been proposed for application to problems of urban growth, world population, long-range coal supplies, natural resource depletion, the United States energy system, chemical processes, narcotics, economic development, regional employment, air pollution, occupational program planning, terrestrial ecosystems, education, crime in Washington, D.C., the dynamics of world peace, private home markets in the United Kingdom, financial planning, gypsy moth populations, urban traffic, and even the cultural structure of pre-Christian Rome.[2]

Some of the fields that system dynamics has penetrated had little prior exposure to formal modeling. Others had their own style of modeling. It is not surprising to find practitioners in these fields rebuffing the system dynamics intruder who appears to malign the traditional theories, methods, and norms of the field, and take liberties with the principles of the scientific method to which workers in the field adhere.

Lawrence Klein expresses an econometrician's reaction in commenting on the attempt by displaced aerospace engineers to move into economics in the late 1960s: "The invasion of quantitative economics by engineers" has been disastrous from the point of view of preserving standards of research. They have "jumped much too boldly without joining forces with econometricians."[3] To Klein, engineers like Forrester are "boy economists" (an epithet economist Paul Samuelson applied to Secretary of State Henry Kissinger when Kissinger proposed a floor on the world price of oil).

With his work in the late 1960s on the urban dynamics model, Forrester

---

[1] Jay W. Forrester, *Industrial Dynamics* (Cambridge: The M.I.T. Press, 1961).
Jay W. Forrester, *Urban Dynamics* (Cambridge: The M.I.T. Press, 1969).
Jay W. Forrester, *World Dynamics* (Cambridge: Wright-Allen Press, 1971).
Donella H. Meadows et al., *The Limits to Growth* (New York: Universe Books, 1972).
[2] For more information on these applications and others, see *System Dynamics Newsletter* 11, System Dynamics Group, Alfred P. Sloan School of Management, M.I.T., Cambridge, Mass., December 1973, pp. 9–47.
[3] Klein made his remarks during the course of an energy modeling conference in June 1974.

began to move out from modeling industrial systems to modeling a city. Finding little useful in the researches of sociologists and urbanologists, Forrester relied on the practical knowledge of former Boston mayor John Collins for an understanding of the city from which to build his model.[4] Forrester believes the principles of system dynamics are universal in the entire sweep of systems that change through time. "Identical structures recur as one moves between apparently dissimilar fields," says Forrester, and "these identical structures behave in identical ways wherever they are found."[5]

Forrester's purview grew (and so did the controversy) from industrial to urban to world systems. His efforts since 1972 to apply system dynamics to the national economy continue the pattern.[6] Detractors and supporters agree on the impact of the work (they disagree on its productiveness), and they acknowledge the attention it has drawn to important problem areas. The world models, for example, focused concern on the finiteness of the Earth, the question of human survival, and the interrelatedness of the basic problems of population growth, ecological abuse, and dwindling supplies of natural resources.

The relative explicitness of a formal computer model has a way of provoking controversy, especially when the model gives the appearance of quantitative precision on sensitive issues that are poorly understood. The debate that followed *World Dynamics* and *The Limits to Growth* was not entirely due to their projections of disaster. These studies were not the first to draw such conclusions. Harrison Brown advanced similar conclusions nearly twenty years earlier in *The Challenge of Man's Future*[7] without arousing the same degree of public controversy. Of course, times were different in 1954. The future appeared brighter then, and the prophecy of doom was easier to ignore.

Brown's book is a careful, scholarly treatment of man's future. It cites Reverend Thomas R. Malthus whose 1798 essay on population growth[8] "was destined to precipitate one of the longest and at times one of the most heated controversies in history . . . unfortunately . . . on an emotional level rather than on a logical one . . . [with] . . . widespread dissemination of opinion disguised

---

[4] Collins' views on urban policy are stated in John F. Collins, "Managing Our Cities: Can We Do Better?" in Nathaniel J. Mass (ed.), *Readings in Urban Dynamics*, 2 vols. (Cambridge, Mass.: Wright-Allen Press, 1974), 1: 3–11. Some urbanologists dismiss the urban dynamics model as a computerized construction of Collins' prejudices.

[5] Jay W. Forrester, "Systems Analysis as a Tool for Urban Planning," *IEEE Spectrum* 8, no. 1 (1971): 50.

[6] Jay W. Forrester, "A National Model for Understanding Social and Economic Change," *Simulation* 24, nos. 4 and 5 (1975). See also Jay W. Forrester, "Understanding Social and Economic Change in the United States" (and four related papers), *Proceedings of the 1975 Summer Simulation Conference* (La Jolla, Calif.: Simulation Councils Inc., 1975), pp. 1465–1515.

[7] Harrison Brown, *The Challenge of Man's Future* (New York: The Viking Press, 1954).

[8] Thomas R. Malthus, *An Essay on the Principle of Population and a Summary View of the Principle of Population* (Middlesex, England: Penguin Books, 1970).

as scientific fact, and ... confusion."⁹ Brown's points are similar to those made in *The Limits to Growth,* but his approach is different. Says Brown:

> It is clear that the future course of history will be determined by the rates at which people breed and die, by the rapidity with which nonrenewable resources are consumed, by the extent and speed with which agricultural production can be improved, by the rate at which the underdeveloped areas can industrialize, by the rapidity with which we are able to develop new resources, as well as by the extent to which we succeed in avoiding future wars. All of these factors are interlocked, but in order better to understand the ways in which each of them operates, we must consider them separately.¹⁰

Using a computer model, *The Limits to Growth* considered together the same factors Brown considered separately. *The Limits to Growth* is more sharply drawn than Brown's book. It shakes the reader with the force of its computer projections of disaster, presenting its conclusions as if newly discovered, with only passing reference to Malthus.

There have been many other attempts to model the world system by computer. Kenneth Watt at the University of California at Davis has been modeling energy, population, land-use, pollution, and natural resources on both state-wide and global levels, leading him to call for massive injections of foreign capital to the underdeveloped countries to avoid an energy shortfall in the developed world.¹¹ Other world modeling efforts include the cooperative international LINK project coordinated by Lawrence Klein,¹² the GLOSAS project, promoted by Takeshi Utsumi in Japan,¹³ the second Club of Rome study led by Mihajlo D. Mesarovic and Eduard Pestel,¹⁴ another Japanese-based project headed by Y. Kaya,¹⁵ and the Bariloche project under A. Herrera in Argentina.¹⁶

None of these efforts have had (and many have not sought to have) the powerful impact of *The Limits to Growth.* Polemical works often either refer

---

⁹ Brown, pp. 5 and 7.
¹⁰ Ibid., pp. 66–67.
¹¹ See K. E. F. Watt, "A Model of Society," *Simulation* (1970): 153–164; and N. R. Glass and K. E. F. Watt, "Land Use, Energy, Agriculture, and Decision Making in Human Society: Progress Report," (Davis, Calif.: Interdisciplinary Systems Group, University of California, December 1974).
¹² Klein has been attempting to link together existing macroeconomic models of the countries of the free world along with specially built models of socialist and less developed regions. For documentation, see L. R. Klein, G. Moriguchi and A. Van Peeterssen, "World Trade Forecasts 1971–73: Retrospect and Prospect," Annual Reunion of the Canadian Society of Economic Science, Ottawa, October 13–14, 1972. Several other internationally linked economic models are being built around the world, including Canadian-American, Austrian-German, and Common Market models. Jean Waelbroeck discusses these projects in Section 7 of "A Survey of Short-Run Model Research Outside the U.S.A.," in Gary Fromm (ed.), *Papers in the Brookings Econometric Model Conference* (Amsterdam: North Holland, 1975), chapter 10.
¹³ Utsumi has been developing a world modeling effort called Global Systems Analysis and Simulation (GLOSAS) which uses satellite telecommunication between Japanese and

to authoritative data, reproducible experiments, and established facts to prove a point (e.g., *The Challenge of Man's Future*); mix facts and speculations so as to give the appearance of scientific validity (e.g., the new "pseudo-science" books, such as *Chariots of the Gods?*)[17]; or make no attempt to prove statements, relying instead on dramatic suggestions (e.g., George Orwell's *1984*). The *Limits* book seemed to its supporters to fit the first category, even though its conclusions were derived from an uncorroborated model. Critics put the book in the second category. Said Peter Passell, "All the conclusions are built in the assumptions, so we get an enormous mass of pseudoscience to arrive at the conclusion that was made very transparently from the first."[18] Adds Michael H. Rothkopf, such models "... should be viewed as no more than the sincere opinions of their builders. They should not be presented as scientifically justified conclusions. If they are, decision makers may place excessive trust in them—and this may lead to bad decisions."[19]

One way of examining or challenging a computer model is by a process we call "counter modeling." This involves testing structure, assumptions, sensitivities, and biases by running and studying strategically altered versions of the model. Counter modeling does not necessarily lead to greater truth or understanding, although that is one of its intended uses. It may serve more as a vehicle for expressing a different point of view, and so widen the scope of debate. Thus, Leo P. Kadanoff in counter modeling Forrester's urban dynamics model warned the reader that his conclusions should not

> be considered a reliable result of a careful analysis which has been based upon a fully evaluated model. On the contrary, the results are different in point of view and in substance from the stated conclusions of Forrester's examination of

---

American modeling teams (later to include other countries) for interfacing regional and national energy models. Participant countries build their own models to receive the output of foreign models as exogenous inputs. See Takeshi Utsumi and E. A. Eschbach, "Joint USA/Japan Project on Global Systems Analysis and Simulation (GLOSAS) of Energy, Resources and Environmental (ERE) Systems," *Proceedings of the 1974 Summer Computer Simulation Conference*, Houston, Texas, July 9–11, 1974, pp. 343–353.

[14] Mihajlo Mesarovic and Eduard Pestel, *Mankind at the Turning Point: Organic or Cancerous Growth Path?* Second Report to the Club of Rome (New York: E. P. Dutton, 1974).

[15] Y. Kaya, "On the Future Japan and the World: A Model Approach," *Towards a Global Vision of Human Problems* (Tokyo: Japan Techno-Economics Society, 1973). See also Yoichi Kaya and Yutaka Suzuki, "Toward a Global Vision of Human Problems: Global Constraints and New Vision for Development," (Tokyo: Japan Techno-Economics Society, 1973).

[16] A. Herrera, "Latin American World Model: Progress Report," (Rio Negro, Argentina: Fundacion Bariloche, 1973).

[17] Erich von Daniken, *Chariots of the Gods?* (New York: Bantam Books, 1971).

[18] Interview with Leonard M. Ross and Peter Passell in Willem Oltmans, *On Growth: The Crisis of Exploding Population and Resource Depletion* (New York: G. P. Putnam's Sons, 1974), p. 97.

[19] Michael H. Rothkopf, "World Models Won't Work," *Simulation* 21, no. 2 (1973): 60–61.

the very same model. He and I have each used the model to explain our different points of view and to put our reasoning in numerical form.[20]

Counter modeling can be a time-consuming, costly, and difficult process. Daniel Babcock devoted much of his doctoral thesis to such a study of *Urban Dynamics*,[21] and the Science Policy Research Unit of the University of Sussex conducted an extensive analysis of the *Limits to Growth* model.[22] These are only a few of a very large number of critiques that taken together illustrate an important fact: models are easier to create and run than to analyze and appraise. They are simpler to construct than to comprehend.

We will review a number of the attempts to understand, assess, and use the urban and world models in the following pages. The review tells a story, but not a story of heroes and villains or of right and wrong. If anything, it is a story of misunderstandings. If it yields a lesson, it is of the need for better ways of encouraging and performing dispassionate analyses of policy models. This requires astute nonadvocates who have the talent and temperament to entertain diverse approaches and keep an open mind to viewpoints that differ from their own. We will develop this idea further in Chapter 10.

URBAN DYNAMICS

The reader already has been introduced to the urban dynamics model as an example in Chapter 4. The model was used to simulate the consequences of traditional urban programs covering jobs, training, financial aid, and low-cost housing. The simulation procedure was first to run the model until an initial equilibrium was attained at around 250 years of simulated time, then to represent a selected urban program in the equilibrated model and allow the model to run for an additional 50 years until it was nearly in equilibrium again. This method of "comparative statics" was used to compare one policy program with another.

Conclusions of the Urban Dynamics Model

The urban programs were represented as follows in simulations of the model. Each year, the job program gave one year jobs to 10 percent of the underemployed in the city, the training program moved 5 percent of the under-

---

[20] Leo P. Kadanoff, "From Simulation Model to Public Policy," *American Scientist* 60, no. 1 (1972): 79.

[21] Daniel L. Babcock, *Analysis and Improvement of a Dynamic Urban Model*, Ph.D. Dissertation, U.C.L.A., 1970.

[22] H. S. D. Cole et al., *Models of Doom: A Critique of The Limits to Growth* (New York: Universe Books, 1973); published in Great Britain as *Thinking About the Future*.

employed into the labor category, a tax subsidy (from state or federal funds) increased the taxes available to the city by a fixed amount, and the low-cost housing program created (at no cost to the city) new low-cost housing units for 5 percent of the underemployed. The programs turned out badly in the simulations. Changes due to the job program, although relatively small, were "nearly all in an unfavorable direction."[23] The training program increased the annual flow of laborers out of the city by 81 percent and the annual flow of underemployeds into the city by 43 percent. The tax subsidy did nothing to improve fundamental conditions within the city and caused an unfavorable shift in the proportions of population, housing, and business. The low-cost housing program was the most detrimental of all.[24]

One recommendation coming out of the simulations was for a 5 percent per year demolition of slum housing together with discouragement of worker-housing construction to achieve a healthier state of equilibrium. Forrester warned his readers not to take these policy conclusions seriously without further study, yet he recognized the unavoidability of some doing just that.[25]

Forrester, himself, was not averse to making policy recommendations on the basis of his modeling work. In October 1970, he appeared before the Subcommittee on Urban Growth of the House Committee on Banking and Currency to urge Congress to discourage continued urban growth. "Population grows until stresses rise far enough, which is to say that quality of life falls far enough to stop further increase. Everything we do to reduce those pressures causes the population to rise further and faster and hastens the day when expediencies will no longer suffice."[26] Forrester proposed that the Subcommittee on Urban Growth change its name to the Subcommittee on National Equilibrium.

Response to Urban Dynamics

The publication of *Urban Dynamics* in 1969 met with strong reactions, both positive and negative. Among the critics, physical scientists, mathematicians and operations researchers found fault with the structure of the model and with the mechanics of its assembly. Urbanologists and social scientists objected to the study's disregard of urban data and previous work. Economists looked in vain for the familiar landmarks of estimated coefficients and statisti-

---

[23] Forrester, *Urban Dynamics*, p. 55.
[24] Ibid., pp. 60 and 65.
[25] Ibid., p. 2.
[26] Jay W. Forrester, Testimony for the Ad Hoc Subcommittee on Urban Growth of the Committee on Banking and Currency, House of Representatives, 91st Cong., 2nd sess. on Industrial Location Policy (July 23, September 23–24, October 6–7, November 18–19, and December 2–3, 1970), p. 228. Forrester is here addressing national urban policy. See also Mass, pp. 245–255, 257–271.

cal measures of fit. Many of the negative responses took the form of counter modeling critiques, several of which were presented at a simulation conference in 1971 at the University of Pittsburgh.[27]

Many early reviews tended to be qualitative and emphatic, one way or the other. Donald A. Krueckeburg called the model "substantive, understandable, complete, cohesive, and directly instructive to what we are trying to do as planners."[28] Richard Rochberg called it "speculative sociology" and charged Forrester with harboring "violent elitist prejudices and a manifest contempt for poor people."[29] As time passed, the reviews became more reasoned in tone, with less overstatement and more counter modeling.[30] A similar pattern of response was to follow the world models.

Many reviewers of the urban model were appalled at the absence of data supporting the assumptions. Aaron Fleisher commented that *Urban Dynamics* "... neither records nor cites one datum in support of the qualities of the interactions attributed to the components. Purveying no such evidence, it can lay no claim to history past or future.... As an appraisal of policy *Urban Dynamics* is, in its present state, entirely groundless. But," added Fleisher, "it is, nonetheless, a valuable work. Forrester has shown how a complex urban system can be formulated and its history traced. He has provided a language in which different disciplines can argue together precisely. These are accomplishments without precedent."[31]

Gregory Ingram[32] complained that Forrester "did not ask representative members of the lower economic classes how they behaved or what pressures they responded to, but rather seems to have depended on his collaborators for those insights."[33] James Hester charged that "Forrester's mechanisms for both industrial growth and population migration strongly contradict existing

---

[27] This conference was devoted almost entirely to presentations of papers analyzing Forrester's urban work. See *IEEE Transactions on Systems, Man, and Cybernetics*, SMC-2, no. 2 (1972).

[28] Donald A. Krueckeburg, "Review of Urban Dynamics," *Journal of the American Institute of Planners*, September 1969, p. 353.

[29] Richard Rochberg, "Some Questionable Assumptions in the Model and Method of Urban Dynamics," Second Annual Pittsburgh Conference on Modeling and Simulation, March 29-30, 1971, University of Pittsburgh, Pittsburgh, Pennsylvania, p. 154.

[30] One of the earlier counter-modeling critiques is Harvey A. Garn and Robert H. Wilson, "A Critical Look at Urban Dynamics: The Forrester Model and Public Policy," Paper No. 113-39 (Washington, D.C.: Urban Institute, December 1970). The Urban Dynamics Group responded in Alan K. Graham, "Understanding *Urban Dynamics:* An Analysis of Garn's Interpretation," pp. 121–137 in Mass. An abbreviated version of Garn and Wilson appears as "A Look at *Urban Dynamics:* The Forrester Model and Public Policy," *IEEE Transactions on Systems, Man, and Cybernetics*, SMC-2, no. 2 (1972): 150–155.

[31] Aaron Fleisher, "Review of Jay W. Forrester: *Urban Dynamics*," *Journal of the American Institute of Planners* 37, no. 1 (1971): 54.

theories, and he offers no empirical evidence to support his divergent formulation."[34]

To these criticisms, the urban dynamicist replies that time series data do not normally contain the kind of information needed for parameter identification in long-term dynamic models, since the separate effects expressed by the model are compounded in the data, so "one cannot fault *Urban Dynamics* for not attempting to incorporate such data."[35]

The omission of suburbs in the urban dynamics model also came under attack. Economist John Kain charged that

> the model's most serious weakness is that the suburbs never explicitly appear in it ... [yet the] ... city strongly influences its suburbs and vice versa. ... Although Forrester's model reflects no awareness of this aspect of metropolitan interdependence, suburban governments are all too aware of it. Indeed, much of the urban problem today is a result of suburban governments' successfully pursuing precisely the kind of beggar-thy-neighbor policies Forrester advocates for the central city.[36]

Urban modeler David Birch claimed that "by forcing the core [of the city] to be self-contained, Forrester's model precludes the very economic specialization on which many central cities are now depending for survival."[37] Walter Helly, an operations researcher, asserted that the model described "a relatively self-contained walled medieval town"[38] better than it did a modern American city.

Physicist Leo P. Kadanoff expanded the urban dynamics model to incorporate both suburbs and other metropolitan areas, and reported obtaining different results from those obtained by Forrester. To Kadanoff, the training

---

[32] Gregory K. Ingram, "Review of Jay W. Forrester: *Urban Dynamics,*" *Journal of the American Institute of Planners* 36, no. 3 (1970): 206.

[33] Indeed, Forrester makes a point of using high level managers and administrators as a primary source of information and insight. Many of the ideas of *Industrial Dynamics* came from popular business publications and conversations with businessmen. Forrester's subsequent works have continued the practice. Forrester uses such sources to flesh out the details of his own conception of how the system works. In his preface to *Urban Dynamics,* Forrester says (p. ix): "I approached these discussions knowing the conceptual nature of the structure being sought, but not the specific details of the structure or the institutional components of behavior to be fitted into it. The others brought the knowledge of the pressures, motivations, relationships, reactions, and historical incidents needed to shape the theory and structure of the specific social system."

[34] James Hester, Jr., "Systems Analysis for Social Policies," *Science* 168 (1970): 694.

[35] Louis A. Alfeld, "*Urban Dynamics* and Its Critics," Paper D-1611 (Cambridge: System Dynamics Group, M.I.T.), p. 3.

[36] John F. Kain, "A Computer Version of How a City Works," *Fortune,* November 1969, p. 243.

[37] David L. Birch, "Review of Jay W. Forrester: *Urban Dynamics,*" *Industrial Management Review* 11 (1970): 68.

[38] Walter Helly, "Review of Jay W. Forrester: *Urban Dynamics,*" *JORSA,* July–August 1970, p. 750.

program discarded by Forrester was in fact "quite effective in holding down the number of unskilled workers and decreasing their unemployment rate,"[39] while the clearance program favored by Forrester was "almost totally ineffective."

Kenneth L. Rider constructed an economic model of the housing market of New York City, taking the urban dynamics model as a starting point. He replaced Forrester's housing sector with an economic model of his own design incorporating New York City data on housing stock, rent levels, operating expenses, and return on capital. He allowed housing construction and demolition to proceed according to basic economic forces. Rider ran four different housing policies under three different sets of assumptions about family size and operating costs. His model was much less responsive to policy changes than the urban dynamics version, leading him to conclude that housing policy alone "is not sufficient to significantly alter the course of the city." In Rider's model, Forrester's favored policy of slum demolition, according to Rider, resulted in an "underemployed removal scheme ... [and was] ... nothing more than a way to get rid of underemployed people by depriving them of a place to live."[40] Rider did not get the increase in upward mobility, availability of jobs, and influx of labor population that Forrester had obtained in his simulations under the slum-demolition policy.[41]

Counter modeling allowed Kadanoff and Rider to express their reservations about the urban dynamics model in more precise terms than those of earlier reviews. Counter modeling turns the tables on the modeler and demands a response made on an equivalent technical basis. But the counter modeler may not provide enough documentation to permit a careful check. This, plus the considerable time and effort required, helps to explain why many counter models go unanswered. To respond to a counter modeling challenge, the modeler faces the same set of problems that the would-be counter modeler faces in the first instance, in greater or lesser degree depending upon how well the counter modeler explains and documents the contrary results.

Urban dynamicist Walter W. Schroeder did undertake a modeling effort to respond to the criticism about suburbs. He came to conclusions generally op-

---

[39] Leo P. Kadanoff and H. Weinblatt, "Public Policy Conclusions from Urban Growth Models," *IEEE Transactions on Systems, Man, and Cybernetics*, SMC-2, no. 2 (1972): 164. Martyn Cordey-Hayes, of the Centre for Environmental Studies in London, obtained similar results for a three-city version of the model (Martyn Cordey-Hayes, "On the Feasibility of Simulating the Relationship Between Regional Imbalance and City Growth," *Proceedings of the London RSA Conference* 1972).

[40] Kenneth L. Rider, "An Examination of Four Housing Policies for New York City," *OMEGA, The International Journal of Management Science* 1, no. 5 (1973): 577–589.

[41] *Urban Dynamics* has been criticized for recommending a policy of slum demolition that would drive underemployed out of the city. In fact, the urban dynamics simulations show a net flow of underemployed *into* the city under the demolition program. The reduction in the number of underemployed is due to underemployed moving into the labor category, not out of the city. See Forrester, *Urban Dynamics,* pp. 99–103.

posite to those of Kadanoff.[42] When Forrester examined the Kadanoff model, it appeared to him to be based on an unreasonable assumption about the nature of population growth. As far as Forrester is concerned, no one has yet shown why an explicit treatment of suburbs would alter the conclusions obtained from their implicit treatment in the urban dynamics model.

Other critics of *Urban Dynamics* challenged its emphasis on housing availability as a force in intercity migration. To migration researchers like Peter A. Morrison of Rand, the housing factor is not very consequential. To Daniel Babcock, an engineer by training, the relationship between housing supply and in-migration of the unskilled is "difficult to quantify but certainly much weaker than Forrester has assumed it to be."[43] Economist Gregory Ingram reported that "most empirical studies of migration patterns in the United States have not found housing availability to be significant in explaining migration flows.... Variables relating to economic opportunity are the best predictors of migration."[44]

Louis Alfeld counters that those who deny the effect of housing "adduce no empirical evidence to the contrary. Nor do they suggest alternative counterbalances to migration."[45] One empirical study was conducted by economist Janet Pack. Relating the white migrants in her study to Forrester's labor-manager arrivals and the nonwhite migrants to Forrester's underemployed arrivals, Pack concluded that Forrester "may have placed too heavy an emphasis on the importance of housing" for underemployed arrivals, although not for labor-manager arrivals.[46] Pack's comparison is summarized in Tables 5-1 and 5-2.[47]

In his counter modeling analysis of the urban dynamics model, Babcock

---

[42] Walter W. Schroeder, "Urban Dynamics in Lowell," D-2025 (Cambridge: Sloan School, M.I.T., July 1974). Also see excerpts of Schroeder's work in *Simulation in the Service of Society* 5, no. 1 (1975): 4–6, and see Alan K. Graham, "Modeling City-Suburb Interactions," Mass, pp. 155–168. Graham finds the qualitative response of his city/suburb model to be "very similar to that of the original model" (p. 164). Volume 2 of *Readings in Urban Dynamics*, W. Schroeder, L. Alfeld, and R. Sweeney (eds.), publication pending, 1975, contains more detail on the Lowell project and its treatment of suburbs.

[43] Daniel L. Babcock, "Critical Analysis of a Dynamic Urban Model," Paper presented to the Seventeenth North American Meetings, Regional Science Association, Philadelphia, Pennsylvania, November 7, 1970, p. 15.

[44] Ingram, p. 207.

[45] Alfeld, p. 2. To Peter Morrison, the burden of proof is on urban dynamics. He believes that migrants will live in trailer parks if there are jobs, and no kind of housing, however attractive economically and otherwise, will compensate for the absence of jobs.

[46] Janet R. Pack, "Models of Population Movement and Urban Policy," *IEEE Transactions on Systems, Man, and Cybernetics*, SMC-2, no. 2 (1972): 195.

[47] Michael R. Goodman and Peter M. Senge followed up the migration debate in "Issues of Empirical Support for the Migration Formulation in *Urban Dynamics*," Mass, pp. 87–101. Goodman and Senge present several difficulties in using statistical inference techniques to derive parameters in the urban dynamics model. They compare the urban dynamics model to Pack's formulation and to the Lowry model (see chapter 4).

Table 5–1: Explanatory Variables in Order of Importance

Forrester's Labor-Manager Arrivals	Pack's Study of White Migrants
1. Jobs	1. Jobs
2. Housing	2. Housing
3. Population in Class	3. Public expenditure and taxation
4. Taxes	

Table 5–2: Explanatory Variables in Order of Importance

Forrester's Underemployed Arrivals	Pack's Study of Non-White Migrants
1. Housing	1. Non-White Population
2. Jobs	2. Economic Variables
3. Public Expenditures	3. Housing
4. Mobility	4. Public Expenditures

replaced nine rate constants with ones he found more consistent with empirical evidence. His simulations produced an equilibrium unemployment rate of 23 percent for the underemployed instead of 45 percent. Babcock concluded that fully half of the previously predicted unemployment was due to "choice of demographic constants inconsistent with urban literature."[48] He charged that built-in biases drove the urban dynamics model to produce excessive amounts of underemployed population and low-cost housing, and that the "inevitable conditions" of the mature city predicted by Forrester "are in no way proven by the Forrester model, but are instead created by a set of *a priori* assumptions."[49]

Nathaniel J. Mass counter modeled Babcock's counter model. Mass retained Babcock's assumption that the rate at which housing of a particular class becomes available to the next lower class depends in part upon the housing demand of the next lower class, so that fewer premium houses become available to the workers when worker housing is in excess and more become available when worker housing is in demand. According to Mass, other system reactions compensate. After obtaining equilibrium values "remarkably similar to those specified in *Urban Dynamics*,"[50] Mass concluded that Babcock's addition of "demand from below" was an unnecessary addition to the model.

Another issue raised by critics like Michael J. Stonebreaker, a computer scientist, is that the urban dynamics model is excessively complicated. Stonebreaker removed about half of the model's structure, including the tax sector and all perception delays. The reduced model replicated almost all of the behavior modes of the original model and matched the equilibrium values of the original model to within an average of 6 percent. Since the same infer-

---

[48] Babcock, p. 12.
[49] Ibid., pp. 18–19.
[50] Mass, pp. 141–154.

ences about policy could be made with either model, Stonebreaker concluded that much of the detail in the urban dynamics model is superfluous and the model's results are easier to understand when the excess complication is removed.[51]

Forrester contends that one should include all potentially important items in a model whether or not they appear to affect a particular policy issue under study, for to do otherwise might bias the causal structure of the model. Forrester asserts that social systems and their representation by his models are "counterintuitive" in that their responses to stimuli are often opposite to expectations.[52] But critics charge that a model is only counterintuitive when it is not fully understood. They feel models should be as simple as possible and they applaud efforts like Stonebreaker's to make models more understandable.

Many reviewers found merit in the *Urban Dynamics* project. Gregory Ingram thought the study worked out the implications of urban policy "more fully and explicitly than they ever have been before."[53] Both Kadanoff and Rider, who differed with the conclusions, nevertheless accepted the urban dynamics model as an appropriate basis for further work. Kadanoff's view is interesting: "Despite these criticisms of Forrester's conclusions, I would argue that his model making is so brilliant and beautiful that his ideas are certainly worthy of examination and further development."[54]

Applications of Urban Dynamics

There is some evidence that a number of the urban land-use models of the 1960s are being adapted for use in planning by cities and regional governments.[55] With this in mind, we conducted an informal survey of attempts to apply the urban dynamics model.[56] The search was disappointing. For the most

---

[51] Michael Stonebreaker, "A Simplification of Forrester's Model of an Urban Area," *IEEE Transactions on Systems, Man, and Cybernetics,* SMC-2, no. 4 (1972): 468–472.

[52] Jay W. Forrester, "The Counterintuitive Behavior of Social Systems," in D. L. Meadows and D. H. Meadows (eds.), *Toward Global Equilibrium: Collected Papers* (Cambridge, Mass.: Wright-Allen Press, 1973), pp. 3–30. Appeared first in *Technology Review* 73, no. 3 (1971).

[53] Ingram, p. 206.

[54] Leo P. Kadanoff, "An Examination of Forrester's *Urban Dynamics,*" *Simulation,* June 1971, p. 262.

[55] See chapter 4 for an account of urban land-use models. A survey of their use is found in Janet R. Pack, *The Use of Urban Models in Urban Policy Making,* 2 vols. (Philadelphia: The Fels Center of Government, University of Pennsylvania, January 1974).

[56] Our informal survey was based upon leads obtained from three sources: 1. John Strongman, "Summary of Urban Dynamics Applied Research," Task I.d of HUD Contract H-2000-R, March 6, 1973; 2. *System Dynamics Newsletter* 11 (1973), Sloan School, M.I.T., Cambridge, Mass.; 3. Published reports of urban dynamics research in the public literature. Where possible, we held telephone interviews with those involved to determine the scope and purpose of their work and to learn their future plans. The survey was limited primarily to North American projects.

part, the activities we were able to locate consisted mostly of theses, papers, and classroom exercises, all isolated from policy makers in municipal governments.[57]

One exception was Walter W. Schroeder's application of the urban dynamics model to Lowell, Massachusetts. Here, city officials were directly involved in trying to fit the model to their city, largely through the efforts of James L. Sullivan, city manager of Lowell during the early 1970s. Sullivan is a long-time friend of former Boston mayor John Collins, whose practical experience provided the data base for the urban dynamics model. Sullivan learned of the model while city manager of Cambridge, Massachusetts, home of M.I.T., where Sullivan lectures from time to time and Forrester teaches. Sullivan regarded urban dynamics as academic, yet potentially useful for the analysis and solution of policy problems. He invited the urban dynamics group to work with the city of Lowell during the summer of 1971 to determine the model's applicability there. Forrester and Collins asked Schroeder, an M.I.T. master's student at the time, to explore the possibilities.[58]

Lowell, Massachusetts, is in many ways an ideal place in which to apply urban dynamics. It is an old New England industrial city whose decaying textile mills and dwindling population reflect the symptoms of urban stagnation that the urban dynamics model, based on Boston, another old Massachusetts city,[59] was meant to examine. Lowell's population grew rapidly in the 1800s due to the nine textile mills located on the Concord and Merrimack Rivers. The population peaked about 1920 and has since declined as other mill towns flourished and then as foreign competition virtually wiped out the domestic textile industry. Lowell's population fell to some 19,000 less than its peak of 113,000. Its economy stagnated and it experienced an unemployment rate of as much as 14 percent.

Schroeder did not have to alter the structure of the urban dynamics model to represent the historical rise and fall of Lowell's population.[60] To match Lowell's characteristics, he modified several of the model's parameters, including land area, family size, and population densities. To produce Lowell's fast growth in the early 1800s, he temporarily quintupled the normal construction

---

[57] A typical example is H. R. Porter and E. J. Henley, "Application of the Forrester Model to Harris County, Texas," *IEEE Transactions on Systems, Man, and Cybernetics,* SMC-2, no. 2 (1972): 180–191.

[58] Walter W. Schroeder III, "Lowell Dynamics: Preliminary Applications of the Theory of Urban Dynamics," Masters Thesis, M.I.T., February 1972.

[59] For a discussion of how the urban dynamics model produces results consistent with population growth patterns in the greater Boston area, see Wilbert Wils, "Metropolitan Population Growth, Land Areas, and the *Urban Dynamics* model," in Mass, pp. 103–114.

[60] Preliminary efforts to apply the urban dynamics model to Lowell are covered in Walter W. Schroeder III and John E. Strongman, "Adapting *Urban Dynamics* to Lowell," in Mass, pp. 197–223.

rates of new enterprises and housing. Lowell's pattern of growth in the 1800s, followed by a population peak in the early 1900s and subsequent decline, is characteristic of many old cities in the eastern half of the United States.[61] If the urban dynamics model had not been able to generate this pattern, it clearly would have been unacceptable. The fact that it could, however, is not by itself sufficient grounds for acceptance of the model.

The Department of Housing and Urban Development (HUD) supported the application of urban dynamics to Lowell from mid-1972 to 1974. HUD, interested in testing the applicability of the model to the problems of American cities, sponsored urban dynamics work in Lowell in three areas: establishment of feasible goals for a city, use of the model to help a city identify policy options relating to these goals, and further refinement and extension of the model.

In 1974 Sullivan left Lowell to return to his job as city manager of Cambridge. With his departure, the city's interest in the application of urban dynamics to Lowell subsided. According to one city official, Sullivan's successor did not share his predecessor's ardor for computer models.

Schroeder reports that a number of policy recommendations developed with the aid of urban dynamics were implemented in Lowell.[62] One was the city's decision to employ an unused industrial facility as a means of attracting new industry to Lowell. The AVCO Corporation, whose 1,000 Lowell employees were engaged in the development of guidance systems for MIRV missiles, closed its Lowell operation after the MIRV system was cancelled in 1971. Unable to dispose of its plant, AVCO offered to sell the building to Lowell for use as a school. Lowell needed better educational facilities and did lease the building as a school for a year while city officials debated whether to buy it outright.

Based on their analysis of Lowell's problems, Schroeder and his teammates had established two goals for the city: improved employment and more benefits for current residents (as opposed to in-migrants or commuters).[63] They were not asked for a "yes-or-no" recommendation on purchase of the plant, but they say they were called upon for their opinions based on their experience in modeling the city. They believe they convinced Lowell officials that it would be unwise to convert good factory space into classrooms. In April 1974, the MOSTEK Corporation bought the plant with plans to employ 1,500 persons there by 1976. With the subsequent downturn in the economy, the plant was still vacant in mid-1975, and MOSTEK was reported to be seeking a buyer for the building.

Schroeder cites other policy actions taken by Lowell as evidence of the in-

---

[61] Albert Harlow, Jr., "Urban Population Data and Urban Dynamics," *Simulation*, October 1973, pp. 125–127.
[62] Schroeder, p. 1.
[63] Ibid., pp. 78–79.

fluence of the urban dynamics model. These include a "tax title program" that inventories and publicizes delinquent tax properties and a code enforcement program that "places extra pressure on the owners of older, low quality property to either upgrade or demolish their structures."[64] On May 16, 1972, Sullivan decided to stop sales of city land to the Lowell Housing Authority for low-income public housing. He feared the housing would attract unemployed persons to the city. Opposed only by local building contractors, his decision stood and Lowell terminated construction of low-income housing. In a related action, the city rezoned a forty-four-acre residential urban renewal area as an industrial park to create a thousand new job opportunities. Again because of the economic downturn, no land for the park had yet been purchased by developers by mid-1975.

City officials in Lowell say their actions had nothing to do with *Urban Dynamics*, even though they were consistent with the book's recommendations. Much of the reason for Lowell's interest in *Urban Dynamics* is found in the kindred policy positions and personal relationships of Forrester, Collins, and Sullivan, coupled with Sullivan's strong leadership in Lowell. While Sullivan was in office, urban dynamics modeling served an educational problem identifying function in Lowell. It was never a direct decision making tool, but as the urban dynamicists would want to point out, it was never intended to be. Today, with Sullivan and federal funding gone, urban dynamics has been put aside by city officials, many of whom consider it to be more appropriate for the "academics" than for Lowell.

Another attempt at applying the urban dynamics model was directed by D.M. Ingels, of Harvey Mudd College, for the city of Anaheim, California.[65] Anaheim is a very different kind of urban setting from Lowell. It is a young western city, founded in 1859, already larger than Lowell and still growing. Western migration, Anaheim's aggressive growth policies, the creation of Disneyland, and the opening of the Santa Ana freeway have all combined to multiply the city's population six-and-a-half times in the past twenty years.

Michael Kono, project leader under Ingels, was not able to duplicate Schroeder's success in making the urban dynamics model fit. He felt exogenous forces were much stronger in Anaheim's case than in Lowell's. His adaptation of the urban dynamics model consistently underrepresented the past growth of Anaheim. When he altered only the parameters changed by Schroeder, he obtained extremely poor agreement with census data. Even changing other parameters in the model did not provide a satisfactory match with Anaheim's

---

[64] Ibid., pp. 66–67. Lowell officials say urban dynamics had little if anything to do with formulation of these programs.

[65] Michael E. Kono, F. S. Bauman, and D. H. Eusey, "Examination of the Urban Dynamics of Anaheim," M.S. thesis, Harvey Mudd College, 1973. (See also D. M. Ingels, "Verifying Urban Simulations," presented at the 1973 Summer Computer Simulation Conference, Montreal, July 17–19, 1973.)

history. Increasing normal housing construction parameter values by factors of from five to ten, for example, had a negligible effect on the fit. The model predicted an imminent population decline, yet Anaheim's planning department expected the population to continue to rise. Whether the urban dynamics group could have obtained a better match is a moot question at this point.

As in Lowell, the Anaheim project team worked with city officials. It also received federal support (through the National Science Foundation's Technical Incentive Program). Unlike Lowell, the effort did not successfully represent Anaheim's behavior nor did it have ready entrée to top policy levels of the city. Ingels terminated the Anaheim project in June 1973.

Nature of the Responses

In summary, reactions to *Urban Dynamics* take three forms. First are outright rejections of the methodology and denunciations of the policy conclusions. Not always, but often, these attacks appear emotional in character, ideologically motivated, and frequently based on misinterpretations or superficial readings of the urban dynamics study. These negative responses are balanced by positive endorsements similar in character and no more substantial.

Second are the more thoughtful critiques. These frequently are counter modeling studies that accept the methodology but not the model (as originally formulated) or the conclusions. Here, too, there is sometimes evidence of insufficient understanding—if not of the original model, then of the art of producing such a model and appropriately altering it.

Third are the attempts to apply the model to municipalities. Most of these attempts did not get outside the classroom. Of those that did, some (as in Anaheim) could not make the model fit the city. In Lowell, where this was not a problem (partly because Forrester and his colleagues were directly involved), the urban dynamics model and the ideology that accompanied it got a good reception and fair hearing. Lowell may have been more than a bit flattered by the attention it was receiving from Washington and other parts of the country because of urban dynamics. But the bloom faded; even in Lowell, urban dynamics' imprint is debated and its future dim. Changing fashions, changing administrations, personal rivalries, and the vagaries of the political process all undoubtedly played a role in its fall from favor.

When HUD funded the urban dynamics study in 1972, its aim was to obtain an objective assessment of the criticisms that had been raised of *Urban Dynamics* since its publication in 1969. It wanted the urban dynamicists to modify the model as appropriate to the criticisms that were valid, and it wanted the assumptions of the model to be better grounded in empirical data. HUD tried to promote these objectives by seeing to it that the project included an advisory board containing prominent urbanologists, namely Britton Harris,

Gregory Ingram, Jerome Rothenberg, and George Sternlieb, all of whom had been critical of *Urban Dynamics*.

The initial meetings of the advisory board included policy-oriented people who, according to one participant, mixed with the technical advisers "like oil with water." Subsequently, the technically oriented people met by themselves. HUD and the advisers agreed that the process did not work. They saw Forrester and his associates as immovable. The urban dynamicists viewed it differently; to them, the problem was one of "misinterpretation" and "semantic differences." They considered the criticisms of urban dynamics as stemming more from misunderstanding than "model defects."[66]

One adviser admitted that the unfamiliarity and idiosyncracies of the system dynamics modeling format did present impediments to outside observers. The urban dynamics model is closed, largely self-contained, and highly aggregated compared to most other urban policy models. It does not relate easily to prior work and is inhospitable to more traditional modes of thought. Unless the observers are willing to make what may be for them an extraordinary effort to think about and work with the model on its terms, they are likely to find it inscrutable, naive, or just plain wrong—especially if its behavior runs counter to their prior conceptions.

This is not to say that making a special effort to study a system dynamics model at length will convert a nonbeliever into a believer. But the question is moot so long as those willing to take the trouble are already disposed to believe, whereas those not so disposed begrudge the time required.

Urban dynamics continues to be used in research studies and continues to attract government funding. Some of the same group that conducted the Lowell project, for example, later applied urban dynamics to a study of the long-term effects of revenue sharing[67] and the long-term dynamics of housing allowances.[68] The findings of these two studies were largely in keeping with the policy conclusions of *Urban Dynamics*.

THE WORLD MODELS

There are two major system dynamics models of the world: World2, by Forrester,[69] and World3, its successor, by Meadows and the *Limits to Growth* team.[70] True to their heritage, the world models are basically similar in struc-

---

[66] John F. Collins, Walter W. Schroeder, and Norman K. Kidder, "Long-Term Effects of Revenue Sharing on Communities," Paper No. D-2177-1 (Cambridge: System Dynamics Group, M.I.T., May 20, 1975), p. 15.

[67] Ibid.

[68] John F. Collins and Walter W. Schroeder, "Analysis of the Long-Term Dynamics of Housing Allowances," Paper No. D-2095 (Cambridge: System Dynamics Group, M.I.T., October 2, 1974).

[69] Forrester, *World Dynamics*.

ture to the urban dynamics model. Whereas the urban dynamics model has over twenty level variables, World2 has only five: population, natural resources, capital investment, capital investment in agriculture, and pollution. World2 also contains a measure of performance of the world system labeled the quality of life, an index that is dropped in World3.[71]

World3 differs from World2 in several other ways: it has investment broken down into service, industrial, and agricultural capital; population divided into four age cohorts; and land separated out from natural resources as potentially arable, arable, and urban-industrial. Over the course of a World3 simulation, land flows from potentially arable to arable to urban-industrial, population cohorts age, and natural resources become depleted. Like the urban dynamics model, the world models are not spatially disaggregated.

Simulation of World2

In simulating possible world futures, Forrester first makes a standard run of the World2 model from year 1900 to year 2100 with all parameters set for the assumed current state of affairs. The earth depletes its fixed stock of natural resources causing world population to decline after year 2020. But the natural resources factor is not the only one limiting world growth. Forrester alters the model to uncover other effects. Reducing by 75 percent the required rate of resource consumption per unit of production beginning in 1970 only results in greater industrialization and a skyrocketing of pollution. Pollution puts the brake on growth, and world population plummets by the year 2040.

Next, Forrester sets the rate of natural resource usage to zero and lowers the rate of pollution generation by 90 percent in 1970. Now population rises steadily before flattening out in the twenty-second century because of the next limit to growth, world crowding. In this simple model, population increases to several times its 1970 value without drastically affecting the quality of life. The severe alterations made to suppress the effects of pollution and resource depletion are clearly distorting. Forrester eliminates the effect of crowding to demonstrate food shortage as still another possible limiting factor.[72]

World Dynamics, like *Urban Dynamics* before it, is a critique of standard responses to social problems. The World2 simulations portray increased capital investment as exacerbating the pollution problem, birth control as being powerless by itself to counter adverse forces in the long term, and pollution control as merely postponing the onset of the pollution crisis, allowing popula-

---

[70] Dennis L. Meadows et al., *The Dynamics of Growth in a Finite World* (Cambridge, Mass.: Wright-Allen Press, 1974). The World3 model is also described in Meadows et al., *Limits to Growth*.
[71] Forrester, *World Dynamics*, p. 60.
[72] Ibid., p. 86.

tion to grow larger in the meantime so that more people ultimately suffer the consequences. Increased agricultural productivity likewise leads to greater population growth as well as to a shift of capital out of food production into material goods. The result is to bring on a pollution crisis even earlier than before.

Combinations of such programs also fail, except when the rate of capital investment is diminished rather than increased at the same time that natural resource usage is reduced. This allows population to equilibrate after 1980, but at too high a level to maintain the quality of life enjoyed prior to 1970. A lowering of food productivity coupled with a program of birth control depresses population enough to give quality of life the desired boost. Forrester's final set of changes involves reducing the rate of consumption of natural resources by 75 percent, the generation of pollution by 50 percent, capital investment by 40 percent, food production by 20 percent, and the birth rate by 30 percent. "The result is to drop population slightly below the 1970 value and increase the quality of life."[73]

As attractive as this outcome may seem compared to the prior scenarios, recommending the reduction of food production sounds to people in many countries of the world like advocating food deprivation—an impression corroborated by close inspection of the simulation runs (e.g., reduced food production causes death rate to rise by almost 30 percent in 1970). The idea has come under bitter attack. In fact, the reduction of food production is not really essential for the results obtained.

Forrester goes out on a limb in promoting the use of the World2 model for policymaking, more than he did with the urban dynamics model. He argues that we cannot avoid the use of models, whether mental or otherwise, in the making of decisions. We ought therefore to choose the models in which we have greatest confidence.

> Having defined with care the model contained herein, and having examined its dynamic behavior and implications, I have greater confidence in this world system model than in others that I now have available. Therefore, this is the model I should use for recommending actions.[74]

Simulation of World3

Results of running the World3 model are reported in *The Limits to Growth* (published prior to full public presentation of the model), and then again, with a few changes and in somewhat muted form, in *Dynamics of Growth in a Finite World* (the official documentation of the model).[75] World3 is largely an extension of World2 and lends itself to conclusions parallel to those of the

---

[73] Ibid., p. 120.
[74] Ibid., p. ix.
[75] Meadows et al., *Dynamics of Growth*.

System Dynamics—A Controversial Newcomer

earlier model. The "standard" runs for the two models are very similar. The authors state "with some confidence that, under the assumption of no major change in the present system, population and industrial growth will certainly stop within the next century, at the latest."[76]

Running the World3 model assuming twice the known natural resources of 1900 causes the world to fall victim to pollution. Reducing pollution by 75 percent after 1970 produces a food shortage and another collapse of the world population. Doubling agricultural productivity and resources leads once again to crippling pollution. Instituting birth control, instead, results in a food crisis. Trying all of these policies together provides only a temporary postponement of the crisis.

With birth rates equal to death rates, capital investment rates equal to depreciation rates, reduced pollution, recycling of materials, and preservation of the soil, the World3 model predicts a stable and prosperous future, according to *The Limits to Growth*, without any reduction in food production (in fact with a "highly capitalized agriculture"). But if the recommended policies are implemented in the year 2000 instead of in 1975, the situation will have deteriorated too far to be recovered. *The Limits to Growth* concludes that if corrective measures are not taken soon, it may be too late to attain a viable equilibrium and save the Earth. *Dynamics of Growth* sounds the alarm more softly.

> Even a twenty-five-year postponement of the combined social and technological policies of the two previous runs will severely reduce their effectiveness.... Society will attain a more favorable and sustainable equilibrium state the sooner it begins to manage the transition to global equilibrium.[77]

Response to World2

It is not difficult to raise questions about the World2 and World3 models. Their internal relationships, in the form of integral equations and table functions, are specified initially never to be altered once the simulation starts. The relationship between world birth rate and standard of living, for example, is locked into the model and used once each period, regardless of the state of the model. Increasing standard of living causes birth rates to drop in the World2 model, whereas when the world system begins to collapse, the falling standard of living immediately causes birth rates to soar. Critics charge that this pattern contradicts the traditional response of populations in times of war, depression, and other stress, and throws "doubt upon even the general trends" of the simulation results.[78]

---

[76] Meadows et al., *Limits to Growth*, p. 126.
[77] Meadows et al., *Dynamics of Growth*, p. 549.
[78] S. Fred Singer, "The Predicament of the Club of Rome," *EOS: Transactions, American Geophysical Union* 53, no. 7 (1972): 699.

Presentation of the system dynamics models of the world stimulated a flood of reviews, book reports, journal articles, newspaper stories, and counter modeling efforts. A partial sampling of responses to *The Limits to Growth* study in the ten months following its release in early 1972 numbers well over two hundred items, including some thirty foreign pieces, with an average of over five new items appearing each week. Articles continue to be published with some regularity several years after the work was unveiled. One purpose of *The Limits to Growth* was to provoke public debate. Its success in that respect has been overwhelming.

The critical furor that broke like water through a bursting dam in March of 1972 began with a trickle in 1970 as newspapers reported on Forrester's computer model of the world.[79] The fact that "the giant electronic computer" was serving humankind by modeling the world attracted more interest at that point than what the computer model had to say.

In January of 1971, Forrester published an article in the M.I.T. magazine *Technology Review* on what he called the counterintuitive nature of social systems, based on the urban dynamics study. As an illustration, he presented seven runs together with a schematic diagram of the World2 model.[80] He expressed the opinion that today's society may be "nonsustainable" or "self-extinguishing," and that resource and food shortages, excessive pollution, and physical and psychological crowding would inhibit further progress. Forrester received an unexpectedly large number of requests for copies of the article.

World Dynamics was published in June 1971. Dennis Meadows, then involved in building the World3 model, published an article in August 1971 entitled "The Predicament of Mankind"[81] in which he described the M.I.T. model and speculated that sometime within the next sixty years world population would undergo a profound and very possibly traumatic deceleration. Meadows further predicted that the vast majority of those living in the developing countries would have no possibility of ever attaining the material standard of living enjoyed by the developed nations, and that the western world might witness a marked decline in its own material standard of living.

A few of the initial reviews of *World Dynamics* suggested ways in which the World2 model could be improved,[82] but most focused more on the model's conclusions than its technical merits. Several expressed skepticism about the assumptions and manner of analysis. An editorial in the *Wall Street Journal,* for example, dismissed Forrester's "prophecy by technology" as a form of "sophisticated guessing."[83]

---

[79] *New York Times,* December 6, 1970, Section 4, p. 14.

[80] Jay W. Forrester, "Counterintuitive Behavior."

[81] Dennis L. Meadows, "The Predicament of Mankind," *The Futurist* 5, no. 4 (1971): 137–144.

[82] Jon D. Roland, "The Disturbing Implications of World Dynamics," *The Futurist* 5, no. 4 (1971): 145–150.

[83] *Wall Street Journal,* September 28, 1971, p. 18.

Hazel Henderson spoke of Forrester's "gloomy scenarios" as the latest entry in the controversy between economists and ecologists that went back to Harrison Brown in 1954.[84] Environmentalists and conservationists saw in Forrester's work a useful weapon to wield against developers, polluters, and overpopulators of the planet. The ecology movement that blossomed in 1962 with Rachel Carson's *Silent Spring*[85] welcomed Forrester and Meadows as compatriots.

Yale economist Martin Shubik was one of the first to draw blood publicly for the opposition. His review of *World Dynamics* in *Science* called the book "blatant and insensitive advocacy for unsubstantiated model building on a very large scale" whose "behavioral-scientific content is virtually zero."[86] Shubik referred to Forrester's approach as "energetic, simplistic, and superficially attractive, but nonetheless dangerously wrong."

At this early stage, reactions were inclined to be instinctive and emotional in tone. Reviewers who agreed with the conclusions tended to dwell upon them at length, whereas many critics chose to ignore them almost entirely. The background and leanings of the reviewer usually gave a reliable indication of whether a review would embrace the model or denounce it. The same pattern of criticism followed the publication of *The Limits to Growth*.

One early review that did address technical as well as philosophical points was by William D. Nordhaus, a Yale economist. Nordhaus decried Forrester's lack of reference to data or existing empirical studies and called the economic theory put forth in *World Dynamics* "a major retrogression from current research in economic growth theory." He also disparaged Forrester's "lack of humility toward predicting the future."

> Can we treat seriously Forrester's (or anybody's) predictions in economics and social science for the next 130 years? Long-run economic forecasts have generally fared quite poorly. Marx predicted the immiseration of the working class under capitalism; Keynes guessed that capital could have no net productivity by the present year [1973]; Galbraith assured us that scarcity is obsolete. And now, without the scantest reference to economic theory or empirical data, Forrester predicts that the world's material standard of living will peak in 1990 and then decline. *Sic transit gloria.*[87]

Nordhaus privately circulated forty-odd copies of an early unpublished version of his paper in 1971. Forrester was sent at least three of them from secondhand sources as far away as Italy and England. This was the first review that bothered Forrester enough to cause him to prepare a personal rebut-

---

[84] *New York Times,* October 24, 1971, Section 3, p. 14.
[85] Rachel Carson, *Silent Spring* (Greenwich, Conn.: Fawcett Publications, 1962).
[86] Martin Shubik, "Review of Jay W. Forrester: *World Dynamics,*" *Science* 174 (1971): 1014–1015.
[87] Williams Nordhaus, "World Dynamics: Measurement Without Data," *The Economic Journal* 83, no. 332 (1973): 1182–1183.

tal. Forrester treated Nordhaus' criticisms one at a time, charging Nordhaus with misunderstanding the system dynamics methodology and also reality.[88] Nordhaus takes account of Forrester's rebuttal in the final published version of his paper, but it is clear that neither player is willing to engage in the contest according to the rules and terms the other player has set. Forrester provides some illumination of how the apparent relationship between birth rates and standard of living is affected by the behavior of other variables in his model—thus effectively countering one of Nordhaus' objections—but for the most part the match is conducted on two separate courts, with each player scoring points on his court at will.

The Limits to Growth

Other works besides *World Dynamics* set the stage for publication of *The Limits to Growth* early in 1972. In England, *The Ecologist* produced an issue entitled "A Blueprint for Survival," presenting many of the same views that Forrester and Meadows were espousing in the United States.[89] Endorsed by over thirty of Britain's most prestigious and distinguished scientists, including biologist Julian Huxley, economist E. J. Mishan, naturalist Peter Scott, and geneticist C. H. Waddington, the "Blueprint" was described as "a major contribution to current debate" in a letter to the London *Times* signed by fifty more scientists, Fellows of the Royal Society, and university science professors.[90] Citing *The Limits to Growth* study as complementing their own, the authors of the report claimed that "if current trends are allowed to persist, the breakdown of society and the irreversible disruption of the life support system on this planet, possibly by the end of the century, certainly within the lifetimes of our children, are inevitable."[91] Unless the developed nations considerably reduce their consumption of such disproportionate amounts of protein, raw materials and fuels, "there is no hope of the undeveloped nations markedly improving their standards of living."[92] One reviewer came away from the report feeling the need for "something akin to religious conversion; an emotional shock affecting the very ground of man's being."[93]

Aurelio Peccei, head of the Club of Rome, is another person very concerned about the world's disaster course. In a 1969 book, Peccei talked of a coming "tidal wave of global problems" and speculated that "the worsening popula-

---

[88] Jay W. Forrester et al., "The Debate on *World Dynamics:* A Response to Nordhaus," *Policy Sciences* 5 (1974): 169–190.

[89] Edward Goldsmith et al., "A Blueprint for Survival," *The Ecologist* 2, no. 1 (1972): 1–43.

[90] Letter to the editor, *Times* (London), January 25, 1972, p. 15.

[91] Goldsmith, p. 1.

[92] Ibid., p. 4.

[93] Right Reverend Hugh Montefiore, letter to the editor of *The Ecologist* 2, no. 4 (1972): 4.

tion-food situation may reach an economically or ecologically *irreversible state of imbalance* in twenty years" and *"entire populations might be destined literally to die of starvation."*[94] Peccei called for an objective diagnosis of the serious world situation and a rationalizing of the basis for long-term action, with models being used "whenever possible."

For Peccei and his colleagues in the Club of Rome, *The Limits to Growth* was "a commando operation. It was aimed at breaking a stalemate situation and transforming it into one of dynamic debate as a prelude to action... a means to arouse our awareness... not an instrument for planning or decision making" nor an impassive, scholarly treatise like Brown's *Challenge* or the "Blueprint." "The Club of Rome was aware that the research would probably conclude with a very serious warning that unless a great change of direction does occur, mankind is heading towards a series of grave crises—possibly of unprecedented dimensions."[95]

Not everyone saw it that way. To economist Henry C. Wallich, economic growth is "positively enjoyable."

> It is an alarming commentary on the intellectual instability of our times that today mileage can be made with the proposal to stop America dead in her tracks. Don't we know which way is forward?... Growth is a substitute for equality of income. So long as there is growth, there is hope, and that makes large income differentials tolerable. The environment will also be better taken care of if the economy grows. Nothing could cut more dangerously into the resources that must be devoted to the Great Cleanup than an attempt to limit resources available for consumption.[96]

Wallich argued that faster growth would give the government the revenues to help care for the poor, the aged, and the unemployed.

Thus a "Doomsday Debate" developed. Anthony Lewis wrote editorials attacking Wallich,[97] and biologist Barry Commoner gave mankind the option of either a "rational, social organization of the use and distribution of the earth's resources, or a new barbarism."[98] But *Nature* editor John Maddox scolded the alarmists and suggested that there is a good chance that "the problems of the 1970s and 1980s will not be famine and starvation but, ironically, the problems of how best to dispose of food surpluses in countries where famine has until recently been endemic."[99]

The formal presentation of *The Limits to Growth* study at the Smithsonian

---

[94] Aurelio Peccei, *The Chasm Ahead* (London: Macmillan, 1969).
[95] Aurelio Peccei and Manfred Siebker, " 'The Limits to Growth' In Perspective," a paper submitted at the request of the Economic Committee of the Parliamentary Assembly of the Council of Europe, December 1972, pp. 17–19.
[96] Henry C. Wallich, "Zero Growth," *Newsweek*, January 24, 1972, p. 62.
[97] *New York Times*, January 29, 1972, p. 29, and January 31, 1972, p. 41.
[98] Barry Commoner, *The Closing Circle: Nature, Man and Technology* (New York: Bantam, 1971), p. 295.
[99] John Maddox, *The Doomsday Syndrome* (New York: McGraw-Hill, 1972), p. 5.

Institution is reported on in Chapter 1. The drama of the event so powerfully affected journalist David Hacker that he was moved to write, "Mark March 2, 1972, on your calendar as a day that history may record to be as important to mankind as the Council of Nicaea in 325 and Martin Luther's tacking his ninety-five theses on the church door in Wittenburg, Germany, in 1517. This was the day *The Limits to Growth* was unveiled to the public."[100] Humorist Russell Baker had a somewhat different reaction.

> Now it appears that it wasn't a joke after all. The world really is coming to an end. We have it from a computer, which has examined or processed or done whatever computers do to, or with, or at, a mathematical model of the world. (How typical, how depressing that most of us, dependent upon a computer and a mathematical model for news of doomsday's imminence, don't even know what a mathematical model is, or what a computer does with it, or to it, or at it).... "The mind boggles," said Elliot Richardson, Secretary of Health, Education, and Welfare, who was there. He was right. Just reading about the prospect from a safe distance is enough to make the mind boggle. And yet, the mind stops boggling very soon, absorbs the fact—"Yes, the world really is coming to an end this time"—and resumes functioning on the old ante-doomsday assumption that everything is going to come out all right in the end.[101]

Classifying the Responses

The week of the Smithsonian presentation marked the start of an avalanche of reactions to *The Limits to Growth*. Robert Gillette called the debut "the first but probably not the last act of a remarkably successful venture in the mass marketing of neo-Malthusian economics."[102] *The Economist* said the report "represents the highwater mark of an old-fashioned nonsense, because the M.I.T. team has pumped into its computer so many dear, dead assumptions."[103] In general, the responses fall into four schools of thought: Malthusian-pessimists, technological-optimists, economic-optimists, and confrontationists.

The Malthusian-pessimists, consisting of Forrester, Meadows, their followers, many ecologists, and certain public officials, see a world with fixed resources threatened by growing population, pollution, famine, resource depletion, and overcrowding. Malthusian-pessimists are also variously referred to as the no-growth school, ecomilitants, environmaniacs, neoMalthusians, and doomsayers. Ecologist Garrett Hardin, a member of the group and a defender of *The Limits to Growth* study writes, "Most of the population con-

---

[100] *National Observer,* March 11, 1972, p. 12.

[101] *New York Times Magazine,* March 5, 1972, p. 13.

[102] Robert Gillette, "The Limits to Growth: Hard Sell for a Computer View of Doomsday," *Science* 175 (1972): 1088–1092.

[103] "Limits to Misconception," *The Economist,* March 11, 1972, pp. 70–72.

troversy is waged between those who have thought about population and those who have not."[104]

> People who ... believe that ... technology will continue to improve as it has during the last two centuries will be proven wrong (if ever) only by our reaching the limits of technology. By the time we do that, it will be too late to survive as a species without a dreadful "crash."[105]

Paul Ehrlich adds that "abuse of the environment must soon halt if catastrophic increases in human misery are to be avoided."[106] Sicco L. Mansholt of the Netherlands, former president of the Common Market Commission, warns of disaster if growth rates are not checked. "Obviously, the society of tomorrow cannot be based on growth, at least not in material goods."[107]

Technological-optimists (sometimes referred to demeaningly as "cheermongers"), in contrast, consist of industrialists and technocrats who feel that technology will continue to evolve fast enough to keep pace with the problems of burgeoning population, pollution, and resource depletion. The following remark expresses this point of view: "While no one knows for certain, technical progress shows no sign of slowing down. The best econometric estimates suggest that it is indeed growing exponentially."[108] Even a Club of Rome member, Jeremy Bray, expresses faith in technology: "... moving on from one technology to the next, we have scarcely begun to conceive the possibilities. There is no justification for facile optimism about technological development. But there is still less room for defeatism."[109] In a typical technologically optimistic commentary, a Japanese chemical engineering company claims that "it is through better technology that man will solve the problems caused by industrial progress."[110]

The economic-optimist (or growth) school is closely allied with the technological-optimists. It consists of businessmen and economists like Wallich who feel that growth is necessary for the economic system to be able to handle its problems. "It is growth, after all," writes Tilford Gaines, senior vice-president and economist for Manufacturers Hanover Trust, "that will provide the products and services needed to eliminate want worldwide and to reduce pollution without reducing the real scale of living of people. Also, growth provides the

---

[104] Garrett Hardin, *Population, Evolution, and Birth Control* (San Francisco: W. H. Freeman, 1969), p. 107.
[105] Garrett Hardin, "Limits to Growth," *International Development Review* 14, no. 4 (1972): 37–39.
[106] Paul Ehrlich and J. P. Holdren, "Limits to Growth," 1972, mimeo, p. 1.
[107] *New York Times,* May 14, 1972, p. 12.
[108] Peter Passell, Marc Roberts, and Leonard Ross, "The Limits to Growth; World Dynamics; Urban Dynamics," *New York Times Book Review,* April 2, 1972, p. 1.
[109] Jeremy Bray, "The Politics of the Environment," Fabian Tract 412, 1972, p. 10.
[110] From an advertisement by CHIYODA Chemical Engineering and Construction Company, Ltd., Yokohama, Japan, in *Scientific American,* March 1974, p. 91.

incentive for technological breakthroughs that will restrain our consumption of limited resources by developing economically usable substitutes."[111] Full-length books have been devoted to defending growth.[112] To economists like Robert M. Solow of M.I.T., excessive pollution results from a flaw in the price system: namely, "generators of waste are allowed to dump that waste into the environment... without paying the full cost of what they do."[113] To Howard K. Smith of ABC News, who accused *The Limits to Growth* study of "dour intellectual pessimism" and "linear, wooden logic," economic growth and technical advance are not the "villains of our future," but rather, "the heroes that will save us."[114] But to Malcolm Slessor, Meadows has essentially pulled the carpet out from beneath the economists.

> All their training, their research and their ethos has been concerned with ways in which the economy can be stimulated and expanded. Practically no economist has given serious thought to the problems of economic stability. For one thing stability is read as stagnation, and for another it is hard to find an employer who is interested in economic equilibrium. It has no appeal to governments, politicians, board chairmen, company presidents or even to used car salesmen. As one economist remarked, "If Meadows is right, then we've been wasting our time."[115]

The confrontationists, finally, steer a middle course. They do not espouse a particular ideology but confront specific problems that are becoming critical. Confrontationists do not see economic growth as either inherently evil or as necessary for bettering the lot of mankind. They consider growth good insofar as it aids in the solution of the world's problems and bad to the extent that its side-effects exacerbate these problems. Ronald Ridker of Resources for the Future argues that "the relevant question is not whether to grow or not to grow, but how to channel and redirect economic output... [to] serve humanity's needs." Ridker believes we "appear to have the resources and the know-how both to continue growing and to cope with the problems of growth, if we are willing to adjust our life-styles."[116] Ridker thinks, for example, that pollution in the United States could be controlled by a transfer of .1 percent in the annual growth of GNP into its abatement. The confrontationists treat each area separately as a specific problem needing a specific answer, while noting the

---

[111] Tilford Gaines, "The Doomsday Debate," *Manufacturers Hanover Trust Economic Report*, March 1972, p. 1.

[112] Wilfred Beckerman, *In Defense of Economic Growth* (London: Jonathan Cape, 1974).

[113] Robert M. Solow, "Is the End of the World At Hand?" *Challenge*, March–April 1973, p. 49.

[114] Howard K. Smith, ABC Evening News, March 30, 1972.

[115] Malcolm Slessor, "The Limits to Growth," *The Ecologist*, June 1972, p. 43.

[116] Ronald G. Ridker, "To Grow or Not to Grow: That's Not the Relevant Question," *Science* 176 (1973): 1315–1316.

System Dynamics—A Controversial Newcomer

general direction indicated by current trends. "To ignore the future implications of present-day trends is as irrational as to assume that these trends will continue unchanged."[117]

Environmental administrator Russell E. Train applauded *The Limits to Growth* and "The Blueprint for Survival" for having raised critical issues that demand attention. "One need not accept the dire hypotheses and methods underlying some of the more extreme predictions to acknowledge the fundamental validity of the questions these various groups are asking."[118] The resulting debate has been lively, although too often there "has been a penchant for arguing against positions that the other side hasn't taken"[119]—sometimes through misunderstanding and sometimes through design, which Alan Coddington derides in his paper on "The Cheermongers or How to Stop Worrying and Love Economic Growth."

> The cheermonger's basic tactic for overturning the pessimistic scenarios of eco-militants is fairly straightforward and involves four steps:
> (i) accuse the ecomilitant of oversimplification in his views;
> (ii) complicate one aspect of the issue until it becomes an open question;
> (iii) take an optimistic view about the open question;
> (iv) present this optimism as the product of greater sophistication in thinking about the issue.
>
> What is simply an affirmation of optimism is accordingly disguised as a move to a higher level of sophistication.[120]

Forrester attributes misunderstanding of his work to the nature of social science education and its failure to deal adequately with dynamic behavior, feedbacks, and formal modeling. But educational factors cannot account for all of the disagreement. There is hardly an aspect of the world modeling studies that has not been roundly criticized. Critics balked at the lack of data, the unreliability of what data there were, the failure to distinguish between developed and underdeveloped nations, the high level of aggregation, the different levels of detail in different sectors of the model, the "built-in" Malthusian collapse, the lack of any pricing structure for scarce resources, the fixed limit to natural resources, and the absence of renewable resources. Also criticized were the model's sensitivity to the "wrong" variables, the lack of adjustment of birth rates to death rates, the failure to include societal response to crises, the lack of faith in technology and economics, the failure to specify any practical means for carrying out recommended policy actions, and even the

---

[117] Rudolf Klein, "Growth and its Enemies," *Commentary,* June 1972, p. 41.

[118] Russell E. Train, remarks at the Smithsonian "Sustainable Growth" Forum, November 20, 1972.

[119] Gaines, p. 1.

[120] Alan Coddington, "The Cheermongers, or How to Stop Worrying and Love Economic Growth," *Your Environment,* Autumn 1972.

delay in publication of technical documentation. The Club of Rome took sixteen pages for a partial summary of criticisms and rejoinders,[121] a subcommittee of the House of Representatives published one thousand pages of papers, reviews, and testimony,[122] a special task force of the World Bank produced a ninety-four-page document on alleged shortcomings,[123] the United Nations performed a critical analysis for its World Population Conference,[124] and a collection was made of the comments of some seventy scholars[125]—all this on the issues raised by *World Dynamics* and *The Limits to Growth*.

Forrester asks why it is that a model that seems to have everything wrong with it (according to its detractors) has attracted so much attention, such a determined group of critics, and such a large number of man-hours spent in analysis. His answer is that the issues are of the greatest importance and the model is the most comprehensive and persuasive available. Forrester proposes the world models as stepping stones to better models in the future, but the character of much of the reaction indicates that this is not, for the most part, how they have been received.

Counter Modeling of the World Models

"Counter modeling" is the running of a model under a change of assumptions to produce results counter to those obtained from the original version. It is a new form of policy dialogue based on computer modeling. By publishing and documenting a policy model thoroughly, the modeler becomes subject to counter modeling, the counter modeler to counter-counter modeling, and so on. Unlike many policy models, World2 and World3 are thoroughly documented. They have probably been the most extensively counter modeled of any world models to date.

A group of researchers from Shell Laboratories in Amsterdam produced one of the first counter models of World2. They implemented two types of automatic social feedback in their version of the model: as pollution rises, more capital is allocated to pollution control; as natural resources become scarce, more money is spent to increase the amount of economically recoverable reserves by means of exploration, recycling, and the development of substitutes.

---

[121] Peccei and Siebker.

[122] *Growth and Its Implications for the Future, Part 1,* Hearings Before the Subcommittee on Fisheries and Wildlife Conservation and the Environment of the Committee on Merchant Marine and Fisheries, House of Representatives, 93rd Cong., 1st sess., May 1, 1973, Serial Number 93-7.

[123] Mahbud ul Haq et al., *Report on the Limits to Growth,* a study by a special task force of the World Bank, September 1972.

[124] Nicholas G. Carter, "Critical Review of Recent Population-Resources-Environmental Models," United Nations Economic and Social Council, August 24, 1973.

[125] Oltmans.

The results show "a much more stable future outlook, which is less prone to crises than the World2 and World3 models." The pollution feedback has "a strongly stabilizing effect" on the model's behavior, and "different but reasonable assumptions about future discoveries [of resources] and the influence of technology on these can yield a spectrum of future outlooks that are not all *a priori* unattractive." Even under "relatively moderate assumptions, the population level stabilizes and no dramatic effects occur before 2100."[126]

In another counter modeling effort at about the same time, Robert Boyd of the University of California at Davis introduced the technological-optimist point of view into the Malthusian-pessimist World2 model to see if it would change the results. He did this by adding a technology factor that aided food production, pollution control, and resource conservation. In Boyd's version of World2, technology is increased as capital investment rises and as quality of life falls. His results "are exactly what a technological-optimist would predict. Technology increases productivity, which in turn increases the standard of living. This eventually drives birth rates low enough that a 'Utopian' equilibrium is reached."[127]

Boyd concludes that the World2 model cannot contribute to clarifying the technological-optimist/Malthusian-pessimist debate—that it merely reflects the opinions of the model builders.

> With neoMalthusian assumptions, the world model yields results which are qualitatively the same as those the neoMalthusians produce without the use of computers; with assumptions of a technological optimist, the model yields a technological optimist's results. Thus, in the absence of any additional empirical input, the model does very little to help us decide between the two positions.[128]

In his counter model, Boyd assumes that a quadrupling of the 1970 level of world technology will produce zero usage of natural resources and zero production of pollution. Forrester takes exception to these assumptions, and contends that a slight relaxation of the absolute zero assumptions causes the Boyd model to revert to the behavior of World2.[129] Forrester calls Boyd irresponsible

---

[126] T. W. Oerlemans, M. M. J. Tellings, and H. DeVries, "World Dynamics: Social Feedback May Give Hope for the Future," *Nature* 238 (1972): 251–255. Another counter model of the pollution sector of the World2 model (by M. R. Berg in 1971) is cited in Kan Chen, "An Evaluation of Forrester-Type Growth Models," *IEEE Transactions on Systems, Man, and Cybernetics,* SMC-3, no. 6 (1973): 631–632.

[127] Robert Boyd, "World Dynamics: A note," *Science* 177 (1972): 517. For a similar counter modeling study of the World2 model introducing the level variable "knowledge" instead of "technology," see Jerrold H. Krenz, "World Dynamics: An Alternative Model," *IEEE Transactions on Systems, Man, and Cybernetics,* SMC-3, no. 4 (1973): 272–275.

[128] Robert Boyd, Letter to the editor, *Science* 180 (1973): 1238.

[129] Jay W. Forrester, "Educational Implications of Responses to System Dynamics Models" (Cambridge, Mass.: Wright-Allen Press, 1974), p. 9. System Dynamics Information Interchange No. 2, D-2021, May 30, 1974.

for presenting assumptions in which he, himself, does not believe. Boyd does consider zero resource usage plausible in view of the fact that "new" resources such as uranium have actually increased the quantity of available resources over the past century. But he is not, himself, a technological optimist and he agrees that the assumption of zero pollution generation might be unfair. (One scientist charges that this assumption violates the second law of thermodynamics.)[130] Boyd asserts that his results are unchanged when pollution generation is taken to be 1 percent of the 1970 level.[131]

Boyd's optimistic assumptions also drew criticism from Peter Boyce and Thomas Boyle. They replaced Boyd's zero pollution and zero resource usage with the assumption that "each fourfold increase in technology produces a tenfold decrease in resource usage and pollution."[132] Boyce and Boyle say that population in their version "grinds on in standard Malthusian fashion," reaching fifteen billion in the year 2100, while quality of life continually remains below the 1970 level.

Support for Boyd's technologically optimistic assumptions comes from a study of data on past technological progress.[133] From fluorescent lights to cyclotrons to computers, the study indicates a consistent historical pattern of overall exponential growth of technology despite a leveling off in the capacities of individual technologies. The study predicts that repeated inventions of new types of technology will more than compensate for future rises in population and pollution.

Another counter model of the World2 model, called GLOBE 5 (later expanded to GLOBE 6), is "more stable and notably less sensitive to the generation of pollution" than World2.[134] The relative insensitivity to pollution is due to the fact that the time constant governing the rate at which the environment absorbs pollution is taken to be independent of the amount of pollution present, thus eliminating a strong positive feedback loop and a possible source of pollution "runaway" in World2.

The first counter modeling of the World3 model, appearing almost a year after publication of *The Limits to Growth*, was a comprehensive interdisciplinary sector-by-sector analysis by the Science Policy Research Unit of the University of Sussex, England.[135] Part of the Sussex analysis was done on World2 because of its relative simplicity. But most of the study was based on

---

[130] Paul E. Damon, Letter to the editor, *Science* 180 (1973): 1236.

[131] Boyd, "Letter," p. 1239.

[132] Unpublished letter by Peter B. Boyce and Thomas J. Boyle, Lowell Observatory, Flagstaff, Arizona, in reference to Boyd.

[133] Chauncey Starr and Richard Rudman, "Parameters of Technological Growth," *Science* 182 (1973): 358–364.

[134] Robert Burnett and Paul Dionne, "Globe 6: A Multiregion Interactive World Simulation," *Simulation*, June 1973, p. 193.

[135] Cole.

a preliminary description of the World3 model, sent out to six groups thirty months before final, official documentation of the model was released.

A different individual or group in Sussex critically analyzed each sector of World3 (nonrenewable resources, population, agriculture, pollution, capital, and industrial output). According to Sussex, the model is "very sensitive to input parameters which have a wide margin of error" and "a high rate of growth is just as likely as a catastrophic collapse." The model is "very sensitive to relatively small changes in the industrial output/capital ratio and other economic relationships which are assumed, with very little empirical justification, to be constants. Relatively small changes to this ratio can prevent any economic growth occurring or, at the other extreme, lead to collapse by 1970."[136]

Sussex takes account of possibilities for recycling and natural resource discovery by adding a fixed per annum rate of discovery to World2. By another per annum rate, it represents an increasing technical ability to control the emission of pollution. One percent per annum rates postpone collapse from resource shortages significantly, while 2 percent per annum rates postpone it "indefinitely." To test the validity of using world averages, Sussex divides World2 into a pair of models representing the developed and underdeveloped regions of the world. "When run separately, the two models do not generate good histories of their respective regions nor does the total match the trends of the original model." To improve the fit, Sussex provides for "flows of capital, resources, and pollution between the two regions.... Both resource and capital flow have to be in the direction of the developed region. Pollution transfer is in the opposite direction."[137]

Based on its counter modeling of the World3 model, and assuming that future advances in technological, economic, and sociopolitical activities will be made continually, Sussex concludes that a halt to growth during the next two centuries is not inevitable because of physical limits. Sussex feels that:

> Forrester's claim that computer models are necessarily superior to mental models is not borne out by either World2 or World3. Decision makers concerned with, say, pollution control, agriculture or natural resources might have very simplified and imperfect mental models but, given their first-hand knowledge of the subject matter, they might also have avoided the rather elementary mistakes made in the assumptions of World2 and World3.
>
> Perhaps the best result one could hope for from any model like the two discussed here is that they contain the seeds of their own destruction—and of their replacement by superior models. Worlds2 and 3 may prove to be useful stepping stones to better models.
>
> There seems to be no reason why mathematical models (including system

---

[136] Ibid., p. 130.
[137] Ibid., pp. 119–120.

dynamics models) should not eventually become an important tool for structuring, classifying and communicating ideas in the social sciences, as they already are in the natural sciences. What does seem especially important, however, is that the work of modelers (and their critics) should not be viewed as a totally objective or apolitical statement of real world situations. Neither should modelers pretend that it is.[138]

The World3 team took issue with Sussex, charging that "the basic points of our modeling effort, as described in *Limits,* have been misunderstood or distorted by the Sussex group, or ignored by them in their attention to nonessential details of the World models."[139]

One of the allegedly "nonessential details" was Sussex's attempt to run the World2 model *backwards* from 1900 (by setting the time increment negative) to see if the model would reproduce earlier history. The result was an absurdity, namely that the twentieth century seemed to lie in the aftermath of a catastrophic population collapse occurring about 1880. The World3 team points out that when the model is run in reverse, negative loops become positive loops and normally insignificant errors eliminated by negative feedback accumulate, a problem that Sussex acknowledges but considers irrelevant to its conclusions. Says Sussex,

> as a model is a mimic of reality, it should reflect mechanisms and trends for the period of interest. If the same mechanisms were important in the past (before that period of interest) it is only reasonable to expect that a model should "backcast" or extrapolate into the past.... To argue that one may not backcast using a model is to say that mechanisms were in fact different in the past.... To argue that one should not attempt to backcast using a system dynamics model, while at the same time admitting that the same mechanisms operated in the past, is to say that such models are beyond the reach of normal scientific criticism.[140]

According to Richard D. Wright, "There is no set of reasonable 1880 initial values to yield behavior consistent with the 1900 starting point of *World Dynamics.*"[141] But Wright believes that backcasting is too perilous a vehicle to be used for testing models.

Harold A. Linstone believes most people have a very short planning horizon and heavily discount occurrences much beyond the immediate future. To

---

[138] Ibid., p. 134.

[139] D. H. Meadows et al., *Models of Doom,* p. 231.

[140] H. S. D. Cole and R. C. Curnow, " 'Backcasting' with the World Dynamic Models," *Nature* 243 (1973): 64. Cole and Curnow argue that backcasting is only valid under certain numerical conditions (fulfilled in the case of the World2 backcast). They contend that Meadows' point on the reversal of positive and negative loops is irrelevant to the issue of World2's structural as opposed to numerical instability.

[141] Richard D. Wright, "Retrodictive Tests of Dynamic Models," *Proceedings of the 1973 Summer Computer Simulation Conference,* Montreal, July 17–19, p. 1091.

make his point, Linstone applied several discount rates to the population and pollution curves of the World3 model. Discounting at 5 percent per year reduces the population and pollution crises to minor significance; at 10 percent, the crises are barely perceptible.[142] Linstone feels that prevention of crises is made very difficult by our inability to perceive their seriousness until they are almost upon us.

Counter modeling can provide a check on the accuracy of the original modeling effort. Thomas J. Boyle was translating a preliminary version of the World3 model from one programming language (DYNAMO) to another (FORTRAN) when he chanced upon a typographical error in the pollution-generation-multiplier-from-output table. Whenever world industrial output per capita fell in the range of $800 to $1,200, the error caused pollution generated to exceed by ten times its intended value.[143] Boyle charged there were major discrepancies in three of the twelve runs published in *The Limits to Growth* traceable to this error. The Meadowses, while acknowledging the error and its quantitative effect on the runs, say that "it does not influence the system instability reflected in those runs, nor does it invalidate or even address any of the basic assumptions in the model. . . . Pollution crises occur . . . where the error is not even present."[144]

O. Rademaker, J. G. M. Cuypers and their colleagues at the Global Dynamics Group in the Netherlands have been conducting a continuing and intensive counter modeling effort of the World models. They agree that unlimited growth of population and prosperity is not possible and that the message of the Club of Rome must be studied seriously and thoroughly. Yet their enthusiasm for system dynamics is qualified: "The method is in principle of the best kind available, and it is of great potential interest to try to improve it and to get what one can out of it. But at the same time it is clear that one must be extremely careful in attributing to the results the slightest realistic value."[145]

Cuypers and Rademaker derived a simple linearized version of the World2 model by taking a first-order Taylor-series approximation of the equations of the model, replacing the table functions with linear segments over appropriate

---

[142] Harold A. Linstone, "On Discounting the Future," *Technological Forecasting and Social Change* 4 (1973): 335–336.

[143] Thomas J. Boyle, "Hope for the Technological Solution," *Nature* 245 (1973): 127–128. The error was corrected in January 1972 and does not appear in any published account of the World3 model equations.

[144] Donella H. Meadows and Dennis L. Meadows, "Typographical Errors and Technological Solutions," *Nature* 247 (1974): 98. The Meadowses were highly incensed at Boyle's having obtained his program listing without authorization.

[145] O. Rademaker, "Project Group Global Dynamics Progress Report No. 1," IV (Eindhoven, The Netherlands: Technische Hogeschool Eindhoven, April 23, 1972), pp. 6–7. Previously we quoted Henri Theil on the same point: "Models are to be used but not to be believed." Henri Theil, *Principles of Econometrics* (New York: John Wiley & Sons, 1971), p. vi.

domains, and discarding insignificant terms.[146] The reduced model gives insight into the larger model. For example, it suggests:

> only capital investment has positive feedback, i.e., that from 1900 to a considerable time after 1970 it grows more or less exponentially, and that the population, as also all other state variables, have a net negative feedback, in other words, they have no inherent inclination to exponential growth. The more or less exponential growth of population and pollution from 1900 to after 1970 is, indeed, not brought about by an inclination to growth within these sectors themselves, but because they are, so to speak, "driven" by the more or less exponentially growing production.[147]

Cuypers and Rademaker dispute Forrester's claim that the behavior of his models is "counterintuitive," calling some of his modeling exercises "counterrealistic rather than counterintuitive," and asserting that insistence on counterintuitive behavior "can mean but one thing, namely that the model is not understood well enough."[148]

The Global Dynamics Group distilled the World2 model down to five strong relationships and the World3 model to eight. The resources and capital sector in the simplified World3 model, as in the simplified World2 model, "develops largely autonomously and exerts a significant influence on the population sector."[149] In addition, the simplified World3 model obeys a "law of Total Possible Industrial Output"; i.e., the total industrial output from 1900 on is almost completely specified by the amount of natural resources in 1900. Attempts to raise this output hasten collapse; slowdowns in output postpone collapse.

Counter modeling and critical review of the world models shows little sign of abating. *The Limits to Growth* hit a nerve. As Robert Socolow puts it, "... the amount of commentary—pro, con, and orthogonal—has exceeded the original text by a factor of several hundred. Like *Love Story* and *Greening of America*, it is simply not permissible to have nothing to say about *The Limits to Growth*."[150]

---

[146] J. G. M. Cuypers and O. Rademaker, "An Analysis of Forrester's World Dynamics Model," U16 (Eindhoven, The Netherlands: Technische Hogeschool Eindhoven, May 1, 1973). Also published in *Automatica* 10 (1973): 195–201. Our own analysis of the Cuypers-Rademaker linearization suggests that they were somewhat lucky to be working with the standard World2 model in 1970. Under a change of parameters and at different times, their linearization procedure may not be successful.

[147] O. Rademaker, "Project Group Global Dynamics Progress Report No. 2," V2 (Eindhoven, The Netherlands: Technische Hogeschool Eindhoven, December 21, 1972), pp. 11–14.

[148] Cuypers and Rademaker, p. 2.

[149] O. Rademaker, "Project Group Global Dynamics Progress Report No. 3," V3 (Eindhoven, The Netherlands: Technische Hogeschool Eindhoven, March 31, 1974), p. 13.

[150] Robert H. Socolow, "Ruminations on *The Limits to Growth* and the Fractured Academy," *Journal of Dynamic Systems, Measurement, and Control*, March 1973.

Another Club of Rome Project

The Club of Rome had mixed feelings about *The Limits to Growth* study. The study achieved the club's goal of sounding an alarm, but the criticism it drew makes club members uncomfortable. Some members feared that people identify the system dynamics World models and their faults with the Club of Rome itself, damaging the club's credibility. As if partly to uncouple itself from system dynamics, the Club of Rome sponsored several other world modeling efforts that used different methodologies. A Dutch project entitled "The Problems of Population Doubling" used an input-output framework to investigate problems of the human race during the next two-decade period when world population was expected to double.[151] In Japan, Yoichi Kaya and the Japan Work Team of the Club of Rome used a hierarchical approach to model Japanese social events, the Japanese economy, and the world economy.[152] The Dutch and Japanese projects disaggregated the variables of the World3 model by such categories as geographical region, agricultural and manufacturing production, pollution generated, and per capita income. In Argentina, the Bariloche Foundation sponsored a normative "alternative" model of the world to suggest world policies that might allow every world citizen his proper allocation of food, shelter, education and health.[153]

A few years after publication of *The Limits to Growth*—the "First Report to the Club of Rome on the Predicament of Mankind"—two Club of Rome members, Mihajlo D. Mesarovic and Eduard Pestel, produced a "Second Report" entitled *Mankind at the Turning Point*. The authors experimented with an econometric-based world system computer model based on Mesarovic's "hierarchical approach to the analysis and control of large-scale complex systems."[154] There are many similarities between the two reports. They have the same sponsor (The Club of Rome), the same financial backing (The Volkswagen Foundation), both report on models of the world system, neither contains much technical documentation, and both are exhortatory and predict dire consequences for the planet if action is not taken to harness growth. Yet the second report separates itself from the first, mentioning it only twice (once in a figure and once in a footnote) and pointedly declaring that its own analysis is "*based on all available data.*" Also, its model is "... fundamentally different from any previously developed, for it recognizes the diversity that exists in

---

[151] Hans Linneman, "Report to the Club of Rome on the Project 'Problems of Population Doubling'," The Hague, The Netherlands, September 1973.

[152] Kaya and Suzuki.

[153] Herrera. The project is under the direction of Amilcar O. Herrera. It and other Club of Rome projects are reviewed in Aurelio Peccei, "The Club of Rome: Its Activity and Scope," *Successo,* January 1975, pp. 156–157.

[154] Mesarovic documents the hierarchical approach in two books, *Theory of Multi-Level Hierarchical Systems* (New York: Academic Press, 1970) and "General Systems Theory" (forthcoming).

the world ... reflects the adaptive nature and subjective character intrinsic to any system involving human elements ... [and deals] with issues concretely, rather than in abstract terms."[155] The second report asserts that modeling the world system as a homogeneous monolith "as has been done in earlier world modeling efforts is inaccurate and can be misleading."

The authors disaggregate the world into ten interconnected regions based on similar history, traditions, economic development, political system, and commonality of major problems. The regions are divided into strata (physical, organizational, and individual) and the strata into substrata (the physical into geophysical, ecological, and technological; the organizational into economic, formal, and sociopolitical; and the individual into human conditions and cultural norms). The authors refer to modeling the present as "objective" and modeling the future as "subjective." Their method of "scenario analysis" projects the "objective" part of the model under "subjective" sequences of future scenarios to explore the effects of policy choices. The model, unlike World3, allows the user (presumably a policymaker) to enter value choices and policy actions from a list of policy alternatives after each ten-year period. The authors view their system not as a predictor but as an instrument for extending one's logic and assessing the consequences of implementing one's vision of the future—as a computer-based planning and decision aiding tool rather than as a computer model in the traditional sense: "In order to arrive at a more definite conclusion one tries in general an entire spectrum of alternative scenarios. If the analysis of the computer runs for all of them leads to essentially the same conclusion, such an event could be expected with a higher degree of certainty."[156]

The authors apply scenario analysis to economic development of the third world, population growth, the effect of economic warfare in the Mideast on gross regional product, the food shortage in South Asia, and world energy. They come out favoring what they call "organic growth," by which they mean the cooperative and selective economic growth of regions in a way that mutually meets each other's needs. Organic growth is growth with differentiation, say the authors, as opposed to undifferentiated growth, which is growth in quantity only. The authors draw an analogy between the organic growth of an organization and that of the world system, and use the analogy to make a point: In nature organic growth proceeds according to a "blueprint" encoded in the DNA molecule. There is, so far, no such master plan for the growth of mankind.

The emphasis on organic growth has the effect of further separating *Man-*

---

[155] Mesarovic and Pestel, pp. 1–2, 43 (their italics).
[156] Eduard Pestel, "Multilevel Regionalized World Modeling Project: Motivation, Objectives, and Conceptual Foundation," Delivered at International Institute for Applied Systems Analysis, Vienna, April 1974, p. 12.

kind at the Turning Point from the *Limits to Growth* in that the concept of organic growth may be palatable to the same opponents of the zero growth school who objected strenuously to the type of world equilibrium proposed in *Limits*. (Some see this as a ploy by the authors of *Mankind*.) The disaggregated representation of the world system that the authors put forward allows them to develop explicitly their idea of organic growth. It is not clear how this could have been done in the highly aggregated World3 model.

A VIEW OF THE BRIDGE

The Club of Rome is a humanitarian organization that may be on its way toward earning a place in the history books of future generations. The full measure of its contribution and the real impact of its studies will not be known for years to come. Yet one result of these studies, bearing directly on the subject of this book, is clear today. *Limits* and *Mankind*, among the other studies, have forcefully demonstrated, each in its own way, the dramatic power and political potential of computer modeling in issue making and public debate.

The enormous controversy aroused by *Limits*, and the bitter opposition it has received from the economics profession and many other quarters, cause some people to regard it as a passing storm. Yet we find continued use of the phrase "limits to growth." The Club of Rome is jointly sponsoring a ten-year program of biennial conferences designed to "stimulate ongoing international debate on the limits and alternatives to growth," and has well-known people from around the world participating.[157] The Club of Rome may be having more than a short-term impact. With a strong assist from computer modeling, it may yet succeed not only in awakening public concern, but also in effecting what it most desires—a long-term reordering of national priorities throughout the world.

Mankind at the Turning Point, with its own brand of modeling, has also received a great deal of public attention—and its share of dissent. Two highly regarded econometric modelers who served as advisers to the project counseled the codirectors not to go public when they did in late 1974. The economic advisors believed the project's modeling effort required another year of work before its results could be accepted with reasonable confidence. Their caution was overruled. Model validity and political pay dirt do not move hand in hand. This is not to say that either objective is right or wrong, but they are different.

---

[157] Announcement of the conference "Limits to Growth '75," the First Biennial Assessment of Alternatives to Growth, The Woodlands, Texas, October 19–21, 1975, showed as participants: Elise Boulding, Lester Brown, Edward Goldsmith, Hazel Henderson, Jacob K. Javits, Herman Kahn, Hans Linneman, Gordon J. MacDonald, Sicco Mansholt, Donald Michaels, Lewis J. Perelman, and Ernst F. Schumacher.

Misunderstanding and mischief are possible when the distinction between them is glossed over or when the second goal is pursued to the exclusion of the first.

No one with modeling experience needs to be reminded of how chameleon-like a model can be in outward appearance depending upon the modeler's choice of assumptions and parameter values. The importance of trying to understand why a model produces the results it does—and what is required to alter these results—is known to anyone who has worked closely with a complex model. This leads us to make two related observations. First, policymakers and the general public are not equipped by themselves to assess the significance and reliability of policy modeling. They require interpreters—expert intermediaries, in effect. Second, there must be skilled professionals with modeling experience who understand other people's models well enough to serve this interpreter's function. The role requires intermediaries who can analyze the other fellow's model critically but objectively, test its assumptions, check its results, and assess it for perspective.

There is a need for two kinds of bridges. The first is a bridge across the gulf that divides policy modelers from policymakers. This need, which has both intellectual and institutional aspects, is discussed at length in our concluding chapter. The second need—less obvious than the first but just as real—is for a bridge between modelers of different persuasions and/or methodological backgrounds. This bridge is primarily intellectual in nature. To the extent it exists today, modelers tend to be reluctant to cross it. It is only human to feel most comfortable with one's own ideas and ways of doing things. As illustrated by the volleys between Nordhaus and Forrester over World2—delivered on separate courts with each man following his own set of rules—or as seen in the disagreement between staff and advisers over urban dynamics, there can be no meaningful interchange and learning unless the opposing parties talk the same language with open minds. If this is asking too much, then we need third parties who can speak several languages and understand a range of perspectives and points of view. Third parties may find it easier to open their minds than the modelers themselves.

The spread of system dynamics underscores the importance of model checking and analysis. We believe this may be one of the most important long-run contributions of system dynamics to policy modeling. System dynamics provides a pressing case for model analysis and the erection of intellectual bridges between modelers. The methodology has done this by illustrating the political potency of policy models on timely issues of general concern, unencumbered by the formal data requirements that burden more traditional modelers. At the same time that system dynamics modelers have attracted widespread interest, they have, in effect, challenged other modelers to understand their models well enough to make intelligent comments, appraisals, alterations, and improvements. The frequent response made by critics that the burden of proof is on the system dynamics modelers may be valid, but it sounds very faint, indeed, in the public clamor aroused by the system dynamics models.

Forrester and Meadows presented their models as stepping stones to better models. For this reason, among others, they went to some length to document and explain their models. The urban and world models have certainly been among the best documented policy models of all time—a characteristic made possible by the relatively simple formations of these models and the absence of extensive formal data for estimation. As a consequence, they have also been among the most examined models of all time. But the heavy amount of counter modeling they occasioned did not lead, in general, to better models, partly because that was not the intention of most counter modelers and partly because those being counter modeled did not really appear that eager to be improved upon.

Many counter modelers and critics of the system dynamics models are offended by what they regard as Forrester's tendency to indulge in overstatement and to portray system dynamics as the only worthwhile modeling methodology. To them, Forrester seems to be saying, "All of you other modelers are wasting your time." The resulting resentment stands in the way of cross-methodological communication.

Forrester, aware of the communication problem his manner engenders, has extended the olive branch to his economist adversaries on more than one occasion. Yet by all indications, more heated battling lies ahead. Forrester's most ambitious project to date is a 2,000 state-variable model of the national economy designed to produce, within reason, the economic behavior of the United States from 1800 to the present time, then a forward projection for another seventy-five years or more.[158] Forrester says he wants his model to be equally applicable to the Indian, Russian, or Chinese economy under appropriate changes of parameters. His plans call for a research budget in the millions of dollars over a several-year period. He has attempted unsuccessfully to engage prominent economists as participants in the project. According to one economist, the economics profession is "digging in" to present a united front against this latest system dynamics effort.

If ever an award is made for a fine sense of timing, Forrester surely deserves it, whatever the final judgment on his models. In the 1950s and early 1960s, when there was much interest in modern methods of management and the emerging computer, Forrester created industrial dynamics to use the computer to study the operation of companies and help executives make better decisions. In the middle and late 1960s, when federal programs for social reform were getting a big play in Washington and urban problems were giving government

---

[158] Forrester, "National Model for Understanding Social and Economic Change."

officials headaches, Forrester built the urban dynamics model and became a critic of conventional housing and job training programs. In the early 1970s, with the upsurge of anxiety about environmental abuse and later about food and energy shortages, Forrester modeled the world system and spoke out for a halt to world growth and a transition to world equilibrium. Finally, in the middle 1970s, while business, government, and the economics profession were reeling from a triple barrage of inflation, unemployment, and the most serious setback to the economy since the Great Depression, Forrester was modeling the national economy with special attention to the causes of inflation and recession.

The system dynamics approach is philosophically very different from econometric modeling, the traditional method of modeling national economies and the principal subject in the following chapter. Despite appearances, bridges may gradually be built between these two methodologies. We believe that construction of such bridges, as well as the willingness by opposing sides to use them, could help make policy models more intelligible and useful to policymakers in future years.

6

Econometric Modeling—
A Familiar Oldtimer

The older methodology of econometric modeling offers a striking contrast to the newer methodology of system dynamics in several important respects. To name one, econometric modeling relies heavily on the availability of formal data and adheres to statistical principles in model estimation and testing. For just such reasons, econometric modeling is regarded as conservative where system dynamics is thought of as rash.

Econometric modeling has a rich and distinguished past. Primarily the product of quantitative economists, its development includes the participation and influence of many of the most prominent economists of the twentieth century.

Econometric modeling has been applied to numerous fields, of which one of the most widely publicized is the study of the United States economy. Macroeconometric models of the economy are most frequently used as forecasting devices, but they can also be employed as tools of policy analysis for comparing the effects on the economy of alternative policy actions.

A genealogical charting of the development of macroeconometric models of the economy shows these models originating thirty to forty years ago in an academic and research environment. More recently, they are appearing in operational settings within government and in commercial service offerings. Their history is intriguing as well as instructive. We will review it in some detail.

DEVELOPMENT AND RECENT PROGRESS

American economist Lawrence R. Klein is one of the country's leading econometric modelers and a pioneer in the field. Building on the earlier modeling of Jan Tinbergen (see Chapter 4), the theoretical work of Ragnar Frisch,[1]

---

[1] Frisch is noted for founding much of modern econometric theory. What is less well known is that he formulated a circulation-planning model of an economy in 1932, several years before Tinbergen modeled the Dutch economy (see Chapter 4). Frisch and Tinbergen were cowinners of the Nobel Prize in Economics in 1969, the first year it

and the insights of John Maynard Keynes, Klein formulated an outline of a fully operative macroeconomic model in 1946 and followed it up a few years later with the groundbreaking Klein-Goldberger model of the American economy.[2] But the experience left him less than euphoric about the econometric approach to modeling large complex systems. "A drawback of the econometric method," Klein wrote as recently as 1962, "is that it is time consuming, tedious, and complex." These are the words of a man writing candidly about the methodology he actively uses, a methodology that he was personally instrumental in developing and refining.

> To build a realistic model of the American economy requires a year in data collection and preparation, another year in estimation with much experimentation following both false and fruitful leads, and finally, years more of testing the model, applying it to practical problems. Every two or three years the model must be revised to keep it up to date. The magnitude of the effort involved is a definite drawback of the approach.[3]

Thus, Klein cast a cloud over his own methodology, but in the years following, the sun managed to shine through. Econometric models have been applied to forecasting and analysis of the economy in the United States and other industrial nations more than any other methodology. Klein's own model, the well-known Wharton model, has been forecasting the economy as a continuous service to government and industry every quarter-year for more than a decade. Klein and his modeling colleagues are one of a number of closely watched modeling teams whose views on the economy are cited regularly in newspaper editorials, magazine articles, and business seminars. *Business Week* features annual reports on the forecasts of these modelers, as well as annual post mortems of their prior year's performances. The situation has changed markedly since 1962. Econometric modeling of the economy is still a difficult and uncertain enterprise, but its practice has been substantially refined and streamlined in recent years, due primarily to the major technological advance achieved in computers, communications, and their mode of utilization.

Role of the Computer

In 1962 the computer was still in its so-called "second generation." Large computers of the kind needed to run large models were relatively slow, limited

---

was awarded to economists. The fact that so many of the initial Nobel Prizes in Economics were presented to economists associated directly or indirectly with the development of econometric modeling indicates the importance attached to this activity by the economics profession as well as by persons outside the field.

[2] Lawrence R. Klein and Arthur S. Goldberger, *An Econometric Model of the United States, 1929–1952* (Amsterdam: North-Holland, 1955).

[3] Lawrence R. Klein, *An Introduction to Econometrics* (Englewood Cliffs, N.J.: Prentice-Hall, 1962), p. 269.

in storage capacity by today's standards, and comparatively difficult to use. The results from a computer run submitted to the computation center in the morning might be returned by the end of the day, on a "good" day, or, more normally, sometime the following day. At a few heavily loaded centers, turn-around times ran to a week or longer. Estimating coefficients, experimenting with alternate equations, and statistically analyzing data were cumbersome activities at best. Many modelers preferred using the desk calculator in their offices for developing and testing their models to undertaking a disruptive series of trips to the computation center.

Important changes took place during the following five years. On-line terminals to central time-sharing systems gave remote users fast and convenient access to large computerized data files, programming systems, and computer power. Computers grew faster and less expensive. They increased in memory capacity and improved in data file capability. Moving into their "third generation," computers paid a major dividend to econometric modelers, despite some initial adjustments and user discomfort. Thus, within five years of the time of his earlier statement, Klein was writing with a colleague:

> The modern computer has brought about an enormous technological change in the conduct of modern econometric research.... Only a few years back it was a formidable task to go through the arithmetic of solving the model. Now our computer programs for finding solutions are so efficient and so fast that [we can] present a whole range of forecasts associated with different exogenous assumptions.... This is one of the most powerful uses of macroeconometric models. The computer has not only enabled us to make use of alternative exogenous assumptions, it has also enabled us to revise forecasts quickly as soon as data revisions are known.[4]

An interesting example of the speed with which model revisions became possible took place in August 1971. The Wharton group was preparing its third-quarter forecast.

> The third quarter of 1971 was not an easy period for economic forecasters. The year 1971 through July had been characterized by very high rates of inflation. The implicit price deflator for GNP had grown at a 5.0% to 6.0% annual rate. Unemployment hovered at 6.0% of the labor force. While the economy was showing a recovery from the recession of 1970, in terms of real GNP, the recovery was disappointingly slow. Another nagging problem was that the economy was faced with serious balance of payments problems, due in part to the high rate of inflation.... By July of 1971, it had become clear that significant shifts in economic policy were to be expected in the near future.[5]

---

[4] Michael K. Evans and Lawrence R. Klein, *The Wharton Econometric Forecasting Model* (Philadelphia: Economics Research Unit, University of Pennsylvania, 1967), p. 71.

[5] Michael D. McCarthy, *The Wharton Quarterly Econometric Forecasting Model Mark III* (Philadelphia: Economics Research Unit, University of Pennsylvania, 1972), p. 157.

The shifts occurred on Sunday, August 15 with an announcement by President Nixon of his new economic policy (NEP) calling for a battery of economic measures ranging from cuts in taxes and foreign aid to floating of the dollar and a freeze on prices, wages, and rents.

The Wharton group had produced its preliminary third-quarter forecast on August 2. At the time of Nixon's NEP announcement, only one working day remained before a regular group of government and industry economists was to meet to review the preliminary forecast and suggest refinements. Suddenly, and without warning, there were ten major policy changes that had to be incorporated into the model. The preliminary forecast was now meaningless and useless. Unless a revised forecast that reflected the changes could be devised within a day, the scheduled meeting would be a waste of time.

> Many of these changes required adjustments in several exogenous variables. On Monday, August 16, virtually no information was available on the precise nature of the proposed policy changes. Apparently in some cases the precise nature of the policy change had not been worked out. We were forced to make our own judgments.... In spite of the difficulties involved, an initial set of exogenous changes was formulated by noon of August 16. The first forecast was available shortly thereafter, and refinements were made in the forecast throughout the day. The forecast ultimately resulting from this procedure was dated August 16 (in time) for the meeting and discussions with business and government economists....[6]

To have made possible this high degree of responsiveness required a streamlined computer system that is convenient and simple to use. But machines are not the whole story. The methodology must lend itself to implementation by such a system. To appreciate how it does, we need to take a closer look at the nature of econometric modeling. In the course of doing so, we will compare this relative oldtimer (as modeling methodologies go) with system dynamics, a newcomer.

The Nature of the Method

An example of a simple econometric model was presented in Chapter 4. With any modeling methodology, the road from a mental model to specification of a formal model is paved with a mixture of theory, data, insight, pragmatism, and expediency. In econometric modeling, the first two of these ingredients, theory and data, play a key role.

---

[6] Ibid., pp. 164–165. The DRI and MQEM models, described later in the chapter, also were able to make rapid projections of the effects of the new economic policy. The three sets of results were discussed in a meeting at the Brookings Institution the month after the new economic policy was announced.

Econometric modeling draws heavily on established economic theory, most notably the body of modern Keynesian theory advanced by John Maynard Keynes in the 1930s. This theory was further developed and clarified by Keynes' followers and expositors, including John Hicks, Alvin Hansen, and Paul Samuelson.[7] Some models draw on the monetarist theory propounded by Samuelson's sometime adversary, Chicago economist Milton Friedman. Keynesian theory emphasizes the importance of government fiscal policy in determining aggregate levels of employment and production. Monetarist doctrine regards money supply as a predominant force.[8] Such theories, by suggesting equations and equation forms, provide econometric models with structural content.

Econometric modeling makes heavy use of time series data; it is data dependent. Data give econometric models substance by providing the basis for estimating coefficients and by furnishing starting values and exogenous input for simulation, as illustrated in the example of Chapter 4. Time series data also provide the means for testing the forecasting accuracy of econometric models. Econometricians regard data as the *sine qua non* of their profession. When formal data on the reference system being modeled are unreliable or difficult to come by, as they often are, econometric modeling is at a disadvantage compared to modeling methodologies that are not as data dependent. So, the authors of an econometric model of natural gas write, "One of the difficulties in constructing a model of this sort is that one must work under the constraints imposed by ... data limitations. ... A good deal of compromise was often required in estimating equations between functional forms that were theoretically pleasing and those that lent themselves to the existing data."[9]

System dynamics, as was seen in Chapter 5, makes minimal use of both formal data and the traditional theories of social science, one reason it is frequently a target of criticism. The system dynamics methodology relies heavily on perceptive insight and bold assertion, conditioned by time series data only insofar as they have been absorbed by the modeler. This style of application could change as the methodology matures, as could the style of econometric modeling. It is not unlikely for these two methodologies to move

---

[7] Samuelson studied at Harvard under Hansen and was in turn Klein's mentor at M.I.T. During the period in which Samuelson was a graduate student at Harvard and young assistant professor at M.I.T., Keynesian ideas were coming strongly into vogue. Samuelson was a vigorous proponent and interpreter of these ideas at frequent university seminars and coffee groups in the M.I.T.-Harvard academic community.

[8] Most models of the economy have a basically Keynesian formulation, but with some imprint of monetarist doctrine. A few models, like the St. Louis model discussed later in the chapter, are primarily monetarist in formulation.

[9] Paul W. MacAvoy and Robert S. Pindyck, "Alternative Regulatory Policies for Dealing with the Natural Gas Shortage," *Bell Journal of Economics and Management Science* 4, no. 2 (1973): 476.

closer together in the future, system dynamics becoming more attentive to fundamental methodological issues, econometric modeling freer of formal data restrictions and readier to use nonquantifiable variables.

Viewed as they are practiced today, system dynamics (the newcomer) and econometric modeling (the oldtimer) belong to different philosophical schools. Econometric modeling, with its emphasis on the use of data in estimating and testing, and in its overriding preference for variables that are measurable (employment, interest rate, price, GNP, etc.), fits in the philosophical tradition of the logical positivists and Humean empiricists who ascribed validity only to the empirically verifiable. System dynamics, on the other hand, with its use of equations that are not susceptible to statistical testing, and variables that have no direct measure or operational meaning (attractiveness of a city, quality of life, normal aggregate pollution level, etc.), tends toward the Kantian rationalist school of thought that believed in inescapable structures of knowledge that "transcend" empirical observation. Forrester argues that the best gauge of a model is not how well it reproduces a set of data from the past, but how well its internal structure resembles real mechanisms in the reference system.[10]

Kant had a name for self-evident concepts that defy empirical test. He called them "synthetic *a priori*" propositions and justified them on the basis of pure intuition. An example is the three-dimensionality of space. The synthetic *a priori* notion stirred much controversy in philosophical circles.

> The logical positivists... dispute the very possibility of synthetic *a priori* propositions: if a proposition is synthetic, they argue, then it must be empirical; and if a proposition is true independently of experience (*a priori*), then it must be analytic; hence the concept of a proposition that is both synthetic and *a priori* is really self-contradictory.[11]

There is a similar disagreement between econometric modelers and proponents of system dynamics. Econometric modelers argue that the modeler who does not subject his model to the rigors of empirical testing is unscientific and irresponsible. System dynamics modelers counter that econometricians have a "data hangup." They charge that econometricians do not see the forest for the trees. Variables and equations should be chosen because of their behavioral significance, not on the basis of whether reliable data exist. Some key variables are not even measurable, claim the system dynamicists.

An econometric model literally grows out of the data. Estimation of the

---

[10] Milton Friedman, in contrast, argues that resemblance to reality is irrelevant and the *sine qua non* of a model or theory is its ability to predict. See Milton Friedman, *Essays in Positive Economics* (Chicago: University of Chicago Press, 1953).

[11] Arthur Pap, *Elements of Analytic Philosophy* (New York: Macmillan, 1949), pp. 8–9, 414–433.

coefficients of the model, specification of the equations, testing of the model, all hinge on having a full set of data available on both the endogenous and exogenous variables. The availability of formal data is therefore a critical factor to the modeler in deciding what variables to include. It is no coincidence that the history of econometric models of the economy is linked chronologically with the brilliant conception and construction of the national income and product accounts by Simon Kuznets and others in the United States during the 1930s.[12] This landmark achievement, besides serving President Roosevelt in the management of resource allocation during World War II, provided econometric model builders with an invaluable set of time series on the American economy. These series have been continually maintained, elaborated, refined, and added to by the federal government and the economics profession in the ensuing years. "Econometric models rely heavily on the National Income Accounts because of their conceptual clarity and consistency and their close correspondence to modern macroeconomic theory."[13]

Besides the national accounts, a great deal of other government-collected data are used in econometric modeling. The Bureau of the Census, the Bureau of Labor Statistics, the Bureau of Economic Analysis, the Federal Reserve System, the Federal Trade Commission, the Securities and Exchange Commission, and many other government agencies accumulate, maintain, revise, and publish conveniently tabulated information on the functioning of the economy. This information is provided on a regular basis, making it attractive for use in research and modeling.

Just as the existence of such data has stimulated the development of econometric models of the national economy, its lack has been an impediment to model building elsewhere. Cities and states, for example, have lagged in the building of econometric models until recently, largely because of the data inadequacies of past years compared to the quality and quantity of data at the national level.[14] The situation outside of the United States is similar, with national accounting spreading rapidly, and econometric model building following apace. As in the United States, it seems to take about fifteen years

---

[12] See for example, Simon Kuznets, *National Income: A Summary of Findings* (New York: National Bureau of Economic Research, 1946). The fact that the main work of Frisch, Tinbergen, Keynes, and Kuznets occurred in the years during and following the Great Depression reflects the challenge that economists felt at the time to discover the cause of the depression—or at least, to find a cure and prevent a recurrence.

[13] Otto Eckstein et al., "The Data Resources Econometric Forecasting System—A Preliminary Account," (Lexington, Mass.: Data Resources, Inc., December 1971), p. 3.

[14] "Despite great interest on the part of regional planners and state and local governments, regional [econometric] models have only recently [1973] become practical tools. They pose formidable problems of data collection." So report F. Gerard Adams and David M. Rowe in *Forecasts and Simulations from the Wharton Econometric Model: A Set of Classroom Materials* (Morristown, N.J.: General Learning Press, 1974), p. 10.

from the beginning of national accounting (fifteen years of data) for econometric model building to take hold.[15]

It is interesting to note that "in sharp contrast to the situation in the United States, about half of model building [overseas] ... takes place in official institutions. As a result, modeling work has become less an academic exercise than in earlier years, and its orientation has been strongly influenced by a policy-making context."[16] In the Netherlands especially, modeling plays an important role in government planning. The strong tradition there in the use of models goes back to Tinbergen's work in the 1930s (see Chapter 4), which "is given credit for much of the postwar economic success of the country," according to a 1969 account. "The Netherlands still makes an annual forecast of the country's growth rate based on Professor Tinbergen's model."[17]

As in the United States, a major reason for the growing interest in modeling overseas, in addition to the increasing availability of data, is "the progress of computers, which has improved to an amazing degree the speed and flexibility of model building work" and made it easier to manipulate models "to meet the requirements of practical policy making."[18] We have already noted that one of the several reasons why econometric model building lends itself so well to computerization is the fact that its data occur as time series. The computer can store data in this simplified format compactly, and retrieve, cross-reference, transform, and update it very efficiently. Several large computerized data banks for econometric modeling now exist.[19]

While econometric modeling benefits from the use of time series because of the simplicity of the data format, it also pays a price. Allegiance to time series and other formal (e.g., cross-sectional and spatially distributed) data limits the choice of variables. It also affects the form of the equations and the manner of simulation. The fact that econometric models are sets of simultaneous difference equations follows directly from the use of discrete series. Variables

---

[15] Jean Waelbroeck, "A Survey of Short-Run Model Research outside the United States," in Gary Fromm and Lawrence R. Klein (eds.), *The Brookings Model: Perspective and Recent Developments* (Amsterdam: North-Holland, 1975), p. 423. Waelbroeck points out that active econometric model building centers are now busily operating in Germany, Great Britain, Belgium, France, Italy, Sweden, Austria, Finland, Japan, Canada, New Zealand, and Australia, as well as in the Netherlands, where the Dutch Central Planning Bureau is the "veteran among model building institutions (p. 425)."

[16] Ibid., p. 423.

[17] "Models Bring Nobel Prize," *Science News,* November 1, 1969, p. 397.

[18] Waelbroeck, p. 423.

[19] Some of the larger of the computerized data banks for econometric modeling have been those collected and maintained by Data Resources, Inc., Chase Econometrics Associates, and Wharton Econometric Forecasting Associates, as well as General Electric and the National Bureau of Economic Research. These data banks have been used either for general economic analysis or for the specification, estimation, and testing of models.

must advance in discrete steps equal to the interval of the series. For most economic data this interval is of the order of a month to a year. Each item of data represents a time average over the length of the interval of the aggregate behavior of many different decision units in the economy. But there is a multiplicity of relationships into which each item of data (or variable) enters during the course of an interval. The more important or dominant of these relationships must be spelled out by the econometric model in the form of simultaneous equations.

Having simultaneous equations complicates both the estimation of coefficients and the mechanics of simulation. Simulation requires solving a set of equations and estimation involves special statistical methods. Although many econometric modelers still prefer ordinary least-squares regression (the single-equation estimation technique used for the LR model in Chapter 1), it is theoretically not an appropriate estimation technique for simultaneous equations. Its deficiencies were first studied in the early 1940s by Trygve Haavelmo, a student of Ragnar Frisch, who was inspired by Tinbergen's modeling work for the League of Nations.[20] Haavelmo's work stimulated a great deal of research devoted to the development of estimation techniques specifically designed for simultaneous equations,[21] techniques that go by such formidable names as "indirect least squares," "instrumental variables," "two-stage least squares," "three-stage least squares," "limited-information maximum likelihood," and "truncated full-information maximum likelihood." Although they are straightforward to automate, these sophisticated estimation procedures increase the computational burden of econometric modeling compared, for example, to a methodology like system dynamics that circumvents the estimation problem altogether.[22]

System dynamics seeks to avoid simultaneity by selecting its simulation

---

[20] Trygve Haavelmo, "The Statistical Implications of a System of Simultaneous Equations," *Econometrica* 2 (1943): 1–12.

[21] See, for example, Tjalling C. Koopmans (ed.), *Statistical Inference in Dynamic Economic Models*, Cowles Commission Monograph 10 (New York: John Wiley & Sons, 1950); and William C. Hood and Tjalling C. Koopmans, (eds.), *Studies in Econometric Methods*, Cowles Commission Monograph 14 (New York: John Wiley & Sons, 1953). Koopmans believes that at least as important as the work on statistical estimation was the work on identifiability, a test that has to be met before estimation is possible. See Tjalling C. Koopmans, "Identification Problems in Economic Model Construction," *Econometrica* 17, no. 2 (1949). Contributors to the work on identifiability included Koopmans, Olaf Reiersöl, Herman Rubin, and later, Franklin Fisher.

[22] System dynamics sidesteps both the estimation problem and the related "identification" problem of econometrics although there is a theoretical correspondence between the continuous conceptual models of system dynamics and the discrete representations of econometrics. Some econometricians charge that since system dynamics does not generally use exogenous variables, its models are "underidentified" and hence its coefficients are unable to be statistically estimated. But statistical estimation is already impractical in many system dynamics models by virtue of the unmeasurability of the variables and the fact that the solution interval is variable and arbitrarily small.

interval (DT) arbitrarily small, small enough so that it does not matter. Conceptually, a system dynamics model is a set of integral equations in continuous time. It is represented by a discrete model whose time interval DT is intended to approximate an instant of time. If the length of DT in any way affects the behavior of the model, it should be made smaller, says Forrester. Within each DT, Forrester claims that multiple effects can be ordered serially without doing injustice to the simulation.[23] "Rates" in system dynamics are allowed to depend only on "levels," not on other rates. Forrester contends that no real life process can contain simultaneity in the econometric sense of the word. Rates can only depend upon the results of the integration (accumulation or averaging) of rates, not on the rates themselves, since rates are imperceptible, instantaneous concepts. The equations of a system dynamics model are "serially recursive" rather than "simultaneous," in the sense that one equation follows another, rather than being concurrent with it, in every time period. The simulation is advanced by updating each equation in sequence rather than by solving all equations simultaneously.[24]

Despite the conceptual difference between the simulation of an econometric model and that of a system dynamics model, the two procedures are not actually all that dissimilar. In fact, a parallel can be drawn between them.

The original or natural equations of an econometric model are called "structural" equations, since in this form they display the assumed structure of the reference system. The endogenous variables of the structural equations are jointly dependent and each one normally appears in several of the equations. When linear structural equations are solved for the endogenous variables, a new set of equations results in which current endogenous variables appear only on the left-hand side, one endogenous variable per equation. This is the "reduced form" of the model, as illustrated in the example of Chapter 4. The ordering of the equations in the reduced form is immaterial, since each endogenous variable depends only on predetermined variables (i.e., on given exogenous variables and lagged endogenous variables from previous periods). Ordering may have consequences, on the other hand, in the serially recursive equations of a system dynamics model, where some variables can depend on other variables of the same period.

We are now in a position to compare the simulation techniques for these two types of models. Simulating an econometric model requires solving the

---

[23] Klein has said to us that he feels the kind of simultaneity intrinsic to the behavior of aggregates of economic decision units, such as producers and consumers, cannot be spaced out serially in time no matter how thinly time is sliced. For a theoretical treatment of the subject, see Franklin Fisher, "A Correspondence Principle for Simultaneous Equation Models," *Econometrica* 38, no. 1 (1970): 73–92.

[24] Econometric models can also be partially or even fully recursive (e.g., the classical cobweb model and the LR model discussed in Chapter 1). In a mathematical sense, recursiveness is a special case of simultaneity.

(not necessarily linear) structural equations for the endogenous variables, commonly by a Gauss-Seidel iterative procedure of successive approximations that sweeps sequentially and repeatedly through the structural equations in circular fashion. On each sweep or iteration, the appropriate values of the exogenous and lagged endogenous variables and the most recent values of the endogenous variables are substituted into the equations and the next set of endogenous variables calculated. Suppose it takes an average of i iterations or sweeps through the equations to obtain convergence to the solution. If the simulation is to last for t time intervals, the expected number of iterations required to simulate the model is $i \times t$.

Compare this with the simulation of a system dynamics model. Here, no solution process is required, since no simultaneous effects are explicitly represented. Each sweep through the equations advances the simulation by one DT. Imagine that the system dynamics model has an econometric model as counterpart whose time interval is T. The simulation interval is normally smaller than T (one reason why the coefficients of a system dynamics model are difficult to estimate statistically).[25] Suppose $DT = T/n$, $1/n$ th of the time interval T. Then, to run the system dynamics model for t time intervals, T, requires $n \times t$ sweeps through the equations. Which is larger, $i \times t$ or $n \times t$? If i is greater than n, then the econometric model requires more iterations. If i is less than n, then the system dynamics model requires more iterations. If they are equal, then the two models require the same number of iterations.

We hasten to add that this analysis is very oversimplified. Many other factors must enter into any serious comparison of the two simulation techniques. We only wish to show here the parallel that exists between them. The key point is that both techniques are simple and efficient to automate. With respect to their ease of simulation on a computer, econometric modeling and system dynamics are about evenly matched. For both methodologies, ease of simulation on a computer is a strong point.

Before leaving the subject of the nature of econometric modeling, we will comment on the way this methodology chooses its variables and equations. This is the most time consuming, demanding, and critical activity in econometric modeling. Here, once again, the computer can be of great advantage.

The process of selecting the variables and equations of an econometric model is known as "specification" of the model. It is an iterative process, like the process of simulating the model, but the modeler is in charge in this case, not the computer. In devising and trying out alternative specifications of the model, good human judgment is of the utmost importance. This is the process that Klein described as "time consuming, tedious, and complex" in 1962.[26] It

---
[25] An increasing amount of statistical estimation is being attempted in system dynamics models, despite the difficulties.
[26] Klein, *Introduction to Econometrics*, p. 269.

is still demanding today, but the time-shared computer has been of great help.

Specification is guided by a testing procedure known as *ex post* simulation: simulation of the endogenous variables over a historical period for which the actual values of these variables and the exogenous variables are known. A trial set of variables and equations is chosen; the coefficients of the equations are estimated by standard statistical techniques; the model is simulated over the designated historical period; and a measurement is made of the *ex post* discrepancies or "residuals" between the simulated and actual values of the endogenous variables. The variables and equations are then altered in a manner intended to improve the *ex post* fit, the coefficients are re-estimated, the model is once more simulated, and the residuals again measured. The iterative process is continued until the residuals are as small as the modeler wishes to make them. The fact that the computer has immediate and direct access to the data required for this process is of great advantage to the modeler.

Klein considers the computer indispensable both in specifications of the model and in estimation of the coefficients.

> A vast amount of experimental calculation underlies the structural specification of our model.... We computed thousands of exploratory relationships before we finally decided on the precise set of equations introduced here. The simultaneous estimation of the model by the two-stage least squares method ... was in itself a major computational task that would not have been feasible without computer facility.[27]

Like all good things, the power and convenience afforded by the computer in the specification process can be misused. It is possible to overfit a model; that is, to specify it to match historical data so closely that it is actually less likely to forecast accurately than if it gave a rougher fit but conformed better to the modeler's *a priori* knowledge of the reference system. There are no hard and fast rules on when to terminate the iterative process of specification. The situation today still requires a highly skilled touch; perhaps it always will. Econometric modeling is for the master craftsman.

There are two last points on the subjects of specification and estimation, bearing on the success of econometric modeling as a forecasting tool, that are worth noting. The first, curious as it may seem, is that *ex post* simulations are frequently less accurate than *ex ante* predictions, even though the former use actual values of exogenous variables whereas the latter do not. Some reasons are explained in Chapter 3.[28] The second point is that there has been a re-

---

[27] Evans and Klein, p. 71.

[28] Comparisons of some *ex ante* and *ex post* predictions were made by Victor Zarnowitz, "New Plans and Results of Research in Economic Forecasting," Center for Mathematical Studies in Business and Economics Reprint Series, No. 278 (Chicago: University of Chicago, Graduate School of Business, Department of Economics, September 1971), p. 57.

thinking of the use of ever more elaborate ways of estimating coefficients for simultaneous-equation models. The development that started with Haavelmo may have run its course and reached the point of diminishing returns. Klein sees greater payoff coming today from the incorporation in models of complicated lag structures and corrections for serial correlation than from the use of sophisticated estimation procedures. For many econometricians, ordinary least squares is still good enough. Some believe the refinement of estimation methods was misguided and these methods can give inferior and even absurd results.[29]

MODELS OF THE AMERICAN ECONOMY

It is tempting to attribute human qualities to aggregate econometric models of the economy. A successful model seems to take on an existence of its own. It grows stronger, changes appearance, and almost invariably gets bigger, as it is used, improved, refined, and extended. It ages and becomes obsolete as better models come along to supplant it. And when it is gone, its spirit lives on through successor models that incorporate its strong points and special characteristics.

But anthropomorphizing models neglects the important role played by the modeler himself. The modeling innovator is critical in the life process of the model, particularly in the early stages. It is through his insights, teachings, and persuasions that the idea and meaning of the model become implanted in the imaginations and work of others. So it was with the influence of Tinbergen and Klein, the two men cited in Chapter 4 as innovators for econometric modeling.

Early Models and Genealogy

Tinbergen is credited with origination of the idea of using a system of simultaneous statistical equations to represent an economy. His twenty-four-equation model of the Dutch economy in 1935, discussed in Chapter 4, was the first econometric model of an economy. Samuelson described it as "our fountainhead and source" in tracing the roots of econometric modeling, noting also two of Ragnar Frisch's models, a propagation-and-impulse macro-dynamic model of 1933 and a circulation planning model of 1932 in which Frisch was attempting to "chart an economy and improve" on economic poli-

---

[29] For a general discussion and review, see R. L. Basmann, "Exact Finite Sample Distributions for Some Econometric Estimators and Test Statistics: A Survey and Appraisal," in M. D. Intriligator and D. A. Kendrick (eds.), *Frontiers of Quantitative Economics,* Contributions to Economic Analysis series, vol. 87 (Amsterdam: North-Holland, 1974).

cies and performance.³⁰ Frisch is generally considered more a theoretician than a model builder. That is, he is regarded more as a mathematical economist than an econometrician, even though his contributions to econometrics, including an elucidation of the crucial "multicollinearity problem," are momentous. It may be argued that he deserves to be included on the list of modeling innovators in Chapter 4 every bit as much as John von Neumann, another theoretician who made singular contributions to applied modeling work. Abraham Wold is still another such theoretician.

In the years since Tinbergen's original model, econometric modeling has been applied to many other forms of economic behavior besides a full economy, but modeling of the economy, the first application, has continued to be one of the most important. Tinbergen followed up on his Dutch model with development of a model of the United States economy, in 1939, for the League of Nations.³¹ As noted in Chapter 4, the League of Nations model was an attempt to understand better the forces that led the United States and the rest of the world into the crippling depression of the 1930s. Tinbergen was convinced that it was fruitless to try to unravel the interconnections that underlie cyclic economic behavior without taking a formal approach.

> Tinbergen's main interest in constructing the first aggregative statistical models was to study the characteristics of the trade cycle and to test various cyclical hypotheses. He was interested in the possibility of constructing a statistical dynamic system that would generate cycles of activity or price levels that we commonly associate with the elusive phenomenon known as "the business-cycle." Various mathematical theories had already shown that self-contained systems could be constructed that would oscillate and grow in a way similar to the actual economy. Tinbergen's question was more numerical and specific. He wanted to see if a system with numerical, or statistical coefficients determined from actual economic data would exhibit the ordinary cycle with damped or steady oscillation.³²

Tinbergen's League of Nations model (*TLN*) stands at the base of the genealogical tree of aggregate models of the American economy presented in Figure 6–1. It was an *annual* model based on data with a time interval of one year. It has fifty equations, thirty-two of them stochastic. (A stochastic equation is one whose coefficients are derived statistically.) With fourteen exogenous variables, it was a medium-scale model.³³ The model's coefficients were estimated by ordinary least squares. Table 6–1 lists these attributes for the

---

³⁰ Fromm and Klein, p. 4. The general idea of representing an economy by a set of simultaneous (nonstatistical) equations goes back to Walras in the nineteenth century.

³¹ Jan Tinbergen, *A Method and Its Application to Investment Activity* and *Business Cycles in the United States of America, 1919–1932*, Statistical Testing of Business-Cycle Theories, vols. 1 and 2 (Geneva: League of Nations, 1939).

³² Klein, pp. 181–182.

³³ Any overall measure of the size of a model must be arbitrary and *ad hoc,* since several factors interact in different ways to determine the dimensions of the model.

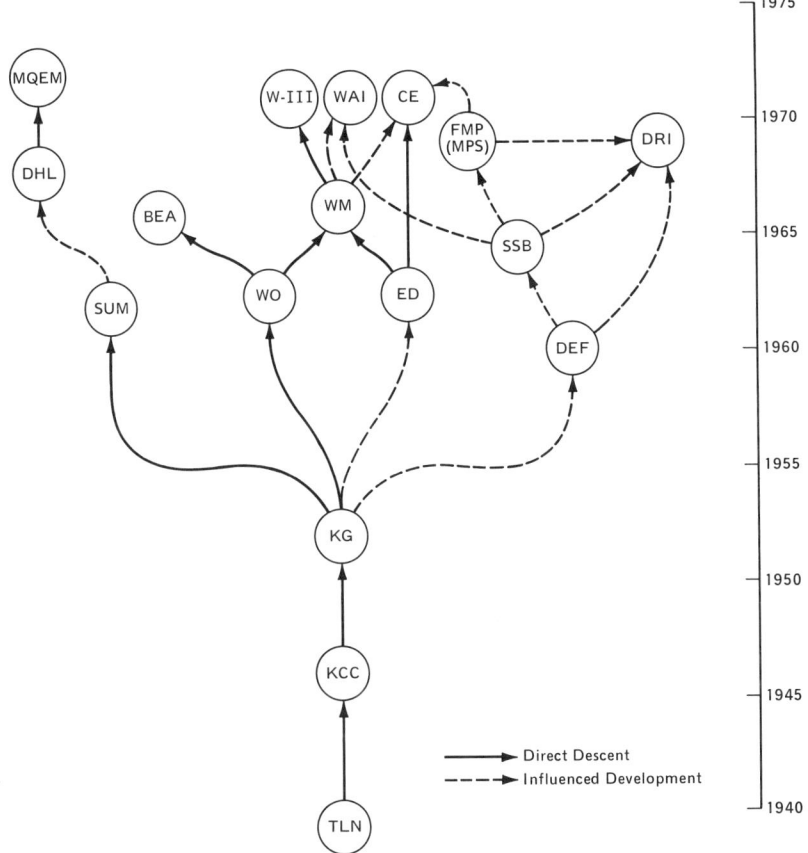

Figure 6–1: Partial Genealogy of Econometric Models of the United States Economy

---

The number of stochastic equations is one measure of magnitude, but the number of variables is also important, especially in determining the data requirements and in indicating the amount of work required to estimate and solve the equations. As a rough gauge, we make the calculation
$$\text{size} = (S + E + X)/3,$$
where S is the number of stochastic equations, E is the number of endogenous variables, and X is the number of exogenous variables. The formula is easy to apply, easy to remember, and has other appealing properties as well. For a single equation model with one dependent and one independent variable, it gives a size of 1. When $S = (E + X)/2$, it gives a result equal to the number of stochastic equations. Since for "complete" models, the number of endogenous variables is the same as the number of equations (i.e., $E = S +$ number of nonstochastic equations), the formula accords endogenous variables almost twice the weight of exogenous variables. Based on our inspection of the characteristics of a variety of models of the economy, we use the following rough classification for size of model: between 1 and 10, "very small"; between 10 and 20, "small"; between 20 and 50, "medium"; between 50 and 100, "large"; over 100, "very large."

Table 6-1: Comparison of Some Selected Models of the United States Economy

Symbol	Model	Date	Stoch.	Eqns.	Exog.	Size	Interval	Est. Proc.
BEA(OBE)	Bureau of Economic Analysis*	1966	36	49	32	M	Q	2SLS
CE	Chase Econometrics	1971	125	175	100	VL	Q	OLS
DEF	Duesenberry-Eckstein-Fromm	1960	10	28	11	S	Q,A	OLS
DHL	Council of Economic Advisors	1967	12	18	15	S	Q	OLS
DRI	Data Resources, Inc.	1969	100	368	120	VL	Q	OLS,2SLS
ED	Evans' Ph.D. Dissertation	1963	30	50	30	M	Q	OLS
FAIR	Fair	1968	14	20	16	S	Q	2SLS(modified)
FMP	Federal Reserve-MIT-Penn**	1969	80	150	138	VL	Q	OLS,IV(iterative)
KCC	Klein Cowles Commission	1946	12	16	13	S	A	LIML
KG	Klein-Goldberger	1952	15	25	14	S	A	LIML
MQEM	Michigan/Hymans-Shapiro	1972	36	59	27	M	Q	OLS,IV
SSB	SSRC-Brookings	1964	119	226	218	VL	Q,A	LIML,2SLS,OLS
St.L	St. Louis Federal Reserve	1970	5	8	3	VS	Q	OLS
SUM	Suits/Michigan	1962	16	33	21	M	A	OLS
TLN	Tinbergen/League of Nations	1939	32	50	14	M	A	OLS
W-III	Wharton Mark III	1971	63	204	105	VL	Q	2SLS
WAI	Wharton Annual Industry	1971	155	346	90	VL	A	OLS,2SLS
WM	Wharton Merged	1966	47	76	42	L	Q	2SLS
WO	Wharton Original	1963	29	37	19	M	Q	LIML,2SLS

Sizes: (See note 33.) VS = very small, S = small, M = medium, L = large, VL = very large.
Intervals: A = annual, Q = quarterly.
Estimation Procedures: OLS = Ordinary Least Squares, 2SLS = Two-Stage Least Squares, LIML = Limited Information,
Maximum Likelihood, IV = Instrumental Variables.

* As with many of the models listed, the attributes given are for an early version. A more recent version of the BEA model contains fifty-six stochastic equations, one hundred and two total equations, and seventy-five exogenous variables, making it a large model.
** The public version of the FMP model is named MPS (MIT-Penn-SSRC).

seventeen models of Figure 6-1 (plus two others) to a first approximation. The table gives a rough measure of how the models compare with one another.[34]

Although Timbergen's League of Nations model was econometric in form and used coefficients estimated statistically from time series data, its objective was closer to that typically found today in system dynamics rather than in econometric models "to measure the cyclical characteristics [of the system] ... and from this possibly devise a scheme for stabilization of the economy." This objective was out of step with Keynesian thinking, then gaining ascendancy, with its "focus of attention on influencing the level of activity at any moment of time rather than [studying] ... the whole temporal shape of a cycle."[35] Economists began to apply Tinbergen's modeling approach to develop reliable short-run forecasts of income and employment as a guide for monetary and fiscal policy. This use of the aggregate econometric model has predominated in the years since the original League of Nations effort.

Two economists in the early 1940s whose thoughts ran along Keynesian lines as they contemplated the potentialities of Tinbergen's pioneering work were Tjalling C. Koopmans and Jacob Marschak, staff members of the Cowles Commission for Research in Economics, a research institute quartered at the time at the University of Chicago. They wanted to bring someone to the Cowles Commission to redo the League of Nations model or develop a replacement using improved current data. They wanted to have the coefficients of the model estimated in a more statistically valid way than the ordinary least squares method used by Tinbergen. Cowles associate Trygve Haavelmo of Norway, stimulated by Tinbergen's work, had shown the inadequacies of the standard single-equation method in estimating the coefficients of simultaneous equations.[36] He and others, such as T. W. Anderson, Jr., and Herman Rubin, were developing more theoretically defensible estimation techniques that Koopmans and Marschak were eager to have tried on a revised Tinbergen model.

At the time, Lawrence Klein was writing a doctoral dissertation under Paul Samuelson at M.I.T. on the "Keynesian Revoluation," an interpretation and integration of Keynesian ideas. M.I.T. had just recently initiated a new graduate program in economics. Samuelson had come from Harvard to teach in the program, and Klein was in the second class of economics students that M.I.T. accepted. After completing his Ph.D. work, Klein accepted an offer

---

[34] For a good rundown of several econometric models, see Marc Nerlove, "A Tabular Survey of Macroeconometric Models," *International Economic Review* 7, no. 2 (1966): 127–175. For a comparative review of the more recent models, see Gary Fromm and Lawrence R. Klein, "A Comparison of Eleven Econometric Models of the United States," *The American Economic Review* 63, no. 2 (1973): 385–393.

[35] Klein, p. 182.

[36] Haavelmo.

from Koopmans and Marschak to join them on the staff of the Cowles Commission.

Klein was strongly influenced by the work of both Tinbergen and Frisch, although he had not yet met either of them. It was Klein's good fortune to have their former prize students as coworkers at the Cowles Commission: T. Haavelmo, Frisch's student, and T. C. Koopmans, Tinbergen's student. Through Haavelmo and Koopmans, Klein had the benefit of the ideas and insights of the two masters.

When completed in 1946, Klein's Cowles Commission model (KCC) was smaller in size than its predecessor, with sixteen equations, twelve of them stochastic, and thirteen exogenous variables.[37] An annual model, its coefficients were estimated by the limited-information maximum likelihood method. The Klein model, when applied to study the effects of the postwar economy, suggested (correctly) that the much expected postwar recession would not materialize, a conclusion that was discounted by numerous prominent economists and government officials committed to the idea that recession was inevitable. The model was also put to use by Alfred Cowles, president of the Cowles Commission, in his capacity as director of the United Fund campaign in Chicago.

When Klein decided to leave the Cowles Commission for the National Bureau of Economic Research in June 1947, Kenneth J. Arrow, then at Cowles, was asked to continue the modeling work. Arrow, whose bent was more theoretical than applied, got interested in other things and the model was dropped.[38] Arrow was another in the long line of distinguished economists and statisticians, like Koopmans, Marschak, Haavelmo, Hurwicz, Rubin, Anderson, Chernoff, Christ, Domar, Debreu, Radner, Brunner, Harberger, Modigliani, Patinkin, and Klein, who spent some of their most productive years working at the Cowles Commission. The institute later moved to Yale University, with Koopmans as its director, and changed its name to the Cowles Foundation for Research in Economics.

---

[37] The first published account of a Klein model of the economy, the KCC model, appeared as an abstract of a talk Klein presented to the Econometric Society in Cleveland, January 1946: "A Macroeconomic System, U.S.A., 1921–1941," *Econometrica* 14, no. 2 (1946): 159–162. Klein describes the KCC model ("Model III") in detail, along with two simpler models ("Model I," with five exogenous and six endogenous variables and three stochastic equations, and "Model II," a reduced form model) in Lawrence R. Klein, *Economic Fluctuations in the United States: 1921–1941*, Cowles, Commission Monograph 11 (New York: John Wiley & Sons, 1950).

[38] Some of the equations were found wanting by others at Cowles in tests of the model against new data. See Carl F. Christ, "A Test of an Econometric Model for the United States, 1921–1947," *Conference on Business Cycles* (New York: National Bureau of Economic Research, 1952). Another early model of the United States economy was reported on by Colin Clark, "A System of Equations Explaining the United States Trade Cycle, 1921–1941," *Econometrica* 17 (1949): 93–124.

After leaving Cowles in the summer of 1947, Klein worked for three months with the Canadian government in developing the first Canadian model,[39] prior to joining the staff of the National Bureau of Economic Research. That appointment evolved into a joint arrangement with the Survey Research Center at the University of Michigan to use the data in the Surveys of Consumer Finances for studies of savings behavior.

As a faculty member at the University of Michigan, Klein founded the Research Seminar in Quantitative Economics with the aid of a grant from the Ford Foundation. Because of new government legislation, private foundations were under pressure at the time to distribute their profits. Klein and the University of Michigan benefited from Ford's compliance with the law. As the major project of his seminar, Klein undertook construction of a new model of the economy in collaboration with his student Arthur S. Goldberger. The Klein-Goldberger (KG) model, small in size, was finished in 1952, with twenty-five equations, fifteen of them stochastic, and fourteen exogenous variables. Like Klein's earlier creation, the KG model was annual and its coefficients were estimated by the limited-information maximum likelihood method. Its big test was predicting the 1953–1954 recession following the Korean War; it passed with flying colors. The Klein-Goldberger model was the best-known and most quoted of the early models of the American economy. It was to inspire and influence a generation of model builders.[40]

The Tinbergen League of Nations model (TLN), the Klein Cowles Commission model (KCC), and the Klein-Goldberger model (KG), form the trunk of the genealogical tree shown in Figure 6–1. In the middle 1950s, the tree began to branch. Dozens of models of the American economy were subsequently developed, and most of them trace back to, and were strongly influenced by, the early work of Tinbergen and Klein in the 1930s and 1940s.

The Klein Line

During the early 1950s, Senator Joseph McCarthy intimidated many intellectuals in the United States, and some found it a propitious time to take a sabbatical abroad. Klein spent the years 1954 to 1958 working at the Oxford Institute of Statistics in England, staying in practice there by developing some econometric models of the United Kingdom.[41] When he returned to the United States in 1958, he joined the faculty at the University of Pennsylvania.

---

[39] Tillman M. Brown, *Specification and Uses of Econometric Models* (New York: St. Martin's Press, 1970), pp. 355–365.

[40] Klein and Goldberger.

[41] Lawrence R. Klein et al., "An Econometric Model of the United Kingdom," Institute of Statistics, Oxford University, Monograph No. 6 (Oxford: Basil Blackwell, 1961).

Work on the Klein-Goldberger model at the University of Michigan, meanwhile, was taken up by Daniel B. Suits of the Research Seminar in Quantitative Economics. His update of the annual KG model was an expanded and reestimated version, but it remained an annual model. One version contained thirty-three equations, sixteen of them stochastic, and twenty-one exogenous variables; a medium-size model.[42] Suits' University of Michigan (SUM) model regularly produced short-run annual forecasts of the national economy and shared the national forecasting limelight for several years with other prominent macroeconomic models. According to one economist, the Suits model was "80 percent Suits and 20 percent model," whereas today the split between modeler and model tends to be closer to "50–50."[43] Suits left the University of Michigan in 1969 and turned to other interests.

Models were not used and probably not much considered at the Council of Economic Advisers until John F. Kennedy became president in 1961. Kennedy brought to his first council and its staff economists James Tobin, Robert M. Solow, and Kenneth J. Arrow, all of whom had strong quantitative and modeling orientations in their approaches to economic problems. But the "pressure cooker" atmosphere of the council called largely for "quick and dirty" solutions. To the harried economists there, small *ad hoc* models were of more interest than large formal models.

Even so, by 1968 three staff members, Thomas F. Dernburg, Saul H. Hymans, and David Lusher had developed a small quarterly model (DHL) for use at the council. Hymans was the principal author of the model. Third-generation computers were commonplace by then, yet the estimation of coefficients for the model was accomplished mostly on a small desktop computer, a commentary on the general inaccessibility of large computer facilities to government agencies at the time. Only the Federal Reserve had a good research computer, which it did make available to the council and other agencies, but since work had to be brought to the site of the computer, its usefulness outside of the Federal Reserve was limited.

The DHL model was used to generate forecasts during 1968, but did not receive much use at the council subsequently, according to Wharton economist F. Gerard Adams, who came there when Dernburg and Hymans left in 1968. Adams was not happy with the DHL model because he felt it had been estimated over a very short, unrepresentative, sample period. He set it aside in favor of single-equation procedures. Hymans, who meantime had returned

---

[42] Daniel B. Suits, "Forecasting and Analysis with an Econometric Model," *American Economic Review* 52, no. 1 (1962): 104–132.

[43] The observation on how much of Suits' forecast was the modeler as opposed to the model was made by Gary Fromm in informal conversation. Suits submits that the "80 percent Suits" was nothing more than the particular care he took with inputs.

to the University of Michigan, brought the DHL model with him. He and his colleague, Harold Shapiro, revised it extensively and continued to run and improve it. A medium-size model, it is now referred to as the Michigan Quarterly Econometric Model (MQEM).[44] At last count it had fifty-nine equations and twenty-seven exogenous variables. It is the forecasting vehicle for the annual University of Michigan Economic Outlook Conference, the continuous series of meetings begun when the Klein-Goldberger model was used in October 1953 to predict the recession following the Korean war. The series of meetings has been carried on since then with the Suits, DHL, and MQEM models.[45]

The Council of Economic Advisers' recent policy has been to consult a number of well-known aggregate models, including an IBM model also in the Klein line. The policy is designed to make certain that the Council not be identified with any one model, but rather be seen as exercising independent judgment with the help of the best models available, whatever their source. According to former member Ezra Solomon, the council does not wish to be tied to any single model or result. Still, it does reconsider from time to time the idea of developing its own model.

After he returned to the United States from England in 1958, Klein embarked on the construction of a quarterly version of the Klein-Goldberger model. With financial assistance from the Rockefeller Foundation, Klein sought to overcome the inadequacies of the annual models. He had already had success in building a quarterly model of the United Kingdom,[46] and once before had tried to use quarterly (prewar) data in a small United States model for methodological purposes.[47]

> Annual models have their place, but their aggregation over time often obscures certain important business cycle developments. For example, real GNP did not fall on an annual basis between 1959 and 1960. Yet there was a recession during 1960 that [only revealed] itself in declining quarterly values of real GNP.[48]

---

[44] Saul H. Hymans and Harold T. Shapiro, "The Structure and Properties of the Michigan Quarterly Econometric Model of the U.S. Economy," *International Economic Review* 15, no. 3 (1974): 632–653. Several consecutive issues of the *International Economic Review*, including this one, contain a description and comparison of a number of econometric models of the United States economy.

[45] Saul H. Hymans and Harold T. Shapiro, *The Outlook for 1970*, Seventeenth Annual Conference on the Economic Outlook at the University of Michigan, November 20–21, 1969, for example, reports on the seventeenth in the series of meetings.

[46] Klein et al., *Model of the United Kingdom*.

[47] Lawrence R. Klein and Harold Barger, "A Quarterly Model for the U.S. Economy," *Journal of the American Statistical Association*, September 1954, pp. 413–437.

[48] Evans and Klein, p. 1.

Klein's quarterly model was the first of a series of models to come out of Wharton. Medium in size, the original Wharton (WO) model[49] had thirty-seven equations, twenty-nine stochastic, and nineteen exogenous variables. It began generating a regular quarterly series of forecasts of the United States economy in the second quarter of 1963. The series has been continued by the group at Wharton ever since.

A version of the original quarterly Wharton model was taken over by the Office of Business Economics in the Department of Commerce, where it was re-estimated with revised data and restructured. Known as the OBE model for many years, it was renamed the BEA model in accordance with the change of name of the office to the Bureau of Economic Analysis. The model has been used regularly in forecasting, not only for the Department of Commerce, but for other government agencies as well, especially the Council of Economic Advisers. It was effective in predicting the 1969–1970 recession, signaling weakness in the economy as early as 1967. The model had forty-nine equations in 1966, thirty-six of them stochastic, and thirty-two exogenous variables, making it medium in size. The two-stage least squares method was used to estimate its coefficients.

Forecasts of the BEA model are kept proprietary, since they often entail reference to alternative government policies under consideration and since they frequently use confidential budget information. The BEA model itself is not closeted. Its developers published its full specification in the open literature,[50] and the BEA modeling team participates in the ongoing NBER-NSF model comparison and criteria seminars conducted under the sponsorship of

---

[49] Lawrence R. Klein, "A Postwar Quarterly Model: Description and Applications," *Models of Income Determination* Studies in Income and Wealth, vol. 28 (Princeton, N.J.: Princeton University Press, 1964), pp. 11–30. See also Lawrence R. Klein and Joel Popkin, "An Econometric Analysis of the Postwar Relationship between Inventory Fluctuations and Changes in Aggregate Economic Activity," *Inventory Fluctuations and Economic Stabilization,* Part 3, Joint Economic Committee, 87th Cong., 1st sess. (Washington, D.C.: U.S. Government Printing Office, 1961), pp. 71–89.

[50] For an account of the Office of Business Economics model, see Maurice Liebenberg, Albert A. Hirsch, and Joel Popkin, "A Quarterly Economic Model of the United States: A Progress Report," *Survey of Current Business* 46, no. 5 (1966): 13–39. One of the initial custodians of the model was George R. Green, who left the BEA staff in May 1971 to work with the Wharton Mark III model as executive director for Short-Term Forecasting at WEFA. Green, Popkin, and Hirsch all worked under Klein at the Wharton School. Green returned to the BEA staff in July 1974. At WEFA, the daily routine of short-term forecast production and customer relations tended to be much more hectic than the atmosphere at BEA, where Green took charge of longer-term projections and began developing an expanded (150–200 equations) version of a BEA long-term model based on the work reported on by Lester C. Thurow, in "A Fiscal Policy Model of the United States," *Survey of Current Business* 49, no. 6 (1969). Thurow's original model had 28 stochastic equations, 35 equations in all, and 52 exogenous variables.

the National Bureau of Economic Research and the National Science Foundation. Analysis of the BEA model is also part of the continuing study of economic forecasts conducted for the American Statistical Association by Charlotte Boschan and Victor Zarnowitz of the National Bureau of Economic Research.[51]

While Klein was producing his quarterly model, Michael K. Evans, a graduate student at Brown University, was becoming (in his own words) "fascinated" by the Klein-Goldberger model. Evans has been modeling economies ever since. For his Ph.D. dissertation, in 1963, he produced a postwar model of the United States economy using quarterly data, as Klein was also doing. The model that Evans constructed in his dissertation impressed Klein.[52] In June 1963, Evans joined the University of Pennsylvania faculty to work with the Wharton group.

> When Mr. Evans joined the faculty of the University of Pennsylvania... we proceeded cautiously by making joint forecasts—one from the Evans model and one from the Wharton model. Apart from the desire to have a check on our work, we looked for some complementarity because the Wharton model made significant use of anticipatory variables (investment expectations, housing starts, and consumer attitudes), while the Evans model did not.... After a year of joint forecasting from these two models, we set about the task of forging one single model that would combine the best features of each.[53]

The Wharton "merged" (WM) model (called that for a time until being christened the Wharton EFU model)[54] had forty-seven stochastic equations of the seventy-six in all, and forty-two exogenous variables; a large-size

---

[51] The ASA-NBER surveys are conducted quarterly and appear with comments by Zarnowitz in the AMSTAT news of the American Statistical Association, *Economic Outlook USA* of the University of Michigan Survey Research Center, and *Explorations in Economic Research* of the National Bureau of Economic Research.

[52] Michael K. Evans, "A Postwar Quarterly Model of the United States Economy, 1947 1960," Ph.D. dissertation, Brown University, 1964. Evans says the model was published as "Multiplier Analysis of a Postwar Quarterly U.S. Model and a Comparison with Several Other Models," *Review of Economic Studies,* date and issue unavailable.

[53] Evans and Klein, p. 1.

[54] EFU stands for Economic Forecasting Unit. It was formed in the summer of 1963 as a subunit of the Wharton Economic Research Unit (ERU), a research entity set up by University of Pennsylvania faculty members in 1961 with financial assistance from the Ford Foundation. F. Gerard Adams, ERU's head, is a former student of Klein and Suits at the University of Michigan. Klein persuaded him to come to Wharton after receiving the Ford grant. ERU's purpose is the support of Ph.D. students and dissertation research. When the Ford money began to run out, Klein and his colleagues established EFU as a vehicle for attracting replacement financing from companies like General Electric, Bethlehem Steel, IBM, and Standard Oil. EFU was the forerunner of Wharton Econometric Forecasting Associates (WEFA), discussed elsewhere in the chapter.

model.⁵⁵ It used a two-stage least squares estimation procedure. It was reestimated in late 1968 and early 1969, and then revised two years later as the Wharton Mark III (W-III) model.

> Given the rate at which new ideas in econometric modeling have been coming forth, it appears that now and for some time to come existing models will require significant rethinking every two to three years. Not surprisingly, it was clear by the summer of 1970 that the 1968–1969 version of the model was beginning to be outdated. It was consistently not predicting as much inflation as the economy was actually experiencing.⁵⁶

But the Wharton (WM) model did have its successes. A *Business Week* article that described the consensus developing across the country in late 1970 on forecasts for 1971 GNP, reported that the Wharton model, in November 1969, had predicted a recession-level 1970 GNP of $980 billion, real growth of 0.3 percent, and a price increase of 4.8 percent for 1970. "That is about as close as anyone could have gotten to the economy's actual performance: $977 billion GNP, slightly negative real growth, and a price climb of 5.2 percent."⁵⁷

Klein and his associates wanted to add a detailed financial sector to the Wharton model as well as other improvements featured in newer models. The result was the Wharton Mark III (W-III) model, with 63 stochastic equations, 204 equations in all, and 105 exogenous variables, the first of the very large models in the Wharton family. Its coefficients were estimated using a modified two-stage least squares procedure, required because of the large size of the model relative to the limited amount of data available. Mark III was later replaced by the still more comprehensive Wharton Mark IV model, illustrating how econometric models tend to continue to grow in size.

Wharton has an even larger model, known as the Wharton Annual and Industry (WAI) Forecasting model, that incorporates input-output information within a simultaneous equation framework to represent the behavior of industries.⁵⁸ The WAI model uses annual data to produce long-term (ten-year) forecasts differentiated by industry, whereas the Mark III model uses quarterly data to provide short-term aggregate forecasts for an eight-quarter

---

⁵⁵ There are two full accounts of the Wharton merged (WM) model available. The first appears in the Evans-Klein book, and the second appears in a textbook by Evans that develops the subject of macroeconomics by explaining the WM model step by step: Michael K. Evans, *Macroeconomic Activity: Theory, Forecasting, and Control* (New York: Harper and Row, 1969).

⁵⁶ McCarthy, p. 3.

⁵⁷ *Business Week,* December 12, 1970, p. 70.

⁵⁸ Ross S. Preston, *The Wharton Annual and Industry Forecasting Model* (Philadelphia: Economic Research Unit, University of Pennsylvania, 1972). Preston has been working on a new version of the model, parts of which are described by him in "The Wharton Annual and Industry Forecasting Model: Input/Output Within the Context of a Macro-Model," *International Economic Review* 16, no. 1 (1975).

period. These two models form the core of the forecasting service Wharton provides to business and government through the nonprofit firm of Wharton Econometric Forecasting Associates (WEFA), described later in the chapter.

Klein has an interesting technique for incorporating the experiences and insights of a broad sampling of experts into the Wharton model before producing a final forecast. He first prepares a preliminary forecast and distributes it to the business and government economists who are clients of WEFA. He then calls a meeting of these economists and proceeds to draw them out on how the assumptions and results of the preliminary forecast jibe with their opinions and with whatever specialized information they are privy to in their organization. As a result of the group's interaction, the Wharton staff makes a set of modifications to the model prior to generating the final forecast. The example given earlier in the chapter of the crisis at Wharton brought about by announcement of Nixon's New Economic Policy, and the sudden need for a revised forecast, took place on the occasion of just such a meeting.

SSRC-Brookings Model

There were three recessions in the first dozen years after World War II. Each one awakened memories of the 1929 crash, but in no instance did the economy fall victim to a depression. Economists spoke confidently of the economy's being depression-proof and much more stable than before the war. Economists James S. Duesenberry, Otto Eckstein, and Gary Fromm, all at Harvard at the time, decided to explore the question by building an econometric model of quarterly movements of GNP with particular attention to such factors as tax and transfer payments whose high postwar levels were considered to have a stabilizing effect over changes in business investment and government expenditure.

The Duesenberry-Eckstein-Fromm (DEF) model included equations relating inventory, consumption, and personal income to GNP, and disposable income to personal income. Unlike most other econometric models, the DEF model was completely recursive in formulation, which meant it could be simulated in a step-by-step manner like a system dynamics model. Several parameters of the model were estimated from data drawn exclusively from periods of recession. The model was applied primarily to the understanding of recession, rather than to recovery or prosperity, a major difference from the Klein-Goldberger model by which it was influenced.

Simulations of the DEF model suggested that tax and transfer payments did indeed have a stabilizing effect, although they did "not have the power to return the system to full employment," a conclusion borne out in subsequent years. The report on the model ended on a hopeful note to would-be modelers: "The model simulated the 1958 recession closely, using only data from earlier periods, suggesting that it has some predictive value. Obviously, better models, using a lower degree of aggregation, can, and should, be built.[59]

The authors went on themselves to build bigger and better models of the economy. First Fromm made the DEF model into a more complete structure for the Joint Economic Committee.[60] Soon Duesenberry and Fromm were part of an ambitious collaboration of numerous economists to construct the most comprehensive model to that time, eventually to be known as the Social Science Research Council-Brookings (SSB) model. A few years later, Eckstein put together a team to build another very large model, this one for commercial application (the DRI model). Both the Brookings and DRI models were influenced by the DEF model, as it in turn had been influenced by the Klein-Goldberger model. The DRI model was influenced by the Brookings model as well, as were the two most recent Wharton models (W-III and WAI). The lines of influence are shown by dotted lines in Figure 6–1, to distinguish them from the solid lines of direct descent.

The seed for the Brookings model was planted at a Social Science Research Council (SSRC) conference held in June 1959 at Ann Arbor to discuss the stability of the American economy.

> There was general agreement that econometric models should play a central role in the analysis of business-cycle problems and stabilization policies. It was also agreed that econometric models tend to become rapidly obsolete unless there is some arrangement to adjust the equations to data revisions and new research results. The need for larger-scale models with more detail than previously used was generally recognized.[61]

After the conference the SSRC established a committee on economic stability and with the committee's approval agreed to sponsor the cooperative development of a large-scale econometric model that would be

> acceptable to a wide variety of macroeconomic theoreticians and usable for stabilization policy. The spark ... came from the whetting of appetites by the DEF model and a realization that other available models did not have wide enough appeal and were not finely enough attuned to short-run (quarterly) business cycle analysis.[62]

In the course of two summer seminars at Dartmouth in 1961 and 1962, sectors of the economy were parceled out to specialists for component research.

---

[59] James S. Duesenberry, Otto Eckstein, and Gary Fromm, "A Simulation of the United States Economy in Recession," *Econometrica* 28, no. 4 (1960): 809.

[60] Gary Fromm, "Inventories, Business Cycles, and Economic Stabilization," *Inventory Fluctuations and Economic Stabilization* (Washington, D.C.: U. S. Congress, Joint Economic Committee, April 1962).

[61] James S. Duesenberry et al., *The Brookings Quarterly Econometric Model of the United States* (Chicago: Rand McNally, 1965), p. v.

[62] Fromm and Klein, p. 13.

By 1964, the sector contributions had been brought together into an integrated model of the economy. The model, referred to initially as the SSRC model, later became known as the Brookings model or the SSRC-Brookings (SSB) model, after the Brookings Institution agreed to accept custodianship of the project with encouragement from a $250,000 National Science Foundation (NSF) grant for continued work on the model. Duesenberry and Klein, original cochairmen of the project, were joined as project leaders by Edwin Kuh of M.I.T. and by Gary Fromm, who came to Brookings to supervise the work in the spring of 1963.

The first version of the Brookings model in 1964 had 226 equations, 119 of them stochastic, and 218 exogenous variables, making it the largest model of the time. A few years later a version with 216 equations, of which 156 were stochastic, and 105 exogenous variables, was said by its modelers to be "much larger in scale—on an order of seven to eight times—than any other econometric model" of that period.[63] The estimation procedures using a block recursive approach were limited-information maximum likelihood (where possible), two-stage least-squares, and when an equation had only one unlagged endogenous variable, ordinary least-squares.[64]

In reflecting on the significance of the project a decade after its beginnings, Klein wrote

> The original idea that a widely accepted working model for applications in contemporary analysis would be available never really materialized, ... for that kind of work shifted to other centers of econometric analysis. However, ... the research contributions of the Brookings model project ... did indeed play a large role in shaping applied econometric work throughout the world.[65]

The research contributions cited by Klein include: (1) use of input-output analysis to integrate the industrial structure within the traditional Keynesian framework of a macroeconometric model, a technique adopted and extended in the Wharton (WAI) model and the DRI model; (2) detailed modeling of the financial sector, an effort that was elaborated and refined later in a major model, known as the Fed-M.I.T.-Penn (FMP) model, developed for the Federal Reserve System; (3) application of the Gauss-Seidel iterative procedure for simulating large dynamic nonlinear models, a fast and simple technique now employed at econometric centers throughout the world; (4) organization of numerous diverse data files into a large integrated computerized data bank (the Brookings Model Data Bank) that was subsequently taken to form the basis for the initial DRI data bank; (5) specification and estimation research

---

[63] Gary Fromm and Paul Taubman, *Policy Simulations with an Econometric Model* (Washington, D.C.: Brookings Institution, 1968), p. ix.

[64] Duesenberry et al., p. 682.

[65] Fromm and Klein, pp. 13–14.

in the areas of investment, production, fiscal policy, and foreign exchange that has since been incorporated in many other models; and (6) policy research procedures[66] that open "new horizons for the whole subject of analysis of economic policy... [and] are now a standard part of work on econometric model projects." Klein concludes his review of the SSRC Brookings Project by observing that in

> contrast with the original intent of developing a consensus-based working model for short-run analyses of economic fluctuations, the Brookings model project became a research center of econometric model building.... Research efforts have now shifted to various specialized centers, and there is less need at this time for one large-scale project to serve the nation or the world econometric community in a concentrated way. Moreover, the computer technology, which is essential to macroeconometric research, is now highly developed, accessible to almost any serious researcher, and distributed through new remote access modes... [alone enough to] stimulate the dispersal of research effort.[67]

Brookings terminated its custodianship of the project around 1970. Brookings is very policy oriented and likes its research projects to have a clear and direct relevance to current policy issues. Its management felt uncomfortable with the methodological flavor of the SSRC-Brookings modeling effort and with the fact that this effort was neither generating current forecasts like the Wharton and Michigan models nor tying in with the policy-oriented work of the senior research staff. Gary Fromm left Brookings for a joint association with American University and a new econometric modeling company, Data Resources, Inc. He continued to work on the SSB model in collaboration with Klein under reduced NSF support to integrate a flow-of-funds model into the overall Keynesian framework.[68]

Federal Reserve Modeling

A major beneficiary of the Brookings model project is the Federal Reserve Board, which in past years has been one of the most supportive of all government agencies in the development of models and other tools for policy research. Its former chairman, William McChesney Martin, Jr., although not himself personally familiar with the workings of modeling tools, had faith that they could be useful and believed that associating with university researchers was healthy for his economists. His director of research, Daniel H.

---

[66] Procedures for doing policy research are set forth in Fromm and Taubman.
[67] Fromm and Klein, pp. 24, 27.
[68] Fromm left DRI in 1974 to found and direct the Washington office of the National Bureau of Economic Research, while continuing his association with American University and his work with Klein.

Brill, well known in the academic world, was trying to build up the Federal Reserve's image in academic circles. Its reputation, high in the 1930s, suffered during the 1940s and 1950s because of a depreciating attitude within the FRB about the value of academic research. Whatever his own personal views, Brill was determined to get professors like Paul Samuelson at M.I.T. to send him their A students instead of their C students, as had become the practice. With freedom from the annual budgetary hassle with Congress, the Federal Reserve had the financial ability to support innovative research projects and to build a first-class research team. An aggressive and successful recruiter, Brill made the most of this freedom with help from Federal Reserve governor George Mitchell.

Several governors and former governors of the Federal Reserve have been professional economists: George Mitchell, Arthur Burns, Robert Holland (formerly Brill's deputy in the research division), Andrew Brimmer, and Sherman J. Maisel, who was responsible for formulation of the housing sector of the Brookings model. From the Federal Reserve staff, Frank F. deLeeuw, a modeler-economist in the research division during the 1960s, was the developer of the financial sector of the Brookings model. Brill, himself, was one of the organizers of the Dartmouth conferences early in the development of the Brookings model, and he advised on specification of the financial sector.

With such close involvement in the SSRC-Brookings endeavor and with a generally progressive research orientation under Martin, Mitchell, and Brill, it was not surprising to find the Federal Reserve establishing its own macroeconomic modeling project. In 1967, Brill, at the suggestion of University of Pennsylvania economist Albert Ando and M.I.T. economist Franco Modigliani, initiated an ambitious research effort to model the monetary sector of the economy. Brill knew that Frank deLeeuw and his Federal Reserve colleague Edward M. Gramlich were also eager to develop a model to integrate several of the analytical research efforts within the Federal Reserve. Brill asked Ando and Modigliani to be coleaders of the project, with responsibility for making the major design decisions, and had deLeeuw and Gramlich join them as chief modelers for the Federal Reserve. The modeling team of very able persons and equally strong personalities was not without its tensions between inside staff and outside experts. As the project expanded, differences of opinion developed over such touchy matters as research direction, priorities, deadlines, and component specifications. On several parts of the model, two renditions were maintained in competition with each other.

By late 1969, three years and over $500,000 dollars after the start of the project, the model was united and essentially ready for application. Known as the FRB-MIT-Penn (FMP) model, it was the most comprehensive formal representation of the United States monetary system and monetary flow in existence.[69] The year the model was ready marked the beginning of the Nixon administration. Federal Reserve Chairman Martin was succeeded by Arthur F. Burns. Brill, deLeeuw, and Gramlich also departed the Federal Reserve.

Chairman Burns, a developer, with Geoffrey Moore, of the "leading indicators" school of economic research, was considerably less supportive of modeling than his predecessor, but did not halt the research division's use of the FMP model in performing its forecasting activities for the Federal Open Market Committee, the basic policymaking body of the Federal Reserve.[70] Once the model was ready to be used as an input to policy decisions, the Federal Reserve wished to shield its workings from public view. It declared the FMP model proprietary, to be kept separate and distinct from the version available to the academic community.

The public version, taken over by M.I.T., the University of Pennsylvania, and SSRC, was called the MPS model. With 150 equations, 80 of them stochastic, and 138 exogenous variables, it was a very large model. Structural changes made by Ando and Modigliani to the MPS version were incorporated in the FMP version, and vice versa, so the basic structures of the two models tended to remain the same, except for special equations used to predict a few troublesome and crucial variables such as the stock market. The main interest of the Federal Reserve was in operating its model for input to policy discussions, but it also devoted a great deal of attention to testing, studying, and improving the model, particularly its stability properties. Despite the fact that the internal version of the model was kept private, the Federal Reserve sought to maintain active communication with the academicians in its own self-interest.

An opportunity to test the still incomplete FMP model arose in 1968. After

---

[69] For descriptions of the FMP model, see Frank deLeeuw and Edward M. Gramlich, "The Federal Reserve-M.I.T. Econometric Model," *Federal Reserve Bulletin,* January 1968; Frank deLeeuw and Edward M. Gramlich, "The Channels of Monetary Policy," *Federal Reserve Bulletin,* June 1969; Franco Modigliani, Robert Rasche, and J. Phillip Cooper, "Central Bank Policy, the Money Supply and the Short-Term Rate of Interest," *Journal of Money, Credit and Banking,* May 1970; Albert Ando, Franco Modigliani, and Robert Rasche, "Appendix to Part One: Equations and Definitions of Variables for the FRB-MIT-Penn Econometric Model, November, 1969," in Bert G. Hickman (ed.), *Econometric Models of Cyclical Behavior* 2 vols. (Cambridge, Mass.: National Bureau of Economic Research, Inc., 1972), 1:543–598; Albert Ando, "Some Aspects of Stabilization Policies, the Monetarist Controversy, and the MPS Model," *International Economic Review* 15, no. 3 (1974): 541–571.

[70] The Federal Open Market Committee is composed of the seven members of the Board of Governors and five of the twelve presidents of the Federal Reserve regional banks. The twelve-person committee sets policy for the daily open market purchase and sale of government securities from the Federal Reserve's trading desk in New York City. These transactions, by influencing the level of commercial bank reserves, are the primary means by which the FRB exercises control of interest rates and money supply.

two years of urging of fiscal restraint by Keynesian economists, the federal government was about to institute a 10 percent tax surcharge. Economic forecasters were asked to predict the effect of the surcharge on consumer spending. There was general expectation that the surcharge would act as a depressant on spending, a view that was supported by projections of the DHL and OBE models and, some believe, by experimental forecasts from the incomplete FMP model as well. (This, the FMP modelers deny.) In the light of subsequent events, it would appear (using the parlance of the trade) that the fiscal multipliers implied by the models were too large. Some fault the models on their timing.

In any event, the Federal Reserve, fearing that the surtax might dampen consumption excessively, adopted a policy of easy money in order to stimulate the economy and avoid a "surtax overkill." The way it turned out, the surtax did not have the anticipated effect and the increase in money supply was ill-timed. Spending on automobiles and housing rose rather than fell. There are those who charge that formal modeling misled the Federal Reserve. Ando does not see how experimental forecasts made by the FMP model as early as 1968 could be taken as anything but an attempt to analyze the characteristics of the model. Gramlich claims that had the FMP model been running at the time, it would have predicted less of a decline in consumption than other models, since it used a "permanent income" form of the consumption function that gave little weight to temporary surtaxes and strong weight to the (then rising) stock market.[71]

The fact is that modeling, if a culprit, was not the only one. Judgmental forecasters inside and outside the Federal Reserve were also wrong.[72] When asked about the surtax episode, Brill calls it "an unpleasant subject." He says that Keynesian economists (among which he includes himself) did not have

---

[71] Indeed, the rising stock market in 1968 did show the consumption function of the FMP model to good advantage, but the falling stock market in 1969 showed it at a disadvantage with respect to the consumption functions of other models. See Saul H. Hymans, "Consumption: New Data and Old Puzzles," *Brookings Papers on Economic Activity* (Washington, D.C.: Brookings Institution, 1970), no. 1, pp. 117–126.

[72] For a postmortem on the effect of the surtax, see Arthur M. Okun, "The Personal Tax Surcharge and Consumer Demand, 1968–70," *Brookings Papers on Economic Activity* (Washington, D.C.: Brookings Institution, 1971), no. 1, pp. 167–211. Okun, a former chairman of the Council of Economic Advisers, found that the DRI, DHL, BEA, and Wharton models showed that it takes time for tax changes "to build up their complete direct impact on consumption" (ibid., p. 200). One may surmise that the spending on automobiles and housing in the first few months after passage of the surtax was due to a shift in how people chose to hold their wealth, as well as to the easing of money and credit. That is, the increase was not in the normal consumer spending that is related to current income by a Keynesian consumption function, but rather in a type of investment spending that is related to wealth. The anticipated fall-off in normal consumer spending did materialize the year after the surtax was passed.

an adequate consumption function. Even though they could fit historical data satisfactorily, tying consumption as closely as they did to current income was a mistake. "Only the monetarists were right in 1968," says Brill.[73]

Gramlich insists that the FMP model did not tie consumption to current income. Ando affixes the problem in the FMP model not to the consumption function but to the investment function, which he points out has since been reformulated. But Brill believes the surprise in investment behavior occurred only after businessmen saw that consumer spending was not falling off as expected. "Businessmen lost caution," Brill surmises.

After deLeeuw and Gramlich left the Federal Reserve, Jared J. Enzler, a former economics student at the University of Pennsylvania, took charge of the FMP model. Enzler spent much of his time initially getting the model working, maintaining it, and putting it on a time-shared computer (a CDC 6400 in Rockville, Maryland) so that it could be used from computer terminals at the FRB and at district banks of the Federal Reserve. He was also successful in putting the model on the Federal Reserve Board's own time-sharing computer facility. Later, Enzler had more time to work on revisions of the model with Ando and Modigliani. Their work led to modifications in the structures of both the public and private versions.

When deLeeuw left the Federal Reserve, James L. Pierce replaced him as chief of the section in which the modeling project was housed. Pierce was the principal author of the Federal Reserve critique of the LR model (discussed in Chapter 1) supplied by Arthur Burns to the Joint Economic Committee when the committee was trying to understand how the Nixon administration had come up with its GNP forecast of $1,065 billion. Consistent with his review of the LR model, Pierce had reservations about reliance on models.

> There is a real danger of giving more credence to model results than they deserve, especially if a particular policy trajectory is highly influenced by the choice of a model. The problem lies not only with uncertainty concerning the true value of model parameters, but also with the structure of models themselves. I cannot state with much certainty that we have a good approximation to the economy with our models at the Federal Reserve Board. I have even more doubt about other models that are used for policy analysis. My particular

---

[73] Ando and Modigliani had been involved during the middle 1960s in a celebrated controversy with Milton Friedman and David Meiselman (known as the AM-FM debate) over whether it was fiscal policy (the AM position) or monetary policy (the FM position) that exerted the dominant force on consumer behavior. Interest in the issue has since subsided. Most economists today are ready to concede that both fiscal and monetary actions play important roles in determining consumption. See Albert Ando and Franco Modigliani, "The Relative Stability of Monetary Velocity and the Investment Multiplier," *The American Economic Review* 55, no. 4 (1965): 693–728; "Reply," by Milton Friedman and David Meiselman, ibid., pp. 753–785; "Rejoinder," by Ando and Modigliani, ibid., pp. 786–790.

concern involves whether or not we have correctly approximated the impact of monetary policy in the models. For example, we have found that with some relatively minor changes in the specification of our quarterly model—changing just three or four equations—we can importantly alter its policy multipliers.[74]

To illustrate his point, Pierce showed how "the short-run impact of a change in the money stock predicted by the model will depend rather crucially on the money demand function selected." Said Pierce, "We simply have no reliable guidelines to help us choose among the functions available."[75]

Two different groups within the Division of Research and Statistics at the Federal Reserve produce policy forecasts: the modelers who use formal models, and the judgmental forecasters, who do not. Years ago, all forecasting was judgmental, but modelers have gradually gained in influence despite the recognized limitations of their models. There is an interesting mixture of cooperation and rivalry between the two groups, with more than a little mutual respect and noticeable complementarity developing.

> Judgmental forecasters at the Fed usually have a very good feel for what is going on in the economy, and they often make better short-term forecasts than the models do. The judgmental forecast is compared to the model forecast. The differences between the two forecasts often lead to insights and revisions in each....[76]

On aspects of the economy where the modelers' record has been good, their forecasts are given greater weight; on aspects where the modelers' record has been poor, the judgmental forecasts have greater influence. The disagreements that judgmental forecasters have with modelers on short-term forecasts tend to get resolved in favor of the former. But only models are well-equipped to estimate systematically the implications of alternate monetary policies. Models also have the advantage when it comes to forecasts going out beyond three or four quarters. But even the models are unreliable beyond about six quarters into the future. "Not much credence is put in longer-run forecasting," says Pierce, because of the "high degree of uncertainty concerning future values of exogenous variables."[77]

In addition to the FMP model, the Federal Reserve had a monthly money market (MMM) model "designed to provide insights into the short-run behavior of that market and to provide predictions of the short-run consequences for the monetary aggregates and short-term interest rates of alterna-

---

[74] James L. Pierce, "Quantitative Analysis for Decisions at the Federal Reserve," *Annals of Economic and Social Measurement* 3, no. 1 (1974): 15. Pierce's point is supported by the findings of many other policy modelers.

[75] Ibid., p. 16.

[76] Ibid., p. 12.

[77] Ibid., pp. 11 and 15.

tive monetary policies."[78] It was a small model consisting of approximately thirty variables and twelve stochastic equations. The monthly time frame of the model was chosen in an attempt to highlight the relatively wide short-term fluctuations hidden in more aggregative quarterly and annual models. The time frame also happened to mesh well with the schedule of monthly meetings of the Federal Open Market Committee.

The Federal Reserve Board has taken the position that "it is always necessary to bring judgment to bear on a model."[79] This attitude is in full agreement with that of most operators of large macroeconomic forecasting models.[80] But just as judgment enhances the usefulness of models, models have served an important purpose that goes beyond the part they play in producing forecasts and assessing the merits of alternative policies.

> While simulation results help directly in policy analysis, models have also encouraged people who are not involved in model building to think in terms of a system of equations in a general equilibrium framework. Thus, the effects of a policy action are more apt to be thought through for the entire economy, rather than for just one sector or element in isolation.[81]

Commercial Models and Auxiliary Services

In the late 1960s, the entrepreneurial pulse of the nation was running fast. The economy was doing well to outward appearances, expansion was the order of the day, and technology was in high vogue. The computer industry was a particular favorite. Wall Street investment houses seemed to gush over almost any new business activity having anything at all to do with computers. Time-sharing companies were propagating at a furious pace. The roof would soon fall in for the shakier companies, but it was an exciting time while it lasted: a time for daring, experimentation, and innovation.

Much of the creativity that flowers during such a period eventually wilts and is lost. But a certain portion takes root and grows into important new business. Commercial econometric modeling got its start during this period. From every indication, it is likely to endure. It has been well-received by its customers in industry and government; it weathered the 1969–1970 recession without a bruise; it has prospered and appears to have a bright future.

The largest of the econometric modeling firms is Data Resources, Inc. (DRI), headed by Otto Eckstein, who earlier had collaborated with Duesen-

---

[78] Thomas D. Thomson, James L. Pierce, and Robert T. Parry, "A Monthly Money Market Model," *Journal of Money, Credit and Banking* (in press), p. 1.

[79] Thomson, Pierce, and Parry, p. 44.

[80] Note, though, that the St. Louis Bank of the Federal Reserve has had a different view, as has Ray C. Fair.

[81] James L. Pierce and Thomas D. Thomson, "Short-Term Financial Models at the Federal Reserve Board," *The Journal of Finance* 29, no. 2 (1974): 357.

berry and Fromm in development and analysis of the DEF model. While an assistant professor at Harvard, Eckstein served as staff director for a Congressional Joint Economic Commitee study of employment, growth, and price levels. During the Johnson administration, as a member of the Council of Economic Advisers, he received quick and abundant access to a wide variety of economic data, which he missed after returning to Harvard in 1967. He needed good data for the consulting and economic forecasting he was doing for the financial community. Recognizing a repeating pattern in forecasting that lent itself to automation, he saw the makings for a new commercial service. Ten years before, while he was working on the DEF model, he had discussed the idea of going into the econometric modeling business with colleagues Duesenberry and Fromm. Having put aside the idea at the time, he was encouraged by the rapid strides that had been made in the intervening years in computer and communications technology. He began to experiment with time-sharing, which he felt provided a promising vehicle for making data and modeling services available, useful, and practical to business and government clients.

Eckstein founded DRI in late 1968 with Donald B. Marron who arranged the financing and provided business and organizational know-how. Eckstein assumed the presidency of DRI and Marron became chairman of the board. They located in Lexington, Massachusetts, along Boston's circumferential Route 128, the home of numerous research and development firms started by former students and faculty of Harvard and M.I.T.

Gary Fromm, involved in the formation of DRI, terminated his stewardship of the Brookings model project. Fromm had put together a data bank and statistical analysis system in a batch-processing mode that was advanced for its time. Eckstein hired one of the Brookings model programmers, John Ahlstrom, in the summer of 1968 to begin to develop the data bank system for time-sharing. James A. Craig, data bank manager of the Brookings model project, joined DRI in January 1969 and quickly built a 6,000 series data bank, starting with 350 series in the Brookings collection. Fromm left Brookings to set up DRI's Washington office and simultaneously to join American University.

DRI needed more than the data bank to offer a usable information system. It needed statistical and computer programming facilities for specifying an econometric model, estimating coefficients, and running the simulation, and it needed a model of the economy. A package of statistical regression routines, known as the Time Series Processor (TSP), developed by Robert E. Hall, seemed to DRI more flexible and powerful than any of its counterparts at the time, including the statistical routines used for the Brookings model. Eckstein requested Hall to convert his package of routines to the DRI time-shared system. The result was the Economic Programming Language (EPL), an extension of TSP that provided DRI with a comprehensive estimation system for econometric model building. Robert Lacey developed the MODEL and MODSIM time-sharing programs to facilitate the use of large national models in combination with the microsatellite models of user organizations.

The requirement for a model of the economy was more difficult to meet. DRI considered the Brookings model, but its structure made it too elaborate and cumbersome for the purpose. Eckstein sought to avoid unnecessary competition and had active discussions with Klein about the Wharton model, but decided that DRI had to have its own model. He and Klein did agree to make the Wharton model available on-line as a supplementary DRI service.

Eckstein collaborated with several students and colleagues in developing the DRI model, most closely with former Wharton student Edward W. Green, who developed the consumption equations; Harvard economists Martin E. Feldstein, who developed the initial version of the financial sector of the model, and Allen Sinai, who extended it; and M.I.T. economist Lester C. Thurow, who developed the initial investment equations. An academic consultant group, including Fromm, Dale Jorgenson of Harvard, and Marc Nerlove of the University of Chicago, collaborated in developing this and other DRI econometric models. By mid-1969 the quarterly model was running. By the fall of 1969 it was producing forecasts for DRI clients.

The DRI Quarterly model at one point had 368 endogenous variables and 120 exogenous variables, of which 162 of the endogenous variables were not central to the model's mechanism.[82] The large size is attributable to the breakdown by industry. The model had separate production equations for forty industries, interrelated by a table of input-output coefficients. A later version of the model in 1975 had 299 exogenous variables and 1,424 equations, of which over 300 were stochastic. The 1975 version, called DRI-II, resulted from DRI's extensively reworking its model to account for the high levels of inflation in 1974.

The DRI model was programmed initially for a time-shared Burroughs B5500 computer, since upgraded several times to larger computers (in 1975 a four-processor B7700) to accommodate DRI's growing business. The model was made available to customers on-line, via DRI's time-sharing service, over a national telephone network operated by the TYMSHARE company. Customers had the ability to insert their own assumptions and derive their own

---

[82] Carl F. Christ, "Econometrics and Model Building, 1967–1972," *The Annals of the American Academy of Political and Social Science* 403 (1972): 161. See also Christ's earlier paper, "Econometrics and Model Building," *The Annals of the American Academy of Political and Social Science* 370 (1967): 164–175. For a description of the DRI model, see Otto Eckstein, Edward W. Green, and Allen Sinai, "The Data Resources Model: Uses, Structure, and the Analysis of the U.S. Economy," *International Economic Review* 15, no. 3 (1974): 595–615.

forecasts (but they could not change equations, since the model was precompiled). Customers could also tie in simulation of the DRI model with simulation of their own company models.

Eckstein used the model to produce a forecast for customers monthly, and more frequently during periods of special interest. The computer run contained many judgmental elements. Eckstein had no compunction about overriding the computer's results when they failed to agree with his intuition. After carefully analyzing recent equation and model errors, he made alterations called "add factors."[83]

Eckstein's reputation stemmed primarily from his expertise as a macroeconomist and his sense of the workings of the economy, not from his performance as a modeler per se. Yet, his modeling activity and experience have contributed significantly to his knowledge and judgment. Eckstein's attitude about models has been decidedly utilitarian. He has rarely hesitated to subordinate the model to his visceral reactions. Models for him have not been principally instruments for expressing ever more refined economic theories; they have been tools and foils for helping to fill in detail, challenge intuition, and construct forecasts that are comprehensive, self-consistent, and as accurate as possible. According to Eckstein, "forecasters with models beat forecasters without models."

With hard-nosed pragmatism, Eckstein comes across as a strong advocate of the value and practical usefulness of models—at least *his* kinds of models. As for other kinds, like system dynamics, Eckstein dismisses them with a wave of the hand and another aphorism, "Only in econometrics are models for real." Eckstein bases this conclusion on what he regards as econometrics' healthy regard for the factual record.

In the first half dozen years of its existence, DRI grew rapidly in numbers of employees and clients, as much as 50 percent a year or more. Customers included industrial firms like AT&T, financial institutions like Morgan Guaranty and Commercial Credit, and government agencies like the Council of Economic Advisers. As of the summer of 1972, each customer was paying a subscription charge of from $1,500 a year (for access to a limited set of DRI's services) to $12,000 a year (for access to a full set). Average fees paid by customers tended to rise as the range of DRI services expanded. In addition to forecasting, DRI furnished its clients on-line access to a large computerized data base of economic time series. Much of these data originated in

---

[83] Eckstein, for example, added about $9 billion to the DRI model's 1971 forecast for GNP. Frank Ripley of DRI's Washington office told us he considered use of the Cochrane-Orcutt correction for autocorrelation in modifying the DRI model to take account of consistent forecasting errors, but found that the technique creates difficulties in long-run simulations and can be justified only for short-run forecasting. Ripley was a staff member of the Council of Economic Advisers for three years in the early 1970s, working with Herbert Stein in short-term forecasting.

the offices of DRI's government customers, but were not drawn together by them. The data bank service has been critical to DRI's operation and success.

DRI has also offered a general time-sharing computer service with special statistical software that allows customers to analyze time-series data on-line and form and run their own regression models.[84] DRI has issued periodic reports on the economy and has conducted quarterly conferences and regular technical seminars. The company has also made consultants available to help customers estimate equations, generate forecasts, and develop an overall economic base for management decisions. It has been company policy not to "take over" in these consulting assignments. The DRI consultant is told to work with the customer's analyst or economist so as to assist him, not replace him.

Occasionally DRI has built a complete model for a customer, such as the Hudson-Jorgenson model, produced for the Ford Energy Policy Project, to explore the probable effect on national income and employment of a long-run reduction in the country's rate of energy growth.[85] The finding that a gradual reduction in overall energy growth would have only a minimal impact directly supported the strong energy conservation recommendations made in the Ford project's final report.[86] Had the model not supported these recommendations, one may wonder about the significance that would have been attached to it, especially in view of the skepticism that the director of the Ford project is said to have had about aggregate econometric models.[87] As it was, the DRI model and its conclusions were highlighted in the report and in the publicity attending its release.

DRI has shifted the emphasis of its business by expanding outward from macroeconomic forecasting of the economy to the modeling of operations in particular industries such as chemical products and steel. DRI vice president Charles B. Warden, Jr.,[88] said it took them a long time to realize that to be taken seriously they had to be directly useful to company management in financial planning and decision making. When the president of a chemical

---

[84] Laffer and Ranson used the DRI time-sharing system to run the LR model and obtain the results that enter into the story reported on in chapter 1.

[85] The Hudson-Jorgenson model is described in Edward A. Hudson and Dale W. Jorgenson, "U.S. Energy Policy and Economic Growth, 1975–2000," *The Bell Journal of Economics and Management Science* 5, no. 2 (1974): 461–514.

[86] Energy Policy Project of the Ford Foundation, *A Time to Choose: America's Energy Future* (Cambridge, Mass.: Ballinger, 1974).

[87] The skepticism of the Ford Energy Policy Project's director is said to stem from the presentation and refutation of the Wein model at the Permian Basin hearings of the Federal Power Commission in the early 1960s. An account of this episode is contained in Joseph L. Steele, *The Use of Econometric Models by Federal Regulatory Agencies* (Boston: D. C. Heath, 1971).

[88] Warden served as special assistant to several chairmen of the Council of Economic Advisers (Ackley, Okun, and McCracken) before joining DRI as a vice president in 1969.

company wants to know whether or not to build a new plant, a macroeconomic forecast will probably be meaningful for his decision. But what he really needs is a clear picture of the future market for his product and how it interrelates with the markets for related products. And he also needs a solid understanding of how financial markets will affect his special capital needs.

DRI has developed generic models of the chemical and steel industries designed to inform companies on how their marketplaces operate in conjunction with the marketplaces of interdependent industries. These models, not always strictly econometric, sometimes include other methodologies such as quadratic programming. DRI maintains ownership of the models and uses them, along with its other proprietary models, to perform analyses for customers at a fee. DRI may run the models for the customers, or the customers may run and alter the models themselves on DRI's computer system and with DRI's assistance. The contract with customers forbids redistribution of the model, its equations, or any of the data that DRI makes available. The charge for use of the steel model has been $15,000 a year, including support in the use of the model. DRI refers to this offering as its "steel service."

By virtue of the changing nature of its business and the major inroads it has been able to make with what are, in effect, management advisory services, DRI now considers its potential market to be five or six times what it had originally estimated. At a time when the nation was in a recession (1975), DRI was still growing, with about 300 employees in offices around the country and a revenue approaching $10 million.

DRI is not the only firm specializing in the business of providing econometric forecasts and modeling services. Within about a year of DRI's founding in 1968, and not unrelated to it, two competitive companies were also getting started.

After teaching elementary economics seventeen times without a break during the six years he was at the Wharton School, Michael Evans, codeveloper with Lawrence Klein of the Wharton WM model, decided to leave the joys of academic life for private enterprise. In September 1969, without benefit of outside financing, Evans formed a one-man firm, MKE Associates.[89] His first project was to turn a number of the ideas that he had stored up since his last major model building effort six years earlier (along with some concepts from the FMP model of the Federal Reserve) into a new quarterly model of the economy. Among the prospective customers to whom Evans made presentations of his new model toward the end of 1970 was the Economics Department of the Chase Manhattan Bank in New York City. Evans, unable to expand his firm because of lack of capital, was beginning to have doubts about

---

[89] Philadelphia Research Associates is the name under which Evans issued some of his early forecasts. Evans informs us that these forecasts were actually produced by MKE Associates.

the wisdom of going on without financing. When John Wilson, head of Chase's Economics Department, called him back with an offer to buy the company, Evans was ready to talk business.

Chase Econometric Associates, a subsidiary of the Chase Manhattan Bank, was formed in early 1971 with Evans as president and Wilson as chairman of the board. The model Evans had developed, now called the Chase Econometrics (CE) model, has about 100 exogenous variables, 175 endogenous variables, and 125 stochastic equations. It became the central pin in an expanding line of customer services.

Evans acknowledges that Eckstein's founding of DRI was an influential factor in his own decision to go into business. But Evans did not have Eckstein's reputation. In his own words, he had to "muscle his way" into contention. He was aided by good forecasts and a good press. The *New York Times* noted in a special 1972 year-end feature on the coming year's economy that "Chase Econometrics has had a remarkably accurate track record in its forecasting during the last few years."[90] Such reports clearly helped. The association with Chase Manhattan was another plus.

In addition to its standard macroeconomic CE model, Chase Econometrics also ran a large industry model for customers. Where DRI stressed interactive data analysis and modeling via time-sharing, Chase Econometrics emphasized industry reports and straight subscription accounts. Because of the significantly different character of its business, Chase Econometrics could have more customers than DRI (in 1975 it had over 500), but on the average it received a good deal less per client than did DRI. Many customers had both services. Evans takes pride in the fact that no more than 5 percent of Chase's business was with the federal government. DRI's percentage was much higher. Chase Econometrics did not operate its own computer facilities, as did DRI. It subcontracted to a time-sharing vendor: originally Rapidata, later Cyphernetics. An interactive customer signed two contracts: one with the vendor and one with Chase. Evans considered his decision not to get into the time-sharing business as one of his wisest moves. It saved Chase from some of the computer and telecommunication headaches that typically beset time-sharing companies, but also constrained the firm's potential market.

An interesting legal question is whether Chase Econometrics is barred from entering the field of management consulting (as DRI has done). The One-Bank Holding Act in New York permits banks to engage in certain nonbanking activities through subsidiaries.[91] Time-sharing is an allowed activity but management consulting is not because of the potential for conflict of interest. Evans, with a hint that the question is of more than academic interest to him, says he will "leave it to the lawyers" to decide.

---

[90] *New York Times,* December 31, 1972, Section 3, p. 1.

[91] Chase Econometrics is a subsidiary of the Chase Manhattan Bank, not of the holding company.

Whatever its ultimate boundaries, Chase Econometrics has been expanding. It appears to have been growing at about 40 percent a year in revenue. Its projected 1975 revenue was in excess of $4 million, compared to $9 or $10 million for DRI. Chase Econometrics had about 100 employees to DRI's 300. Since these figures are all unofficial and unsupported, one can only guess at the relative size of the two companies. Chase would appear to be about 40 percent as large as DRI. Says Otto Eckstein, "Chase Econometrics is our most serious competitor."

The rivalry is echoed by Evans. "This is a two-firm industry," he declares. Yet there have been a number of other companies offering similar services, including parts of Battelle and General Electric, and forecasting groups in Georgia, Michigan, and England. Most significant of the other firms in the industry is Wharton Econometric Forecasting Associates (WEFA), the nonprofit corporation formed by Lawrence Klein and his colleagues at the Wharton School in 1969, the same year that DRI got started and the same year that Evans left Wharton to go into business for himself.[92] WEFA initially made its model available over the DRI service, "in retrospect a mistake," says Wharton economics professor F. Gerard Adams, the firm's secretary-treasurer, who was convinced that to survive in the business one needs to offer timesharing. WEFA let its contract with DRI expire and contracted with Boeing Computer Services to provide remote access to WEFA's time-sharing data bank, estimation, and simulation system called DAMSEL.

From Adams' point of view, econometric modeling was (at least), a *"three-firm industry."* As evidence, Adams noted that WEFA was a thriving enterprise with over 135 clients and a rapidly growing activity in tying its macro models to satellite models it is building for regions (Pennsylvania, Mississippi, Philadelphia), industries (steel, petroleum), commodity markets (nonferrous metals, rubber), and energy. Yet, said George Green when he was with WEFA, "making money is not our main goal." WEFA's primary objective, says Adams, is to contribute to national forecasts and policy research. Adds Klein emphatically, "we are not a commercial firm."[93]

Klein feels that commercial modeling firms have done a disservice to the field by putting profit ahead of scholarship. Another point of view sees the commercialization of modeling as having placed models within reach of a wide class of decision makers and as having made them potentially more useful than ever before. Klein acknowledges that up to 1962 "it was a continual battle to get econometric models accepted." He did not then foresee the day

---

[92] Wharton Econometric Forecasting Associates is wholly owned by the University of Pennsylvania. Its activities have been discussed earlier in the chapter. The Research Seminar in Quantitative Economics at the University of Michigan, nonprofit proprietors of the MQEM model, is a very similar, though smaller, operation.

[93] WEFA, together with EFU (its still-functioning predecessor) has contributed over $100,000 a year (from about $1 million in gross annual revenue) to the support of Ph.D. students and dissertation research.

when "just about every company and every country" would be wanting to have its own model. Klein attributes this development to the "computer age." DRI and Chase Econometrics are products and instruments of the computer age.

Two Small Models

Besides the Wharton model, DRI has also made the monetarist St. Louis model available to its customers on-line. Although it too was an aggregate econometric model of the economy, the St. Louis model differed sharply from the other macroeconomic models (except for the LR model described in Chapter 1). As a monetarist model, the St. Louis model was non-Keynesian in formulation. It was based on the modern quantity theory of money that regards money stock as the major influence on the collective behavior of economic units. Created in 1970 and maintained by the Federal Reserve Bank of St. Louis, it was not designed as a replacement for Keynesian macroeconomic models, but as an additional entry to the modeling field.[94] Nor was it intended as a tool for short-term forecasting. Beginning in the early 1960s, the St. Louis bank began emphasizing the use of monetary aggregates in economic analysis. The St. Louis model was a direct outgrowth of this movement. Its primary purpose was to assist "in the development and evaluation of stabilization policies" and to assess the impact of alternative monetary and fiscal measures.[95] It was intended to help government authorities evaluate the short- and long-run effects of alternative monetary and fiscal actions on output, employment, prices, and interest rates.

With but eight equations, five of them stochastic, the St. Louis model was very small. It had only three exogenous variables: change in money stock, change in federal expenditures at high employment, and potential full-employment output. It was smaller by a factor of thirty than the Brookings and DRI models, and almost as small as the LR model (with its three equations, all stochastic, and six exogenous variables.)

Because of its small size, the St. Louis model was useful as a standard for comparison. What made it especially valuable for this purpose was that its developers tried to maintain a "hands-off" philosophy. Unlike most modelers, the St. Louis team kept the model's basic form "unchanged so as to permit more accurate assessment of its usefulness and validity."[96] Coefficients were re-estimated as new data became available, and in this sense the model was

---

[94] Leonall C. Andersen and Keith M. Carlson, "A Monetarist Model for Economic Stabilization," *Federal Reserve Bank of St. Louis Review*, April 1970, pp. 7–25.

[95] Leonall C. Andersen and Keith M. Carlson, "St. Louis Model Revisited," *International Economic Review*, June 1974, p. 1.

[96] Ibid., p. 12.

put back on the track each quarter; yet the fundamental specification of the model was kept the same.

The tendency with larger models is for the modeler to strive to improve the performance of the model by a continual process of modification, enlargement, refinement, and, as previously discussed, by imposing judgment and intuition on it. Klein alters the Wharton model and the exogenous input for it on the basis of a users' conference called before the final run to discuss the results of a preliminary simulation. Hymans and Shapiro do the same with the Michigan model. Eckstein adds adjustment factors to the output of the DRI model to bring it into line with his personal feel for the economy. The Federal Reserve adjusts the constant terms in equations of the FMP model "that have not been tracking well," blends the model's forecast with a judgmental forecast produced by its judgmental forecasters, derives a consensus forecast, and then again adjusts the individual equations of the model "so as to force its sectors and totals to agree quarter by quarter with the consensus forecast."[97]

While such subjective adjustments have tended to improve the forecasts and keep them consistent with economic developments not reflected by the model, they have also made it difficult to cross-evaluate the performance of models as opposed to modelers. Indicative of the problem is the previously cited remark about the SUM model at the University of Michigan, whose forecasts were said to be 80 percent Suits, 20 percent model. Under the circumstances, it is wise to have some forecasts available for comparison that are "mostly model" (although the reader should take that phrase with a grain of salt).

The monetarist St. Louis model was one relatively objective model. Another, this one in the Keynesian tradition, was developed in the late 1960s by Ray C. Fair, a Yale economist who took his Ph.D. in economics from M.I.T. in 1968. Fair kept his model deliberately small and comparatively simple. It contained twenty equations, fourteen of them stochastic, and sixteen exogenous variables. It had no tax variable and almost no financial sector, taking market interest rate as an exogenous variable. Consumption was a function of GNP, not disposable income. Fair called his model of the economy a short-run "forecasting model" as opposed to a "structural model" (a model designed more to explain the structure of the economy than to predict its behavior). Fair made extensive use of expectational variables such as investment expectations and consumer buying plans. He avoided making subjective adjustments and maintained a hands-off policy, preferring to "stick by his guns and let the chips fall where they may."

> The model is free from the use of subjective methods in that, given data on the exogenous variables of the model, the forecasts can be generated in a determi-

[97] Pierce, p. 12.

nistic way. The forecasting ability of the model can thus be analyzed in objective terms, with some confidence placed on the assumption that the past forecasting performance of the model will be capable of achievement in the future. The disadvantage with informal forecasting techniques is that they are difficult to quantify; and it is thus difficult to determine the likelihood of their future success given their past forecasting performance.[98]

Fair did not really object to the use of subjective adjustments by other modelers, but believed it essential to have unadjusted or mechanically adjusted models as well. Fair's goal was to contribute to the development of better macroeconometric models that come ever closer to approximating the laws that govern the behavior of the economy. He had faith that these laws exist and are stable. To him, a model that was subjectively adjusted did not provide as solid a basis for improvement in specification as one that was not subjectively adjusted.[99]

In the past, Klein has differed with Fair on several counts. Klein believes that "best predictions will be made from best structural models," an opinion that Fair would share only with respect to the long run. Klein feels that models must be large enough "to accommodate taxes, transfers, price level, wage rate, interest rate, foreign trade, and all the main components of GNP," as well as tax law changes, shifts in monetary policy, and other "environmental changes." Klein defends *a priori* adjustment of constant terms in the equations of a model as a way of keeping the model in very close touch with reality on an updated basis, according to the recent history of error terms in the model and a knowledge of special events likely to occur. Fair claimed that his model was "better at tracking the economy" during the 1960s than either the Wharton or BEA model. But its performance fell short of the other models in the 1971–1972 period. Whereas Fair put the blame on the period, calling it "abnormal" because of the General Motors strike, Klein contends that as a "critical" period it was an excellent time for testing the strength of a model. Klein believes a model needs to spell out the car market in enough detail to be able to take account of the adjustments caused by strikes and other disturbances. He feels modelers should seek out, not avoid, "abnormal" situations as testing grounds for their models.[100]

Klein, expressly opposed to small models as serious forecasting instruments, sees a need for building highly technical pieces of nonstatistical institutional information into model specifications: *a priori* information on official budgets, social security legislation, tax codes, the Eurodollar process, certificates of

---

[98] Ray C. Fair, *A Short-Run Forecasting Model of the United States Economy* (Lexington, Mass.: Heath-Lexington Books, 1971), p. 2.

[99] Ray C. Fair, "An Evaluation of a Short-Run Forecasting Model," *International Economic Review* 15, no. 2 (1974): 285–303.

[100] Lawrence R. Klein, *An Essay on the Theory of Economic Prediction* (Helsinki: The Academic Book Store, 1968), pp. 99, 80, 50.

deposit, environmental constraints, and the like. That is why he favors big models. One cannot build very much institutional detail into small models.

Fair's views no longer seem as much at variance with Klein's as they once did. Fair agrees that the model builder should welcome abnormal situations for testing his model, although Fair's definition of an abnormal situation is not exactly the same as Klein's. Fair also appears readier than he used to be to sacrifice smallness of size for forecasting accuracy. He has put his small model to rest and has built a new model of the economy that incorporates microeconomic effects and is four times larger than the twenty-equation model.[101]

In sharper philosophical disagreement with Fair is Arthur M. Okun, who has thought about modeling from the perspective both of a macroeconomic forecaster and a government official. Okun served as chairman of the Council of Economic Advisers under Lyndon Johnson. For Okun, any sensible model builder should want to amend the results of his model and confront it with subjective judgment much of the time.

> Take an automobile demand equation, for example. The equation says: Tell me disposable income for the last three quarters, lagged auto consumption, the existing stock of cars, some interest rate, and a couple of wealth or liquidity variables, and I will tell you what to believe about future expenditures on cars; and nothing else in the world that you could possibly know should make any difference whatsoever in your estimate of automobile expenditures for the next four quarters.
>
> Now, what a foolish equation. How can it be so absurd? How can it have such a limited perspective on what can be relevant in determining the course of automobile expenditures? Anyone working on September 15 to project automobile demand for the fourth quarter of 1971 should have asked himself searching questions about how to assess the impact of the proposed repeal of the automobile excise tax, both while it was pending in the Congress and after it became law. Similarly, he would have had to judge what it meant to consumers that 1972 automobile prices had been rolled back, but might go up again subsequently. Nobody knows how to weight such issues objectively and systematically. But we know zero is the wrong answer. And zero shouldn't be the answer in any forecast meant to guide policy.[102]

---

[101] Ray C. Fair, "A Model of Macroeconomic Activity," vol. 2: "The Empirical Model," (New Haven, Conn.: Yale University, first draft, May 1975). Fair describes the new model as "not in any direct sense an expanded or revised version of my forecasting model" (p. ix). The new model contains eighty-two equations, twenty-six of them stochastic, and seventy-eight exogenous variables (p. 95), making it large by our measure. In a letter sent out July 21, 1975, along with his twenty-first forecast based on the small model, Fair writes, "I have decided to make this my last regular forecast with the [small] model.... The new model ... is on much firmer theoretical grounds ... and also appears to be more accurate." Fair adds, "if I do eventually release *ex ante* forecasts with the new model, the forecasts will not be subjectively adjusted."

[102] Fromm and Klein, pp. 367–368.

Okun's observation, noted at the end of Chapter 3, is worth repeating here. "The model as a forecasting device is not an alternative to judgment. It is not a product in and of itself. It is a tool in the hands of a trained economist." Says Okun, "Larry Klein can perform better when he has his model."[103]

Recapitulation

So the battle lines are drawn—for intellectual disagreement, for business competition, and through both, for collaboration, innovation, and forward progress. We need the small models as standards of comparison and as instruments for evaluating alternative strategies of control. We need the large models for the detailed level of understanding and the greater flexibility they afford. We need the objective "hands-off" approach as a measure of what models can do by themselves and as a basis for improvement. We need subjective "fine-tuning" and judgment for making the forecasts as good as possible. We need the commercial enterprises for packaging modeling and data services and bringing them to the point of application. We need the research and educational institutions for advancing the state of the art of modeling, for innovating, and for training modelers for the campaigns ahead.

There is no best model. We should use many models, both for cross-checks and for coalitions. A study of the predictive records of the Chase Econometrics, DRI, Fair, and Wharton models for nine major economic variables over a three-year period found that no one model dominated the rest. Chase Econometrics had the best overall record for current dollar GNP and also for forecasts of business fixed investment, but its forecasts of residential construction were inferior. DRI had the smallest computed errors for the unemployment rate, total consumption expenditures, and business inventory investment, but it also had the least accurate forecasts of fixed business investment. The Fair model, because of its small size and its renunciation of subjective adjustments (even in the face of an auto strike and price freeze), tended to have the poorest forecasts. Yet its estimates of expenditures on consumer durables were generally the most successful, as were its estimates of changes in business and fixed investment. Wharton ranked first in real GNP and investment in residential structures, but it had relatively large error accumulation in its forecasts of inflation and the unemployment rate.[104]

---

[103] Ibid., p. 362.

[104] Stephen K. McNees, "The Predictive Accuracy of Econometric Forecasts" and "A Comparison of the GNP Forecasting Accuracy of the Fair and St. Louis Econometric Models," *New England Economic Review,* Federal Reserve Bank of Boston (September-October 1973), pp. 3–34. McNees, in the second cited study, compared the GNP forecasts of the Fair and St. Louis models, finding that the former were consistently superior, but noting that the St. Louis model has been very successfully used in studies of stabilization policy, the purpose for which it was designed.

A comparison was also made between the forecasts generated by the models as a group and a set of judgmental forecasts submitted by thirty-six professional economic forecasters, most of whom "do not rely primarily on formal econometric models." The results of the comparison were "rather inconclusive," but overall the median judgmental forecast seemed to be "about as accurate as the median econometric forecast."[105] The fact is that just as most modelers adjust the results of their models judgmentally, many judgmental forecasters avail themselves of model forecasts in deriving their estimates. Paul Samuelson speaking for nonmodelers says, "our judgment has been formed and is kept tuned up by looking at computer forecasts." Before "tackling the back of an envelope" Samuelson has regularly consulted a number of the well-known macroeconomic models. He says, "We dwarfs of judgment see as far as we do because we stand on the shoulders of computer giants."[106]

In 1974, economic forecasters, modelers and judgmentalists alike, took a severe trouncing. They predicted that inflation would average about 6 percent, with only a slight dip in production, and that economic recovery would begin by late fall. Instead, inflation soared to double digits and the economy plunged into a deep, prolonged recession (some economists called it a depression) that did not begin to abate until well into 1975. Poor crops domestically and an oil cartel internationally provided excuses for those who wanted them, but a more productive route was to examine why and where the models had failed. Visibly shaken, econometric modelers began to take second and third looks at their models for deficiencies and weak spots.

Confirmed in his beliefs by the poor performance of econometric models, and convinced that traditional econometric modeling is the wrong approach, system dynamics modeler Jay Forrester worked with determination on his most ambitious model to date—a 2,000 state-variable model of the national economy focusing on the causes of inflation and recession.[107] Econometric modelers were busy too. Otto Eckstein launched a thorough overhaul of the

---

[105] Ibid., p. 23. In a later study, McNees found that model forecasts with judgment generally outperformed mechanical approaches. See Stephen K. McNees, "How Accurate Are Economic Forecasts," *New England Economic Review,* Federal Reserve Bank of Boston (November-December 1974), pp. 2–19. Accuracy, however, is not the whole story. In another comparison of models, it was found that "though the models forecast well over horizons of four to six quarters, they disagree so strongly about the effects of important monetary and fiscal policies that they cannot be considered reliable guides to such policy effects...." Carl F. Christ, "Judging the Performance of Econometric Models of the U.S. Economy," *International Economic Review* 16, no. 1 (1975): 54.

[106] Samuelson, p. 9.

[107] Jay W. Forrester, "Understanding Social and Economic Change in the United States," *Proceedings of the 1975 Summer Computer Conference* (La Jolla, Calif.: Simulation Councils, 1975), pp. 1465–1473. Also see Nathaniel J. Mass, *Economic Cycles: An Analysis of Underlying Causes* (Cambridge, Mass.: Wright-Allen Press, 1975).

DRI model to increase its sensitivity to financial conditions and make it better able to explain the instabilities of the preceding years.[108] Michael Evans, agreeing with the sentiments of economist-government official John T. Dunlop, questioned the validity and usefulness of aggregate models by themselves and began putting more of his firm's efforts into industry studies of production bottlenecks, raw material prices, wages, and markets. Ray Fair set aside his diminutive model for a grander one that incorporated microeconomic effects and many more variables. Lawrence Klein endeavored to bring a greater number of institutional factors into the Wharton model and to link it up with macroeconomic models of Japan, the European nations, and other countries of the world.

The general trend was to move away from the unitary, aggregate model of the macroeconomy in two directions simultaneously. There was a move toward greater detailing of industry, institutional, and microeconomic factors, and there was a concurrent move toward systems of national models that took account of increasing international dependencies. The next few years will be interesting. We will not have "Big Brothers" in 1984, but we are likely to have Big Model Systems if current trends continue. Some of these systems will be very large, indeed, by traditional standards.

---

[108] The rebuilt DRI model, called DRI-II, was three times as large as its predecessor and contained an elaborate stage-of-processing model that traced price effects from the basic resource and agricultural-product stage through to the retail stage. The model also contained detailed flows on international trade and business financing.

7

An Institute for Policy Modeling: The New York City-Rand Institute

One kind of bridge between model builders and decision makers is the econometric modeling firm discussed in the last chapter. Although very useful, the services such a firm provides cannot answer all needs.

Forecasts and analyses of the macroeconomy are clearly of central importance to government officials in the Federal Reserve and the Department of Commerce, as well as to executives of many companies, but they cannot be of more than peripheral interest to an urban bureaucrat planning a hospital expansion program or to a fire commissioner seeking a means for increasing the efficiency of his firefighting units.

This leads us to wonder whether there are other organizational innovations that might provide an effective linkage between the world of modelers and, for example, the operations of municipal agencies. The Rand Institute was an attempt to forge just such an organizational link. Although very successful in some respects, when measured by the hopes and expectations of its originators, it failed.

In this chapter we will review the life cycle of the Rand Institute—from its birth in 1968, through its seven years of active working on the problems of the city of New York, to its demise as an organizational entity in 1975. The two chapters following are also on the Rand Institute. In all three chapters we will look for clues as to why a mediating institution like Rand often has so much trouble operating on the treacherous boundaries between research, bureaucracy, and political action.

MEDIATING INSTITUTIONS

Modern marketing specialists long ago discarded the notion that a man needed only to build a better mousetrap to attract the world to his doorstep.

NOTE: Unless otherwise noted, all direct quotes in the chapter are drawn from personal interviews with participants in the events described, some of whom do not wish to be identified as sources.

Better computer models, like better mousetraps, do not automatically find a way into the hands of their users. And since models are designed to fulfill highly sophisticated needs, the process of delivering models and their by-products to the policymakers who can use them is considerably more complex than the job of supplying mousetraps to the world. Yet, the institutional arrangements for accomplishing this task have not advanced very far beyond the mousetrap stage. Builders of models find that the means for reaching the appropriate policymakers are uncertain, and policymakers, even if they are so inclined, generally lack the necessary information to beat a path to the most suitable model.

Communications between public officials and modelers are usually indirect and often fortuitous. Having an office adjacent to that of an ex-mayor-turned-academician, for example, helped to acquaint Jay Forrester with the information needs of urban policymakers. His modeling efforts became known to these policymakers indirectly by way of the academic community, a published book, and the national press. Forrester reached urban decision makers by broadcasting his study and results widely to anyone willing to listen. Likewise, the econometric modeling firms offer their services to anyone willing to pay for them. Their audience is also large and diverse, though more specialized than Forrester's. The marketplace is their communications medium.

The Need for More Institutional Bridges

The attention of modelers is frequently drawn to the same issues that preoccupy public decision makers, even though no deliberate arrangements have been made to link the concerns of the two groups. Some public problems, after all, are so important or so widely publicized that they capture almost everyone's notice, and it is hardly surprising that modelers and policymakers should be dealing with them simultaneously. It usually happens that these attention-getting issues are the ones that provoke the policymaker's largest demands for information, analysis, and expert advice. Unfortunately, these are also the issues that tend to create a political setting in which the application of research results to policy decisions becomes especially difficult (see Chapter 2).

So long as modelers rely on big issues to bring them together with policymakers, it is not easy to avoid this dilemma of policy research. Yet without established institutions to coordinate the activities of modelers with the information needs of decision makers, policy modelers at universities some distance removed from the locus of policymaking will continue to be drawn to the most visible, tumultuous issues. Some modelers behave as though only by riding the wave of public concern about an issue of great moment can they carry their models from the university to the point of policy impact. Once over the crest of the wave, however, there is a good chance that the model will wash ashore and be abandoned, if not from a shift in political concerns and public attention, then from deficiencies in the model itself that might have been avoided had the model originated closer to the policy arena.

The rate of mortality for models conceived and developed in purely academic settings is very high when they reach the stage of policy application.[1] Many of these models may still serve useful purposes, but usually different purposes from those intended. If modeling institutions were more closely linked to policymaking institutions, modelers might feel less inclined to hitch their models to momentous policy issues. Or if they did, the nearer range and clearer vision that comes from greater proximity might make for easier entry and greater effect in the policymaking process.

The best way to shorten the distance between modeling and policymaking is not by moving universities to Washington, D.C., or next to the local city hall. It is by establishing mediating institutions that form bridges between government and academe. The Brookings Institution and the Urban Institute in Washington, D.C., and the commercial econometric modeling services with their networks of computer lines into the offices of clients, are examples of the kinds of institutions that could, and to an extent already do, perform this mediating function. They provide new settings for the modeling process closer to the field of policymaking than the university.

Modeling, more than most other forms of policy research, lends itself to changes of organizational environment. Models are explicit, self-contained packages of data, theory, and assumptions. As such, they are relatively portable products of policy research. A model created and developed as part of a university research project can be taken over by a mediating institution that refines and maintains it—often with the help of the model's originators—and adapts it to fit the particular needs of policymakers.

There are several possible types of mediating institutions. One is the nonprofit research organization like the Urban Institute or Brookings. Its experts appear at congressional hearings, run seminars for political officials, write position papers, do thoughtful policy studies, and publish scholarly books. Another type is the econometric modeling company. It distributes modeling results to policymakers as a general commercial service. On occasion it performs special studies and provides consultative assistance. While reluctant to become directly involved in the business of their clients, these companies strive to gain a clear understanding of the client's needs by working closely with designated persons, often the chief economist or forecaster, within the client's organization.

When models are based at mediating institutions, their entry into policy is

---

[1] Gary Fromm, William L. Hamilton, and Diane E. Hamilton, *Federally Supported Mathematical Models: Survey and Analysis* (Washington, D.C.: National Science Foundation, 1975), p. 32.

not so likely to depend on the occurrence of policy crises and momentous issues. The modeling process can be tuned more closely to the less visible but more durable problems of public decision makers. If there is hope for modeling to earn for itself a secure place in the everyday business of policymaking, it would seem to be in the further development and strengthening of mediating institutions.

In some policy areas, modeling has already moved well along in this direction. Today, for example, the managers of the national economy turn to the forecasting models of the commercial services as a matter of course. Some government agencies like the Federal Reserve Board and the Bureau of Economic Analysis operate their own economic models but stay in touch with the academicians who developed the models and (while being careful to protect the privileged aspect of their internal modeling activities) participate in intermodel seminars with their academic friends. Along with other government organizations, these agencies also subscribe to the services of the econometric modeling firms.

The success of the modeling firms shows that it need not take a momentous issue like the urban crisis or the energy shortage to create a market for modeling. Modest commonplace subjects of investigation, including operational problems of a relatively routine nature, are being modeled every day in increasing numbers.

Forging Appropriate Connecting Links

The history of macroeconometric models of the economy in Chapter 6 suggests how modeling is becoming institutionalized as part of the policy process. Econometric modeling firms are important mediating institutions. The three main firms—Data Resources, Chase Econometrics, and Wharton—were all founded by academic economists who had considerable experience as modelers. The models around which these economists developed their businesses were elaborations or reformulations of models they had designed and used during the course of their academic careers. The models were primary resources of the firms during their fledgling years, and they continue to be central to the firms' offerings. The models are made available to potential users in government, business, and industry with the help of computer time-sharing technology and through the mechanism of the marketplace. Unfortunately, this fitting device for modelers of the national economy is not as promising or appropriate for other kinds of policy modeling.

In order to make its way on the open market, a model must meet the information and decision needs of a relatively wide range of potential users. The financial survival of a modeling firm depends on its ability to develop a broad clientele for the modeling and information services it sells. The conditions are favorable in the case of national economic models. An extensive, well-developed body of economic theory provides a common framework for the conduct of national economic policy deliberations and for producing and running models. There is general acceptance of the national income and product accounts and related concepts and data. Econometrics supplies a standard repertoire of techniques and routines for analyzing the data and creating models. Abundant time series are carefully tabulated and regularly updated by government agencies. The data are in the public domain; they are made available without charge, are well-known, and widely referenced. The field of macroeconomics is blessed with a virtual standardization of user requirements and concerns, making it both feasible and profitable for the modeling firms to serve many users from the same economic model and data bank through the open market. Industry models command similar interest.

In other policy areas where the requirements of users are more diverse and the supply of data less plentiful, it is cumbersome to try to serve a multitude of customers with a single model. A model designed to satisfy a large variety of users may satisfy no one in the end.[2] The complexity of the model, the special features it requires in order to be general in application, and the enormous amount of data necessary to keep it running, all present obstacles to its effective operation and use. No well-defined set of standard needs or strong commonality of interests naturally exists in such social policy areas as urban development, education, poverty, health, environment, drug abuse, and crime. A commercial modeling service would have a difficult time gaining and retaining wide acceptance in these areas.

THE RAND INSTITUTE

To link modeling and decision making in some policy areas requires other kinds of institutional arrangements than those provided by the commercial modeling firms. One interesting organizational mechanism is the semiofficial research auxiliary attached to particular public agencies or other decision making units. The New York City-Rand Institute, formed in the late 1960s, is an example of just such an organization. In the present and two succeeding chapters we will examine its seven-year history as one possible pattern for the design of these auxiliaries.

The institute was a partnership between a particular governmental unit (the City of New York) and a nonprofit research organization (the Rand Corporation). The work of the institute was tailored to meet the policy problems

---

[2] See Douglass B. Lee, Jr., "Requiem for Large-Scale Models," *Journal of the American Institute of Planners,* May 1973, p. 164. Lee points out, for example, that trying to use a single model to achieve many purposes at once usually means that all purposes are likely to be poorly served.

and information needs of specific clients in city government. Many of the institute's modeling efforts concentrated on the operational problems of particular city agencies, not something that results in products easily resold on the open market. Such modeling efforts cannot succeed without the close cooperation of the agency in question. The data required, the administrative practices to be analyzed, and the problems demanding solution tend to be distinctive to the agency, so the modeler must become intimately acquainted with the agency's operation and its working environment.

The Rand Institute was designed to foster close working relationships between modelers and their clients in New York City. It did not manufacture its mousetraps first and then wait for the world to beat a path to its door. As Gotham's own think-tank, its research projects were made to order for a specific user. One of the early goals of the Rand Institute was to develop models and techniques which could be usefully extended to other cities. Little progress was made in this direction, however, save for some aspects of Rand's work in special areas.

The Rand Institute set out to reshape the relationship between policy research and the policy process. It takes more than elegant design or the technical skill of a modeler to place a model and its results in the policy arena. Some models enter the policy process almost by accident, some because a modeler has the personal prestige and determination to call the attention of public decision makers to his work. In other cases, policymakers themselves are responsible, as when, for example, the pressure of political circumstances caused George Shultz to invoke a modeling effort in support of the economic position of the Nixon administration (see Chapter 1).

In order for policy modeling to mature and for policymakers to make more systematic use of models, the path from model to user must be shortened and made more direct, which suggests a more institutionalized and regularized relationship between modeling and policymaking. The New York City Rand Institute was an early attempt at providing such a relationship, one reason why it deserves close examination.

The Stated Plans and Objectives

Designing computer models was only a small part of the institute's business. It used a variety of techniques "to enlarge what is known about the city's problems and opportunities; to devise timely and realizable recommendations based on that knowledge; and to help improve the process through which city agencies routinely make decisions."[3] These were the formal aims of the institute as stated in its annual reports. The list does not reveal all of the purposes that Rand was intended to serve.

---

[3] The New York City-Rand Institute, *First Annual Report,* October 1970, p. 2.

The institute, a joint venture of the Rand Corporation and the New York City government, was established to overcome some of the shortcomings of more conventional institutions for policy research. It was an organizational hybrid, designed to combine the advantages of an internal research group and an outside consultant, without the deficiencies of either. The institute maintained a semiautonomous status as an outside adviser to city government by keeping its identity as an arm of the Rand Corporation and having its own board of directors. Its researchers were not employees of any city agency and were not to serve at the command of agency executives to fulfill the day-to-day information needs of the municipal bureaucracy. By and large, the Rand analysts were expected to reserve their talents for more ambitious tasks—not to smooth out the day-to-day operation of existing policies, but to suggest new policies. In order to embark on such enterprises, Rand was accorded a degree of autonomy in the development of its research agenda and its researchers were to be protected from daily demands for immediately useful information and advice so as to make possible the sustained research efforts needed to prepare the way for significant changes in municipal policy. Some capacity for long-term research commitments, it should be noted, is a prerequisite for most nonroutine uses of models in policy analysis, since modeling projects typically require considerable time and patience.[4] Early discussions between city officials and representatives of Rand anticipated projects of this kind.

As an outsider, Rand "was to be independent enough to be critical of city policies" and "insulated enough from city hall's daily operational concerns to work persistently on underlying problems."[5] But the role of outside consultant can present difficulties as well as advantages. If Rand's access to the internal operations of a city agency were restricted, so would be its ability to conduct policy research. "Since the consultant must have information to conduct his study, and often only the bureaucracy possesses that information, by selectively cooperating with the consultant, the bureaucracy can effectively scuttle desired change."[6] A policy analyst must have easy access to the public agency—not only to collect data about agency operations, but also to gauge the receptivity of agency officials to alternative changes.

It may also be desirable for an analyst to participate in the process of implementing a recommended change. Autonomy may make it possible to "work persistently on underlying problems" and to produce unbiased results

---

[4] See Aaron Wildavsky, "Consumer Report," *Science* 182 (1973): 1335–1338.
[5] Peter Szanton, "Analysis and Urban Government," in Alvin W. Drake, Ralph L. Keeney, and Philip M. Morse (eds.), *Analysis of Public Systems* (Cambridge: The M.I.T. Press, 1972), p. 20.
[6] R. W. Archibald and R. B. Hoffman, "Introducing Technological Change in a Bureaucratic Structure," The New York City-Rand Institute, P-4025, 1969, p. 15.

of high quality, but it does not help assure that these research results will subsequently be incorporated into public policy. An academician who makes his policy recommendations from a university campus may enjoy considerable autonomy and prestige but is poorly situated with respect to the process by which policy recommendations are transformed into action. Likewise, an outside consultant whose work with a public agency is confined to a single research project is seldom in a favorable position to influence the acceptance and implementation of research results.

Thus, Rand could not afford to be so independent of municipal government that it became remote. It would have to be "close enough in its working relations with city agencies to devise recommendations that were timely, realistic, and usable." The duration of a partnership between Rand and a particular city agency was not to be limited to a single research project. Unlike the typical outside consultant, Rand was to "work steadily with city agencies on a broad range of their problems" so that the institute's researchers would become generally knowledgeable about the operations of city agencies and develop mutually congenial relations with agency officials.[7]

The Rand Institute was an arrangement intended both to assure that policy research would flourish and to facilitate the translation of research results into public policy. It was designed to provide an environment congenial to the use of models in policy research and the use of this research in the fashioning of public policy. Rand was an organizational arrangement that, were it to work as conceived, would have provided modelers with both the opportunity to use their skills and a direct route of entry into the policymaking process.

Unstated Objectives

The institute had other objectives as well. Rand made its debut in New York in 1968, two years after John Lindsay became the city's mayor. Rand's design was closely tied to Lindsay's goals. The mayor began his administration in 1966 by declaring war on "bureaucracy," special interest "power brokers," and the obstructive alliance between them. Lindsay promised a program of reform that would liberate municipal agencies from the control of the special interests (chiefly, the municipal employee unions) and make it possible to streamline and rationalize the operations of the city government. Most of the reform measures advanced by the Lindsay administration proposed to curb the influence of special interests by enlarging the powers of the mayor—in particular his ability to direct the activities of the city bureaucracy.

One of the earliest of these measures consolidated about fifty city agencies into ten "super-agencies," each of which was charged with responsibility for

---

[7] Szanton, p. 20.

directing a number of related, but previously separate governmental activities. The new administrative arrangement was intended not only to achieve a more effective coordination of public programs, but to reduce the number of department heads who reported directly to the mayor so that he could exercise more forceful control over the administrative operations of the city's government.

Other innovations aimed at the same result. Lindsay directed one of his deputies to establish within the mayor's office a special staff of analysts who were to devise more efficient ways of delivering city services. The city's Budget Bureau, through which the mayor could control municipal agency expenditures, was enlarged and given a more influential role in the making of agency program decisions. Among the bureau's new functions was the establishment of a program-planning-budgeting system (PPBS) for the city of New York—a system that was supposed to bring key policy decisions to the highest levels of the governmental hierarchy.

The Budget Bureau soon became the lynchpin of a Lindsay administration effort to make the city bureaucracy more manageable and the mayor more powerful. Without defining precisely the kinds of administrative innovations it desired, the bureau orchestrated a three-part campaign designed to make municipal agencies more receptive to change.

One of these parts the bureau played itself. Through its budget examiners, it continued to perform its traditional role as an advocate of economy in agency expenditures. At the same time, a newly created staff of Budget Bureau program analysts scrutinized agency activities for gaps in service, performance, or resources. Within the agencies themselves, Budget Director Frederick O'R. Hayes was able to plant a number of young management specialists recruited from outside the city government. These newcomers to the municipal bureaucracy were not Lindsay espionage agents, but neither were they agency loyalists. It was hoped that from their strategic positions inside various city agencies they would stimulate some important departures from business-as-usual. Collectively, these inside men represented the second element in the administrative reform effort coordinated by the Budget Bureau.

The third element was Rand. Budget Director Hayes attempted to solicit Ford Foundation support for a "Rand-type corporation" in New York a year after the start of the Lindsay administration. When these efforts did not bring immediate results, Hayes approached the Rand Corporation directly. In discussions during late 1966 and early 1967, he suggested to receptive Rand officials that there might be a role for Rand researchers in New York City.

Twenty years after its inception as an Air Force research organization, the Rand Corporation was still almost wholly dependent on income from contracts with defense agencies. Its executives were anxious to diversify its research activities. The growth of President Johnson's Great Society program suggested new opportunities for Rand analysts. Shortly before Hayes approached the corporation, Rand's executive board had made a formal decision to devote some of the think-tank's attention to urban problems. Hayes could hardly have chosen a more appropriate time to advance his proposal. The New York venture would enable Rand to develop some expertise in urban studies and, possibly, build a reputation in the field that might attract other clients. Hayes' plan for an urban research organization would then serve Rand's interests as well as Lindsay's.

The Beginning

By mid-1967, Hayes and Rand had reached a loose agreement for the corporation to embark on some preliminary research projects in New York City. In January 1968, under television lights in Gracie Mansion, Mayor Lindsay announced the signing of six-month contracts between Rand and four city agencies—the Police Department, the Fire Department, the Housing and Development Administration, and the Health Services Administration. The agreements, said the mayor, would "greatly assist our introduction into city agencies of the kind of streamlined, modern management that Robert McNamara applied in the Pentagon with such success in the past seven years.... I regard this as the most important development in the search for effectiveness in city government in many, many years."[8]

It would be some time before the Rand enterprise bore fruit, but the mayor and other city officials appeared to understand that long-term research efforts seldom produce short-term results—and they were patient. Peter Szanton, a Harvard-trained lawyer-historian, who formerly had served with the Office of Management and Budget in Washington, directed Rand's New York project office. He emphasized the need for forbearance when the corporation's first six-month contracts with the city came up for renewal.

> We are not bound to produce specific results at specific times, and we wouldn't have accepted such a contract. There may not be any usable solutions in the first six months or even a year. It's like building a big hospital which can take years. If after the first six months someone asks you how many patients you're treating, you have to answer "zero."[9]

Budget Director Hayes was content with that answer. Although Rand's efforts had not yet produced any measurable results, its progress, he said, had been "very satisfactory." And when a newspaper reporter asked whether the city's chronic budget difficulties might result in a reduction of funds for Rand, Hayes replied that "one of the last things you want to cut is the kind of brain

---
[8] *New York Times,* January 9, 1968, p. 31.
[9] *New York Times,* April 29, 1968, p. 32.

power that will help you out of a tight squeeze."[10] Not long afterwards, the city renewed Rand's contracts for a full year at $2.4 million, about four times the amount of the original six-month agreements.

If city officials were more patient with Rand than with other consultants, they had loftier expectations. Unlike most city consultants, Rand was not being retained on a short-term basis to solve a specific problem. Rand's relationship with the city was intended to be long-term and comprehensive. "We are willing," said Szanton, "to work first on more immediate and operational problems," but these short-term projects would be pursued "with the idea that we will gradually build up to the grand system for approaching problems."[11] The city's dealings with Rand were to be more intimate than its relationships with other consultants. "A common failing of consultative relationships," Mayor Lindsay said in 1969,

> is that the consultant has little interest in implementing the programs it has helped to develop. This is often fatal when it turns out that the hardest part of implementation is retaining the character of the original idea in the actual program. Compared to previous experience, we see a welcome willingness on the part of Rand to leave model building long enough to assist in the application of their new systems in a real agency in a real city.[12]

Rand's role was to be different from that of other consultants hired by the city, but its official status was initially the same. It was a private contractor providing professional advice to public officials.

In mid-1969, however, Rand's distinctiveness was formally recognized. Its New York project office was converted into the New York City-Rand Institute, a nonprofit corporation with Szanton as president and two "members," one to be appointed by the city of New York and the other by the Rand Corporation. Each of these members would appoint an equal number of directors to the institute's board. It was hoped that the new arrangement would permit the Rand effort to "become the basis for something more useful than a series of single shot studies." The problems of the city were complicated and "would yield, if at all, only to persistent effort, to sustained evaluation, experiment, change and re-evaluation." It was thought that a continuing relationship between Rand and the city would facilitate such persistent efforts; "at the same time, analyses ... of simpler problems would profit from a continuous and steadily deepening experience."[13] With the launching of this joint venture, Rand became, in the words of one New York administrator, "the think-tank of choice as far as the city was concerned."

---

[10] Ibid.
[11] Quoted in Paul Dickson, *Think Tanks* (New York: Ballantine Books, 1971), p. 249.
[12] *New York Times,* March 16, 1969, p. 49.
[13] Rand Institute, pp. 1–2.

Incorporation of the Rand Institute was also an important component of the change-inducing apparatus that Hayes had been constructing in and around the city bureaucracy. The Rand researchers were linked to that enterprise in two ways. First, the Budget Bureau was party to each of the agency contracts with Rand and much of Rand's preliminary work was designed to serve the purpose of the bureau—chiefly, the bureau's efforts to introduce PPBS to the municipal bureaucracy. Affirming Rand's close ties with the bureau, Budget Director Hayes was appointed as the city's member of the new nonprofit corporation. Second, the officials that city agencies designated as their ambassadors to Rand were often the same youthful management specialists recruited to the city government through the efforts of the Budget Bureau and the mayor's office. Rand was not a lonely missionary of "modern streamlined management," but part of a loosely coordinated campaign to convert the municipal bureaucracy to the latest management methods—a campaign that might also enhance the mayor's influence over city agencies.

The Problem of Constituencies

Rand was identified from the beginning with the cause of John Lindsay. Those New York politicians inclined to challenge the authority of the mayor were therefore also inclined to challenge Rand. The institute may have been the think-tank of choice in the circle that surrounded the mayor, but it was not so highly favored in other circles. In its early days there was little Rand could do to cultivate support outside the executive branch of the city's government.

To Peter Szanton there seemed to be compelling reasons for Rand to refrain from advertising itself and its activities. "First," says Szanton, "we sensed as we came into the city an overenthusiasm on the part of some people... the notion that Rand possessed somewhere in its computers a magic [and] that once we had figured out how to apply it to cities, it would have immediate and profound results." There was a danger, in other words, that Rand had already been oversold, and further efforts to promote the enterprise might only aggravate that problem. A second reason for maintaining a low profile was inexperience. "We were, in the first year, learning our way around the city," says Szanton. "We were really very ignorant people. Fortunately, we were aware of that, and we did not want to display our ignorance." But even if the Rand researchers became street-wise and politically sophisticated New Yorkers, it would still be best to remain unobtrusive. "It seemed to us," Szanton recalls,

> that we were not primary actors. We were not going to be the innovators. We were not going to be the people who could force change, that would pay for change, or manage change. We were going to have the easy job of proposing it,

and that meant a couple of things. One was that ... we didn't deserve credit for the change. And the converse of that was that other people—the people who *were* going to be responsible for it, like agency heads or legislators—ought to get identified with what was happening. It ought to be their change, not ours.

Rand's business was "to make other people look good." Sometimes the "other people" might find it convenient to make Rand look bad. If a proposed innovation were especially unpopular, an agency official could give the Rand analysts full credit for it. If it were popular and effective, agency officials could take the credit themselves. So charged one Rand analyst engaged in research for the Fire Department, when he claimed that "the department has chosen to say that a recommendation was their own or ours according to their own convenience."

Rand's situation did not provide many opportunities to develop a constituency external to the Lindsay administration. An organization devoted to making other people look good might have few chances to look good in its own right. It was true that the Rand analysts were not always faithful to the humble role in which Szanton had cast them, and the organization's own annual reports exhibited less modesty than one might expect. But it was difficult for Rand to make conspicuous overtures to the general public or cultivate the good will of local interest groups and political leaders whose disfavor could be dangerous to the institute.

Both the city council and the city comptroller, as it turned out, would pose threats to the survival of the Rand enterprise in political skirmishes with Lindsay. Their opportunity came in 1970 when a serious dispute erupted over the mayor's authority to dispense city contracts to private consultants. City Comptroller Abraham Beame, later elected Lindsay's successor, had been defeated by Lindsay in the mayoral election of 1965. He charged that the city's annual expenditure for outside consultants had risen from about $8 million to almost $70 million since Lindsay took office. A series of articles in the *New York Times* had disclosed evidence of impropriety both in the granting of contracts and in their fulfillment. Beame suspended the city's payments to all consultants—among them, the Rand Institute—on the grounds that the consulting contracts had not been open to competitive bidding, nor approved by the city's Board of Estimate.

The attack was joined by a committee of the City Council, which launched an investigation of the city's dealings with private consultants. Some councilmen had already expressed resentment over the mayor's monopoly of Rand expertise. Six months before the outbreak of the consultants' controversy, ten councilmen filed suit against the mayor demanding that they be granted access to the results of a secret Rand study of the city's rent control system. Their resentment surfaced again during the investigation of city consultants. Although the bulk of the city's expenditure for expert advice had gone for architectural and engineering consultants, with only a tiny portion going to Rand, the institute received a disproportionate share of the council's attention during the inquiry. The committee, for example, called in Peter Szanton for a four-hour grilling he did not expect.

In the end, the committee acknowledged that the basic research and analysis for which Rand was known must be a basic component of modern municipal government, but the committee suggested that the job of basic research could be performed more cheaply and more effectively by homegrown experts at the City University of New York than by the Rand Institute.[14]

The attack on Rand by Mayor Lindsay's political antagonists was more than disconcerting. Rand remained unpaid for its work, by order of Comptroller Beame, from July 1970 to the late summer of 1971. It was sustained financially during this period by funds from the Rand Corporation and by part of a $900,000 grant it had received from the Ford Foundation in 1969. Rand officials recognized that support of this kind could not continue indefinitely and twice set a date for shutting down the institute's operations. Finally, in mid-1971, the city comptroller and the Board of Estimate agreed to pay Rand for most of the work done the preceding year. The institute no longer faced the immediate prospect of closing its offices, but there could be no mistaking the fact that the enemies of Rand and the mayor had brought the institute to its knees.

The experience raised troubling questions for Rand. "One of the more difficult issues a policy analyst may face," Szanton later wrote, "is that of his responsibility to persons and organizations other than his client." In the eyes of the City Council, Rand researchers worked only for the executive branch of the city government, and more particularly for the mayor and the mayoral establishment. The exclusive identification with Lindsay produced problems for Rand. "Information," Szanton observed.

> is an element of power. Analysts working for one branch of a city government, where that branch can restrict to itself access to the results of the work, disturb the balance of power. Where the work addresses problems of little social importance, the disturbance will be correspondingly trivial. But the more important the subjects of research, the more likely are the other branches—especially legislative—to observe the imbalance and to respond. The response will be one of two kinds. The legislature will seek either to provide itself with a corresponding analytic capability, or to strike such an instrument from the hands of the executive.[15]

In New York, the response was to lash out at the mayor's analysts.

---

[14] The City Council of New York, Committee on Charter and Governmental Operations, *Report on Consultant Contracts,* December 21, 1970, pp. 9–10.

[15] Szanton, p. 29.

For Rand, one means of protection from these antimayoral attacks was to develop its own base of political support outside the mayor's office. Szanton had been reluctant to launch Rand on a campaign of constituency-building, but after he resigned as president of the institute in late 1971, his eventual successor, Bernard Gifford, exhibited much less reluctance. Gifford may have been selected for the job (at Szanton's recommendation) with an eye to Rand's need for political allies in New York City. A young black Ph.D. biophysicist, Gifford not only possessed the academic credentials expected of a Rand researcher, but he was a native New Yorker and political activist in good standing with some of the city's powerful Democratic party leaders.

During his tenure of little more than a year, Gifford pursued a course that diverged sharply from Szanton's low-profile strategy. "My feeling," said Gifford, "is that if ordinary people don't know what we're all about... we'll never build a constituency." Rand, he was convinced, would "have to come out of the dark." The institute had "nothing to be ashamed of. I think our work is something that's credible, and I think our work will be a hell of a lot more useful if more people know about it." Gifford's promotional efforts were to be directed, not only at the general public, but at "special interest groups" and local political authorities as well—the Board of Estimate, the City Council, borough presidents and others. Gifford was confident that "a good case [could] be made for analysis in government," but it could not be made by "hiding in the back pocket of the mayor of New York and becoming a political captive."

While Gifford attempted to move Rand into the limelight, powerful considerations pushed in the opposite direction. One was the interest of municipal agencies in keeping their internal affairs and problems from public scrutiny. Agency executives were disinclined to cooperate with Rand researchers when they had reason to believe that information provided the analysts might find its way into the newspapers or into the hands of politicians and interest groups.

Rand's supporters in the mayoral establishment had their own reservations about the institute's efforts to develop a public constituency and to cultivate a working arrangement with the City Council. One former Budget Bureau official expressed concern about the risk to the mayor in his relationships with the City Council and with major community groups or unions "on anything as vulnerable as a research effort, dealing with people who are as apt to get chewed up in the political process as the typical Rand analysts are." The mayor's office was not prepared to "share" the services of Rand with city councilmen or other local politicians. Still, the mayor was a powerful ally, and as long as he remained in office, the institute would have some assurance of survival. But Lindsay would not last forever, and there was reason for Rand officials to be apprehensive about the future.

The New Mayor and the Demise of the Institute

The test of Rand's ability to sustain itself politically, independent of mayoral support, came after John Lindsay was replaced in 1974 by his comptroller, Abraham Beame, a man conspicuous in his lack of enthusiasm for the Rand enterprise. When Rand's contracts with the city expired in 1974, the Beame administration had the opportunity to terminate the institute, once and for all. Influential Beame lieutenants were inclined to do precisely that, but Rand was given a reprieve and its contracts were renewed for another year at a reduced level. The final death blow came during the municipal budget crisis of 1975.

During its seven-year life, Rand conducted research for a wide variety of city agencies beginning in 1968 with the Police and Fire Departments, the Health Services Administration, and the Housing and Development Administration, and later with the Department of Corrections, the Water Resources Administration, the Human Resources Administration, the Economic Development Administration, and others. Rand's most important constituency was its clientele, but not all of these clients were equally ready to lend their support to the preservation of Rand. The municipal bureaucracy is not a homogeneous interest group. Each agency has its own organizational tradition, administrative structure, personalities, and political environment, and each differs from the others both in the extent of its demand for research and in the extent to which it is able to put research recommendations to use.

The agencies for whom Rand conducted research were not selected according to any narrow principle. According to Peter Szanton, Rand tried to find situations where there was an agency interested in having policy-oriented research done for it and there were Rand staff people with relevant analytic skills who were interested in the substance of that agency's work. Given these criteria of selection, it is not surprising that Rand's bureaucratic clientele was heterogeneous. Still, the selection standards were not so broad that they permitted Rand to make every agency its customer. The Municipal Services Administration, for example, would have welcomed a Rand study of the uses of the city's radio station WNYC, but Rand declined the invitation because it had no staff members equipped to conduct such a study. Rand employed a number of specialists, on the other hand, competent to analyze the city's air pollution problems, but the Bureau of Air Quality Control was already conducting its own research program and saw no need for the institute's services. In other cases, the structure of city government prevented Rand from acquiring a potential client. For example, Budget Director Fred Hayes regarded the city school system as fertile ground for Rand research projects, but the educational system was a relatively autonomous bureaucracy, not under the direct control of the mayor. Mayoral backing was not enough to make the public schools a Rand client.

These and other omissions notwithstanding, the list of Rand clients is impressive for its diversity. And since the institute conducted its policy research for a variety of clients in a variety of organizational settings, a consideration of its work helps to reveal how various kinds of policymaking circumstances and organizational conditions can affect the fortunes of policy analysts and their recommendations. We will not attempt to recount the institute's history or conduct a general evaluation of its work, but will concentrate instead on how policy research fared in a few Rand projects that used models or related analytical tools. Many of the projects did not. The operations of Rand's outpost on the Hudson offer us further opportunity to find out why models are used in policy research, how they are used, and what they are likely to yield in varying bureaucratic settings.

In addition, an examination of Rand's experience permits us to look behind the broad outlines of policy research and policymaking to consider the kinds of relationships that arise between individual researchers and decision makers. The fact that this experience occurred within the scope of a single governmental jurisdiction and involved a single research organization makes the record conveniently compact and simplifies the task of identifying the conditions that produced differential results in the performance of modelers and their models.

The two chapters that follow examine some major Rand research projects in which modeling played a part. The first case history concerns Rand's work for the New York City Fire Department, the second, for the city's Health Services Administration. We shall see that the quality of the Rand-client relationship was drastically different in the two cases, as were the results. The traditions, organizational setting, and political environment on the client side were instrumental in shaping these relationships, as were the attitudes and personalities on both sides of the consultative agreement. We cannot escape the conclusion that these predominantly nontechnical factors were decisive in determining the success and failure of the work that ensued.

8

Putting Out Fires in the Fire Department

CLIENT MEETS CONSULTANT

For some public agencies, crisis and disaster are the stuff of everyday business. Their job is to deal with dangerous and usually unexpected events—accidental injury, mayhem, natural disaster, or conflagration. The job of preparing for these crises is inevitably a difficult one. If we could be fully prepared for emergencies, after all, they would no longer be emergencies; the job of preparing for them is made more difficult still by the fact that one can seldom rely on traditional trial and error techniques in order to devise responses for these occurrences. Where life and limb are at stake, there may be an understandable reluctance to experiment with untried policies that could result in errors. Indeed, there may be a reluctance to depart at all from long established ways of doing business. But if the process of trial and error can be transferred from the actual operations of an agency to a computer model, the high costs of error may be considerably reduced. It may be possible to simulate an emergency, as well as the response to it, and thereby estimate the effectiveness of the response without actually endangering life or property. Where public policies must deal with extraordinary and unusually dangerous events, simulation models may provide an important way—perhaps the only way—to test those policies.

The Department and Its Difficulties

Computer simulation was one technique chosen by the New York City Fire Department in 1968 to test some of its current and prospective policies for coping with the dangers of urban conflagration. Those dangers, of course, were hazards that the department had always faced, but by 1968, a further danger had arisen. Long accustomed to dealing with other people's disasters, the Fire Department seemed to face an impending disaster of its own. During the decade preceding 1968, the annual number of fire alarms in New York

---

NOTE: Unless otherwise noted, all direct quotes in this chapter are drawn from personal interviews with participants in the events described, some of whom do not wish to be identified as sources.

had nearly tripled, but the department's uniformed manpower had increased by only about 16 percent. And the men were unhappy.

In areas, such as the South Bronx or Bedford-Stuyvesant, which had registered especially large increases in fire alarm rates, the crushing workload had driven firefighters to the limits of their endurance, and many of them were determined to tolerate no more. Rank-and-file discontent surfaced within the two major labor organizations representing firemen—the Uniformed Firefighters Association and the Uniformed Fire Officers' Association. In mid-1968, the firemen's resentments exploded. "Our people finally threw up their arms," reports one union official, "and they literally had a revolt here ... the men themselves threw out most of the Executive Board by election ... and they submitted demands to the Executive Board that if something were not done to relieve the workload ... they should take a strike referendum."

The threat of a strike or slowdown by firemen converted the department's already serious workload problems into an emergency. To the union leaders, the only satisfactory solution was the most obvious one—to hire large numbers of additional firefighters. But the department's managers were unwilling to accept the proposal. To create seventy-five new fire companies, which the unions demanded, would add an estimated $46 million to the department's $200 million annual budget. Like many other local officials, the officials of New York were reluctant to make substantial increases in public expenditures, especially since wage contracts with many uniformed employees were scheduled to expire in October 1968. Fire Department executives and other city officials insisted that the firemen's workload could be reduced by means other than the addition of new manpower—most notably, by the less expensive alternative of making changes in departmental policies and management practices.

Changes, however, do not come easily in the Fire Department. More than most municipal agencies, the fire service is a creature of tradition. In New York, for example, one fire fighter on each ladder truck is still designated as the "whip," a holdover from the days when fire engines were drawn by horses.[1] A mayoral committee in the early 1950s cited criticism of the department as "reactionary and mossbacked,"[2] and such criticisms are not surprising. The men who run the agency have rarely been administrative innovators, trained in the techniques of modern management; they are former fire fighters themselves, trained in the management of hoses and ladders and promoted through the ranks of the department's tight, quasi-military hierarchy. Set off in their "closed, tradition-oriented bureaucratic society," they will not be hurried into innovations.[3]

---

[1] Dennis Smith, *Report from Engine Co. 82* (New York: McCall Books, 1972).

[2] Mayor's Committee on Management Survey, *Modern Management for the City of New York*, 2 vols. (New York: The Committee, 1953), 2:783.

[3] Wallace Sayre and Herbert Kaufman, *Governing New York City: Politics in the Metropolis* (New York: Russell Sage Foundation, 1960), p. 268.

Yet the circumstances of the Fire Department in 1968 demanded rapid and substantial changes in the agency's management and allocation of work. Although by outward appearances the department hardly seemed a likely candidate for change, a closer look might have revealed a few openings for innovation. For one thing, although the department might appear reactionary and mossbacked to some observers, it had in fact been rather innovative—for a fire department. "New York's Bravest" had pioneered the use of super-pumpers and tower-ladders, and the department, in 1967, had installed the first fire department computer.[4] Moreover, the operational chief of the department, John T. O'Hagan, was regarded as a skilled and progressive manager, receptive to change. O'Hagan had been in the department for seventeen years when, in 1964, having scored highest on the qualifying examinations, he was promoted over the heads of more senior officers to become departmental chief. At 39, he was the youngest fire chief in New York's history. It was under O'Hagan's regime that the Fire Department had acquired its computer, and the chief had other changes in mind as well. In a speech before the International Association of Fire Chiefs in 1967, he proposed to his professional colleagues that they establish their own staffs of management analysts to examine and streamline departmental operations in their respective cities. O'Hagan had already asked Mayor Lindsay to provide funds for just such an analytic group in New York. But according to one observer, O'Hagan "really didn't know what he wanted, and the mayor didn't have any clear idea what he was talking about." For the time being, at least, O'Hagan would have to do without his own management planners and analysts.

Such planners and analysts as the department had were lodged in the office of O'Hagan's administrative superior, Fire Commissioner Robert Lowery. While Chief O'Hagan exercised operational control over fire fighting and fire prevention activities, Commissioner Lowery had overall responsibility for the administration of the agency. Lowery was a veteran fire fighter, with more than twenty-five years of service in the department, and most of his staff members had similar backgrounds. One exception was Paul Canick who joined Lowery's staff as assistant commissioner for program budgeting at the beginning of 1968. Canick, a management consultant with a degree in electrical engineering, had never responded to a fire alarm. He had not been recruited by the Fire Department, but by the mayor's office and the Budget Bureau, and sent off among the firemen with an uncertain mandate to bring modern management to the fire service. Just how he was to do this remained unclear. He was given neither a staff nor a secretary, and for some months after his arrival, says Canick, "there were times when I would actually be star-

---

[4] Edward Blum, "The New York City Fire Project," in Alvin Drake, Ralph L. Keeney, and Philip M. Morse (eds.), *Analysis of Public Systems* (Cambridge: The M.I.T. Press, 1972), p. 97n.

ing out the window of the municipal building on Chambers Street, wondering what the hell I was doing there and what was going to happen. . . ."

Rand's Fire Project

On the same day in January 1968 that Paul Canick assumed his new and largely undefined duties, the Rand Corporation also went to work for the Fire Department. The department was one of four municipal agencies with whom Rand had signed six-month contracts "to undertake analyses of some of the problems of policy and operations facing New York City."[5] As in its contracts with other agencies, Rand was expected to develop a program-planning-budgeting system for the department. Its project agreement with the fire officials also outlined four other areas of investigation. First, Rand was to review technological developments in building construction and fire fighting that might improve the department's ability to prevent fires or to put them out once started. Second, it was to investigate and design alternative communications systems that would meet the department's future needs at a reasonable cost. Third, it was to develop a method for predicting when and where different types of fires were likely to break out. And finally, it was to investigate ways of measuring the Fire Department's efficiency and effectiveness. This preliminary investigation, it was hoped, would lead to the development of a model of departmental operations that might be used to compare alternative response and deployment policies.

Rand's research program was worked out during the latter part of 1967 in discussions among officials of the Budget Bureau, the Fire Department, and Rand itself. The program agreed upon did not go far in specifying the kind of work that Rand was to do, but by comparison with Rand's other contracts in New York, it was a rather detailed statement of research responsibilities. "In fire," according to one Budget Bureau official who participated in the contract negotiations, "the work program, while generalized, was in fact more defined than the others." Its specificity may have reflected the fact that important parts of the research program had already been sketched out during the months before Rand's arrival in New York. Steven Isenberg, one of the Budget Bureau's young program analysts, had discussed the Fire Department's research needs with Chief O'Hagan and with Fred Hayes, the city's budget director. In the process, the budget officials "worked out . . . an idea of how things ought to proceed; it was based on the notion that there were two problems that had to be gone at, and it involved some fairly sophisticated research and model building. The first one was . . . the fire response model. The second aspect of it was the whole question of the predictability of fire incidence" re-

---

[5] The New York City-Rand Institute, *Annual Report* (1970), p. 1.

quiring the construction of a so-called "threat model." The tentative research plans were designed to meet both problems. The threat model would be an instrument for predicting the demand for fire fighting services. The "response model" would deal with the department's ability to meet that demand. It might be used to test policies for increasing departmental efficiency, minimizing fire response times, or reducing the firemen's burden of overwork.

During the fall of 1967, Steven Isenberg discussed these research plans with fire fighting experts at the National Academy of Sciences and in several private consulting firms. At the same time, the development of the plans themselves continued to go forward during contract discussions between city officials and the Rand Corporation. For the moment, however, no steps were taken to put the scheme into effect. "We didn't want to proceed," says one budget official, "until we had somebody in the Fire Department who really had a technical understanding of the problem." The hiring of Paul Canick in early 1968 was intended to fulfill that need, and the simultaneous arrival of Rand provided the Fire Department with the capability to carry out a research program. From Rand Corporation headquarters in Santa Monica, Edward Blum moved to New York to take charge of Rand's research effort in the Fire Department. Blum, a chemical engineer, had been an active participant in the drafting of the fire project agreement. Paul Canick was to serve as the Fire Department's liaison with the Rand analysts.

Animosities and Alliances

The people needed to carry out the Budget Bureau's "idea of how to proceed" were now in place and ready to proceed. They proceeded rapidly, but not smoothly. Within a few months, a certain animosity had arisen between the Rand analysts whom Blum had hired and Paul Canick, their supposed accomplice within the Fire Department. Some observers in the Budget Bureau attribute this falling out to a tendency among the Rand analysts to "play the role of the kid in the sixth grade class who always has his hand up." The analysts saw Canick, whose training and background were similar to theirs, as a rival in the struggle for intellectual preeminence. "Rand," it is argued, "has tensions with any other intellectually sophisticated group with which they deal."

The tension with Canick, however, may also have had other, more specific sources. Canick, after all, was initially an alien in the Fire Department, with hardly any administrative allies, no clearly defined functions, and no staff. It was understandable that he might treat the Rand project team as a surrogate for the research staff that he lacked, and that he might regard the Rand enterprise as an essential component in his own effort to find a useful role in the department. During Canick's first months at the department, one of his few supporters in the agency was the head of the Bureau of Fire Communications. The two men were evidently drawn together by their common background in electrical engineering. In order to assist his would-be ally, Canick attempted to guide the Rand analysts into research projects dealing with the departmental communications system—in particular, studies that were likely to produce relatively quick results. In April 1968, for example, Canick persuaded the reluctant Rand research team to prepare an analysis of the costs and benefits of consolidating the four Fire Department Communications Offices into one facility.[6] The study was to be a short-term effort. "It was important," says Canick, "to focus on some things that would show that it was possible to get a report done in a few months, rather than looking ahead." Quick research results might earn Rand a reputation for effectiveness; they might also help to cut short Canick's uncertainty about his own position within the Fire Department.

Canick may have been right about the need for producing research results rapidly, but members of the Rand staff saw things differently. "Paul," says one of them, "was trying to pick a couple of minor targets of opportunity to make a splash on," whereas the Rand analysts had their sights on more distant objectives—specifically, the development of simulation models that might be used to test the department's command and control policies. Accordingly, although the Rand researchers acceded to his request for a cost-benefit study of a consolidated communications facility, they resolved to "get out of the slot that Canick was trying to put [them] into." Their determination to do so was based not only on a distaste for the research projects that Canick had recommended, but on strategic considerations as well: "We didn't want to be tied to Paul because Paul was clearly still, in the department's view, an outsider, and for us to be attached to somebody who was an outsider would ... in the long run have been disastrous. We wanted to get more attached to O'Hagan and to the commissioner's staff, and to various other people at operational levels who were the people we had to work with and get information from and influence, and with whom Canick didn't necessarily get along all that well."

The job of "building bridges to all spectrums of the department" fell, in large part, to Rae Archibald, one of the first analysts to join the Rand project team. Archibald had originally been hired to work on a program-planning-budgeting system for the fire service and in "fringe areas of operation research work"—preparing cost-benefit analyses in connection with the recommendations that arose from Rand research and dealing with organizational problems that might be encountered in putting those recommendations into effect. Gradually, he became the middleman in Rand's dealings with the Fire Depart-

---

[6] See G. S. Levenson and A. J. Tenzer, "The Service Facilities of the Bureau of Fire Communications: A Cost Analysis of a Proposed Consolidation," The New York City-Rand Institute, RM-5726-NYC, September 1968.

ment, a "translator" who attempted to overcome "differences in knowledge and perspective between the fire fighting group and the analysts." In the process, Archibald made contacts for Rand among the operating officials of the department, especially in Chief O'Hagan's office. Canick apparently adjusted gracefully to the changed situation. He, too, began to seek out allies in O'Hagan's office. "It wasn't clear to me," he says, "whether Rand worked for me or whether I was supposed to determine what course of action they were supposed to follow. It became clear finally that I wasn't going to be able to do that.... It took me about six months to figure out where my strength was and who my natural allies were. It became clear to me after that time that John O'Hagan was a very positive, supporting type of person, and that Rand would be very much worth working with...."

John O'Hagan had research interests of his own, and in certain respects they were similar to Canick's. O'Hagan, like Canick, was concerned about the condition of the department's communications bureau. The communications system that dispatched tower-ladders to rescue the residents of high-rise buildings in 1968 still strongly resembled the one that had sent horse-drawn engines to tenement fires at the turn of the century. Much of the communications equipment was obsolete, and the operation of the system itself seemed unnecessarily cumbersome. But the communications function also seemed to be an important point of leverage in New York's fire fighting system.

As the demand for fire fighting services increased, it became more and more difficult for the department to mount a quick response to fire alarms. Time lost in responding to alarms could be expensive or fatal, but means for reducing the department's response time could also be expensive. Increasing the number of available fire companies, for example, was the one way to subtract valuable minutes or seconds from the time that it took for fire fighters to reach the scene of an emergency. It would take a number of additional fire companies, however, to bring about any appreciable reduction in response times, and the annual cost of operating each company would be between $600,000 and $700,000. At the same time, the annual cost of operating the communications office for the entire borough of Brooklyn was only about $400,000. It might be considerably less expensive to save seconds of response time in the processing of alarms by communications offices than to save them through the creation of additional fire companies.[7] The communications offices were strategic points for the introduction of time-saving innovations into the fire fighting system.

Even before the Rand analysts went to work, Fire Department officials had been laying plans for the renovation of the communications system. High on the list of proposed changes was the acquisition of new equipment. The de-

[7] Arthur J. Swersey, "Reducing Fire Engine Dispatching Delays," The New York City-Rand Institute, R-1458-NYC, December 1973, p. 41.

partment's antiquated telegraphic system was to be replaced by voice communications, and more ambitious renovations were being considered. In particular, Chief O'Hagan and his staff had begun to explore the possibility that the processing of alarms in the communications offices might be computerized. The arrival of Rand analysts who were familiar with computer systems increased the attractiveness of computerization. Rand's reputation for sophisticated technological skills made the task of computerization seem a near-perfect assignment for the Rand researchers, and the Rand analysts apparently regarded the project favorably themselves. In the early spring of 1968, at a meeting in Commissioner Lowery's office, the Rand representatives recommended that the job of computerizing the communications offices be a major focus of Rand's work for the Fire Department.

Other participants at the meeting objected. Whatever Rand's reputation, there were those who believed that the Rand fire research team was not sufficiently expert to undertake the computerization project. They claimed that Rand had seriously underestimated the likely cost of the effort. The objections came from computer experts serving on the city's Operations Research Council, a body organized by Deputy Mayor-City Administrator Timothy Costello. Its opposition to the Rand research proposal, while not decisive, could be embarrassing.

The council's involvement in the Rand enterprise was a by-product of palace politics in the Lindsay administration. Rand had made its debut in New York under the auspices of Lindsay's budget director, Fred Hayes. Until Mayor Lindsay publicly announced the city's signing of an agreement with Rand, Hayes had never discussed the venture with Deputy Mayor Costello, who had previously assembled his own team of management planners and analysts in the city administrator's office. Understandably, Costello and his staff were "out of sorts with the fact that things had been initiated" without their knowledge. As a conciliatory gesture, Hayes suggested that Costello's Operations Research Council, a group of seventeen prominent management specialists who donated their time to the city, be assigned to "monitor" the Rand work.[8] Two council members, both computer experts, were named to oversee Rand's research for the Fire Department. It was their criticism that temporarily stalled Rand's computerization project.

Chief O'Hagan, offering encouragement, suggested that the Rand representatives present their case for computerization again at a subsequent meeting, taking care to answer the objections raised by the experts from the Operations Research Council. The interested parties reconvened in May 1968 at

---

[8] On the functions of the Operations Research Council, see Philip Finkelstein and Sigmund G. Ginsburg, "Innovations and New Directions in Administration: Recent Developments in New York City's Office of Administration," *Urban Affairs Quarterly* 3 (1967): 54–68.

Budget Director Hayes' office. Again the experts criticized the Rand proposal, concentrating on what they regarded as unrealistically low cost estimates. The computerized alarm processing system, they said, might cost twice what the Rand researchers were predicting, perhaps ten or twelve million dollars, plus as much as one million dollars a year to operate. One of the experts turned to Chief O'Hagan to ask if he would be willing to spend such an enormous sum on the proposed system. With Budget Director Hayes sitting on the opposite side of the desk, O'Hagan was not about to deny the desirability of spending money on his own agency. Few municipal administrators were given such felicitous opportunities to justify new expenditures in the presence of the city's budget director. O'Hagan, already favorably disposed toward the computerization of his department's communications system, rose to the occasion and delivered a lengthy argument on behalf of computerization. When it was over, Budget Director Hayes informally assured O'Hagan that money would be made available for the project. At subsequent briefing sessions, members of the Operations Research Council were seldom present.

O'Hagan therefore had reason to be grateful for the Rand enterprise. While it had not yet produced any research recommendations, it did seem to strengthen his position with the Budget Bureau. The Rand analysts provided support for modernization of the communications offices. They also endorsed O'Hagan's earlier request that he be provided with his own management planning and analysis staff. Rae Archibald, Rand's middleman in its dealings with the Fire Department, had pointed out to the Budget Bureau that the appointment of two or three planning officers to assist O'Hagan would provide Rand with a useful avenue of access to the chief's office and to the operating levels of the department. This time, the Budget Bureau granted the chief's request for a planning staff. By mid-1968, according to one Rand analyst, O'Hagan was beginning to "warm up" to Rand.

A PRELIMINARY USE OF MODELS

Redefining the Problem

Rand did not immediately fulfill O'Hagan's expectations by designing a computer system for the processing of fire alarms. Instead, Rand's own research efforts began to raise questions about the desirability of computerization and to stimulate interest in other, less expensive improvements that might be made in the department's communications and dispatching system. The temporary shift in research priorities began one day late in the spring of 1968 when Edward Blum and Peter Szanton were touring the Fire Department's Manhattan communications office. They were accompanied by Arthur Swersey, a new member of the Rand staff who had just completed graduate course work in operations research. Civil disorder was the subject of conversation. Only two months before, Martin Luther King's assassination had triggered riots in New York, as in most big cities, and the limited resources of the Fire Department had been severely taxed. Szanton observed that the communications office was virtually unprotected. A Molotov cocktail or a mob attack could easily put it out of operation and paralyze fire fighting efforts in the borough. He suggested that Swersey prepare a memorandum on the vulnerability of the communications offices to disruption.

Swersey went to work exploring possible ways in which communications offices might be "hardened" against attack. At the same time, he considered what might happen if an attack succeeded in shutting down a communications center. Such a disaster would make it necessary, at least temporarily, for one of the communications offices in another borough to assume the workload of the destroyed office. It was an open question whether any communications center could absorb this additional burden, and soon Swersey began to wonder whether the offices could handle the burdens that they already had. A call from a union official alerted Swersey to the possibility that the increasing demand for fire fighting services was pushing the department's communications system to the breaking point. The union spokesman implied that fire dispatchers were already forced to ignore alarms in periods of peak demand. In short, it did not take a race riot to overload the department's communications system.

Swersey redirected his research from the security problems of the communications offices to their workload problems. His days were spent in the Brooklyn communications center, the busiest in the city, where he observed the fire dispatchers at work—to their annoyance. The dispatchers resented his presence and were suspicious about the work he was doing. But in time, says Swersey, "I think I got a certain amount of respect . . . because I was there so long that I knew what the system was like. I understood it." Understanding (or even perceiving) the system was not easy—just "so much noise and people running around in different directions." Gradually, Swersey was able to identify an underlying order amid the confusion. At the suggestion of Edward Blum, he decided to deal with the workload difficulties of the communications system as a queueing or waiting-line problem: in effect, the incoming fire alarms lined up waiting to be processed and responded to. The problem was to locate and remove the critical bottlenecks that slowed the movement of the line.

Swersey identified three stages in the process. The first was the handling of alarms as they came into the office. When a fire alarm box was triggered, it set off a bell in the communications office. (The bell system has now been replaced by voice communications.) A fire dispatcher then counted the number of times the bell rang to determine the identification number of the alarm box and retrieved an alarm assignment card for that box from an index file. The assignment card showed where the alarm box was located and listed the companies that might be sent out in response to the alarm. The dispatcher then handed the card to a colleague (the "decision maker") to begin the second stage.

While there might be several fire dispatchers working simultaneously to receive alarms and retrieve assignment cards, only one man at a time served as decision maker in the Brooklyn communications office. His job was to compare the fire companies on the assignment card with those listed as currently available or unavailable on a status board to determine which units should respond to the alarm. Finally, in the third stage of the process, a telegrapher tapped out a signal to the units selected indicating the number of the alarm box that had been triggered.

Swersey decided to ignore this third stage. His observations convinced him that it was not a bottleneck; the time needed to send telegraphic messages to fire houses remained fairly constant no matter how busy the communications office. He began to collect data on service and waiting times in each of the other two stages. The first of these, the receiving of alarms, caught the notice of any visitor to a communications office: "There is a great deal of noise associated with ringing boxes and telephones, and there is much activity related to counting boxes ... and determining the location of an incident reported by telephone." This part of the process, more repetitive and routine than the decision making stage, had been regarded as a prime candidate for computerization. If it could be shown to be the bottleneck, a strong case could be made for a computer system as a solution to the workload problems of the communications offices.

Models and Intuitions

In order to examine the behavior of the dispatching system at different workload levels, Swersey constructed a two-stage simulation model. Running the model, he hoped, would tell him which stage of the dispatching process was responsible for waiting line delays in periods of peak demand for fire fighting services. He chose a simulation model rather than an analytic model because he was not aware of any queueing models that would produce analytic solutions for two successive waiting lines.

Swersey's initial modeling effort produced unsatisfactory results. Guessing that the first stage of the process was responsible for dispatching delays, he had assumed a constant service time for the second, decision making stage. The decision making process seemed very rapid to him, while the job of receiving alarms seemed more time-consuming. But most of his observations were made during the daytime, when the Brooklyn communications office was not especially busy. He had assumed that he could extrapolate his daytime observations to the more hectic nighttime hours, but he was mistaken. The simulation results showed no substantial increase of waiting line delays in the alarm-receiving process as the number of incoming alarms mounted, contrary to Swersey's intuition. "I was looking for some answers that made sense," says Swersey, "and I wasn't really getting very much out of that model, and that told me that ... something must be wrong."

The unsatisfactory results caused Swersey to look at the second, decision making stage of the dispatching process to see if it was more sensitive to increases in the volume of business than he had originally assumed. Swersey returned to the Brooklyn communications office for more observations, this time during the busy nighttime hours. Based on the new observations, he produced a revised model that did not assume a constant service time in the decision making stage. Swersey found the decision making process tended to become more time-consuming as the number of incoming alarms increased. As each new alarm came in, the decision maker had to compare it with recently processed alarms to make sure that it really signified a new incident. The more incidents underway, the more time it took both to complete this checking process and to identify available fire companies for dispatching.[9] Service times in the decision making stage increased as the number of incoming alarms increased. This meant that waiting line delays would increase as well.

According to Swersey's new modeling results, the decision making process could indeed be a bottleneck. Delays increased gradually until the alarm rate reached twenty or twenty-five per hour; beyond that point delays began to increase sharply. At thirty-five alarms per hour, Swersey predicted an average elapsed time of nine minutes between the alarm's sounding in the communications office and the issuance of dispatching orders. In 1968, the alarm rate seldom reached thirty-five per hour, but it was mounting. Swersey's curve suggested that delays could soon be expected to increase sharply; the dispatching system was approaching a breaking point.

Swersey's major recommendation for averting a breakdown in the communications system was to attempt to ease the flow of alarms through the decision making stage of the dispatching process. Swersey proposed that the borough of Brooklyn be divided into two parts, with a separate decision maker assigned responsibility for incidents in each part. The recommendation, says Swersey, did not come from the modeling results: "The model was more important as a framework for looking at the problem than as something that was going to give you results. The results ... helped me and supported my intuition, but at the time the results came through I knew what needed to be done."

---

[9] Swersey, pp. 16, 19, 37.

Swersey's intuition was shaped in part by the results of his first, unsuccessful modeling effort, which revealed that the alarm-receiving process was not a significant source of delays. This insight raised obvious questions about the proposals to computerize this part of the dispatching system. Although there might be other good reasons for automating the system, saving time in the processing of alarms was not one of them. Swersey went further: he suggested that even in the second, decision making stage of the process, computerization was not likely to bring an appreciable reduction in the time it took to process alarms. His own recommendation was less expensive and sufficient to ease the burdens imposed by the increasing alarm rate.[10]

The Findings and the Fire Dispatchers

Swersey learned that devising recommendations was not the same as getting them carried out when he attempted to put his suggestions to the test in the Brooklyn communications office. The test was scheduled for an evening in February 1969. When the time came, Swersey found the dispatchers uncooperative. They disregarded the procedures that he had devised and complained that the innovation was unnecessary. To make matters worse, the night turned out to be a relatively tranquil one for Brooklyn's firemen. Swersey's new dispatching system never got the opportunity to show how it would do under heavy traffic. The leader of the dispatching team wrote a memorandum to the head of the Bureau of Fire Communications asserting that the test had demonstrated that there was no need to adopt the changes suggested by the Rand study. Swersey challenged this conclusion, but made little headway with the bureau chief. For the time being, at least, business would proceed as usual in the Brooklyn communications office.

Resistance to Swersey's recommendations probably arose from a number of sources. In the first place, the Fire Department had already made plans for extensive changes in communications equipment. Swersey's innovations were not part of those plans, and it was not clear just how they could be incorporated into the department's modernization program. Among the dispatchers themselves, other factors probably helped to make Swersey's recommendations seem unattractive. Men who have done their jobs in the same way for many years are not likely to accept changes readily, and the changes proposed by Swersey might prove uncomfortable for the dispatchers. Under the existing system, the decision maker set the pace for the entire dispatching team. He was the nerve center that controlled the system. Swersey's recommendations would not only speed up the pace of the dispatching operation, but give it two nerve centers. It would therefore undermine the single decision maker's strategic position in the dispatching process. In short, the proposed

---
[10] Ibid., p. 40.

change may have encountered resistance because it represented a threat to the existing distribution of status and control within the work team.

Whatever the reasons for resistance, they were not insurmountable, and Swersey soon had another opportunity to test his recommendations. The chance came in May 1969, when routine statistical reports from the Brooklyn communications office indicated that the alarm rate was fast approaching the point at which Swersey's model predicted a sharp increase in the likelihood of breakdowns and overloads in the dispatching system. Careful scrutiny of the statistics hinted that such overloads might already be occurring. Swersey found some evidence that incoming alarms were occasionally being "lost" or ignored by the fire dispatchers. He brought this evidence to the attention of the chief of the Bureau of Fire Communications and, as a result, received permission to test his recommendations once again. This test fell afoul of the same resistance that Swersey had encountered in his first attempt. However, Swersey won permission for a third trial—this one to be conducted by a dispatching team with which he was on especially good terms. The third test was not free of problems. A particularly troubling one had to do with the physical rearrangement of people and equipment made necessary by Swersey's recommendations. In the end, however, these problems were overcome, and the department officials and Rand representatives who were present as observers watched the modified dispatching system operate for three hours on an especially busy night. During one hour of the test, the communications office received forty-three alarms, a workload which almost certainly would have produced dispatching delays under the old system. But the modified system, with the two decision makers recommended by Swersey, handled the heavy burden without difficulty. No alarms went unanswered, and there were no significant delays. The chief of the Bureau of Fire Communications was sufficiently impressed to agree to the adoption of Swersey's recommendation in the Brooklyn office. In July 1969, the change went into effect. The department's plans for equipment modernization were modified subsequently to incorporate Swersey's two-man decision making arrangement.

The innovations that resulted from Swersey's study could hardly be characterized as sweeping. They did not even extend beyond the Brooklyn communications office. In other boroughs, alarm rates were seldom high enough to warrant the adoption of Swersey's recommendations, and in one or two of the offices, existing administrative arrangements or equipment problems made the two-decision maker dispatching system inconvenient or unnecessary. Still, Swersey's findings had significant implications—and not only for the Brooklyn communications office. They showed that the best solution for a problem was not always the most obvious one—in this case, computerization. Swersey's research also demonstrated to Fire Department officials the possible utility of Rand analysis. The study of the Brooklyn communications office

MODELING IN A LABOR DISPUTE: RAND'S "SUPREME ACHIEVEMENT"

The Unions on the Offensive

The most serious problems of the Fire Department in 1968 were its heavy workload and its troubled labor relations; in fact, they were one problem. While Arthur Swersey was still at work designing a simulation model of the fire dispatching system, the two major unions representing fire fighters launched a determined campaign to reduce the burdens imposed upon their men as a result of the rapidly increasing fire alarm rate. The campaign was triggered by intense membership discontent. Most of the leaders of the Uniformed Fire Officers Association (UFOA) were turned out of office in a union election in July, and a more militant set of officers took their place. In August, the newly installed officials, responding to the insistent complaints of their followers, filed a formal grievance with the city's Office of Collective Bargaining, charging that fire officers were dangerously overworked. The UFOA demanded that the city hire an additional 2,500 firemen. Within days, the Uniformed Firefighters Association, a larger union representing the rank-and-file firemen, joined the UFOA in its grievance.

The emergent labor dispute was an unusual one. It promised to broaden the scope of collective bargaining in New York City's municipal agencies beyond the traditional issues of wages and hours to include questions of manpower, workload, and work assignments—matters previously regarded as "management prerogatives." Under the existing system of labor relations in New York City, it was not clear that the city was obliged to negotiate on such matters with municipal employee unions. The Board of Collective Bargaining, a quasi-judicial body made up of labor, management, and "impartial" members, took the matter under consideration. In November 1968, after months of deliberation, the board issued its decision: the city was bound to negotiate with the fire fighters' unions in order to settle the workload dispute. Although management decisions usually lay outside the range of collective bargaining, the board ruled that this was a case in which management decisions had a "practical impact" on city workers. And under the city's labor-management regulations, the practical impact of management decisions—if not the decisions themselves—was a proper subject for collective bargaining. The board's ruling went even further: if the city did not promptly provide relief from the "practical impact" of the Fire Department's manpower and workload policies, the city and the unions should immediately begin negotiations on ways of reducing the firemen's burdens. In negotiations concerning "methods of relief," of course, decisions previously reserved for departmental managers would inevitably become issues for collective bargaining. Furthermore, the board warned that if these negotiations resulted in deadlock, it would appoint an impasse panel with the authority to make recommendations covering the means for reducing the workload of firemen.[11]

Fire Department officials, who had long enjoyed an almost military authority over their agency's affairs, now faced the prospect of having to bargain about their decisions with labor leaders, and justify those decisions before third-party arbitrators. Departmental managers resented this intrusion upon their prerogatives. The situation was made more difficult by the fact that the firemen's wage contract expired in October 1968, and while negotiations on the union's workload grievance went forward, a simultaneous set of negotiations was under way in the wage dispute. In no time at all, the atmosphere became acrimonious. By January, the parties had taken to the newspapers in order to trade public charges and denials. Union officials claimed that Fire Department equipment was obsolete and dangerous, that Fire Commissioner Lowery was harassing fire fighters in an effort at "penny ante union busting," or that the department was cutting back its building inspection program by forcing some of the inspectors to retire. The department's managers peremptorily rejected each charge as it was made.[12]

Workload and wages may not have been the only issues that simulated labor-management animosity. The union officials, their positions threatened by increasing rank-and-file militance, had reason to fear that a conciliatory approach to the wage and workload disputes might cost them their jobs. Rank-and-file rebellion could be headed off only by pre-empting the militant style and demands of the potential rebels. For the rank-and-file unionists themselves, militance may have reflected more than discontent about too much work and too little pay. Subsequent developments, a year or two after the initiation of the workload dispute, betrayed a more visceral resentment. In late 1970, when the Lindsay administration refused to increase expenditures for fire protection because of "budget drains," one union leader delivered a bitter response: "There's a drain all right, and who's getting it? We know. Welfare has gone from 10 percent to 22 percent [of the budget]—there's plenty of money for that." Overworked firemen who had been stoned in slum neighborhoods felt ill-will toward the nonworking slum residents. According to some observers, labor-management relations in the Fire Department became tinged by "underlying racial and class issues."[13] In the work-

---

[11] See Raymond Horton, "Municipal Labor Relations: The New York City Experience," *Social Science Quarterly* 52 (1971): 684.

[12] *New York Times,* January 7, 1969, p. 27; January 21, 1969, p. 38; January 29, 1969, p. 21.

[13] *New York Times,* December 20, 1970, p. 1.

load dispute, therefore, much was at stake besides the workload. For Fire Department officials, the issue was one of managerial authority; for union leaders, it was the ability to remain in command of their own organizations; and for the firemen, it was perhaps a matter of self-esteem. The stakes were also high for Rand's fire project team. The workload dispute was to become a decisive test of Rand's ability to deliver useful research to public policymakers.

The Department Calls on Rand

Late one afternoon in January 1969, at Rand's New York City headquarters, Edward Blum received an urgent telephone call from one of Chief O'Hagan's aides. The chief was scheduled to meet with Herbert Haber, head of the city's Office of Labor Relations, the following morning. Haber's job was to represent the city in municipal labor negotiations, and he was holding discussions with Chief O'Hagan in order to sketch out a bargaining position for the city in its upcoming workload negotiations with the fire fighters' unions. Unless the city could bring some concrete proposals of its own to the bargaining table, it would be difficult to defend against the unions' expensive demands for additional manpower. Chief O'Hagan wanted the Rand analysts to devise a reasonably precise way of measuring and defining workload and some proposals for reducing workload without hiring large numbers of additional firemen. And he wanted it by 8:00 A.M. the following day.

All that night, members of the Rand staff worked to assemble the materials requested by Chief O'Hagan. At 8:00 A.M., they briefed O'Hagan; at nine, O'Hagan met with Haber. And later that afternoon, Blum received another call from Chief O'Hagan's office reporting that the commissioner of labor relations had been favorably impressed with the Rand suggestions. Rand's all-night effort initiated a series of contributions to the department's defense against union demands.

The Rand analysts were not thrust into the workload dispute completely unprepared. Their initial recommendations to O'Hagan had been preceded by almost a year's work. From the beginning, the department's use of manpower and equipment had been the central concern of the Rand project team. During the first year of Rand's partnership with the Fire Department, more staff time had been spent in examining the deployment of men and equipment than in any other research task. Originally, it had been Blum's intention to evaluate alternative deployment policies by estimating their likely impact on the loss of life and property through fire. But it soon became apparent that the data and "theoretical base" needed for this were simply not available.[14] Blum and his staff therefore decided to abandon the fruitless quest

---
[14] Blum, p. 116.

for these "global measures of effectiveness" and to concentrate instead on so-called "internal measures," like the number of units responding to an incident, the time that it took each one to arrive, and, significantly, the workload of the firemen.[15] In retrospect, the decision to make workload one of these measures of effectiveness was extremely fortunate, but not fortuitous. From the early days of the fire project, it was apparent to fire officials and Rand analysts that the department's workload problems were becoming more and more acute.

In order to determine the effects of departmental deployment policies, the Rand project team used a series of computer models whose development could be traced back to early discussions of a Fire Department "response model" between Chief O'Hagan and Steven Isenberg of the Budget Bureau. Under the ministrations of the Rand project team, the notion of a response model broadened into plans for two different kinds of models—one descriptive, the other prescriptive.

The prescriptive models were intended to identify "optimum" deployment policies for the Fire Department. Separate models would be designed to provide answers for different kinds of deployment questions. Where should the fire companies be located? How many companies should be dispatched to an incident? Given the number of units to be dispatched, which companies should be sent?

But optimizing models were not sufficient by themselves. "Optimization in the usual sense," writes Edward Blum,

> does not apply to the problems and issues that have proved most important. Too many objectives matter for any one to be selected as paramount, and there is no operationally reasonable way of combining them all into a single index, especially when they conflict. Moreover, and perhaps more important, fire departments' prime responsibility is to provide emergency, contingency protection. They must perform at a high level under quite diverse conditions and circumstances, and the flexibility and adaptability required to do so must be gained at the expense of "optimality" in any narrow sense.[16]

It was not clear exactly what should be optimized. Furthermore, optimizing models have to make simplifying assumptions to yield analytic solutions. A policy that appears to be "optimum" on paper may turn out to be undesirable in practice.

To overcome the shortcomings of analytic, optimizing models, the Rand project team proposed to construct a large simulation model of Fire Department operations. The simulation model would be used to estimate the consequences of policies prescribed by other models or suggested by common sense.

---

[15] Ibid., p. 117; Grace Carter and Edward Ignall, "A Simulation Model of Fire Department Operations: Design and Preliminary Results," The New York City-Rand Institute, R-632-NYC, December 1970, pp. 9–11.

[16] Blum, p. 116.

For example, one might test a policy that was supposedly "optimum" with respect to fire response times in order to find out whether it also had acceptable consequences for the workload of the fire fighters or for the availability of fire fighting equipment.[17]

The simulation and analytic models were interdependent components of an overall research strategy. The simulation, by itself, would not produce policy recommendations because, as one Rand analyst observed, "it can only try out what somebody tells it to try out." The analytic models on the other hand, would suggest the policies that might be worth trying out, and these could then be tested on the simulation.

Rand's Simulation Model

Chief O'Hagan's request for assistance in the workload negotiations did not cause Rand to abandon its research strategy, but it did bring some changes in emphasis and timing. After answering O'Hagan's initial inquiries, says one Rand staff member, "we focused everything on the workload issue. We structured our models so that they would be able to discriminate among the policies that were being proposed" to alleviate the firemen's work burden. When the workload dispute came to a head in the latter part of 1968, Rand's simulation model was already well on the way to completion, but the Rand staff had not yet produced analytic models capable of generating "optimum" policy recommendations. Throughout the workload controversy, the policies tested through simulation were generated by common sense rather than by analytic models. The search was not for "optimum" deployment policies, but for policies that would produce better results than the ones currently being used by the Fire Department.

The simulation model provided the Fire Department with something it did not previously have—a systematic means for testing proposed policy changes. The department had in its possession much of the raw material needed to construct such a model. The agency had kept a punched-card record of every incident since 1962 to which the department had responded. Each punched-card summary included the date, time, and location of the incident, how it was reported, the nature of the incident, the number of engine and ladder trucks that responded to it, the number of units actually used at an incident, and a few other pieces of information. These Fire Department records provided the Rand analysts with most of the information needed to construct their simulation model of departmental operations. Other sources of information included the journals kept by individual fire companies, which

---

[17] Edward H. Blum, "The New York City Fire Project: Research Review and Projection," The New York City-Rand Institute, D-17363-NYC, July 5, 1968, p. 11.

recorded the length of time that each unit worked at a particular fire. These documents were essential for measuring the workload of the firemen.[18]

Rand's early work on the simulation model consisted largely of information discovery and collection. In mid-1968, the construction of the model began in earnest. At that time, two new members were added to the fire project staff. One was Edward Ignall, a faculty member in operations research in the School of Engineering at Columbia University. The other was Grace Carter, previously an operations researcher for Bell Telephone, who subsequently did most of the computer programming for the Fire Department simulation. Carter and Ignall were responsible for the design of the simulation model, based on the general outlines that had earlier been decided upon. But almost all the members of the Rand project team participated in the effort. Defining the measures to be used, for example, was a task in which many of the Rand analysts had a hand. In addition, members of the Rand staff made frequent field tours of Fire Department operations and facilities—riding to fires with battalion chiefs or observing what went on in a fire station, a communications office, or at the scene of a fire. During the summer of 1968, staff members prepared brief memoranda of the observations made on these expeditions into the field, and these reports, too, became grist for the modelers' mill.

Carter and Ignall chose to simulate departmental operations in a single borough—the Bronx. Some of the busiest fire companies in the city were located there. In the South Bronx, particularly, the increase in the fire alarm rate was adding significantly to the department's burdens. The simulation model included a hypothetical representation of the Bronx in which the locations of fire stations and alarm boxes were fixed, at first, according to a system of grid-square coordinates. Later, the representation would be refined to reflect actual street locations of alarm boxes and fire houses and actual routes that fire trucks might take to the scene of a fire. An analysis of Fire Department records made it possible to simulate the demand for fire fighting services in the borough—the rate at which given alarm boxes were likely to produce alarms and a probability distribution of the types of incidents likely to be reported from particular boxes. The journals kept by fire companies provided a basis for estimating the workload generated by each type of incident—the number and kind of units required to deal with it, and the length of time each company's services would be required. This analysis of incidents was primarily the responsibility of Ignall. Its end-product was an "incident tape" that served as input for the second stage of the study: simulating the department's response to alarms.

This second phase of the modeling effort took up where Swersey had left off. Swersey modeled the dispatching process, from the initial report of an incident to the transmission of dispatching orders to a fire station. Carter and

---
[18] Carter and Ignall, p. 14.

Ignall included a simplified representation of these steps in their model, but went further to follow the subsequent progress of incidents through the fire fighting system, from the departure of engines to their return.

The simulation began with the simulated outbreak of a fire. Then, at a time determined from the incident tape, an alarm is received at the dispatching office. According to a dispatching policy prescribed by the modelers (and subject to variation), certain fire companies are sent to the location of the fire. After their arrival, the dispatching office receives a report from the men on the scene concerning the state of the fire. If too many companies have been sent, the excess units are returned to their fire houses and become available for dispatching to subsequent incidents. If the fire is a serious one and more equipment is needed, additional companies are dispatched. After an interval determined in part by the work times specified on the incident tape, the fire companies are released from duty. They return to their fire houses and become available for service in other incidents.[19]

This abbreviated account enumerates only the most important steps in the simulation. The model, for example, also allowed for the possibility that a fire truck might have an accident on its way to a fire. It took account of the fact that some companies might be called out of the borough to fight fires in other sections of the city. It allowed firemen a period of recovery after strenuous duty at serious fires. And a later version of the simulation provided for the relocation of units into fire houses left vacant when their usual occupants had been called away for extended service at major fires.

Using the simulation, different policies could be tested under the same conditions (number of alarms, types of incidents, sequence of incidents) to see, for example, which of two alternative deployment policies produced shorter response times or lighter workloads. Carter devised a series of computer programs to aggregate and analyze the mass of information generated by each run of the simulation.

The ability to interrupt the simulation to monitor the state of the fire fighting system provided the modelers with a way of evaluating the department's preparedness for especially serious fires—in particular, those in which lives were likely to be lost. Such disasters occur infrequently. In New York City only one in a thousand fires was responsible for a loss of life during 1968. But it was obviously important to find how proposed deployment policies might affect the department's ability to cope with those emergencies as well as the more common trash and automobile fires. The solution was to stop the simulation at regular intervals to examine how many companies would be available for service in the immediate vicinity of a potentially fatal fire if one were to occur at that moment.[20]

---

[19] Ibid., pp. 20–21.
[20] Ibid., pp. 12–13.

By late fall of 1968, the model designed by Carter and Ignall was ready for preliminary runs. Many shortcomings remained to be overcome; travel time between fire stations and fire scenes, for example, was calculated on the assumption that trucks would move at an average speed of 20 miles per hour along grid-square coordinates. It was not until 1970 that Rand analysts would be able to measure the actual travel times of fire trucks on the streets of the Bronx. The grid-square representation of the Bronx itself was merely a hypothetical construct. The model would not reflect the actual geography of the borough until late 1969, and it was not until 1970 that modelers would attempt to take account of the fact that a delay in the arrival of fire engines was likely to result in a more serious fire. Had the time been taken to introduce such refinements in 1968, it is unlikely that the Rand model would have been of much use to the Fire Department in its workload dispute with the unions.

Testing Proposed Policies

The department did not demand quick results. Indeed, for some time, most fire officials seemed largely uninterested in Rand's modeling efforts, and some were mildly contemptuous of the project. One of the departmental managers who dealt frequently with the Rand analysts had a picture of a scantily clad woman on the wall of his office; it was labelled "The Rand Model." Other fire officials did not exhibit even this level of interest. "We came in by fiat of the mayor," explains one Rand staff member. "We were a gift, maybe a Trojan horse." As a result, he says, there were few demands for the services of Rand model builders. "A good deal of the first year that I was on the project was sort of 'free,' " says one analyst who joined the Rand staff in mid-1968. "No one in the Fire Department was asking, 'What did you do today and what good is it doing me?' "

The indifference of the fire officials was not entirely unwelcome; it allowed the Rand modelers to launch their project without being interrupted by day-to-day demands for immediately useful information. Until the workload dispute exploded in early 1969, there was only one significant occasion on which the modelers were required to make a formal presentation of their findings to Fire Department officials—a major Rand briefing in September 1968. But in September, the modelers did not yet have any findings to present. "I think we teased the department," says one of them, and implied "that we did know a few things, but didn't tell them anything." According to one member of the Rand staff, "nobody knew that we had anything to offer. Nobody came to us."

Until the spring of 1969, the Rand modelers proceeded with their work, still largely free from the scrutiny of Fire Department officials. The analysts' attention had turned from the design of the simulation to the testing of alternative deployment policies. Two policy proposals in particular received attention. One would have created a small number of extra part-time fire companies (later known as tactical control units). These would be housed in fire stations where the workload was especially heavy during the hours of peak demand for fire fighting services. A second proposal was to modify the existing dispatching policy so that fewer units would be sent to some alarms. The department's policy had been to dispatch a "standard response" of three engines and two ladder trucks to all alarms, unless the units were unavailable. But most alarms did not call for the standard 3–2 response. In fact, approximately one-third of all the calls for assistance received by the Fire Department turned out to be false alarms. Under the proposal, those alarm boxes would be identified from which only minor fires or false alarms were likely to be reported. When these selected street boxes were triggered, only two engines and one ladder truck would be dispatched.

Fire Department officials had made the proposal for a reduced or "adaptive response" in a Fire Department submission to the Budget Bureau in the spring of 1969. Uncertainty about its consequences, more than departmental conservatism, was the major obstacle to adoption of such a recommendation. Unravelling the likely consequences of such proposals could be an extremely complicated task. For example, although the department's standard response to an alarm was to dispatch three engines and two ladders, there were many occasions on which fewer trucks were sent out—simply because the units normally dispatched were not available. Frequently, in fact, only one engine and one ladder truck would answer an alarm. In these circumstances, the "reduced" response of two engines and one ladder truck would actually be an increased response, and would not lighten the fire fighters' workload.

More important, an adaptive response might dangerously delay the arrival of fire fighters at serious fires. The response times for the initial two engines and one ladder truck would not be adversely affected, and might even be reduced, but if any additional fire companies were needed, they would not be dispatched until after the first units on the scene had called in a request for assistance. Such delays might be avoided by a larger initial response, such as that prescribed by the department's existing policy.[21]

Proposals so vulnerable to objections were not likely to bear up well against union demands for additional full-time fire companies, or the scrutiny of Budget Bureau program planners, or the anxieties of a public aroused by visions of late-arriving rescuers and fiery death. The department needed evidence to justify such proposals—to show that they would actually reduce the workload of fire fighters without endangering the public. The evidence would

---

[21] Grace Carter, Edward Ignall, and Warren Walker, "A Simulation Model of the New York City Fire Department: Its Use in Deployment Analysis," *Proceedings of the Winter Simulation Conference,* San Francisco: January 1973, pp. 8–9.

have to reveal not only the consequences of each proposal by itself, but the combined result of using reduced responses and part-time companies. The problem was too complex for paper-and-pencil calculations. The Rand simulation model—or something like it—was needed to trace out the results of the proposed policy changes. At an all-day briefing in July 1969, the Rand analysts unveiled the first results of their simulation experiments before an audience of about thirty people—Fire Department administrators, Rand staff members, and Budget Bureau officials. The meeting room was equipped with a computer terminal so that questions or suggestions arising during the course of the session could immediately be put to the model. The audience took a lively interest in the proceedings. Workload negotiations with the unions had reached a critical stage, approaching deadlock; Chief O'Hagan and his staff were looking for ammunition, and the simulation results provided it.

They showed, for example, that the additional full-time fire companies demanded by the unions would not provide the workload reduction the unions wanted. Much of the additional labor would be expended to fill out the "standard response" that the department was currently unable to mount during the busiest hours of the day. Fire companies presently overworked would receive little relief at precisely the times when their burdens were heaviest. Adding units would mean sending more engines to fires, not reducing work for existing fire companies. For the hard-pressed companies, in fact, the most significant change resulting from the union proposal for additional manpower would be that already over-taxed units could respond to alarms which they had previously been too busy to cover. Creating additional units carried small promise of a reduction in workload. The benefits, such as they were, would go disproportionately to those fire companies that were not seriously overworked, but were located on the fringes of areas where the incidence of alarms was high. The addition of new full-time companies would reduce the likelihood that these fringe-area units would have to be called in to cover alarms in high-incidence regions.[22]

While the simulation results raised serious doubts about the wisdom of union demands, they did not provide solid support for management proposals either. The reduction in standard response recommended by the Fire Department would not give much relief to the most seriously overworked fire companies. Instead, the simulation results once again showed that the chief beneficiaries would be units located on the periphery of a high incidence area, not the heavily burdened units in the center. Reducing the three-engine-two-ladder response to two engines and two ladders, for example, would save the third engine the time and trouble of a response, but it was usually the one located furthest away from the site of the alarm. The result was that dispro-

---

[22] Blum, p. 127.

portionate workload relief would go to fire companies on the edges of especially busy areas.

Nor would the addition of new full-time fire companies provide substantial relief for the most seriously overworked firemen. But adding part-time companies during the peak demand hours, from 3:00 P.M. to 1:00 A.M., could be effective, if the department also reduced the standard response during these peak demand hours.[23] The reduced response would assure the labor of these new part-time companies would not be drained off in order to fill out the traditional 3-2 response. They would provide relief for the currently overworked fire companies. Furthermore, the simulation results indicated that a reduced or adaptive response would not delay the arrival of additional units at serious fires. In fact, the additional apparatus would arrive more quickly. Since fewer engines would be dispatched to all alarms, additional companies were more likely to be available close at hand when they were needed for an especially serious fire.

These proposals could not be attributed to Rand. Rand analysts themselves concede that fire fighters had been thinking about such innovations for some time. The ideas were "floating around in the department" when the modeling effort got underway. No one is certain exactly where they originated, but Rand analysts could claim at least to have helped make them respectable. The Rand simulation experiments provided a way to put untried policies to the test and generated evidence that could be used not only to support a particular policy change but to suggest possible refinements in it. Chief O'Hagan and his aides could now go off to the workload negotiations armed with specific policy proposals and with detailed estimates of policy consequences for both the department's and the union's recommendations.

As the parties maneuvered from one position to another during the course of bargaining, additional simulation runs were made to test each succeeding set of proposals put forward by the two negotiating teams. At the same time, weak points in Rand's July briefing were shored up with new evidence. At the time of the July presentation, for example, Carter and Ignall had not yet had the opportunity to simulate the deployment policies currently being used by the department so that they could be compared with alternatives proposed by the union, the department, or Rand analysts. Instead, the consequences of the current policies had been roughly estimated through a "probabilistic analysis" completed during the day and a half preceding the July briefing. Later, the simulation model was used to generate more accurate estimates.

Rand's findings were transmitted to the Fire Department's labor negotiators as they were needed through Rae Archibald, Rand's emissary to the workload negotiations. Archibald did not sit in on the bargaining sessions, but held

---

[23] These part-time companies were later known as "tactical control units."

himself ready offstage to supply up-to-date simulation findings and other needed pieces of information. Archibald must have gotten along well with the fire officials. When Paul Canick resigned from the Fire Department to take a job as Deputy Police Commissioner, Archibald was hired to take his place.

The Unions, the Negotiations, and the Settlement

Edward Blum hoped that Rand might establish equally amicable relations with the fire fighters' unions and become a trusted source of expert advice for both sides in the workload negotiations. These hopes, though never realized, were not entirely groundless. During the late spring of 1969, when the Rand modelers were beginning to test alternative deployment policies, one union official met informally with them on several occasions to keep abreast of their progress. David McCormick, a veteran fire fighter, a battalion chief in the department, and an official of the Uniformed Fire Officers Association, had acquired some familiarity with modeling and operations research while earning a business administration degree. He would later become president of his union. After the Rand analysts briefed departmental officials in July, McCormick requested that union leaders receive a similar briefing. "My belief," he says, "was that the union people representing the rank and file should have as much communication with the consultants as possible" because the Rand analysts might help to illuminate the "many areas in which we could agree."

Observers in the Fire Department saw other intentions behind McCormick's request. A shrewd union leader might find a way of "using Rand for union ends." And if that failed, there might be other advantages in hearing the Rand analysts make their presentation: "McCormick apparently thought that by trying to make Rand sell its case, by listening to all these naive kids talk about fire, he could destroy their case. A bright union guy like McCormick could raise a lot of petty objections." McCormick, according to this account, wanted to bring the "naive" Rand analysts out into the open where their expertise and their model could be attacked directly. Once the analysts had been discredited, the department's negotiators would be less able to use the Rand model or its findings to support their position.

Whatever McCormick's intentions, Fire Department and Budget Bureau officials were suspicious, and they were reluctant to authorize Rand to brief the unions. But the Rand analysts were eager to deal directly with the labor leaders. The Rand staff, says one observer, "wanted to see its work get implemented," and the cooperation of the unions would probably be an essential prerequisite. Moreover, since no Rand representative participated directly in the workload negotiations, there was no way for Rand researchers to find out exactly how their work was being presented to the union bargainers. By briefing the union officials themselves, they might be able to correct any misunderstandings about their work. In the end, Fire Department and Budget Bureau officials gave in to Rand and to the urging of a mediator who had been appointed by the Office of Collective Bargaining to preside at the workload negotiations. Rand was authorized to present its findings directly to the labor representatives.

A briefing for the unions was held about two weeks after Rand made its formal presentation to the Fire Department managers. The Rand analysts did not have an easy time of it; among the union members who attended, says one observer, there was "strong suspicion... of the management consultants." The Uniformed Firefighters Association, in particular, was represented by some "people who took a pretty hard labor line, and they figured the hell with [Rand]." The contingent from the Uniformed Fire Officers Association was not much more friendly. It included "some pretty crusty old chief officers" whose animosity toward Rand crystallized when they took "one look at this dimpled kid about 23 years old, with glasses that looked like milk bottle bottoms and hair down to his shoulders." The union hostility became evident to the Rand representatives as dozens of objections were raised against the Rand model and its results. The union men, for example, attacked Rand's estimates of travel time between fire stations and fire scenes. And they questioned estimates of the work time required for various kinds of incidents. After all, says one member of the Rand staff, "they'd been to thousands and thousands of incidents, and for us to say, for example, that a certain type of incident required twelve minutes of company time sounded to them like management mumbo-jumbo."

The Rand analysts weathered the attack of the unionists, but made no subsequent attempts to cultivate the good will of the labor organizations. "The union people became very suspicious," says David McCormick, "not only of Rand, but also of me. They felt that they weren't getting all of the information that the department was. Rand would only release what was well-laundered material, and the department continued to receive confidential reports. So the union really wasn't in there as a partner or as an equal, and that caused part of the resentment." Union men regarded Rand as an agent of the opposition, and union leaders who had attempted to keep themselves informed about the progress of Rand's work found it expedient to curtail their dealings with the analysts.

Rand's research continued to play a role in the workload negotiations; in fact, during the final months of bargaining, the Rand-supported recommendations became the main subjects of labor-management discussion. It was difficult to avoid them; both Fire Department officials and union representatives agreed that excessive workload was the most serious problem faced by the fire service, and they recognized that some significant action would have to be taken in order to deal with the problem. No one assumed that business could continue as usual. Once the parties agreed on the need for change, it was apparent that the proposed changes supported by Rand research had undergone more careful analysis than any others, and some were difficult to dispute. It was difficult, for example, to argue against a reduction of the standard response because it was well known that the department was already dispatching less than the standard response on many occasions. Moreover, the recommendation for part-time fire companies was one that made concessions to both sides in the workload dispute. For the unions, it represented a step toward the creation of additional fire fighting units. For management, it promised a cost savings. The part-time units, according to Rand, could produce the same impact on workload as full-time companies at 40 percent of the expense.

It is debatable whether Rand's research was responsible for moving the workload negotiations off dead center, but most observers are willing to acknowledge that it was helpful in resolving the dispute. As late as June 1969, one month before Rand presented its findings, the Uniformed Firefighters Association was still publicly demanding that the Fire Department hire an additional 2,000 men.[24] After Rand analysts presented their simulation results, the focus of bargaining changed. The Rand-supported proposals gradually became the core of an emergent settlement between the unions and the department.

Finally, in September, the negotiators joined Mayor Lindsay in a press conference at city hall to announce that the workload dispute had been resolved. The city would create ten part-time fire companies (tactical control units) to relieve the burdens of overworked fire fighters during the hours of peak demand. In addition, the Fire Department's standard response would be reduced to two engines and two ladders during the peak hours of the day. In order to get union consent for the workload package, the city promised to create eight new full-time fire companies and agreed that the new Tactical Control Units would be manned only by volunteers. The reduction in the department's standard response was not as substantial as the one initially considered by the Rand analysts, yet the impact of the Rand simulation model was significant. It was, according to one Fire Department official, Rand's "supreme achievement in the city of New York."

THE AFTERMATH AND SOME CONCLUSIONS

The Impact of Rand's Research

Shortly after the unions and the department reached a settlement, several Rand-supported recommendations went into effect. In mid-November, the

---

[24] *New York Times,* June 11, 1969, p. 45.

first three tactical control units began to function on a trial basis in the South Bronx, and for ten hours a day the "adaptive response" designed by Rand analysts became the department's standard response. No serious problems arose during these field experiments. Two weeks later the innovations were extended to some parts of Brooklyn. The changes made a tangible difference to fire fighters in overworked units.

"Until recently," one fireman in the South Bronx wrote,

> my company and Engine 85 responded to many of the same alarms. Then, two years ago, we responded a record number of times. Engine 85 went out 8,386 times in a twelve-month period. Ladder Company 31 went to 8,597 alarms, and my company, Engine 82, went to 9,111. The Fire Department saw that a change was needed, and arranged that engines 82 and 85 would not respond to the same alarms [under the adaptive response proposal]. The plan worked. Last year my company's responses dropped to 6,377 and Engine 85's to 5,012. But the plan worked only for the engine companies; Ladder Company 31's responses increased to 8,774. Another plan was then discussed, and Tactical Control Unit 712 was created to respond only within the high incidence hours between three in the afternoon and one in the morning. The four companies on Intervale Avenue are now averaging 700 runs a month.[25]

There were other factors besides the Rand-supported work arrangements that helped to reduce the fire fighters' burdens. The fire alarm rate did not continue to increase after 1969, for example, at the rapid pace it had followed during the preceding decade. In 1972, in fact, the alarm rate actually declined slightly for the first time in memory, but then it resumed its climb. Apart from this temporary reduction in the alarm rate, whatever workload relief the firemen experienced can reasonably be attributed to the changes made under the labor-management agreement of 1969.

Not all parts of that agreement were implemented as rapidly as the adaptive response and tactical control units. The city's promise to create eight new full-time fire companies remained unfulfilled when wage negotiations with the unions were reopened late in 1970. The unkept promise was one of many irritants that contributed to the bitterness of a year-long battle between the department and the unions—a struggle marked by work slowdowns and repeated strike threats. One of the most intensely fought issues in the conflict was the department's demand for a change in duty tours for firemen. Rand supported the proposed rearrangement of work shifts—called the "concurrent two-platoon system"—with simulation results.

The two-platoon system was designed to insure that two overlapping shifts of firemen would be on duty during the high alarm hours from 3:00 P.M. to midnight. Fire fighters were strongly opposed to the new work shifts, as were

---

[25] Smith, p. 12.

their unions, and Rand became a target for public attacks by union officials. The president of the Uniformed Fire Officers Association referred to the Rand analysts as "itinerant data diddlers." The president of the Uniformed Firefighters Association charged that the annual expenditure of $600,000 for Rand research might have been used more profitably to hire additional firemen.[26] The unions went further. They ordered the men who had volunteered for duty in tactical control units to withdraw from the part-time companies. In the end, the department not only failed to carry out the concurrent tours program, but forfeited the tactical control units as well.

Rand's work nevertheless continued. The optimizing models that Blum envisioned as part of the Rand research effort began to produce results. The simulation model now included many refinements. On the basis of their simulation experiments, the Rand analysts proposed further changes in Fire Department deployment policies—strategies for the relocation of units into fire stations that had been stripped of coverage, procedures for determining which units to dispatch to an alarm, methods for deciding where to locate fire houses. Rand also recommended a comprehensive management information and control system that would permit departmental officials to adjust their deployment and allocation policies to match shifts in the incidence of fire alarms. The proposed $20 million system represented an extension and refinement of Rand's initial proposal for the computerization of the department's communications offices.

Rand's work for the Fire Department was coming to be regarded by fire officials, some union leaders, and by the Rand analysts themselves as a generally successful enterprise. In 1970, during City Council hearings on municipal contracts with consultants, Fire Department officials testified that Rand's work for their agency had saved the city about $7 million a year.[27] While there may have been some differences of opinion about its magnitude, there was surprising agreement about the nature of the achievement. Rand's chief contribution was not to invent policy innovations but to test them and thereby supply the evidence necessary to win their acceptance. "The idea that response should be reduced," says one former member of the Rand staff, "was clearly initiated, long before Rand, by the departmental management. But they didn't know about the consequences of sending less. They didn't know how many were actually being sent under the present system. They didn't know the details of the process."

Rand provided the needed information. Its role was to clarify and refine the intuitions of departmental managers—to convert untested but plausible hunches into convincing policy proposals. Just who needed to be convinced

---

[26] *New York Times,* February 21, 1971, p. 26.
[27] *New York Times,* October 29, 1970, p. 25; Blum, p. 94.

is a matter of some uncertainty. The Rand analysts themselves tend to assume that their research reports and briefings persuaded union officials that certain policy proposals were worthy of adoption. Some union officials, however, believe that the persuasive power of Rand's research findings had its chief effects in other quarters. One union leader observes that Rand "had great credibility in city hall.... Here in the fire service, we could say 'this is the problem and the solution is that we should reduce the responses to these boxes during certain hours.' But it took the sophisticated presentation of the Rand group to sell the idea." Chief O'Hagan thinks both the unions and the city administration were influenced by Rand's "sophisticated presentation." Justifying the Rand enterprise before a city council subcommittee, O'Hagan asserted that "the only way we could sell" the administration and the firemen on "changes in our adaptability was by having carefully thought-out, data-supported studies."[28]

In retrospect, the Rand-supported suggestions must have seemed obvious or old-hat to many veteran firefighters. Some felt the institute's analysts had simply marshaled evidence behind other people's ideas—ideas that departmental officials had been discussing before Rand arrived with experts and computer models. Of course, there had been many ideas under discussion in the department. Fire officials, says Blum, had "proposed numerous ... approaches to the department's problems. Given the tools then at hand in the fire profession, however, most competing theories seemed more or less equally plausible, depending perhaps on who advocated them. Thus, policy debates often ran aground on vital but unanswerable questions, and all but conservative ideas tended to lose impetus."[29] Rand analysts, according to Blum, provided the material necessary for a more productive debate. Their research helped to refine the intuitive hunches of departmental managers and to identify the hunches that were likely to work.

In the process, the Rand analysts developed their own intuitions about the operations of the Fire Department. Arthur Swersey, for example, guessed the location of a bottleneck in the dispatching system before he developed the simulation model that could demonstrate where it was. His intuition was formed as a result of experiments with an earlier simulation model. The analysts who worked on the Fire Department's deployment policies intuited a successful combination of policies even before their simulation model reached a state of refinement sufficient to test their intuitions. These intuitions grew out of early experiments with a primitive version of the model. The process of designing a model and making it work helped the Rand analysts develop their own intuitive understanding of the fire fighting system.

---
[28] *New York Times,* October 29, 1970, p. 25.
[29] Blum, pp. 96–97.

The Impact of the Research Setting

Some of the most widely publicized successes of Rand's fire project made no use of computer models. One of Rand's earliest contributions to the Fire Department, for example, was in the field of chemistry. Project leader Edward Blum suggested the use of a chemical additive that would allow water to move more rapidly through fire hoses. By using "slippery water," firemen would be able to increase the volume of water directed at a blaze, and the department would be able to cut its expenditures by purchasing fewer large-diameter hoses. There was no need for computer models here; Rand's ability to introduce innovations into the Fire Department did not depend on the use of a particular research technique. A critical factor was the nature of the organizational environment in which the research took place.

The environment was congenial to modeling and quantitative analysis. Among municipal agencies, says a leader of one fire fighters' union, "there's nothing more quantifiable... than the Fire Department, because we rely so heavily on numbers and whatnot—more than any other group." For that reason, the agency offered numerous opportunities to the "bright young men of Rand, with their very strong backgrounds in statistics and in the ability to quantify problems." The Fire Department also has clear objectives that are relatively unambiguous, noncontroversial, and highly visible. There may be some debate about the relative importance of fire fighting and fire prevention, but there can be little doubt that the overriding objective of the department in New York City is to put out fires.[30] The clarity with which the function is defined simplifies the task of measuring its performance. There is no need for drawn-out deliberations to determine the department's mission.

The clarity and measurability of the Fire Department's objectives undoubtedly made it easier for Rand analysts to conduct their studies of departmental operations. But this does not mean that it was also easier for Rand to get its recommendations adopted by the Fire Department. In fact, the department appears to be less receptive to change than most other municipal agencies. It is a quasi-military bureaucracy where rules and regulations are published regularly like "orders of the day" and where the leadership selects its own successor, singling out for advancement those candidates "whose values are closely aligned with their own." Other kinds of candidates are likely to be scarce. Since would-be leaders must pass through a long process of acculturation in the ranks, "there is little likelihood that individuals with values much different from those of the organization will survive to become candidates for leadership." The initiation of changes, "always difficult in a bureaucracy, is even more difficult" in such "in-bred" and "self-perpetuating" organizations.[31] In the New York City Fire Department, according to Sayre

---

[30] Sayre and Kaufman, pp. 267–268.

and Kaufman, the fire commissioner himself does not have the ability to lead his agency toward innovation.[32] If the department's own executives lacked the power to introduce change, how could the inexperienced outsiders from Rand hope to stimulate innovation in the fire service?

One possible explanation for their ability to do so, of course, is that the conditions faced by the department in the late 1960s were different from those of ten years before, when Sayre and Kaufman were writing. The increasing cost of fire protection and the rapidly growing demand for it imposed a severe strain on the Fire Department. It was becoming evident to many that the old ways of doing business would no longer suffice. When the fire fighters' unions triggered the workload dispute, the old ways became simply untenable. "The Fire Department," says one of its officials, "had an incredibly pressing problem at the time, and everybody was chafing. It was really driving everybody to distraction."

What was a nightmare for the Fire Department was "an analyst's dream" for Edward Blum and the members of his research team. "Our research began," writes Blum, "in an environment in which many were aware of the general need for change but unsure of the direction that change should take. ... The issue from the time we began ... was not whether change would take place but what change and how." In the fire service, there were almost no research precedents to guide innovation. "To have strong pressures for change and a nearly virgin research territory" was as much as any analyst could ask.[33]

Fire Department officials recognized that their agency faced a major problem. Like other administrators in similar circumstances they looked to research to find solutions. But the conditions that create a demand for policy research may also prevent its results from being put to use. (See Chapter 2). Large-scale problems that increase an organization's appetite for research also stimulate widespread efforts to influence solutions. A proliferation of interested parties increases the difficulty of adopting significant innovations and interferes with a researcher's opportunities to gain the ear of a policymaker. How could Rand's research team deal with this dilemma?

Anyone who looked at a Fire Department organization chart in 1968 might easily have been persuaded that the commissioner's office would be Rand's logical point to contact with the fire service. Overall responsibility for the affairs of the agency was lodged here. Here, too, was the responsibility for departmental planning and budgeting as well as many other staff functions. Research, a staff function itself, might reasonably have been grouped with

---
[31] R. W. Archibald and R. B. Hoffman, "Introducing Technological Change in a Bureaucratic Structure," The New York City-Rand Institute, P-4025, 1969, pp. 8–9.
[32] Sayre and Kaufman, p. 268.
[33] Blum, pp. 101–102.

these other staff activities. In fact this appears to be precisely what city officials initially decided to do. Paul Canick was added to the commissioner's staff to act, among other things, as the middleman between the department and Rand.

But in an agency like the Fire Department, being in a "staff" position can have its disadvantages. Rae Archibald, before he joined the fire project team, had enumerated some of these disadvantages in a paper written with a colleague at Berkeley: "[One] aspect of police and fire bureaucracies is the slow, reluctant acceptance of staff positions as meaningful complements to organization structure. The majority of police and fire departments are strongly biased in favor of line duty." Staff positions usually lie to one side of the path to promotion; they are not sought after, and their occupants seldom carry much weight in organizational decision making.[34]

Rand's entry into the Fire Department would not be auspicious if it were sponsored by members of the commissioner's staff. Very soon after its arrival, therefore, the project team made an effort to put some distance between itself and Paul Canick. Rae Archibald was directed to cultivate other contacts in the Fire Department—especially in Chief O'Hagan's office, which exercised control of the department's line operations.

Rand's new anchorage in the Fire Department offered an escape from the disadvantages of the commissioner's staff. In Chief O'Hagan's office there were no staff experts who might compete with Rand in supplying research to the chief. The small planning staff that the chief subsequently acquired, with Rand's support, did not present a threat to the project team's research monopoly. From these departmental planners, says a Budget Bureau official, "we were not going to get specialized analytic skills.... We were dealing with fire officers, [and] at best you were going to get technical fire fighting skills and managerial capacity." The chief's planning staff did not obstruct Rand's access to the chief and other line officers.

O'Hagan provided the Rand analysts with an avenue of access into the heart of the Fire Department. From the commissioner's office, it would have been difficult to "pierce the chain of command running down from fire chief to deputy chief to battalion chief to captain to lieutenant to fireman." The operational hierarchy is self-contained and does not readily admit influences from outside or above.[35] Through Chief O'Hagan's office, however, the recommendations of Rand analysts could pass directly into that hierarchy, and the project team could establish contact with the "people at operational levels who were the people we had to work with and get information from and influence...."

Rand positioned itself in the Fire Department so that it could have a clear shot at line operations. The nature of the target made it especially susceptible

---

[34] Archibald and Hoffman, pp. 10–11.
[35] Sayre and Kaufman, p. 267.

to Rand's influence. The same insulated, quasi-military character that made the Fire Department seem an unlikely candidate for innovation could also facilitate innovation under some circumstances. "The other side of the coin," observes Blum, "is that fire departments also can be tightly organized, relatively monolithic organizations that may respond quickly to leadership initiatives in situations having commonly perceived outcomes and widely perceived goals."[36] In the tightly organized hierarchy of the Fire Department, where the workload dispute was "driving everybody to distraction," an innovation that promised relief and received the sanction of top executives might be carried out in spite of resistance in the ranks.

In some other agency, whose openness and disjointedness might appear to offer greater opportunities for innovation, the process of adopting innovations might be more difficult. A program of innovation prompted by major policy problems would almost certainly mobilize many interested parties in a contest to control the course of events. In the scramble, the advice of analysts and researchers might be smothered by the advice of more influential participants. In the Fire Department, by contrast, the Rand analysts had attached themselves to the most insulated part of an insulated agency. The same barriers that shielded the department from outside interference also gave the Rand analysts a measure of protection from the rough and tumble of political scrambles. Rand could not escape all controversy, of course, but the self-contained character of the Fire Department meant that the controversies which arose tended to be limited in scope and of a fairly predictable kind—labor-management disputes, for the most part. Rand was operating in a highly structured political environment, a setting in which the kinds of objections that might be raised against a proposed innovation could usually be anticipated and where those who raised the objections were likely to be well-known participants in the closed system of departmental politics.

The institute's ability to work its way into this sheltered political environment was increased by the fact that it was not an ordinary consulting firm. Its partnership with the Fire Department was to outlast the conduct of any single study. There was time for Rand analysts like Rae Archibald and Arthur Swersey to become well-acquainted with agency officials and to be recognized as legitimate participants in the department's business. If Rand had been a conventional consulting firm engaged in a single project for a limited period of time, it would probably have been unable to achieve such a firm footing. The institute had been designed so that analysts could achieve just this sort of access to the innermost parts of municipal agencies—to facilitate the collection of information and to enable them to follow up on the implementation of their recommendations. In both respects, the fire project lived up to its promise.

---

[36] Blum, p. 100n.

The Rand Institute was designed to combine these advantages of access with the benefits of autonomy. The fire project team was not intended to become the department's house research staff. Its independence enabled the Rand group to fend off most of Paul Canick's early requests for short-term projects. And when the disadvantages of association with the commissioner's office became evident, Rand was able to detach itself and seek out more useful allies. In other instances, the benefits of autonomy did not live up to expectations—expectations that were probably unrealistic. In the workload dispute, for example, the institute's independence from departmental managers was not sufficient to convince union leaders that Rand was an impartial supplier of information. At the same time, the degree of autonomy that Rand enjoyed may have made it easier for some union officials to give serious consideration to its research findings.

In summary, the special organizational arrangements made for the Rand enterprise in New York City served their intended purposes effectively in the fire project. Here, Rand earned a reputation for success. A number of factors contributed to that success. First, the Fire Department's operations were well documented, easily quantified, and had unambiguous objectives, making them an ideal subject for Rand's modeling techniques. Second, the department's managers, faced with serious and complex problems of administration, were already convinced that they could not continue to conduct business as usual and that significant operational changes would have to be made. Like other administrators confronted with unfamiliar issues, they lent their support to research efforts. But unlike many other administrators, they were somewhat protected from the diverse political pressures that tend to accumulate when public officials are considering major shifts in policy—pressures that frequently make it difficult to translate research findings into concrete decisions. The emphatically hierarchical character of the Fire Department and its political insularity helped to minimize such pressures, though not to eliminate them entirely. Finally, the organizational arrangements of the Rand Institute itself and the kind of connection that its research team managed to establish with the Fire Department helped the analysts exploit the advantages that were offered by the department's distinctive organizational characteristics.

The relative success of Rand's research venture in the Fire Department occurred under circumstances that could hardly have seemed more unfavorable at first glance. A stolid, tradition-bound, quasi-military agency was to be linked with a think-tank known for its use of sophisticated research methods, its intellectual fashionability, and its unconventional style of work. It was an unlikely partnership. The mismatch between institutional cultures was reflected at the individual level in the contrast between "crusty old chief officers" and the young, highly trained but largely inexperienced analysts from Rand. In fact, however, it was the differences between Rand and the Fire Department that helped their partnership succeed. Had the department resembled Rand more closely, it would hardly have been able to carry out the Rand-supported recommendations so expeditiously. The sharply drawn differences between Rand and its client helped to minimize confusion about their respective roles. It also reduced the likelihood that either party would regard the other as a threat to its own dominion. In these and other ways the sharp distinction that existed between the researchers and their clients contributed to the success of the fire project. The importance of this factor can be perceived more clearly by examining one of Rand's less successful enterprises in New York, which we will do in the next chapter.

9

Health, Hospitals, and Hostilities

CONFLICTING PERSPECTIVES

Rand and the Health Services Administration

The contract between the Rand Corporation and New York City's Health Services Administration (HSA) was one of the four initial agreements that Mayor Lindsay announced in January 1968. By mid-1972, when this agreement was dissolved, Rand had more than seventy research notes and written reports to show for its four-and-a-half-year effort, but its labor had left hardly a trace in the programs and administrative policies of the Health Services Administration. "The work that Rand did for us," concluded one HSA official, "was, on an overall basis, rather useless." And Rand officials themselves acknowledge that projects undertaken for HSA were among the institute's least effective enterprises in New York City.

Of the seventy-odd reports that Rand prepared for HSA, only one employed a formal model. But the methodological distinctiveness of this project —a study of bed utilization in New York's municipal hospitals—did not rescue it from the fate of most other Rand investigations; it had almost no effect upon the operations of HSA and its sister agency, the Health and Hospitals Corporation. In short, whether the Rand analysts used modeling or some other research technique seems to have had little effect on their ability or inability to influence the administrative policies of HSA. The obstacles lay elsewhere.

From the perspective of HSA officials, the obstacles were in the Rand staff itself and its style of operation. The health administrators complain that the research interests of Rand analysts were so "abstract" or "academic" that their work could seldom be of any practical use to the agency, that Rand analysts were not bold enough to enter the bureaucratic fray in order to do battle on behalf of their own recommendations, and that the work effort of the Rand staff was not sufficiently vigorous.

NOTE: Unless otherwise noted, all direct quotes in this chapter are drawn from personal interviews with participants in the events described, some of whom do not wish to be identified as sources.

Accusations made by Rand analysts are inverted images of HSA's complaints. While HSA officials charge that Rand's work effort was insufficient, Rand analysts complain that members of the agency were impatient, expecting results in weeks from research projects that took months to complete. While HSA officials fault Rand for its timidity in advancing its own recommendations, the Rand analysts say that implementation of these recommendations was the responsibility of HSA, not Rand. And while agency officials allege that Rand research was too abstract or academic to be useful, the Rand analysts argue, in effect, that what was "useful" to agency officials was also trivial. Health administrators, they declare, sought to employ Rand researchers as "fire fighters" on specific problems that arose in HSA's day-to-day operations rather than on the long-range planning function that the Rand analysts thought they were meant to perform.

Some Rand analysts suggest that these complaints and counter-complaints are symptoms of a general "feeling of competition" that infected the relationship between Rand and HSA. The HSA analysts felt threatened by the experts from Rand—or so it appeared to the Rand people—and it is charged that HSA attempted to supplant the Rand project team with a special staff of its own, organized to meet some of the same long-term research needs that Rand was supposed to fulfill. In this way, allegedly, the agency might bring the process of research more completely under its own control.

HSA officials staunchly deny any intention to push aside the project team from Rand. They point to the development of an internal agency staff for long-term research projects, not as evidence of an attempt to undercut Rand's position, but as one indication of a need to supplement Rand's inadequate research efforts at a cost per man-year that was considerably lower than the cost of the Rand studies.

Whatever the truth of the matter, it is clear that the distinction between researchers and clients was not so sharply drawn in Rand's health project as it had been in the fire project. In the Health Services Administration, Rand analysts confronted people with backgrounds and temperaments similar to their own—people who sometimes performed research functions themselves, not grizzled bureaucratic veterans devoted to the traditions of their craft. Despite the similarities, relationships between the Rand researchers and their fellow analysts in HSA were less than cordial.

Rand and the Health and Hospitals Corporation

While the Rand Institute's dealings with HSA may have been troubled, Rand had hardly any dealings at all, troubled or tranquil, with city administrators directly responsible for running New York's municipal hospitals. Although these hospitals accounted for the lion's share of the HSA budget,

Rand conducted no studies of hospital operations for almost three years after signing the first contract with HSA. In late 1970, when the institute undertook a modeling study of hospital bed utilization, it did so without having established any direct relationship with the city's newly created Health and Hospitals Corporation, a factor that both Rand and HSA officials cite as having prevented the bed utilization study from being put to use. Until 1972, the Health and Hospitals Corporation had established no analytic staff with whom the Rand analysts could discuss their work. Rand could only hope that its immediate client, the Health Services Administration, would bring its research recommendations to the attention of the new corporation. Given the poor standing of Rand research in the eyes of many HSA officials, it is not surprising that this hope remained largely unfulfilled.

What is perplexing, however, is the apparent contradiction between the inferences that have been drawn from Rand's experience with the hospitals corporation and those that could be drawn from its dealings with HSA. Observers report that a significant obstacle to effective coordination with the hospitals corporation was the absence of any agency analytic staff with whom the Rand analysts could consult. In the case of HSA, the chief obstacle was reported to be the presence of such an analytic staff and its competition with the Rand project team. When the client agency lacks a research staff, it fails to provide a point of entry for outside studies and recommendations. When the agency does have a research staff, the work done by outside analysts may fall victim to "competition." But if both the existence and nonexistence of an agency research staff prevent outside studies from having an influence on agency policy, it would be impossible for an organization like the Rand Institute to conduct successful policy research. In fact, we know that Rand did affect the policies of agencies like the New York City Fire Department and the Water Resources Administration. Since the kinds of problems Rand had with HSA were not universal, the explanation for them must lie in some distinctive characteristic of Rand's health project team, or the health agency, or the relationship between them.

PRELUDE TO DISAPPOINTMENT: 1968–1970

Instability in Rand's Research Staff

What caused Rand's problems in the health area? Rand staff members, HSA officials and independent observers identify a number of factors that weakened the institute's research effort in the field of public health and made it vulnerable both to criticism and to dilemmas like the one just described. Rand's health project team, for example, suffered from a remarkably high rate of personnel turnover. From mid-1968, when Rand established the team, to late 1970, when the institute began the study of hospital bed use, three different project leaders directed the research. Before appointment of the team's first leader, two other members of Rand Corporation in Santa Monica were responsible for outlining a research agenda. Altogether, therefore, five different people tried to guide the Rand's health research during a period of less than three years. The team's ability to retain its members was hardly superior to its ability to retain its leaders. By late 1970, only one staff member remained of an original half dozen.

High personnel turnover offset one of Rand's chief advantages over more conventional consulting organizations, namely, its ability to establish a durable relationship with a client that outlasts the conduct of any particular research project. Although the Rand Institute provided an organizational framework for such long-term relationships, the framework by itself was not enough. It was also necessary that the institute's employees be willing to continue working with the same city agencies for relatively long periods of time. In the case of HSA, they were not. Their frequent comings and goings may have contributed to the unhappy state of Rand-HSA relationships, and these unhappy relationships may have been partly responsible for the high rate of departure. The rapid turnover may have been both a cause and an effect of the tension that existed between HSA and the Rand Institute.

Poorly Defined Research Tasks

High personnel turnover was not the only source of tension. Potential points of contention and misunderstanding were built into the Rand-HSA partnership from the very start. The initial agreement between Rand and HSA was loosely drawn and did not specify the functions that the Rand project team was expected to perform. Rand's contract with the Fire Department was not precise either, but it did ask Rand specifically to develop a "predictive tool for estimating number and type of fire incidence and to examine the department's communications system." By contrast, the HSA contract spoke in general terms of Rand's investigating "the delivery of community-based comprehensive psychiatric and psychological care to mentally ill patients" as well as "defining and conducting studies ... in other important policy areas such as reducing the in-patient burden, restructuring the administration of the health services delivery system, and improving the accessibility of ambulatory care." These numerous, imprecisely defined tasks were mentioned merely as examples of the kinds of research Rand might conduct, not as projects the institute was actually expected to undertake. In fact, one of the responsibilities the drafters of the HSA contract gave to Rand was the design of a long-term research program for HSA. While other Rand project teams were ready to embark on research programs, the health project team first had to design such a program.

One would not expect the failure of the HSA contract to specify research tasks to have been a crippling problem for Rand. Rand researchers place a high value on flexibility and freedom, and there should have been an opportunity for the Rand project team to work out a more detailed and coherent specification of research responsibilities in negotiations with HSA officials who wanted particular studies conducted. But this assumes there were some HSA officials who felt a need for Rand research; such administrators were at first difficult to locate.

Health Research and Administrative Hostilities

Rand was not warmly received at HSA. For most of its first year, the Rand project team searched in vain for an agency administrator who cared to use its services. HSA officials were unimpressed by the outsiders, most of whom had no previous experience in health or hospital administration. They were skeptical about Rand's ability to understand the ills of the city's public health system, much less cure them.

Other factors also contributed to Rand's cool reception at HSA. The Budget Bureau had been a party to Rand's research contract with HSA, and many of the project team's research responsibilities were designed to fill the bureau's needs rather than HSA's. Rand was asked to prepare an analysis of "major resource allocation decisions to be made in the proposed 1968–69 expense budget;" it was to devise "measures of output and effectiveness" for health programs that might be used in the city's program-planning-budgeting system; and it was to seek out means to "control costs and performance of suppliers of health care." HSA officials often found themselves in an adversary relationship with the economy-minded analysts from the Budget Bureau, and so they were naturally suspicious of the Rand project team, which they perceived, with some reason, to be an agent of the bureau.

The inability of the Rand project team to locate suitable clients within HSA during the first year of the Rand-HSA contract only served to drive the Rand analysts into a closer alliance with their clients in the Budget Bureau and aggravated their strained relationship with the HSA administrators. The Rand project team spent most of its first year performing PPBS-related tasks for the Budget Bureau, activities that contributed nothing to Rand's popularity within HSA, and further convinced HSA administrators that Rand's work was not directly useful to their agency. When Rand's first contract came up for renewal, few supporters of the institute could be found in HSA. It was only through the influence of the Budget Bureau that the Rand enterprise managed to survive.

The close alliance between the health project team and the Budget Bureau continued up to the last days of Rand's contract with the Health Services Administration. More than most Rand project teams, the health researchers regarded the Budget Bureau as a major client. "We clearly had an equal responsibility to the Budget Bureau," recalls one leader of the health project team, "and this sometimes got in the way. For instance, when we did some kinds of analyses and gave copies to both [HSA and the Budget Bureau], HSA would be upset."

HSA officials were also upset by what they regarded as Rand's refusal to perform "short-term analyses" of pressing agency problems like the reorganization of preventive disease clinics into comprehensive neighborhood health systems, or the impact of Medicaid cutbacks on the finances of New York's municipal hospitals. It was not until 1969 that Rand began to undertake short-term projects of this kind for HSA officials, and even then, only for certain HSA officials. One of these was a newly appointed deputy commissioner in the Health Department (an administrative subdivision of HSA) who was able to persuade the Rand analysts to work on some short studies to design programs for the detection, treatment, and prevention of four diseases: lead poisoning, venereal disease, alcoholism, and schistosomiasis, an illness affecting the city's Puerto Rican population. The most effective of these studies, the lead poisoning study, led to the creation of a $2.4 million screening and prevention program. Although the Rand study was not responsible for convincing Health Department officials that they needed a lead poisoning program, it did help them justify the program and get Budget Bureau approval.

The schistosomiasis study, in its own way, also served a purpose. The Health Department wanted to demonstrate that it was as concerned about the unique health problems of Puerto Ricans as it was about sickle cell anemia among the city's blacks. The schistosomiasis study reported that since the disease could be contracted only in Puerto Rico, and since a health program was already under way on the island that would lead to the eradication of the disease in the near future, there was no need to launch a schistosomiasis program in New York.

Rand's studies of alcoholism and venereal disease had no immediate influence upon agency programs. The same was true of a more comprehensive study conducted by Rand to assess all Health Department services for children and young people. Not only did this study fail to produce results, but for more than two years it failed to produce a final report. The working notes that did appear occasionally only succeeded in convincing Health Department officials that the study would not tell them anything they did not already know.

Officials of the Department of Mental Health and Mental Retardation, another of HSA's constituent agencies, came to much the same conclusion about some of Rand's projects for their department. A study of potential delivery systems for neighborhood mental health services did not provide them with any information that they thought could be put to use. The only research that seems to have found an appreciative audience among the mental health administrators was a compilation of data on the home addresses of patients in city and state mental hospitals. It could be used to identify areas of the city that most urgently needed neighborhood mental health clinics.

Obstacles to Comprehensiveness in Research

By the end of 1969, after two years of studying the health problems of New York City, the Rand Institute had not yet been able to cultivate a substantial or enthusiastic clientele in the Health Services Administration. A few Rand studies had been reasonably well received, and some may have influenced agency decisions, but none dealt with major segments of HSA operations. On those occasions when Rand analysts ventured beyond the narrow confines of a single program—as in the study of child and youth health services or the investigation of alternative delivery systems for community mental health services—the results were pronounced useless by the would-be clients.

Apart from the reports for the Budget Bureau, almost all Rand studies up to 1970 were requested by officials in HSA's constituent agencies, not by the central administrative staff of the super-agency itself. "HSA-Central," which had overall responsibility for public health programs in the city, would have been the logical client for any comprehensive studies Rand might have attempted of the health care delivery system in New York. But the assistant administrator of HSA, who was assigned to handle the super-agency's dealings with the Rand Institute, never mapped out any comprehensive studies for Rand to perform. Instead, he suggested a series of short-term studies to meet the central staff's more urgent and specific needs. The assistant administrator's preoccupation with short-term projects was understandable. The Health Services Administration had not yet established its own analytic staff, and there was almost no one in the super-agency who could produce the short-term studies that HSA administrators needed in order to make informed decisions about day-to-day operations. If these limited and urgent information needs were to be met at all, they would have to be met by Rand's health project team. Rand's refusal to accept these assignments caused frequent irritation among the harried administrators at HSA-Central. But to Rand researchers, these "low-grade" research tasks seemed inconsistent with the more ambitious purposes for which the Rand Institute had been created. They were determined not "to become a job-shop for the Health Services Administration."

The failure to establish a satisfactory working relationship between Rand and the central administrative staff of HSA undermined Rand's ability to resolve the uncertain mandate of its contract with HSA. Without a high-level administrative focus for its activities, Rand was unlikely to develop a substantive research focus, and there was a danger that the project team would be left to dissipate its energies in small, uncoordinated studies conducted in various nooks and crannies of the public health bureaucracy.

The problems that arose from the diffuseness of Rand's contract with HSA were therefore compounded by Rand's difficulties in dealing with HSA administrators. It was not simply that HSA officials were hostile or indifferent clients who were reluctant to supply the Rand project team with specific research assignments. Such reluctance was undoubtedly present—fostered by skepticism about the abilities of the Rand researchers and by resentment over their ties with the Budget Bureau—but even when HSA administrators called upon Rand for assistance, their requests were unlikely to contribute to development of the kind of comprehensive research program envisioned, though not described, by the HSA contract. Officials within the operating subdivisions of HSA were in no position to outline comprehensive research tasks; they were responsible only for the activities of their own subdivisions. Officials of the super-agency, on the other hand, faced immediate research needs that could not be met by long-term investigations. The members of the Rand project team were the only experts available. In the absence of an internal agency research staff to absorb these requests for urgently needed, small-scale studies, HSA's demands upon the Rand project team were governed by a Gresham's law of policy research, and the demand to fill short-term needs tended to drive out the desire for longer-term studies.

ADMINISTRATIVE CHANGES AND A NEW BEGINNING

Organizational Renovation in HSA

Long-term studies could be carried out of course, only by researchers who stayed on the job a relatively long time. But there was high personnel turnover on the Rand health project team and among the HSA officials as well. The city administrators came and went almost as rapidly as the Rand staff members. From the signing of Rand's first contract with HSA until the beginning of 1970, three different administrators headed the agency. It had been created only a year before Rand's arrival in New York, and it was hardly an entrenched bureaucracy. Unlike the Fire Department where officials tended to leave only when they retired and some administrative procedures had remained unaltered for almost seventy years, the Health Services Administration was beset by changes.

One series of changes was triggered in 1969 when Mayor Lindsay requested the resignation of the physician then serving as HSA administrator. After an interregnum of several months, Lindsay appointed Gordon Chase as a replacement. Chase was a city official in his late thirties who had been serving as deputy administrator for management in the Human Resources Administration. He had no previous experience in the field of public health. His appointment reflected the mayor's conviction that what was needed in the costly and far-flung operations of the Health Services Administration was not medical competence or public health experience but managerial skill.

Not everyone agreed. The New York Academy of Medicine and the New York State Medical Society both registered strong opposition to Chase's nomination and their objections were echoed by at least one influential political figure in the city—Bronx borough president Herman Badillo. The opposition was not sufficient to block Chase's appointment, however, and in early January 1970, he was sworn in as the new administrator of HSA. Almost immediately, he began to remake the staff of the super-agency in his own image. Most of his new recruits were management specialists and systems analysts without previous experience in health or hospital administration. The chief responsibilities of this new staff lay in two areas: legislation and program evaluation and planning. To prepare a legislative program for the agency, Chase hired a handful of youthful lawyers. The responsibility for evaluation, planning, and budget administration fell to Robert Harris, an economist who had been executive director of the President's Commission on Income Maintenance. Chase appointed Harris deputy administrator of HSA.

Within a year and a half, Harris' research staff numbered about twenty people organized in two divisions. An Office of Program Analysis was responsible for conducting short-term studies of HSA operations, and an Office of Health Systems Planning, created in 1971, was responsible for planning the agency's capital construction program and for conducting other long-term studies.

While HSA was completing the renovation of its staff, the Rand project team was experiencing some staff changes of its own. In the spring of 1970, a new project leader was appointed: Allen Ginsberg was an economist and systems analyst who had worked previously on a health research project for the Rand Corporation at its headquarters in Santa Monica. Not long after Ginsberg moved to New York City, Ronald Choy, who had just received his degree in urban planning, also joined the Rand project team.

By mid-1970, there were several respects in which the Rand project team and the HSA research staff had come to resemble each other. Both had young members, most of whom were newcomers either to the agency or to the Rand Institute; their training was usually in economics or systems analysis; almost none of them had any extensive experience in the administration of public health programs. But there were a few small differences, too. The HSA staff was weighted more toward economists and business school graduates, the Rand analysts more toward expertise in operations research. The respective quality of the groups is naturally difficult to assess. Not surprisingly, each felt it had the superior staff.

Organizational Turmoil in the Hospitals Department

Before the members of the Rand project team could become well acquainted with their new counterpart in HSA, the agency experienced still another major change in personnel and organization. Disturbed that the mayor had not consulted him about the appointment of a new administrator for HSA, the commissioner of HSA's Hospitals Department, Joseph Terenzio, resigned. Terenzio's departure capped a series of reported disputes with the mayor over the budget of the Hospitals Department and the handling of community protests at a municipal hospital in the South Bronx. Terenzio's resignation represented a serious setback to some laboriously developed plans on the organization of the Hospitals Department.

In 1966, six different investigatory bodies had launched inquiries into the operations of the Hospitals Department, three of them proceeding under the authority of various branches of the state government, and three under the auspices of the city government. One of these groups of investigators—a special commission appointed by the mayor—eventually produced a plan for the reorganization of the Hospitals Department as a public corporation whose directors would include some administrative officials of the city government as well as others to be designated by the mayor and City Council. As a corporation, rather than a city agency, the municipal hospital system would be empowered to raise some of its own revenue through the issuance of bonds, and it would be set free from the city's civil service regulations and purchasing procedures. The result, it was hoped, would be greater autonomy for the administrators of New York's eighteen municipal hospitals, so that they would not have to refer everyday decisions to higher authorities in the comptroller's office or the city's Civil Service Commission.

The plan for reshaping the Hospitals Department had been approved by the state legislature in 1969. The fact that this comprehensive reorganization was in the works had been at least partly responsible for deterring any studies of the department by the Rand Institute's health project team. The plan had also triggered extensive controversy among city politicians. City Council president Sanford Garelik, for example, complained that under the proposed system, the city government would be "abdicating its responsibilities," since "elected officials will no longer be directly responsible for running municipal hospitals." He predicted that the system would become "even more remote from the poor people it is supposed to serve."[1] Other prominent figures in New York politics, like Herman Badillo, made similar predictions.

The resignation of Joseph Terenzio prolonged the uncertainty and debate that the hospital reorganization plan had engendered by removing from consideration the leading candidate for the post of president in the new corpora-

---

[1] *New York Times,* June 28, 1970, p. 31.

tion and thereby postponing the corporation's birthdate. It was not until mid-1970 that Mayor Lindsay and the hospitals corporation board were able to appoint an executive officer for the new hospital system—Dr. Joseph English, a psychiatrist who had been serving as administrator of the Health Services and Mental Health Administration in the U.S. Department of Health, Education, and Welfare. Gordon Chase, as chief of the Health Services Administration, automatically became chairman of the board of directors. After four years of preparation, the new Health and Hospitals Corporation was finally ready to take over the city's hospital system.

For the Rand Institute's health project team, the creation of the Health and Hospitals Corporation helped to resolve administrative uncertainties of several years' standing and thereby made the city's enormous hospital system a suitable field for research. At the same time, the establishment of a research staff in the Health Services Administration promised to reduce the demands that were made of the project team for short-term studies. Demands of this kind, and the Rand analysts' reluctance to meet them, seem to have been partly responsible for the continuing disagreement between Rand and HSA-Central and probably helped to frustrate the development of a comprehensive health research program for Rand. It now remained to be seen whether the Rand research effort would fare better in the presence of the agency research staff than it had in its absence.

THE RAND HOSPITAL BED UTILIZATION MODEL: 1970–1972

The Political Setting

Not long after the birth of the hospitals corporation, HSA Administrator Gordon Chase met with community representatives from the South Bronx to discuss their proposal that a new municipal hospital be built in the Soundview section of the borough. The Bronx was suffering from an apparent shortage of hospital facilities, and several of the city hospitals that did exist in the borough were badly in need of replacement. To make matters worse, the closing of a voluntary hospital not far from the Soundview area seemed to create a special need for hospital facilities in that section of the Bronx, and the city's hospital construction program had not yet made any provisions to meet it.

The Bronx residents' request for a new hospital was supported by two influential spokesmen who accompanied them to Chase's office—Dr. Howard Brown, a former administrator of the Health Services Administration, and Bronx Borough President Herman Badillo, previously an opponent of Gordon Chase's appointment to head HSA, a critic of the plan for the new Health and Hospitals Corporation, and recently named by Mayor Lindsay to serve on the corporation's board of directors. Badillo reported that he had already discussed the financing of the new hospital with members of Governor Rockefeller's staff. Under a state law, the New York State Housing Finance Agency had been authorized to sell low-interest bonds to finance the construction of public hospitals. Hospitals that were built under this arrangement would be leased by the state to municipalities. Several hospitals and hospital additions then under construction in New York City had already been financed by this means, and the Housing Finance Agency was fast approaching the limit of its borrowing authority. Badillo, however, claimed to have reached an agreement with the governor's office under which hospital financing priorities would be reshuffled in order to accommodate the construction of the Soundview facility.

HSA officials regarded this claim skeptically. One of them speculates that the "agreement" which Badillo had secured from the governor's aides was no more than a tentative assurance that the state would consider financing a new hospital for Soundview if the city committed itself to building one. By presenting city officials with the prospect of state financial assistance, it is argued, Badillo hoped to extract just such a commitment from them and thus induce the state government to strengthen its uncertain promise of financial support. The increased assurance that state financing would be available might then help to solidify the city's determination to build a hospital in Soundview. Badillo, says an HSA official, "no doubt would have continued going around in circles, hoping to incrementally get people into making contingent commitments until all parties fell into the trap. We knew it was a potential trap from the first meeting."

In spite of such apprehensions, Gordon Chase moved quickly to prepare his agency's response to the request for a new hospital. His research and planning staff, however, suggested that he use the opportunity provided by the Soundview proposal to conduct a comprehensive study of the need for hospital facilities not just in the South Bronx but in the city as a whole. Before making any decisions on Soundview, Chase and his staff wanted to deal with a more general question—whether or not to embark on a major new program of municipal hospital construction and reconstruction. Preliminary evidence seemed to favor a massive building effort, not because of any overall shortage in the supply of hospital beds, but because many of the available beds were in aging, substandard facilities, or were not located in the neighborhoods that needed them most. The comprehensive study suggested by Chase's staff would permit the agency to examine the construction and replacement needs that resulted from these problems. It might also reveal whether the need for a new hospital in Soundview outweighed the claims that might be made by other neighborhoods. The study was to include an examination of hospital obsolescence and the need for replacement, an analysis of patient flows to determine which neighborhoods the city's hospital patients were coming from, an examination of the length of patient stays in different facilities, and a study of hospital financing. Chase reluctantly agreed to allow three months for these investigations.

The research staff assembled by HSA Deputy Administrator Robert Harris for planning and evaluation was not large enough to complete all of these assignments in the allotted time while performing its other tasks as well. Harris requested Allen Ginsberg, the Rand Institute's health project leader, to provide him with at least one analyst to work on the study of hospital needs. Although the request was of just the sort that Rand had dismissed in its earlier dealings with HSA, Ginsberg agreed to supply the services of Ronald Choy for about six weeks. The arrangement was an unusual one. "Rand," explains a former member of the project team, generally did not "like to do this kind of thing—to lend somebody out." But "the situation being what it was, we decided to tread pretty carefully," taking care not to become too deeply involved in "the day-to-day junk." Choy was to serve as "sort of a scout, because we were all just starting out, and the idea was that we would get tossed into the situation fast, and find out what the problems were, or at least what these guys were thinking. Also, at that time, we didn't have a grand scheme of what we wanted to do."

An Inauspicious Beginning

Choy went to work on the HSA project in October 1970. He was given responsibility for the segment of the study that was to trace the flow of patients from various neighborhoods of the city into the municipal hospital system. By determining where the patients came from and where they went, it was possible to identify those areas of the city in which large numbers of patients were traveling long distances in order to get hospital care. The results of this investigation suggested that there were several New York neighborhoods whose need for hospital facilities might be greater than that of the Soundview section. But Choy also found some evidence that seemed to support another, more general finding: the city in fact already had enough hospital beds to accommodate the patient demand, but those beds were inefficiently used and poorly distributed across the city. With a more efficient system of allocating patients to beds, the city might not need any additional hospitals at all.

Choy suggested to Ginsberg that a Rand study aimed at more efficient bed utilization in the city's hospitals might provide an appropriate starting point for the institute's renewed research effort at HSA-Central. Ginsberg agreed, and Choy supplemented his report on the geographic movements of hospital patients with a short section devoted to the problem of "excess" beds and the inefficient use of beds. The contents of this report, as well as the results of the other investigations of hospital needs, were to have been presented to HSA administrator Gordon Chase at a meeting in December 1970. The meeting was cancelled at the last moment, but not before some of the would-be participants had already assembled. Among those participants was an official of the Budget Bureau, whose approval would be needed for HSA to embark on a hospital construction program. Choy, believing that the Budget Bureau was to receive the results of his study, handed over a memorandum that summarized his findings to the budget official who was present.

The release of Choy's findings to the Budget Bureau caused much irritation among members of HSA's research staff. The irritation was certainly not diminished by the fact that the Budget Bureau subsequently leveled some severe criticisms against HSA's hospital construction proposals. Although Choy's observations about excess bed capacity do not appear to have played any significant part in these criticisms, a few HSA officials perceived a direct connection. HSA administrators were particularly irate about a contention, implied in Choy's memorandum, that Gordon Chase had decided in favor of a hospital construction program in spite of an existing surfeit of hospital beds, and had done so for political reasons. Some agency administrators acknowledge that the contention was not entirely false, since a massive hospital construction program could, after all, have considerable political appeal. But, says one official, "to put such a thing in a document submitting preliminary results of a technical study struck me as outrageous." Speculation about Chase's motives, it is argued, did not belong in a technical report. Besides being inappropriate, "if leaked, such a document could have been very damaging, completely undermining the possibility of doing further good analytic work on the issue of hospital needs."

HSA officials made their displeasure known to Allen Ginsberg, and sought an assurance that future Rand reports and memoranda would be submitted to HSA for review before being forwarded to the Budget Bureau. Ginsberg declined to make any such promises. The Budget Bureau, he argued, was as much a party to Rand's contract as was HSA, and the bureau should therefore have equal access to Rand research.

Agency administrators were clearly disturbed by the way Choy had introduced his proposal to study hospital bed utilization. But while they did not immediately authorize Choy's study, they did not immediately reject it either, and Choy began his research without the agency's specific approval.

Specific approval may not have been necessary; the importance of the issue to which Choy addressed himself had already been generally acknowledged within HSA. The proportion of the city's hospital patients who were cared for in the municipal hospital system had been declining for almost twenty years, largely as a result of the growth in private and public health insurance programs. Patients who were covered by Medicare, Medicaid, or private health insurance often preferred treatment in private-sector hospitals to free care in the municipal system. As a result, there had been a general increase in the number of vacant beds in the municipal system. If some of these empty beds could be eliminated, the underfinanced hospital system might be able to achieve a cost savings. Moreover, if patients from neighborhoods with filled hospitals could be systematically diverted to hospitals with empty beds, the need to build new hospitals might disappear or diminish.

The empty beds represented not only a possible means for saving money, but an occasional source of public embarrassment for New York's health officials. Less than six months before Ronald Choy proposed the bed utilization study, the Citizens Budget Commission, a private agency supported by local businessmen, issued a report charging that the increase in the Lindsay administration budget between 1970 and 1971 was excessive. The commission was especially critical of the allocation of additional funds to municipal hospitals where there was "significant underutilization" of the existing hospital beds. After citing occupancy rates in the municipal system that ranged from 77 to 84 percent, the commission inquired whether the money spent on public facilities might not be better spent on nonpublic hospitals "to which sick people want to go." A member of the mayor's staff responded with an attack on the commission's "insensitivity [toward] the many poor who have no other hospital service available" than the care provided by the municipal system.[2]

In fact, the average occupancy rate in a hospital or in a hospital system does not directly indicate the number of beds needed there. Demand for hospital beds may vary considerably from one day to the next. If the administrators of a hospital were to reduce the bed complement of their facility to equal the average number of patients, they would be forced to turn away patients on days when the demand for hospital services was greater than average. Not all of the beds that lie empty on an average day are dispensable. The number of beds really needed to accommodate the varying demand for hospital services depends partly on the amount of day-to-day variation in the demand and partly on the extent to which hospital administrators are willing to risk turning away patients who need hospital care.

Conducting the Study

The problem of estimating the number and location of "excess" empty beds in the city's hospital system became the central objective of Rand's bed utilization study. The elements of the study were worked out in a few hours by Ronald Choy and Allen Ginsberg following one of their meetings with the HSA research staff. But the job of assembling the necessary data and producing estimates took several months. Choy undertook this responsibility. He was

---

[2] *New York Times,* June 1, 1970, p. 39.

not a specialist in queueing theory, the approach that he and Ginsberg had selected, and he consulted other Rand staff members who were. The decision to employ a queueing model was, according to Ginsberg, easily made: "It was fairly clearly a queueing situation, the data happened to be available, and the assumptions that were necessary to build a model checked out."

One important set of assumptions had to do with estimating the average daily demand for hospital beds and the distribution of demand over time. The city's hospitals collected information only about patients admitted on any given day, not about patients turned away. Since these "lost patients" represented an important part of the demand for hospital services, neither the average demand nor the distribution of demand could be determined from existing hospital records. By using a simple queueing model, however, the average number of "lost patients" and the average daily demand for hospital services could be estimated, given certain standard assumptions about the probability distributions of demand, length of stay, and hospital occupancy, together with available data on the total bed complements of hospitals, the average length of hospital stays, and the average daily admissions.

Once having derived the estimates of demand, Choy was ready to consider just how many beds were needed in municipal hospitals in order to accommodate that demand. The problem was to minimize the average "buffer stock" of empty beds that a hospital had to maintain without running an excessive risk that patients would have to be turned away on busy days. Exactly what risk was "excessive" was not something Choy could determine on his own; it was a matter for hospital administrators and policymakers to decide. Choy surmised that city officials would be willing to turn patients away from municipal hospitals at a rate somewhere between one in a hundred and one in a thousand.

The next step was to determine the "optimum occupancy"—the number of beds a hospital could keep occupied on the average without being forced to turn away patients at an unacceptably high rate. Once this "optimum" occupancy had been determined, the hospital's average occupancy was subtracted from it to calculate how many empty beds on an average day could be filled without exceeding the maximum turn-away rate. These were the hospital's "excess" or "usable empty beds."

A major problem remained. Hospital beds are not necessarily interchangeable. Pediatric patients, for example, cannot be distributed among empty beds in surgery wards. Nor can surgery patients be shifted to general medicine wards. "Excess" empty beds in one service cannot be used to make up for a deficiency of beds in some other service. A hospital that has an optimum occupancy overall may nevertheless face serious occupancy problems in individual departments. Choy attempted to meet this problem by treating each of three major hospital departments, pediatrics, surgery, and general medicine, as a separate unit. He calculated the average number of excess beds for each service individually. Taken together, these services accounted for approximately three-quarters of the beds in the municipal hospital system, of which, Choy estimated, between 8 and 12 percent were excess empty beds.

Choy was now prepared to offer suggestions for handling the "empty beds" problem. He devised several alternative sets of recommendations, each accompanied by an estimate of the cost saving that would result. The job of estimating these savings was complicated by the fact that no one knew what would happen to the "lost patients" presently being turned away from municipal hospitals. If a more efficient system of bed utilization made it unnecessary for city hospitals to turn away these patients, the cost savings that resulted from a more efficient use of hospital beds would be offset, to some extent, by the added cost of treating more people. Of course, the current "lost" patients might not actually be lost at all; after being turned away from one of the city's hospitals, they might gain admission to another. In this case, more efficient bed utilization would not increase the number of patients, but only make it possible to handle the existing patient load with a smaller number of beds. The cost savings that came from increased efficiency then would not be reduced by an added cost of treating more patients.

Whether "lost" patients were really lost also made a difference for the solution of the empty bed problem. If every patient turned away from one city hospital was subsequently admitted to another, the municipal hospital system was already meeting the demand for patient care. The excess empty beds then simply represented excess capacity and could be eliminated. That was the simplest of Choy's remedies. On the admittedly questionable assumption that it cost the hospital system $50 a day to maintain each empty bed, Choy estimated that this simple solution could save between $10 million and $15 million a year for the city's hospitals.

For the possibility that the "lost" patients were really being lost, Choy devised several other remedies, all based on the same underlying principle: "A larger facility can handle a higher optimum occupancy because the variance of its daily census is relatively smaller so that it needs a relatively smaller buffer zone of beds to handle the day-to-day fluctuations of utilization demand."[3] Accordingly, Choy suggested that for the purpose of allocating patients the municipal hospitals be treated as an integrated reservoir of beds, not as separate facilities. If a particular hospital had filled all of its beds, it could refer incoming patients to other municipal hospitals where spare beds were still available. Patient referral systems of this kind could be established for each of the boroughs in the city, or a single referral system could be organized for all of the municipal hospitals in New York. By increasing the efficiency of

[3] R. K. H. Choy, "A Queueing Analysis of Hospital Bed Utilization in New York City," The New York City-Rand Institute, WN-7425-NYC, June 1971, p. 35.

bed utilization, these referral systems would reduce the number of lost patients and at the same time make it possible to eliminate some excess empty beds. The cost savings that would result from filling some of the empty beds and eliminating others would range from an estimated $5 million to $9 million a year if boroughwide referral systems were used and from an estimated $21 to $24 million if a citywide referral system were established.

Problems of Implementation

Choy submitted a final report on his findings and recommendations in June, 1971, about six months after he had begun to work on the empty bed problem. HSA officials were impatient to see the results, and some of them were not completely satisfied with what they finally saw. One member of the HSA research staff perceived several distinct stages in Gordon Chase's response to the study: "His first reaction was 'Where is it, already?' That went on for several months. His second reaction was 'What does it say?' Then his reaction was that it wasn't detailed enough."

In order to assist Chase in understanding what the report said, the HSA research staff prepared a short summary of its findings. Chase sent the summary, together with the report itself, to the president of the Health and Hospitals Corporation. There, the subject of empty beds was not heard of again for almost a year. Chase, as chairman of the corporation's board of directors, exercised both formal and real influence over the operation of city hospitals. "If we do a study," says one HSA analyst, "he's got some leverage to use on the corporation staff to get them to implement it." But the bed utilization study arrived at the corporation's offices at a time when the agency was preoccupied with serious financial difficulties. The immediate problem of maintaining solvency apparently took precedence over the more remote possibility of saving money through efficient use of hospital beds. Moreover, the Choy study, as it stood, could not be implemented. There were essential details absent from the study, as Gordon Chase had pointed out, and the corporation had not yet organized a research staff that could work out these details of implementation.

The details fell instead to the HSA analysts and continued to occupy them for more than six months. In their eyes, Choy's queueing model, though sophisticated, did not add much to what could be gained by simply ordering hospital officials to close down empty beds "to the point where occupancy rates reached 90 percent." In order to go beyond that, says one member of HSA's research staff,

> It would have been necessary to cover services other than the three major services that were included in the study. It would have been necessary to go into all sorts of detailed work—looking at configurations in each hospital, the physi-

cal layout, the staffing pattern, and what could be rearranged. There was no interest at Rand in getting into anything that was that operational.

Perhaps the chief problem for the HSA analysts was to ensure that the elimination of excess empty beds actually did result in cost savings for the municipal hospital system. It was far from certain that the closing of an empty bed would save the city $50. a day, as Choy had assumed. Much depended upon just which beds were closed. If two or three beds were eliminated from a ward of twenty, for example, it was unlikely that the city would save anything. It would still have to pay for heating and lighting the ward; someone would still have to mop the floors; and since most city hospitals were understaffed, there was little hope that such a reduction of the bed complement would allow a reduction of staff. If substantial savings were to be achieved, they would not come from mothballing a dozen or two dozen beds that were scattered throughout a hospital. They would come only from closing down an entire ward or an entire wing—hence the concern about "configurations in each hospital, the physical layout, the staffing pattern, and what could be rearranged."

While they were wrestling with these difficulties, staff members of HSA's Office of Program Analysis were also attempting to extend investigation of the excess bed problem to the city's tuberculosis wards and its obstetrics-gynecology services. In the process, they abandoned Choy's queueing model for less complicated research techniques. "I don't have much faith in computer simulation," explains the official who was director of Program Analysis at the time.

> I think that you can use a lot less sophisticated quantitative techniques a lot more successfully. Frankly, I don't think it's worth the effort—the time, and especially the expense—to do a computer simulation when you can do it a lot less sophisticatedly. And in fact, that's what we did with Choy's analysis.... There was a problem of taking a study that sophisticated and turning it into a policy.... I felt, for our purposes at least, that things were happening so quickly and so rapidly—and Chase was demanding things—that we just couldn't rely on that kind of sophisticated method.

HSA's analysts were more subject to the agency's day-to-day demands than Ronald Choy had been, and they could not afford to use the time-consuming research techniques that Choy had used. Simpler and quicker techniques would have to suffice. One method was to assume that hospitals should operate at average occupancy rates of 90 to 95 percent; where the buffer stock of empty beds was more than 5 or 10 percent of the total complement, the excess could be eliminated. Another technique was examination of the occupancy and admissions figures for city hospitals in order to determine how many beds a hospital would need if it were to meet all demands for admission 95 percent of the time. Beds in excess of this amount could be regarded as expendable.

While the HSA staff was searching for more economical alternatives to Choy's queueing model, work was under way at the Rand Institute to strengthen the model. In mid-1971, Choy had given a seminar on the bed utilization study for his colleagues at the institute. One of them, Peter Kolesar, a specialist in queueing theory, raised some questions about the assumptions of the model, and volunteered to conduct a study to test their validity, especially the validity of assumptions concerning the day-to-day distribution of demand for hospital services. Using detailed data on hospital admissions that had not been available to Choy and a different method for estimating patient demand, Kolesar was able to demonstrate that Choy's assumptions about the distribution of demand, and the other statistical assumptions on which Rand's bed utilization study had been based, were reasonable.

Kolesar took almost a year to complete his analysis of Choy's assumptions because of delays in assembling the necessary data and because of his other research responsibilities. This time, the wait for research results did not strain the patience of HSA officials. They had already discarded Choy's model and were not especially anxious about its validation. Kolesar's work therefore remained somewhat isolated from the parallel studies of hospital bed utilization being conducted in HSA's Office of Program Analysis. Indeed, from the perspective of some HSA officials, Kolesar's inquiry was quite irrelevant to the agency's own efforts. For them, the important task was determining which hospital beds should be closed, in which order, and how much could be saved as a result. In their eyes, Kolesar's painstaking effort to test modeling assumptions was simply "a very academic piece of work, which may have been worth doing, but [it] was not appropriate for the city to pay for it."

The divergence of the Rand and HSA research efforts involved more than a difference of opinion about appropriate methods and subjects of research. It had an important bearing on the fate of Choy's recommendations for dealing with the empty bed problem. In his own research report, Kolesar attempted to convince HSA that short-cut methods for estimating the number and location of excess beds could only identify those beds that were expendable under the existing organizational arrangements of the hospital system, not under a patient referral of the kind that Choy had recommended. A queueing model, he argued, could be used to simulate alternative referral systems and to estimate the number of excess beds that each system would yield, whereas the short-cut research techniques would not permit analysts to test any significant reorganizations of the system. By abandoning Choy's queueing model, Kolesar contended, the HSA research staff had forfeited the opportunity to design a patient referral system of the kind that Choy had suggested in his recommendations.[4]

---

[4] See Peter Kolesar, "An Analysis of HHC Hospital Bed Utilization Data," The New York City-Rand Institute, WN-7851-NYC, July 1972, pp. 1, 15.

Kolesar's warning does not seem to have troubled the HSA analysts. To Kolesar, in fact, it appeared that the agency officials were almost relieved to learn that they were not likely to uncover a substantial number of excess beds in the municipal hospitals unless they embarked on a major reorganization of the hospital system. When he presented the results of his work to a joint meeting of officials from HSA and the Health and Hospitals Corporation, he found that his audience was not especially interested in reorganization proposals, but gratified to discover that so few excess beds could be found under the existing organizational arrangements.

> The major impact of everything that we did was to show that they had enough beds as it was, [and] it looked as if you couldn't really cut back significantly without a major reorganization. My impression was that they were very pleased with that. It showed there weren't that many excess beds in the system. They were not very interested in the reorganization of the system.

Actually, HSA staff members had discussed the proposal for a patient referral system on several occasions and made a deliberate decision to scrap it. The prospects for a referral system, for example, were discussed briefly in the synopsis of Choy's bed utilization study that the HSA staff prepared for Gordon Chase. Such a system, it was noted, would not cost very much, but it would present "a large and complex implementation problem." The "problem" was the elephantine and administratively confused Health and Hospitals Corporation. "It was," says one HSA analyst, "the nature of the way the corporation operates. It's very slow to move." The job of integrating the municipal hospitals into a patient referral system seemed to be more trouble than it was worth. At the same time there was considerable uncertainty about just what the effort *would* be worth. HSA officials were not at all convinced that the cost savings predicted by Choy could actually be achieved, and they were reluctant to embark on an enterprise that seemed as troublesome as the organization of a patient referral system unless they could be reasonably sure that it would result in substantial economies.

The chief recommendation to come from Ronald Choy's bed utilization study succumbed, therefore, to a combination of circumstances. To establish such a referral system would require major changes in the operation of the ponderous Health and Hospitals Corporation, and the HSA staff did not feel confident that the bureaucratic obstructions could be overcome. Moreover, to make such an enterprise worthwhile, it would be necessary to have some assurance that the expected cost savings could actually be realized, and the assurances were insufficient.

There were other considerations that undoubtedly operated to retard any program to eliminate excess beds, whether it included a patient referral system or not. Probably most important were the expected political consequences of closing hospital beds. The residents of New York's neighborhoods were unlikely to regard the beds in their community hospitals as "expendable," whatever the experts from Rand or the Health Services Administration said. A vigorous effort to reduce the bed complement of the hospital system could be expected to provoke a vigorous response. And it did.

By the spring of 1972, almost a year after the completion of Choy's report, HSA's work on the empty bed problem had progressed far enough so that the agency could begin to consider arrangements for disposing of some beds. A leading proposal was to sell one or more of the most underused municipal hospitals to a local corporation that operated a large health insurance plan. Negotiations with the prospective buyer had already begun when a memorandum concerning the proposed sale found its way out of HSA's Office of Program Analysis into the offices of the *New York Times*. Public response came quickly—and sharply. Members of the board of directors of the Health and Hospitals Corporation, some of them prominent New York politicians, expressed surprise that the actions discussed in the purloined memo were actually being considered. Recovering quickly from the shock, they passed a resolution asserting that no one had the authority to negotiate the sale of municipal hospitals without their consent. The resolution went on to criticize the research staff of HSA—and indirectly, Gordon Chase—for not consulting the board about the selling of municipal hospitals. Chase explained that plans for shrinking the bed complement of the city's hospital system had been only "tentative." "We have these staff papers coming out by the dozen," he said. "That's what we pay those guys for. But I could show you other HSA studies that call for expansion of facilities and services."[5]

In any case, it was fairly certain that HSA would not be producing any more staff papers that called for the elimination of hospital beds. Not long after the corporation's board passed its critical resolution, HSA's work on the empty bed problem was concluded. By coincidence, the agency's partnership with the Rand Institute came to an end at approximately the same time. In June 1972, HSA abruptly announced that it was terminating its contract with Rand.

AFTERMATH AND IMPLICATIONS

Although the Rand Institute and the research staff of HSA were no longer directly engaged in bed utilization studies, the empty bed issue was not dead. In mid-1972, for example, the Citizens Budget Commission issued a special report on the city's hospital system, one chapter of which was devoted to the excess bed problem. Much of the material in that chapter had been drawn

---

[5] *New York Times*, April 14, 1972, p. 43.

from Ronald Choy's year-old study. Only a few weeks after the commission released its report, the hospitals corporation succeeded in establishing its own office of program analysis, staffed by former employees of HSA. As its first major project, the corporation's new research staff embarked on an effort to eliminate excess beds from the municipal hospital system. Although the corporation's analysts held a few meetings initially with representatives of the Rand Institute to discuss the empty bed problem, they decided to proceed without Rand's assistance. A year later, after a long series of negotiations with the staff of the various municipal hospitals, they had succeeded in closing approximately 600 excess beds. The closings had been achieved quietly, gradually, and with the active cooperation of hospital administrators.

It is difficult to determine exactly how much the Rand bed utilization studies contributed to the final result, but it does not seem that their contribution was a major one. The corporation did not adopt the patient referral system which had been recommended by the Rand studies. Nor did the corporation's analysts adopt the modeling techniques that Ronald Choy had used to estimate the number and location of excess beds. They relied instead on simpler methods. In fact, the final decision to eliminate a particular block of beds was generally not based on any research method at all, but on a process of negotiation between the corporation staff and hospital officials. Rand cannot even be given full credit for calling attention to the empty bed problem. Months before the Rand Institute began its studies of bed utilization, the Citizens Budget Commission had already registered its dissatisfaction with the large number of vacant beds in the city's hospitals, and New York health officials claim to have been aware of the empty bed problem long before that. One member of the HSA staff concedes that the Rand study "further stimulated our interest in the question of excess beds ... but nothing happened as a result of it." His estimate of Rand's influence is probably a reasonable one.

Organizational Differences

One might have expected a more impressive record of achievement for the Rand research enterprise. The institute's client agency was generally receptive to research efforts. Its own large research staff stood as evidence of a substantial commitment to such activities. Nor was the Health Services Administration such an inflexible and tradition-bound agency that one would expect it to offer rigid resistance to researchers' suggestions for administrative change. On the contrary, it was a relatively new agency, with a youthful staff, and it was adapting to major organizational changes even while the Rand analysts were conducting their studies. In spite of all that, the innovations suggested by the Rand bed utilization studies were never translated into agency policies.

Perhaps the explanation is that the virtues of HSA were also its faults. The newness and disjointedness of the agency meant that lines of authority were not well established. The super-agency was not fully in control of its constituent units, and the reorganization of the municipal hospital system in 1970 seems to have aggravated this condition, especially where the issue of bed utilization was concerned. Because of the hospital corporation's semiautonomous status, it was relatively immune to research conducted under the auspices of HSA—so much so that the HSA research staff despaired of making any attempt to establish the patient referral system which the Rand study had recommended for city hospitals.

Being "innovative" does not necessarily equip an organization to adopt innovations. The contrast between the Health Services Administration and the Fire Department is instructive in this respect. The Fire Department, with its quasi-military hierarchy and its twenty-year employees, may not have been a promising source of administrative inventions, but the organization's long-established system of command and obedience helped to assure that an administrative change, once introduced, would actually be put into effect. The very characteristics that made the Fire Department seem mossbacked and reactionary to some observers—the insularity, the stability, and the solidarity —facilitated the implementation of administrative innovations. Conversely, the very characteristics that made the Health Services Administration seem open and innovative—its newness, internal diversity, and administrative changeability—probably impeded the adoption of Rand-supported recommendations.

The impediments were of several kinds. The internal diversity of HSA, for example, contributed to an ambiguity in agency objectives. As a result, Rand analysts were hard put to discover a focus for their research that was also a focus of agency concern. The Fire Department, on the other hand, was a more single-minded agency than HSA. Here, it was easier for analysts to identify policy questions that could command the attention of agency administrators.

Because Fire Department objectives were more clearly defined, success in achieving them could also be more easily measured. If it was impractical to count the number of lives saved by the efforts of fire fighters or to assess the property damage averted, at least it was possible to estimate the speed with which the department could mount an appropriate response to various kinds of emergencies under different conditions. The ability to treat the central objectives of the agency in quantitative terms gave considerable power to the Rand modeling effort. The absence of this ability in HSA meant that Rand modelers tended to be drawn to peripheral concerns of the agency—problems that lent themselves to quantification but were not necessarily subjects of intense interest among HSA administrators. The problem of excess beds was only one of many subjects that concerned health officials. Other matters, like the issue of health care delivery systems, seem to have commanded higher priorities. With so many other problems to worry about, HSA officials were not prepared to embark on a laborious program of administrative change designed to increase the efficiency of bed utilization.

The diffuseness of HSA's objectives was paralleled by a diffuseness of bureaucratic power. In the Fire Department, authority over agency operations was concentrated in the hands of Chief O'Hagan. With his support, Rand researchers gained access to the tightly organized hierarchy that responded to his commands. In the Health Services Administration, on the other hand, Rand was unable to form a close working relationship with the agency's chief administrator—a fact that contributed to the eventual breakdown of Rand's partnership with HSA. But even the friendship and support of HSA's chief would probably have added little to Rand's ability to make headway in the municipal health bureaucracy. Unlike Chief O'Hagan in the Fire Department, the administrator of HSA did not stand at the peak of a tightly ordered hierarchy.

HSA was a holding company for a collection of health agencies which had previously been autonomous city departments, and which continued to exercise considerable autonomy after being brought under the umbrella of the super-agency. The administrator's office was not a strategic control center from which Rand analysts could readily achieve access to the super-agency's various subdivisions and affect their operations.

While the health bureaucracy may have been relatively unresponsive to the influence of its chief, it was more highly vulnerable than the Fire Department to the influence of outsiders. Its exposure to external political forces became evident when HSA's own internal research group took up the study of bed utilization. The investigation came to an abrupt end when the agency, not yet firmly established or secure from external attack, was criticized for considering the sale of "excess" hospitals. Of course, research efforts in the Fire Department were not immune from attack either, but here the conflict was confined to a more limited arena and occurred within the well-ordered and ritualized framework of labor-management relations. The Fire Department was more impervious to outside influences than HSA. While its insularity may have made it resistant to externally induced change, it also offered a politically sheltered environment in which Rand researchers could operate with some security.

The process of administrative change in HSA was therefore hindered by some of the same organizational characteristics that made the agency appear more receptive to change than the Fire Department. The agency's openness to outside influences meant that the difficult business of innovation could easily be disrupted by unanticipated upheavals in HSA's political environment. The decentralization of administrative authority reduced the likelihood that internal resistance to change might be overcome. And the confusing multiplicity of organizational objectives in HSA made it difficult for would-be innovators to find a suitable target for their proposals. There was no strategic point of leverage for implementing important changes in HSA.

Research Problems

Problems of implementation, however, do not fully account for the differing fortunes of Rand's research ventures in the Fire Department and the Health Services Administration. The differences also had to do with the nature of the research conducted. The fire project and the bed utilization study, for example, both relied on models, but of different kinds. In HSA, Ronald Choy used an analytic model; in the Fire Department, Rand researchers depended on a simulation model. Stated briefly, the difference between these two approaches is that Choy's analytic model produces one mathematical solution covering all possible outcomes, while a simulation model produces single outcomes from a distribution of outcomes. Both types of models rest on assumptions, but in different ways. In the simulation model, an assumption can be modified or relaxed and its effect on the results of the model noted. In the analytic model, certain assumptions may be necessary in order to arrive at a mathematical solution. Changing these assumptions might destroy the possibility of obtaining a result. Assumptions tend to be more binding in an analytic model, and the analytic model is therefore more restrictive in scope.

Technical considerations of this kind can impinge on the usability of research recommendations. If the assumptions of an analytic model cannot be tested, recommendations based on the model are conditional at best, and policymakers should be warned of their conditional nature. Since it is often impractical or impossible to determine whether the assumptions are accurate, policymakers may well be wary, as they were about Choy's recommendations for the municipal hospital system. In the minds of HSA officials, too much remained uncertain to justify immediate adoption of Choy's proposals.

Rand's research problems went beyond matters of modeling technique. A major source of trouble was the relationship between the research activities of Rand and those of HSA's own analytic staff. Creation of the HSA research office was another apparent sign of the agency's flexibility and receptiveness to change. Young and highly trained, the agency's analysts seemed to represent an organizational commitment to innovation, but in the eyes of the Rand analysts, they represented another obstacle to effective policy research and administrative change. One member of the Rand staff who conducted studies for both the Fire Department and the Health Services Administration sees Rand's tie to the HSA planning and evaluation staff as one of the principal handicaps of the institute's health project team:

> I'd always thought that we were working for the wrong people. We were a staff operation working for another staff operation.... If we were going to have any real impact, we should have been working for the Health and Hospitals Corporation, but we didn't have direct contact with the operating agency or with a single hospital.... In health, we were working for a staff group, most of the members of which had no line experience. They were analysts like us. They had virtually no influence on operations. By contrast, in fire, the people we worked with had come up through the ranks. They were taken out of the field explicitly to work with us.

Rand analysts were convinced that the creation of the HSA research staff had placed a barrier between them and operating officials in HSA's constituent units. These officials—not members of the HSA research staff—controlled the information needed by Rand analysts and had the authority to put Rand recommendations into practice. The institute's health project team became "a staff operation working for another staff operation"—an engine racing in neutral. Perhaps more important, because the Rand research staff was working for another research staff, its relationship with its health client always threatened to become a competitive one. The HSA staff, made up of "analysts like us," was able to do on its own much of the work that Rand itself was doing. The two research groups were perfectly capable of carrying on without one another, and after the completion of Ronald Choy's initial queueing study, that is approximately what they did. Had there not been this parting of the ways between Rand and HSA, Rand's research enterprise might have had more useful results.

The same conditions that led to the divergence of the Rand and HSA bed utilization studies eventually led to a more permanent and complete break between the two organizations. After Gordon Chase established his own research staff within HSA, he perceived little need to retain the more costly services of the Rand health project team. The result, says one administrator, was that "as time went on, there was less and less of a need for Rand." "We felt," adds another HSA official, "that we could do much of their work internally ... and draw from selected consultants for particular studies." Rand had become expendable to the Health Services Administration. In mid-1972, Gordon Chase dispensed with the services of the institute.

The "competition" between Rand and HSA research staffs was not equally evident to all parties. "Rand," says one HSA official, "felt competitive with our staff—and they told us so. When they first told us that, I was quite surprised, since I viewed the functions of Rand and the HSA staff as very different." The problem, from the HSA perspective, was that Rand did not perform its expected function well. Administrators complain of the "poor quality of Rand's work," or that Rand analysts "were totally unresponsive" to HSA needs, or that the institute was too "academic." Stated briefly, the objection of the HSA officials is that Rand's efforts were too far removed from the practical concerns of the agency to be useful.

Complaints of this kind might be expected more readily from the crusty veterans of the Fire Department than from the young, research-oriented analysts of HSA. By temperament and training, Rand and HSA analysts were kindred spirits. But it was the fire officials who seem to have adapted more easily to the Rand research enterprise than the analysts at HSA.

Differentiated Roles

In the Fire Department, Rand analysts were dealing with people seemingly very different from themselves. The potential for mutual antagonism and misunderstanding would appear to have been high, diminishing the prospects for effective policy research. The need for harmony between the policymaker's way of thinking and the researcher's is acknowledged almost as a matter of form in the many books and articles which exhort policy researchers and their clients to establish close working relationships for the purpose of facilitating communication or understanding. Perhaps the exhortations have become so frequent because of a widespread conviction that policymaking and policy research call for fundamentally alien modes of thought that cannot be reconciled except by continuous intellectual diplomacy. The confrontation between Rand researchers and officials of the Fire Department would certainly seem to have presented these diplomatic problems in an especially pronounced form.

But the intellectual gap between policymaking and policy research may be narrower than it seems. An inclination to exaggerate the difference between them has been noted by Max Millikan, who detects "a tendency on the part of the researcher to underestimate the intellectual content of the policy process" and to assume "that the man of action is guided to effective decision making by some intuitive process beyond the reach of rational argument."[6] In fact, the intellectual processes by which a researcher reaches a conclusion may not be so different from those by which a practical-minded policymaker arrives at a decision—even in a fire department. We have already suggested, for example, that policymaking and policy research tend to resemble each other when decisions are made incrementally (see Chapter 2). The idealized incremental decision maker introduces limited changes in policy, observes the consequences of these adjustments, and uses the information generated in this way

---

[6] Max Millikan, "Inquiry and Policy: The Relation of Knowledge to Action," in Daniel Lerner (ed.), *The Human Meaning of the Social Sciences* (New York: Meridian Books, 1959), pp. 170–171.

to test or refine his intuitions about how the world works—intuitions which may then suggest further policy modifications. Decision making itself can become an instrument of inquiry.

Researchers and policymakers may be more nearly alike than they realize, but their similarities do not necessarily promote harmony between them. In fact, where the functions of researchers and policymakers are not clearly distinguished from one another, the confusion that results can create serious tensions. Such tensions were likely to be less pronounced in an agency like the Fire Department, where the distinction between researchers and operating officials was sharply drawn, than in an institution like the Health Services Administration, where officials had adopted something of the researcher's outlook and used a scientific approach to support policy positions. In these surroundings, the functions of researchers merged with those of administrators.

This blurring of roles is probably not harmful in itself, but the manner in which researchers and policymakers respond to it can cause difficulties. If the ways of researchers are not recognizably different from those of policymakers, some question is almost sure to arise in the minds of the policymakers concerning the need for professional researchers and their expensive studies. One line of defense available to researchers is the emphatic differentiation of their own responsibilities from those of other participants in the policy process. The determination to be different may manifest itself, as it did in Rand's health project, in a refusal to become involved in the day-to-day routine, or to become a mere job-shop. This effort to hold the client's day-to-day concerns at arm's length, of course, may also impair the researcher's ability to understand and resolve the client's problems. In the work that researchers do, the scientist's concern "with the verifiability of his theory in many contexts" may soon take precedence over the policymaker's interest in "attaining a specific desired outcome ... in a specific space-time configuration."[7]

These and other aspects of the researcher's behavior are signs of a tendency to emphasize the distinctiveness of the research process—a tendency which may serve to reassure researchers that their work does not simply duplicate work of which their clients are capable. Indeed, the more capable the clients are, the easier it becomes to rationalize this tendency. Where research clients are scientifically sophisticated, as they were in HSA, it is not difficult to assume that they should be knowledgeable enough to translate research into action without much assistance in matters of detail.

What is mere detail to a researcher, of course, can be of greatest importance to those officials who have direct responsibility for fashioning policies and carrying them into effect. Such policymakers are liable to respond to the

---

[7] Garry D. Brewer, *Politicians, Bureaucrats, and the Consultant* (New York: Basic Books, 1973), p. 78.

analyst's pretensions by complaining that the researcher has become "totally unresponsive" to agency needs and by insisting on the analysis of concrete problems instead of excessively "academic" ones. These demands reflect the genuine and distinctive needs of policymakers, but policymakers may have reasons for asserting their own distinctiveness too—reasons that are similar to those of the researchers. It is not simply that policymakers feel threatened by research, as some researchers are prone to assume. It seems far more likely that the policymaker's assertion of his own distinctive perspective represents an effort to chart an otherwise confused terrain, to establish who's who. An insistence on quick answers to urgent questions (not ultimate answers for deep-seated problems) may serve to draw the line between policy and inquiry, action and research, and so help to resolve a fluid, ill-defined situation.

In the troubled association between Rand and HSA, a largely unacknowledged problem of policy research became evident—the problem of conducting research for sophisticated clients. The need to blend the disparate perspectives of policymakers and researchers has received so much attention that there has been a tendency to overlook the tensions that arise when the temperamental differences between analysts and decision makers narrow to the vanishing point. The oversight is understandable. So long as formal policy research remained a novelty to policymakers, there was good reason to concentrate on the problem of assimilating this unfamiliar activity to the policy process. But as policymakers become more accustomed to the sometimes showy trappings of research, less overawed by the claims of science, and more sophisticated about the methods and perspectives of researchers, it becomes important to sharpen the boundaries between the functions of policymakers and those of researchers.

Mediating Institutions

Mediating institutions like Rand provide a possible mechanism for establishing such boundaries. The purpose is not to assure that policymakers and researchers pursue their respective functions in self-contained compartments. It is rather to clarify the distinct position of researchers, so that they may not be so inclined to use research itself as a means of effecting separation from other participants in the policy process. A mediating institution for policy research that serves as an organizational container for the function of analysis provides the researcher with a relatively secure footing in the policy process. The fact that the Rand Institute failed to perform this role-defining function in its dealings with the Health Services Administration does not indicate that another mediating institution would fail also. What it does show is that a loosely drawn contract and a high turnover of personnel make it especially difficult to establish a clear division of responsibilities between researchers and their clients.

Mediating institutions can also have other uses, as illustrated by the case of Rand and the Fire Department. In the absence of an external research organization like Rand, it is unlikely that the department would have used the modeling techniques that helped it to find and test remedies for its serious workload and deployment problems. At the same time, if Rand had been a conventional consulting organization, with only a short-term commitment to its client, it would probably have been unable to penetrate the insular fire fighting bureaucracy in order to gain acceptance for its recommendations. The distinctive organizational design of the Rand Institute was therefore well suited to the needs of the Fire Department, and the Fire Department's centralized, hierarchical character made it well suited to carry out the recommendations that resulted from Rand's research.

In the Health Services Administration, the advantages of the Rand arrangement were certainly less evident. But even in an innovative, research-oriented public agency, there may be functions for a mediating institution like Rand to perform. It could provide a setting for the conduct of long-term studies that would be impossible if researchers were exposed directly to the day-to-day demands of administrators for quick answers to urgent questions. Such demands are likely to be particularly harmful to model development projects, which usually require concentrated attention for extended periods of time. They can also impede the maintenance, updating, and running of models once built, activities that tend to be long-term and continuing in nature.

In addition, the problems of implementation that arise in loose-jointed agencies like HSA may also create a need for research organizations of the Rand variety. In the face of administrative confusion, it is especially important that research projects be tailored to fit the client's limited capability to carry out research recommendations. What is needed, perhaps, is not a comprehensive, coordinated research effort of the kind that Rand launched for the Fire Department, but a series of relatively modest research projects, each designed to capitalize on some realistic opportunity for achieving administrative change. Detecting the possibilities for successful innovation in an organization is not something that can be done well or easily by a consultant passing through. It is likely to require the more sustained contact between researcher and client that the Rand Institute was designed to encourage.

Although the Rand Institute was created to deal with the problems of New York City, it also represented an attempt to deal with the more general problem of introducing timely and usable research results into the process of public decision making. In effect, it was an experiment—though not a controlled experiment—in policy research. The results suggest a need for more such experiments.

10

Modeling and the Political Process

The time has come to stand back and attempt to decipher why it is that modeling is not yet living up to expectations in policy application. It is not easy; there are so many different kinds of policy models representing different methodologies, applied to different areas by different people for different purposes at different times under different circumstances. To attempt to distill out of our study something of general relevance to the whole field of policy modeling may be as foolish as it is fearless.

Our first observation has to do with the nature of the relationship between the modeling process and the political process and with the people engaged in these processes. There are similarities and dissimilarities—and there is tension. We will speculate on the reasons for the tension and on whether it can be directed along constructive channels.

This leads us into a discussion of the way policy models are used, and of the central importance of the modeler or modeling advocate. One of the more eye-catching uses of models is their role in policy debate. In disagreements, a human tendency is to oversimplify the issues and view one side as right and the other as wrong. These labels and judgments get applied to the antagonists, their supporters (not the least of whom these days may be modelers), the arguments, and evidence, including model runs. Thus modelers and models also get labeled (and dismissed) as right or wrong, a simplism that distorts the meaningfulness of models and undervalues their full potential as ingredients in the policy process.

The solution we envision is indirect, long-term, and aimed at the roots of the problem rather than the symptoms. It is not solely to create better public education in modeling, or more professionalism among model builders, or a greater exercise of responsibility by policy makers in the commissioning and use of models, or more rigorous standards in model review and documentation, or better organizational devices for bridging the gap between model builders and model users. Each of these measures would indeed help correct current deficiencies; in fact, one is tempted to conclude that the problem must be attacked on all fronts simultaneously. But, in good conscience, we feel there is one line of approach that dominates the others.

In our concluding remarks we will discuss this approach and explain how we believe it can work to meet the problem as identified and ultimately improve the usefulness of models in the policy process.

NATURE OF THE PROBLEM

On August 1, 1970, Willard F. Rockwell, Jr., head of North American Rockwell Corporation, wrote to President Richard M. Nixon with a proposal to develop an "integrated socioeconomic model system of the United States."

> We believe this proposal to be as bold and exciting as Project Apollo, although it lies in a completely different field. If successful, it could achieve an integration and systematization of knowledge about our society comparable in magnitude to the scientific and engineering advances made by the Manhattan or Apollo Projects. The potential values of this knowledge in improved public policies and human welfare are, we believe, even greater.

The previous fall, Rockwell had challenged Bernard D. Haber, his vice-president for research and engineering, with a question frequently posed at the time: "If we can put men on the moon, can we do something about our problems here on earth?" Haber responded with the modeling proposal.[1] In his letter, Rockwell told Nixon that the proposed system would be a "powerful instrument of management" when put in the hands of the new staff organizations, such as the Domestic Council and the Urban Affairs Council, that Nixon had created. It would provide a grand synthesis of a number of existing models and modeling approaches.

Although the White House never made an official response to the proposal, there are indications that it did give the idea serious consideration. Some will see the episode as foreshadowing bright new possibilities, others, ominous trends. Although extreme, the incident provides insight into present-day modeling developments. It delineates the gulf that exists between policymakers and policy modelers, and suggests in a dramatic way just how far some believe that policy models are capable of going.

Though the range of policy modeling has been impressive—from municipal operations to the national economy to the future of the world—the direct impact of models on the process of public decision making is still difficult to pinpoint. More policy models are appearing all the time, yet the true nature and extent of their use by policymakers is clouded. Of one thing we can be sure; there is no foundation for the hope—or apprehension—that New York

---

[1] The Rockwell proposal is entitled, "Proposal for an Integrated Social and Economic Analysis of the United States Leading to a National Socioeconomic Model System," North American Rockwell Corporation, November 20, 1970. The proposal resulted from the efforts of a working group assembled by Haber that included several UCLA faculty members—econometrician Michael D. Intriligator among them.

City, the United States, or the United Nations will soon be run by means of computer models.

But if it is farfetched to expect computer models to control our affairs, it is not unreasonable to inquire whether they might provide useful guidance for decision makers who will face the complex, interrelated problems of public policy likely to be characteristic of life in the fourth quarter of the twentieth century. Many sensible people see in models a possibility for unraveling the intricacies of these multifaceted problems. Yet the position of modeling in the world of policy at the present time makes one question whether the increase in the amount of genuinely useful guidance provided by models will keep up with the increase in the magnitude and complexity of our problems.

Some Simplistic Answers

Before beginning to explore the problem, a caveat is in order. There are getting to be as many different kinds of policy models as there are species in the animal kingdom. Generalizing about them is hazardous at best. The models arise in university research projects, congressional inquiries, regulatory hearings, military planning, agency activities, industry operations, management studies, consulting work, and countless other settings. The models are transferred from one location to another, revised, elaborated, taken over, updated, shelved. They are built and used for an assortment of purposes. The commissioner of the model may have one objective in mind, the model builder another, and the user still another. The motivations behind the model, the constraints imposed upon it, and the political environment that surrounds it can be widely different from model to model.

Yet there is one thing that policy models have in common. Most fall short of their potential as instruments for the clarification of policy issues and the enlightenment of policymakers. There is considerable evidence indicating that modeling is indeed effective in educating policy *modelers*. That has likely been the surest achievement of policy modeling to date. But the use of models in the making of policy decisions is beset with problems. Why?

The quickest and least troublesome answer is the nihilistic one. The world is chaotic. Human social activity is not susceptible to systematic analysis, reduction, and construction by components. Models may be fine for physics, but the world of human affairs is unstable, disordered, and unpredictable. It defies the rational model building approach. Policymakers are not using models because in their pragmatic wisdom they know there is no use in using them.

One's inclination is to dismiss this kind of thinking as anti-intellectual (or, at least, intellectually lazy). But like many an extreme position, it serves a purpose. It reminds us of the equally misguided opposite attitude; namely, the behavior of humankind is neatly deducible from a set of laws and axioms that challenge our genius, only to be discovered. This completely deterministic view is likely to give rise to either fanaticism (if one is a "know-it-all") or still another excuse for doing nothing (if one waits for the Newtons and Einsteins of social science to come along to find the right theories).

There is another too easy, too convenient reply to the question of why models are not more useful and more used in policymaking. It has the same futile tone as the preceding argument, but with a more rational-sounding twist. It is a quality judgment. "The models that are being built are just no good. Policymakers are not using models because the models available are not good enough to be used. They are defective merchandise. They do not live up to the claims of the modeling entrepreneurs who sold the idea to commission them."

Now let us agree at the outset that it is indeed easier to sell a proposed model than it is to build it and make it perform to specification. Moreover, it is far simpler to construct the model than to understand it and fit it to the relevant policy context. The model is apt to have an appetite for data that is difficult to satisfy. It may be enigmatic in behavior, cumbersome in size, awkward to use, and hard to adapt—characteristics that were not mentioned in the project proposal. It is no wonder that the policymaker was readier to commission the model in the conceptual and promotional stage than to seek guidance from it and put it to effective use when it is finished.

There is great appeal in this defective-quality line of reasoning. If most policy models are just no good, there seems little reason to seek any further explanation for their underdeveloped use in the policy process. Their neglect by decision makers is perfectly understandable. It hardly seems worthwhile, after all, to ask why policymakers ignore bad models. The question answers itself. Nor does it seem productive to inquire just how policymakers or policymaking institutions might work to improve the quality of modeling. The search for remedies turns naturally to the scientific community, not to decision makers, administrators, or public officials. The problem is perceived not as one of unsatisfactory organization or inadequate management, but as a failure in technical prowess and scientific achievement.

The Policymaker—An Unknowing Culprit

With just such reasoning as this, a group well equipped and positioned to take corrective action abandons its jurisdiction and share of the responsibility. It is a natural response by busy people confronted with a new and uncertain technology that falls short of their expectations. And, to some extent, the failure to meet these expectations may indeed be explained by a shortage of modeling expertise. The expectations, themselves, may well have been inflated by the exaggerated claims of overzealous model salesmen eager to acquire support for their projects. At present, there are few professional restraints in the modeling field to curb such excessive behavior. There is little in the way of an organized modeling profession to provide any authoritative standards of performance or codes of conduct for modelers. In the absence of a profession, modelers tend to take their cues from the particular political and organizational setting in which they are operating. These cues are at least as decisive in determining the quality of a modeling effort as are the technical skills of the modelers.

The signals that policymakers often unwittingly give to modelers can make the difference between a useful model and a useless one. In seeking to explain why policy models are not more effectively used in government decisions, it is important to consider the nature of the policymaker's job as well as the policy modeler's.

We are reminded of a legislative aide to whom we spoke at a meeting among energy modelers and their clients in Washington. Working for a congressman active in energy matters, he portrayed himself as constantly deluged with work and as having almost no time to get it done. From his description, his office sounded like a cross between a newspaper city room and the floor of the New York Stock Exchange. Unless the results of a modeling study came to him aptly summarized at precisely the moment the issue it addressed was up for consideration—with unmistakably relevant, clearly understandable policy conclusions—there was just no way the results would get used. To him, such havoc was the normal style of operation in every busy policymaker's office in Washington. He saw nothing unreasonable in the demands his frantic pace implicitly imposed on policy modelers. He did complain about the unreasonableness of the demands placed on him by frenetic newspaper reporters.

Policymakers are people under pressure. "The man who tries to keep on top of his responsibilities," says Harold Lasswell,

> is likely to suffer from chronic fatigue and exasperation, and unless he has an exceptional natural constitution, a quick mind, and selective habits of work, he falls farther and farther behind. The more he knows about the full scope of his potential influence, the more bitterly the conscientious man feels about the physical and psychological limitations that constrict his performance. He perceives that his impact falls far short of either need or opportunity.[2]

To deal with the strain, a "subculture of mutual reassurance and support" among decision makers often emerges in which the principal activity is the exchange of praise, congratulation, and exaggerated gestures of esteem. Such

---

[2] Harold D. Lasswell, *A Pre-View of Policy Sciences* (New York: American Elsevier, 1971), pp. 34–35.

fraternities of fellow power-holders serve as an antidote for the policymaker's self-criticism and sense of despair.

Mutual congratulation is relatively harmless compared to other possible responses to the pressures of policymaking. According to Lasswell, some public officials deal with the strain of their responsibilities by making "grandiose demands... on immediate, intermediate, and public circles." One such circle is the scientific and research community. The request for scientific assistance all too often becomes a demand for salvation, and science itself simply another device for managing or displacing the pressures and conflicts that accompany decision making—not "a help in *coping* with hard problems, but... a device for *escaping* them altogether."[3] There is a tendency for policymakers to underwrite research efforts in the vague hope that some technological miracle or scientific breakthrough will bring relief from their perplexities. Such hopes are manifest in the commonly stated expectation, mentioned earlier, that the technical skills which put men on the moon ought to be able to solve the problems of our cities or nation. The Rockwell proposal responded to this expectation.

Those who offer scientific assistance to policymakers may therefore find a ready market for inflated promises. In such cases, they are also likely to find that the assistance they provide seldom results in a satisfied client. Great expectations prepare the way for great disappointments. The policymaker's initial enthusiasm quickly gives way to impatience, irritation, disillusionment, and then repudiation or indifference. Suspicion of scientific advice and cynicism are likely to go hand-in-hand with supreme (and unfounded) confidence in the powers of research. These seemingly contradictory attitudes both reflect a tendency to cope with the near-impossible demands of the policy process by making near-impossible demands of the environment. Such unreasonableness works to undermine the prospects that a model will be well designed and useful to the policymaker.

Responsibilities of the Policymaker

Policymakers need to consider the role that their own attitudes and actions play in leading to the faulty research of which they complain. The responsibility of the policymaker who inaugurates a modeling project begins at the outset of the project. More than likely, this responsibility is delegated to one or more staff members—possibly career civil servants—whose job it is to supply the policymaker with the best information and analyses available. These staff members are rarely expert modelers themselves, but they are in the best position to be knowledgeable about the questions that need illumination—the

---

[3] Robert E. Bickner, "Science at the Service of Government: California Tries to Exploit an Unnatural Resource," *Policy Sciences* 3 (1972): 182.

policy issues. The policymaker's responsibility to the modeling project, as delegated to these trusted aides, is to convey policy insights to the modelers by maintaining frequent two-way communication for the duration of the project. The aides need to comprehend what the modelers are doing. They must make certain that both they and the modelers agree that what is required is realistic and reasonable. And they must constantly review with the modelers whether the project is meeting these requirements.

Expert modelers are usually far more familiar with theoretical formulations and computer operations than with the workings of housing markets, welfare systems, and health programs. A successful combination of modeling skill with practical and political expertise does occasionally occur in the same person, but not often. Policymakers invite disillusionment when they assume these combinations will occur of their own accord. If helpful guidance is what policymakers desire from the modeling project, then helpful guidance is what they must supply to the modelers during the conduct of the effort.

Why do modelers need the guidance of policymakers? To begin with, the key questions to be posed to the model are seldom evident or clearly identified during the early stages of model building. An essential part of the modeling process is the translation of the policymaker's perceived concerns into researchable questions. If the policymaker is inarticulate, aloof, or ignorant of the capabilities and limitations of modeling—or if the modeler lacks empathy with the policymaker—the enterprise may go astray before it has fairly begun.

During the course of the project, the modeler and the policymaker's staff face a succession of problems. Essential data may be unavailable, unusable, or uncollectable. There may be no body of theory to guide the modeler in selecting variables or specifying relationships, and so on. It is in order to bypass these difficulties while satisfying an unrealistic or unreasonable policymaker that a modeler may unwittingly fall from grace by structuring the model so that important but technically troublesome elements of the relevant questions are eliminated, oversimplified, or distorted. This possibility is especially likely when the policy questions are ambiguous or hard to pin down, as they often are.

The result is a widening of the gap between the policymaker's questions and the modeler's replies. Even if the modeler's answers are appropriate to the policymaker's questions, the policymaker may still not find them intelligible unless there has been effective communication during the course of the project. Misunderstanding is inevitable.

Misunderstanding begins when expectations are unrealistic. The same excess of optimism that leads policymakers to expect ready answers from models may also produce misguided complacency about the ability of modelers to identify the central policy questions on their own. Many modelers, for their part, will become generally inattentive to policymakers whose expectations seem fanciful and who give the impression that they don't know what they're talking about. Worse yet, if the modelers fail to recognize the discrepancy between their abilities and the hopes of the policymakers, they may proceed as though the mere exercise of technical competence—a simulation model that runs—is sufficient to satisfy the policymakers' needs. In effect, they trim the problem to fit the technique.

Institutionalizing the Modeling Process

The first order of business in any effort to increase the usefulness of policy models is to improve the relationship between the consumers and producers of models—reduce misunderstanding, facilitate communication, and promote mutual acceptance and respect. These goals sound fine, but how can they be achieved? How, for example, does the policy modeler gain the acceptance and respect of the policymaker? One energy administrator with many years of modeling experience in the Pentagon and other federal agencies considers five factors important as conditions for a modeling study to be accepted.

First, the study must be well timed. At a minimum, its results must be ready prior to the making of the decisions for which the study was intended. (This condition is often not met.) Second, the results must be effectively communicated by a trusted aide of the policymaker in terms the policymaker can understand. Since most policymakers in Washington are lawyers, this usually involves converting technical results into a language comprehensible to lawyers.[4]

Third, there must be compatible personalities at the policy interface.[5] Fourth and fifth, the modelers must be relatively independent of the policymakers and must have a reputation for astute analysis and good sense based on past performance. The fact that these points are last is not accidental. The factors are in order of the importance attached to them by the energy administrator. To him, the first two, good timing and communication, are

---

[4] The energy administrator, A. B. Holaday, cites Eric Zausner at the Federal Energy Administration as someone who has a special knack for translating from the jargon of economics and operations research into "legalese." Further testimony comes from Arthur Okun, former chairman of the Council of Economic Advisers. Okun reports that half his time at the council "was spent as rewrite man trying to translate good staff material about slopes and elasticities into a form that was meaningful to the president." See Martin Greenberger (ed.), *Computers, Communications, and the Public Interest* (Baltimore: The Johns Hopkins University Press, 1971), p. 106.

[5] Former Secretary of Defense Robert McNamara and Federal Energy Administrator Frank Zarb are said to have had excellent working relationships with the presidents for whom they served, whereas Federal Energy Administrator John Sawhill's relationship with the president he served was strained, especially after Sawhill publicly suggested a rise in the price of gasoline as a means of reducing gasoline consumption. Modeling results influenced policy more when McNamara and Zarb were the spokesmen than when Sawhill was, despite the fact that Sawhill was highly intelligent and very sympathetic to modeling and quantitative analysis.

far and away the most decisive in gaining acceptance, while the reputation and ability of the modelers, though significant, is not nearly as critical as the reputation and effectiveness of the political intermediaries. The ability to bring the modeling results to the policymakers clearly, persuasively, and at the right time, is what makes the difference.

Timing, which many agree is most important, is also most troubling, especially for a model building study that is conducted in a political environment to assist in the making of key policy decisions. One can never be sure of what one is getting into at the start of a modeling project. Collecting the data, specifying the model, making it fit, understanding the issues, and so on, are all likely to be imponderables until well into the study. Any one of these requirements can turn out to be unexpectedly time-consuming. Also, the political agenda of a city or of the nation cannot be scheduled like work in a job shop. Issues blow hot and cold, usually without much warning. There is typically not much time between one issue and the next for launching a modeling study and obtaining results that can be used in decision making.

The only practical solution we see to this dilemma is to avoid as much as possible the undertaking of large *ab initio* modeling projects in response to the emergence of new policy issues.[6] There must be support for sustained modeling endeavors so that, over a period of time, there are maintained and available a number of well-understood, well-respected models that can be applied solely or in combination to a wide variety of policy issues. We would not have these models housed and cared for in a government-controlled model shop, but in universities, research centers, and especially mediating institutions that form bridges between the research and political worlds. The models would be alive and continuing in the sense that they would be used repeatedly, kept up-to-date, and modified as needed. In effect, they would become institutionalized. Through their repeated use, these models would gradually become familiar and credible to policymakers and gain their confidence.

Some government officials in Washington cite the tax modeling work at Brookings and the macroeconometric model of Data Resources, Inc., among other examples, as models that are conveniently packaged, highly accessible, straightforward in concept, and well-known by policymakers.[7] These models

---

[6] Present government funding for model building tends to treat policy models like models in the sciences—as though all that was necessary was that they be built, tested, and applied. In fact, policy models need continual care and updating in order to be of ongoing usefulness. A policy model left on the shelf soon becomes obsolete. Energy models consulted in policy discussions before the sharp rise in world energy prices and left in their original form were next to useless at the higher price levels. The situation, in that particular case, was without precedent. There was, at first, no reliable basis whatsoever for re-estimating coefficients or respecifying model structures.

[7] The tax model is discussed in Chapter 3 under microanalytic models, and the Data Resources model is discussed in Chapter 4 under commercial modeling firms.

have been used many times for a variety of policy purposes. Not the least of the reasons for their success is the fact that their spokesmen understand the workings of the policy process and have ready entrée to the inner chambers of the federal bureaucracy.

Despite a growing number of such examples, much of the modeling work done for policymakers is still initiated from fresh starts on a project-by-project basis. The result, as Garry Brewer indicates, is a "tendency to hold out hope that a specific project [or] a particular computer model... will provide *the* much-desired *answer*." Redefining the research effort as a continuing experiment would remove "the onus of having to produce *the* answer" and would moderate the policymakers' unrealistic expectation that such an answer will be forthcoming.[8]

As a mediating institution, the New York City-Rand Institute represented an experimental step in the right direction. The Rand Institute was fashioned so that the relationship between researchers and clients would extend beyond the life of a single project. Rand's initial research responsibilities were defined broadly within subject areas, not in terms of particular tasks. Such an arrangement does not encourage policymakers to invest their hopes in a single research effort designed to produce specified results by a contract deadline. Nor does it stimulate researchers to make inflated promises on behalf of particular projects or models. While the arts of salesmanship are not likely to be abandoned, the compulsion to use them is diminished in a situation where most research teams do not have to live from project to project and where survival depends more on satisfying a current client than on snaring new ones. Since completion of a task does not normally terminate the analysts' dealings with a client, there is a distinct disincentive to promise what might not be deliverable.

The Rand Institute was unsuccessful when measured against its initial objectives. Nor was it sire to a great number of modeling systems that outlived it and continue to be used by municipal agencies in New York City. The institute's design is not what we would recommend for the next such institutional experiment. But we found its aborted life very instructive. Rand's example is valuable for the many lessons it provides those who would seek to improve upon it. We believe more such attempts should be made.

APPOSITION OR OPPOSITION

We have spent a great deal of time attempting to establish what may be obvious: that the effectiveness of policy modeling depends not only on the model and the modeler, but on the policymaker too. Increasing the usefulness

---

[8] Garry D. Brewer, *Politicians, Bureaucrats and the Consultant* (New York: Basic Books, 1973), p. 234.

of models as instruments for enlightening decision makers will require behavioral adjustments by the policymakers as well as by the modelers.

Politics in Modeling

But policy models are not just instruments of enlightenment. For public officials, they can also serve political and administrative purposes. Garry Brewer points out, for example, that policymakers faced with difficult or unpleasant problems may look upon model building as a way of postponing the time of decision—a welcome refuge from responsibility, or a statesmanlike expedient to permit a cooling-off period in turbulent situations. Since the modeling process takes time, the conditions that originally prompted the policymaker's flight to research may have passed away before the modeling effort is completed. Given the high rate of personnel turnover in government, especially among political appointees, the policymakers themselves may have passed from the scene before the modelers have finished their work. A lengthy modeling study must often suffer the repeated replacement of its supposed sponsor. The eventual successor may have little interest in or even knowledge of the project by the time the results are ready to be unveiled. The disruptive effect this turnover can have on the modeling project is considerable.

As a delaying device, modeling is capable of becoming a stylish substitute for the well-worn political tactic of "referring a problem to committee." Policymakers may initiate modeling studies for other reasons also—to justify decisions already made, add a sheen of technical sophistication to their reputations, or simply keep an expensive research staff fully occupied.[9] It is no wonder studies go astray.

The important point is that policymakers often resort to modeling not so much to illuminate the complexities of the world in which they work as to secure themselves against the political pressures and uncertainties of that world. Now, it is tempting to condemn the political use of modeling as the "wrong" use: it can impede the conduct of the research process in numerous ways, not the least of which is to confuse the central policy issues and misrepresent the nature of the problem at hand.

But it does little good to rail against the intrusions of politics into the modeling process. In the first place, policy modeling itself may be an intrusion upon territory that politicians have traditionally regarded as their domain. In the second place, the same kinds of situations that prompt policymakers to turn to models are also likely to foster political controversy and cause political pressure. A complex, far-reaching, and unprecedented policy problem that creates a demand for research may also produce an atmosphere simmering

---

[9] Ibid., p. 84.

with political conflicts and crowded with partisans anxious to influence the political outcome. To expect that policymakers will forswear "political" motives in these circumstances is to ask the impossible.

Since policy modelers cannot escape political reality, they must come to terms with it. They must recognize the points of tension—and the opportunities for accommodation—between the process of modeling and the process of political action.

The Tension Between Modeling and Politics

The two processes are not entirely dissimilar. The modeling process deals with simplified representations of reality. So, too, does the political process—although here the representations are unconscious and implicit. The operation of the national economy, for example, can be represented in reduced form by a formal model; it is also reflected in the political activities and attitudes of voters, interest groups, and public decision makers. In that sense, at least, there is a certain kinship between politics and modeling. Both deal with representations or reductions of systems external to themselves—but there is a sharp difference in the manner of representation.

Formal models are the products of synthesis. In a model, disparate bodies of data and theory are brought together in an effort to mimic the operation of some complex part of nature or society. The model is a repository in which elements of knowledge too numerous to be accommodated simultaneously and assimilated by the unaided human mind are placed in relation to one another within an integrated framework. The model serves as a focusing device. It is an instrument for the intellectual management of multiple relationships among complex phenomena.

The political system is also an instrument of management, but its purpose is conflict management, not intellectual mastery. In politics, there is a tendency to fragment large problems into smaller, more manageable problems. Fractionation, not synthesis, is a hallmark of the political process. A single underlying problem (like the energy shortage) may generate a variety of different political issues, scattered through a multiplicity of policymaking arenas. A particular social or economic phenomenon, such as the public's rising expectations or the problems of the aged or the flight to the suburbs, may be refracted through the prism of politics to produce a wide spectrum of political struggles in the areas of welfare, health, agriculture, fiscal control, urban policy, land-use development, and environmental management—each of which may be fought and resolved separately from the others.

A vivid portrayal of the dispersive nature of the political system was painted for President Gerald Ford at the economic summit conference he called in September 1974, soon after replacing Richard Nixon in office. The inflationary problem was getting out of control and Ford was searching for a solution, or at least for some agreement, from a discussion among a broad cross-section of experts and affected parties.

> President Ford's long-touted economic summit conference began in disarray yesterday as debate over anti-inflation policies promptly gave way to political bickering and demands by varying interest groups for special relief. Rather than building toward any consensus, the 600-odd delegates demonstrated widely disparate views over what policies the administration should follow, with most emphasizing measures to ease recession, not to slow the inflation rate... calling for tax measures and other steps to relieve the impact of current anti-inflation moves.[10]

There were some modelers in attendance and they had their say along with the others. But the conferees were not looking to models to add light to the heat of the proceedings. The inflationary problem was disassembled into particular problems, illustrated by stories of personal adversity and grand displays of emotion and rhetoric.

Modeling, because it is a process of synthesis, is likely to be at odds with the fragmenting ways of politics. The resulting tension between the two processes helps to explain some of the difficulties encountered by modelers and policymakers when they attempt to work in tandem. The political process rarely presents modelers with a coherent, well-defined statement of an overall problem. Instead, there are scattered fragments of problems that the modeler must find a way to integrate in a systematic synthesis. Once the model is complete and producing results, the policymaker may find it necessary to perform the same kind of task in reverse, breaking down the modeling results into politically meaningful components. It is understandable how modelers may misconstrue the questions posed by policymakers, and how policymakers may find it difficult to put the modelers' results to use.

It is also understandable that those apprehensive about political centralization and state planning might regard modeling as a threat to the fractioning and decentralizing processes of American politics. In part, these apprehensions are attributable to the kinds of political circumstances in which policy modeling has risen to prominence: the big, unprecedented issues, the crises in public policy that tend to create a market for modeling. These are also the political conditions that foster centralizing tendencies in the political system. The Great Depression and its aftermath, for example, stimulated the earliest attempts to build econometric models of national economies. The Depression was also largely responsible for the growth of centralism and the spread of bureaucracy in government. Since the Depression, econometric

---

[10] Art Pine, "Disarray Mars Start of Ford Summit," *Baltimore Sun,* September 28, 1974.

modeling has continued to play a policymaking role, not primarily in moments of economic crisis, but in the making of routine economic decisions. In short, models may not cause political centralization, but only accompany it.

Explicitness and Conflict

Modeling can appear a political misfit, not only because it is a process of synthesis, but also because it produces an explicit and (through simplification) highly accentuated representation of reality. "Models are, for the most part, caricatures of reality," writes one scientist, "but if they are good, then, like good caricatures, they portray, though perhaps in a distorted manner, some of the features of the real world. The main role of models is not so much to explain or to predict—though ultimately these are the main functions of science—as to polarize thinking and to pose sharp questions."[11] In scientific research, the polarization of thinking and the posing of sharp questions are unmistakable virtues. The more quantified and highly explicit the model, the more it is valued. But in policymaking, where the resolution of conflict is an abiding concern, ambiguity may often be preferred to explicitness, and polarization is to be avoided. This is another respect in which the process of modeling and the process of policymaking seem to be at odds with one another.

We have seen several instances in which models have been centers of controversy, perhaps even the sources of controversy. General criticism of the Nixon administration's economic forecasts, for example, was quickly transformed into a focused attack when critics were presented with the LR model as a concrete target. And even though no particular policy decision hung in the balance, Jay Forrester's urban and world dynamics models became battlefields for policymakers and would-be policymakers. Models, because they are so explicit, may serve not to resolve differences of opinion, but to sharpen them.

The argumentation stimulated by a controversial model has a positive side. It can shed light on poorly understood issues and arouse the interest of bright but uninformed people. Modeling can help to provide a framework for debate. It can widen the perspectives of decision makers and influence their thinking. By framing positions (as opposed to providing answers), models clarify policy preferences and increase understanding of the similarities and differences among various viewpoints. Models offer hope of elevating the level of political discussion, thus improving the chances for intelligent decisions.

Political authorities with responsibility for budgets and programs may not see things this way. They may come to resent research studies that produce

---

[11] M. Kac, "Some Mathematical Models in Science," *Science* 166 (1969): 699.

contention, attract widespread notice, accentuate disagreements, and aggravate conflict. An unambiguous model gives potential opponents a well-defined target to attack. It may even undermine agreement among potential allies, since it is often easier for supporters to agree on the policy decision itself than on the specific justifications for it.

Models may become especially troublesome politically when the issues under consideration are complex and marked by a high degree of uncertainty and large political or economic stakes. As we have observed before, these are precisely the kinds of issues that tend to elicit modeling efforts. What is called for in such highly charged settings is compromise, conciliation, and mediation, not strong stands and elaborate justifications. In politically delicate situations, the modeler with an explicit model may be as welcome to policymakers as the proverbial bull in a china shop.

Modeling in Debate

In emphasizing the explicit nature of policy models, we do not mean to suggest that models are also single-minded or intransigent. A policy model is not composed of universally accepted theory and data, but of hypotheses and assumptions; much of the information on which it is based is estimated and incomplete. A model can offer a great deal of room for maneuvering and expressing varying shades of opinion. The LR model, for example, was used to support the forecast of a 1971 GNP of $1,065 billion, but it could have been used to support other positions as well, depending upon the historical period used to draw data for estimating the coefficients of the model and the assumptions made about future values of such exogenous variables as the rate of growth of money supply.

Thus, it is incorrect to equate a model with a single policy position, even though a particular application of the model may provide convincing support for a particular point of view. Models are explicit but flexible. The same model that serves to give explicit form to one person's side of a policy dispute may serve, with some changes, to provide just as explicit a formulation to the opinions of the adversary. There is ample room to express one's preconceptions and viewpoints either in the design of a model, as was illustrated by the *Limits to Growth* study, or in the choice of a model, as we found in the Laffer-Ranson episode. A policymaker can elect to adopt or ignore a model depending on the tone of the conclusions to which it leads.

This may sound a bit cynical, but it is a fact of life. We must recognize that models can be used to mislead the unwary. For this reason, some people are inclined to denounce models altogether. But recognizing the power of words to deceive does not render us mute, nor does the knowledge that one can lie with statistics cause us to reject all resort to facts and figures. So it is with models. Their potential for misrepresentation does not disqualify them from use in policymaking.

Because of their flexibility, models can do more than provide a framework for debate. They can become the instruments of debate. We saw numerous instances in the *Limits to Growth* controversy of both counter modeling (the alteration of a model to challenge the original policy conclusions inferred from the model) and multimodeling (the use of a number of models reflecting different viewpoints). Counter modeling and multimodeling are new forms of political dialogue—a kind of "adversary modeling" technique. On the positive side, adversary modeling can help to identify the substantive points of difference between antagonists and thereby redirect political debate from apparent to real areas of disagreement. This does not guarantee a resolution of the conflict; in fact, it can exacerbate the problem. But when the disagreement is found to be based on misunderstanding, ignorance, or the lack of facts, adversary modeling can assist in bringing the opposing interests together by exposing the imagined differences that kept them apart and by neutralizing the emotional content of those differences.

On the negative side, adversary modeling may operate to distract attention from the policy issues to points of technical procedure. Examples are the arguments over "backcasting" that erupted in the *Limits to Growth* controversy (Chapter 5) and the quarrel evoked by the use of seasonally unadjusted data in the LR model (Chapter 1). This does not mean that such technical points are of no consequence and should be ignored, but their consideration, understandably, is of little interest to policymakers. When given prominence in public airings of modeling debates, technical disputes can undermine the role of modeling as a contributor to policymaking by emphasizing minor points of disagreement and neglecting major points of agreement. Modelers aggravate the problem when they become distracted by technical fine points and lose sight of the bearing of these details on the policy issues being studied.

A closely related difficulty comes from the pride that modelers tend to take in their models, especially in the competitive atmosphere of an adversary proceeding. In the Maryland 1972 Brandon Shores Power Plant controversy, the most heated contention was on points not really germane to the ultimate policy question of whether or not to build the plant (see Chapter 3).

A model builder, although possibly in the best position to uncover weaknesses in an opposing modeler's arguments, is in a very important sense the wrong person to make an objective policy oriented appraisal of the alien model. It requires superhuman virtues for model builders who have close personal identifications with their own models to be thoroughly fair and open-minded about someone else's model and to filter out technical points that do not bear significantly on the policy questions at issue. The counter modeling technique, while helpful, is not enough by itself to put a model in intelligent perspective. Quite the contrary, it may reduce the model to a political football, to be punted from one side of an issue to the other (depending on which modeler is kicking) or to be thrown out of the dispute if bruised and battered in play. The two modeling examples of Chapter 1 are cases in point.

Debate and controversy will almost surely erupt when a modeler with an unorthodox approach or striking conclusions (or both) enters a policy area where modeling is no stranger and where sophisticated modelers stand ready to challenge newcomers and mavericks. Economic policy is such an area. It was primarily economists who critiqued and attacked the LR model, and they will be out in force again for Forrester's model of the national economy. In the fray over the urban dynamics model, there were physical scientists among the critics as well. In policy areas where modeling is less familiar, models may remain mysterious and be received, if not with awe or trepidation, then with silent resentment and resolute close-mindedness.[12]

In political debate, things tend to be seen as either right or wrong. These labels get applied to partisans, antagonists, their views, and also the models and modelers that support or oppose these views. Often the name-calling is just for effect, as it normally is when applied to politicians. But when applied to a model, it may have a deeper connotation. It may express the total acceptance or absolute rejection of the model. In most cases, this attitude sells the model short and misconstrues its purpose and nature. To the extent that the attitude is prevalent among policymakers, for whatever political or human reasons, it represents a serious impediment to the full and productive use of models in decision making.

Entrée of the Expert

Despite the problems that beset models, policymakers continue to look to modelers—those masters of cross-disciplinary synthesis—for assistance. A recent example is the federal government's financing of scores of model development projects in its efforts to explore the many aspects of the world energy problem.[13] Behind the showy, eye-catching use of models in debate is their almost routine use in a large number of policy guidance roles.

But playing a role and filling it well are two very different things. Putting models to effective use in policy guidance is clearly much more significant and difficult than merely placing models within reach of policymakers. The condi-

---

[12] In municipal administration, for example, signs of such resistance were evident in the attempts to apply urban dynamics to cities. (See Chapter 5). Even in Lowell, Massachusetts, where urban dynamics got a big boost from the model-supportive city manager, city officials soon grew cold to the modeling approach after the manager left his job to return to Cambridge.

[13] See for example Michael S. Macrakis (ed.), *Energy* (Cambridge: M.I.T. Press, 1974).

tions that lead policymakers to request models or that lead modelers to offer them are not the same as the circumstances required for their effective use.

Models are used in either of two general ways for policy guidance. The first and best-known way is in conditional or unconditional forecasting. Models can be used to forecast GNP, predict the consequences of a policy change, or anticipate economic and demographic conditions that policymakers will face some time in the future. This use ranges from the short-run quarter-to-quarter forecasts of the macroeconometric models of the economy to the long-range qualitative projections of the system dynamics models.

The second way that models are used is for education and exploration. The process of building and running a model may help deepen a modeler's understanding of the reference system it represents.[14] Modeling, from this perspective, is not primarily a technique for forecasting, but a discipline. The model is not itself the source of knowledge. It is a medium through which understanding of the reference system is quantified, integrated, and made available. The reference system must remain the final authority on how things work.

In practice, we find that policy modeling combines both the educational and predictive uses of models, though the two functions may not be equally visible. Most policy models are designed to generate predictions in one form or another, but that is not all they do. Forecasts produced by models rarely enter the policy process directly. They enter through a modeler whose intuitions and instincts about a policy problem are likely to have been shaped by building the model, experiencing its operation, and revising the model in accordance with the observed behavior of the reference system. The process of modeling can sharpen the expertise of a modeler, and this expertise, more than the model or its forecasts, may influence the making of public decisions.

The forecast itself may be subordinated to the expertise of the modeler. Economist Otto Eckstein, for example, does not expose the results of the DRI econometric model to public view until he has first adjusted the model's forecasts to his own intuitions and judgment—formed, in part, by his experience as a model builder and model manager.

The Rand Institute's Arthur Swersey developed an understanding of the New York City Fire Department's communications system by modeling it, then embodied his insights in a revised model that helped to confirm his intuitions about how to solve some of the department's communications problems. Another example is Rand researcher Jan Leendertse, the fluid flow expert who

---

[14] Douglass B. Lee, in commenting on the failure of urban land-use modelers in the 1960s to realize their original ambitious goals of detailed prediction and comprehensive planning, called the use of models for educating lay decision makers the "ultimate come-down." (See Douglass B. Lee, Jr., "Requiem for Large-Scale Models," *Journal of the American Institute of Planners,* May 1973, p. 171.) Although we appreciate the point Lee is making, we believe that learning, especially by the modeler, has been a valuable and redeeming benefit of modeling.

designed a detailed computer simulation model of water and pollutant flows in New York's Jamaica Bay (Chapter 3). The commissioner of water resources in New York City relied heavily on Leendertse's judgment about the effects that proposed construction projects and dredging operations would have on water quality in the bay. Leendertse made these predictions without running the model. He acquired the understanding of the bay on which he drew, during the course of extensive model building and repeated simulations, much as a pilot develops a feeling for flying a plane by repeated training sessions on the ground in a flight simulator.

Leendertse's judgments were highly respected, not only by the water commissioner, but also by federal, local, and interstate authorities whose activities involved them in the problems of Jamaica Bay. It was not Leendertse's model but his expertise that most influenced the course of the policy process. Experts create models, but models also create experts. In policymaking, models function to develop judgment, not to substitute for it.

As a general rule, the modeler is far more important than the model in providing input to policy discussions. Modelers can soften the explicitness of a model and make its results more palatable to nonmodelers. They can season the model's output with their own judgments and intuitions—about the political environment as well as the reference system being modeled. Politically astute modelers may be able to avoid the controversies that models often generate. In the process, however, a serious question arises.

Who monitors the modeler? A model run in a modeler's brain is not accessible to outside critics. As models are being put more to use to advance particular policy preferences, there arises a need for responsible critical review. We will discuss this need in the next and final section and offer some suggestions.

CONCLUDING REMARKS

We started this chapter with a statement of a problem. We come back now to confront the problem once again. The policy usefulness of models appears to us to be lagging. That is, the growth in the useful application of policy models to the problems facing government decision makers is not keeping up with the increase in either the number or complexity of these problems. That is the way it seems to us. At the same time, the use of models for political purposes is expanding noticeably. In other words, the use of models to dramatize or publicize particular points of view is overshadowing their use for the enlightenment of policymakers—and the enlightenment that they provide is not meeting the needs of the nation. What, if anything, can be done about it? How can policy models be made more useful?

A "living" model is a useful model. What can be done to promote the development of more and better living models and to produce an organizational framework in which these models can take root and grow? One line of reasoning would put more emphasis on mediating institutions. The Brookings Institution and the Urban Institute, on the one hand, and the econometric modeling firms, on the other, are performing needed research and translation functions more each year. Perhaps, as these organizations mature further and become more numerous, the mediation and communication they provide between policy researchers and policymakers will encourage a fuller, more familiar use of policy models. On the state and local levels, organizational experiments like the Rand Institute may eventually lead the way to institutional arrangements that convey policy research to cities and states. Governments could be encouraged to launch additional experiments of this kind.

A second line of reasoning argues that more effort must go into correcting current misunderstanding and ignorance of the modeling process, especially among policymakers. Policymakers need to become better informed about models and more realistic about what models can and cannot do. They must be more willing to accept their own part of the responsibility for the disappointments, and they must take the lead in seeing to it that a healthier environment for policy modeling is created. We developed these arguments at some length early in the chapter. The trouble is that one can only make the points, stress them, and possibly suggest a role for education. The attitudes are widespread and deep-seated. The malady will not cure itself and it will not respond to simple prescriptions.

A third line of reasoning focuses not on the policymaker but on the modeler and the modeling profession—or rather, the lack of one. Professional standards for model building are nonexistent. The documentation of models and source data is in an unbelievably primitive state. This goes even (and sometimes especially) for models actively consulted by policymakers. Poor documentation makes it next to impossible for anyone but the modeler to reproduce the modeling results and probe the effects of changes to the model. Sometimes a model is kept proprietary by its builder for commercial reasons. The customer is allowed to see only the results, not the assumptions. Such practices are sure to raise questions and may eventually lead to regulatory remedies.

We believe that all of the defects just enumerated are of legitimate concern. All lend themselves to corrective action to some degree. It is tempting to end the book here by recommending the adoption of an ensemble of measures designed to rectify each of the deficiencies—a multisided attack on the problem. This is possible to do, yet we know how little such a diffuse approach is likely to accomplish.

Instead, we prefer to concentrate on a feature of the problem that we have alluded to many times throughout the book. We think it is central and we feel it presents an opportunity for exercising leverage in efforts to make policy models more useful. It has to do with an observation often made on the present sociology of the modeling field. Modelers mostly build and run their own models: that is where the credits lie. Very few modelers run and analyze the other fellow's model in any systematic way, counter modeling notwithstanding. Modelers are synthesizers and refiners more than analyzers, particularly analyzers of other modelers' models. When possible at all, such secondary analysis is too difficult and unrewarding an activity to generate much interest. As a result, the inner workings of a policy model are seldom understood by anyone but the builders of the model (and not always by them). This is a weak foundation for gaining the reliance and trust of policymakers.

We are not suggesting that model builders be subjected to behavior modification to make them pay more attention to the models of others; model builders perform a vital function and they should be supported in doing their jobs, albeit in a more professional environment. What we do propose, however, is the development of a new breed of researcher/pragmatist—the model analyzer—a highly skilled professional and astute practitioner of the art and science of third-party model analysis. Such analysis would be directed toward making sensitivity studies, identifying critical points, probing questionable assumptions, tracing policy conclusions, comprehending the effects of simulated policy changes, and simplifying complex models without distorting their key behavioral characteristics.

We have definite ideas on how the development of third-party model analysis as a new profession can be brought about. This is not the place to spell these ideas out in detail, except perhaps to say that an appropriate incentive structure for researchers would have to be established. We believe the primary drive and initiative for fostering the development should come from government and policymakers, not from the modeling community. Also, mediating institutions must be involved, and universities obviously have an important role to play.

The model analyzer would be neither model builder nor model user, but in a middle position between the two, empathetic with both. Model analyzers would study and report on new policy models as they are put forward, and would continue to check and stay abreast of the older models. The third-party model analyzing activity, once institutionalized, could do a great deal to bring the "life" and "continuity" to policy models that we consider indispensable to making them useful in policy. It would make policy models more familiar, afford them greater longevity, and give policymakers a place to turn for impartial analysis and assessment when "the time is right" politically.

Third-party model analysis is also likely to have a beneficial effect on the modeling field. It would produce de facto standards of performance for model builders. It would stimulate (and require) improved, open documentation of models and data. And it would promote a generally higher level of professionalism in the modeling trade. If successful, the activity of model analysis would provide an intellectual tie between policy research and policymaking. From this foundation, solid organizational bridges could develop and a new policy-oriented, technically based profession serving the public interest could form.

When all is said and done, the way to make policy models more useful in policy is through greater understanding and generally improved communication between policy modelers and policymakers. Their respective roles and responsibilities need to remain sharply differentiated and well defined—with the tensions which that entails—but there must also be a working harmony between them, a mutual respect, and a concurrence of fundamental goals. The most successful modeling projects are ones in which the relationship between the policy staffs and modelers is marked by trust, mutual respect, reasonableness, frank communication, and common purpose. The disappointments are marked by rivalry, contempt, unreality, lack of understanding, and confused or hidden motives. Third-party model analysis, in our opinion, would help to create the desired harmony by combatting ignorance and suspicion with informed assessment and a continuing process of professional testing and review.

Some see in the use of computer models by government another fad like program budgeting (PPBS)—here today, gone tomorrow. Gunnar Myrdal, for example, in an interview conducted the year before he received the 1974 Nobel Prize for Economics, declared that

> fashion changes in a cyclical way in our field of study. The pendulum has swung lately to abstract model building not only in the United States but also in the rest of the world. Ten or fifteen years from now the institutional approach will again be the new vogue. The recent attempts to emulate the methods, or rather the form, of the simpler natural sciences, will be recognized as largely a temporary aberration into superficiality and irrelevance.[15]

Myrdal may be right about those applications of computer models whose purpose is more scientific affectation than scientific understanding. But modeling is too universal and basic a means of expression to go the way of the common fad. When the dust from the present mix of disenchantment and enthusiasm for modeling clears, a substantial and growing policy modeling activity is likely to be evident—but in a different and probably more institutionalized mode than that practiced today. It is not a question of whether models will be used in policymaking. They always have been, in one manner or

---

[15] Gunnar Myrdal, Interview Number 35 in Willem L. Oltmans (ed.), *On Growth—The Crisis of Exploding Population and Resource Depletion* (New York: G. P. Putnam's Sons, 1974), p. 234.

another. The real questions are how well they will be used, in what form, for what purpose, within what organizational framework, and with what safeguards. While we have tried to address ourselves to some of these questions in this book, it may yet be too early in the development of policy modeling to answer the questions satisfactorily. It is certainly not too early to raise them.

Index

Abelson, Robert, 111
Adams, F. Gerard, 202, 223
Adversary modeling, 334
Ahlstrom, John, 217
Aiken, Howard H., 90
Alfeld, Louis, 151
Algebraic methods of operations research, 102–104
Algorithm, 60
Allen, Jodie T., 113, 114
Allocation function of model, 62, 63
Alonso, William, 118
American economy
   Klein-Goldberger model and, 184
   models of the, 195–230
      table and chart of, 197–98
   Tinbergen's League of Nations model, 196–99
   Wharton model and, 184
Anaheim, California, 156–57
Analog model. See Physical models
Analysis, 49
Analytical models. See Mathematical models
Anderson, T. W., Jr., 199
Ando, Albert, 211
Annual models, 203
Applied Physics Laboratory, 69–70
Archibald, Kathleen, 34
Archibald, Rae, 254–55, 257, 273–74, 282
Arrow, Kenneth, 200, 202
Artichoke effect, 73
AVCO Corporation, 155

Babcock, Daniel, 146, 151–52
Badillo, Herman, 295, 296, 297–98
Baker, Russell, 166
Baltimore Gas and Electric Company, 69
BASS. See Bay Area Simulation Study
Bay Area Simulation Study, 117
Bay Area Transportation Study Commission, 76
Beame, Abraham, 243, 246
BEA model, 204–205
Bellman, Richard, 103
Birch, David, 72, 119–20, 149
Blackett, P. M. S., 99, 102
Blum, Edward, 253, 257, 258, 265, 266, 274, 280
Bonini, C. P., 73
Boschan, Charlotte, 205
Boyce, Peter, 172
Boyd, Robert, 171
Boyle, Thomas, 172, 175
Brandon Shores Power Plant, 69–70
Bray, Jeremy, 167
Brazer, Harvey, 110, 113
Brewer, Garry, 25, 72–73, 118, 328, 329
Brill, Daniel H., 210–14
Bronx, the, 268, 270
   hospital facilities in, 297
Brookings Institution, 233, 338
   SSRC-Brookings model and, 209–10
Brown, Harrison, 143
Brown, Howard, 297
Budget Bureau (N.Y.C.), 239

343

Budget Bureau *(Continued)*
  Fire Department and, 252–53
  Rand-HSA contract, role, 291–92, 300
Burns, Arthur F., 16, 211, 212

Canick, Paul, 251–52, 253–54, 255, 274, 282
Carlson, Walter, 73
Carter, Grace, 268, 270, 273
CE model. *See* Chase Econometrics model
The Challenge of Man's Future (Brown), 143–44
Charnes, Abraham, 96, 103
Chase Econometric Associates, 222–23
Chase Econometric model, 222
Chase, Gordon, 294–95, 297, 298, 300, 304, 308, 313
Choy, Ronald, 295, 299, 300, 301–302, 303, 304
Citizens Budget Commission, 301, 308
CITY computerized games, 118
Civilian agencies, PPBS and, 35–36
Club of Rome, 3, 20, 170
  other world model projects, 177–79
  role of, 179
CLUG. *See* Cornell Land Use Game
Coddington, Alan, 169
Coefficients (in models), 54
Cohen, Murray, 115
Collins, John, 143, 154, 156
Commoner, Barry, 165
Community Action Program, 29
Community Renewal Program model (San Francisco), 129–31
Complexity, 72–73
Complication, 72–73
Computer models, 48, 55–58
  econometric modeling, role of, 184–86
  Jamaica Bay simulation, 79–84
  linear programming and, 95–96
Conditional forecasting, 62
  model use for, 24–25
Consad Research Corporation, 117

Constants (in models), 54
Cooper, William W., 103
Cornell Land Use Game, 117–18
Costello, Timothy, 256
Council of Economic Advisers, 32
  full employment, role of, 10
  models, use of, 203
Counter modeling, 181
  political process and, 334
  of system dynamics, 145–46
  of urban dynamics model, 150, 151–52
  of world models, 170–76
Cowles, Alfred, 200
Cowles Commission for Research in Economics, 199, 200
Cowles Foundation for Research in Economics, 200
Craig, James A., 217
Crecine, John P., 117, 118
CRP model. *See* Community Renewal Program
Cuypers, J. G. M., 175–76

Dantzig, George B., 94–95
Data
  econometric modeling, role of, 187–89
  modeling process and, 70–74
  system dynamics, role of, 187–88
Data Resources, Inc., 78, 216–21
David, Edward E., 2, 21, 92
Decision making
  big decisions, 40–42
  domain of knowledge and, 27–42
    policy analysis and, 29–30
    policy evaluation and, 29
    policy research, role, 28–30
  incremental, 39–40
  operations research and, 100
  PPBS
    inside and outside Pentagon, 33–37
    movement, 32–33
Defense, Department of
  PPBS and, 32–37

Index

DEF model. *See* Duesenberry-Eckstein-Fromm model
Delays (system dynamics), 124
DeLeeuw, Frank F., 211
Derivation, function of model, 62–63
Dernburg, Thomas F., 202
Descriptive models, 59–60
DHL model, 202–203
Discrete programming, 103
Domain of knowledge, decision making and, 27–42
Domain of politics, 27, 28
Downs, Anthony, 44
DRI. *See* Data Resources, Inc.
DRI model, 208, 218, 230
Duesenberry, James S., 207, 208, 209
Duesenberry-Eckstein-Fromm model, 207–208
Dunlop, John T., 230
Dutton, John, 73
Dynamic models, 56–58
Dynamic programming, 103
Dynamics of Growth in a Finite World, 160

Ebbin, Steven, 83
Eckstein, Otto, 207, 208, 216–17, 218, 223, 229, 336
Econometric modeling, 76, 128, 183–230
  of American economy, 195–230
  computer, role of, 184–86
  data role in, 187–89
  development, 183–95
  economic theory and, 187
  Federal Reserve modeling and, 210–16
  Klein's Cowles Commission model, 200
  Michigan Quarterly Econometric model, 203
  national economies and, 189–90
  nature of the method, 186–95
  for policy modeling, 104–107
  recent progress, 183–95
  simulation technique compared to system dynamics model, 192–93
  specification in, 193–94
  SSRC-Brookings model, 207–10
  St. Louis model, 224–25
  Suits' model, 202
  time series data and, 190–91
Econometric modeling company, 216–24, 233
Econometric models, 14, 60
  of housing, 136–39
  simultaneous difference equations and, 190–91
  structural equations, 192
Economic Report of the President, 7–8
  GNP forecasts and, 8–9
Econometrics, 104
Economic Programming Language, 217–18
Economic theory
  econometric modeling and, 187
  input-output analysis and, 87–93
Ehrlich, Paul, 167
Employment Act of 1946, 10
Endogenous variables, 55
Energy crisis, 88
English, Joseph, 297
Enzler, Jared J., 214
EPL. *See* Economic Programming Language
Equilibrium in system dynamics, 125–26
Evans, Michael K., 205, 221, 230
Ex ante forecast, 68
Exogenous variable, 55
Experts, growing role of, 28
Ex post forecast, 68

Fair, Ray C., 225–26, 227, 230
Family Assistance Plan, 37, 38
  TRIM model and, 114
FAP. *See* Family Assistance Plan
Feasibility targeting, 62
Federal funding, land use modeling and, 120

Federal Reserve
  FRB-MIT-Penn model and, 211–14
  modeling and, 210–16
  monthly money market
    model, 215–16
  MPS model and, 212
  surtax episode, 213–14
Feldstein, Martin E., 218
Feldt, Allen G., 117
Fire Department, New York
    City, 249–85
  adaptive response proposal, 271
  compared to Health Services
    Administration, 310–12
  computer simulation, use of, 249
  computerized alarm processing
    system, 256, 257
  departmental communications
    system of, 254, 255–57
  difficulties of, 249–52
  extra part-time fire company
    proposal, 271
  Rand Corporation study and, 252
    differentiated roles, 314–16
    fire dispatchers and findings,
      261–63
  impact of research, 276–79
  impact of research setting, 280–85
    redefining the problem, 257–59
    research problems, 312–14
  Rand model
    testing proposed policies, 270–74
    work load negotiations and, 272–74
Fleisher, Aaron, 148
Ford, Gerald, 330, 331
Ford, L. R., Jr., 103
Forecasting
  Federal Reserve and, 215
  of GNP, 8–9
  models and, 336
  models used for, 24–25
Formal models, 48–59. *See also* Models
  defined, 48–49
  role-playing, 59
  schematic, 49–50
  symbolic, 51–58

Forrester, Jay W., 3–6, 71, 78, 120,
    121–22, 126, 141, 147, 151, 153,
    154, 156, 159, 162, 169, 171–72,
    181, 192, 229
FRB-MIT-Penn model, 211–14
Friedman, Milton, 12, 15, 136, 187
Frisch, Ragnar, 107, 195–96
Fromm, Gary, 71, 207, 208, 209, 217
Fulkerson, D. R., 103
Full employment, 8–9
Full-employment budget, 11
Full-employment model, 52–53

Gaines, Tilford, 167–68
Gale, David, 96
Gaming models. *See* Role-playing
    models
Garelik, Sanford, 296
Gateway Recreation Area, 82
Genealogy, of econometric models
    of the U.S. economy, 197
Gifford, Bernard, 245
Ginsberg, Allen, 295, 299, 300, 301
Global Dynamics Group, 175–76
GLOBE 5 model, 172
GLOSAS project, 144
GNP forecasts, 8–9
  calculation of, 10–11
  hearings concerning, 12–14
  LR model and, 16–17
  political factors in, 9–10
Goldberg, Michael A., 119
Goldberger, Arthur S., 201
Goldner, William, 116, 117, 118, 119
Gomory, Ralph A., 103
Gramlich, Edward M., 211, 213, 214
Graybeal, R. S., 117
Green, Edward W., 218
Green, George, 223
Growth, limits of, 2

Haavelmo, Trygve, 191, 199,
    200
Haber, Bernard D., 320
Haber, Herbert, 265
Hacker, David, 166

Index

Hall, Robert E., 217
Hancock, John, 115
Hansen, Alvin, 187
Hardin, Garrett, 166
Harris, Briton, 65, 157
Harris, Robert, 113, 295, 299
Hayes, Frederick O'R., 239, 240, 242, 257
Health, Education, and Welfare, Department of
system analysis and, 35
Health and Hospitals Corp., 288–89
Health Services Administration (N.Y.C.), 310–12
Fire Department (N.Y.C.), compared to
organizational renovation in, 294–96
Rand Corporation and, 287–88
obstacles to comprehensiveness in research, 293–94
poorly defined research tasks of, 290–91
research and administrative hostilities, 291–92
research problems, 312–14
Heineman, Ben W., 113
Helly, Walter, 149
Henderson, Hazel, 163
Herrera, A., 144
Hester, James, 148–49
Hicks, John, 187
Hitch, Charles, 32, 33
Holland, Robert, 211
Hospitals Department (N.Y.C.), 296–97
House, Peter, 118
Housing
econometric model of, 136–39
microanalytic model of, 128–31
system dynamics model of, 132–36
urban dynamics model, 146–58
Houthakker, Hendrik, 10
HSA. *See* Health Services Administration
HSA-Central, 293
Hudson-Jorgenson model, 220

Huxley, Julian, 164
Hybrid systems, 51
Hydraulic model of Jamaica Bay, 81
Hymans, Saul H., 202–203
Hypotheses as theory, 64–66

Iconic models. *See* Schematic models
Ignall, Edward, 268, 270, 273
IIPS. *See* Vancouver Regional Interinstitutional Policy Simulator
Income maintenance, 37–38
Income maintenance studies, 113–14
Incremental decision making, 39–40
modeling and, 45
Incrementalism, 44
Industrial Dynamics (Forrester), 120, 142
Ingels, D. M., 156
Ingram, Gregory, 148, 151, 153, 158
Input-output analysis, 87–93
national economy and, 108
Integer programming, 103
Intuitions, models and, 259–61
Isenberg, Steven, 252, 253, 266
Issues, attracting public notice to, 43–44
Iverson, Kenneth E., 90

Jamaica Bay simulation, 79–84
Johnson, Lyndon, 28

Kadanoff, Leo P., 76, 145–46, 149–50, 153
Kahn, Herman, 102
Kain, John, 149
Kant, Immanuel, 188
Kantorovich, Leonid V., 93
Kaufman, Herbert, 281
Kaya, Y., 144, 177
KCC. *See* Klein's Cowles Commission model
Kennedy, John F., 202
Keynes, John Maynard, 187
KG model. *See* Klein-Goldberger model
Kimball, George E., 98, 100

Klein, Lawrence, 104, 107, 126, 142, 144, 183–84, 185, 193, 199–200, 201–202, 203, 204, 205, 209–10, 218, 223, 225–26, 230
Klein, Rudolf, 3
Klein-Goldberger model, 184, 201
Klein's Cowles Commission model, 200
Kolesar, Peter, 306
Kono, Michael, 156
Koopman, B. O., 98
Koopmans, Tjalling C., 96, 199, 200
Krueckeburg, Donald A., 148
Kuh, Edwin, 209
Kuhn, H. W., 96
Kuznets, Simon, 104, 189

Lacey, Robert, 218
Laffer, Arthur B., 14, 17–18
Laffer-Ranson model, 14–19, 26, 48, 55, 62, 67
  criticism of, 20
  Pierce, James L., and, 16, 214–15
  political issues and, 19, 20, 21
Land-use analysis, 115–20
  Lowry model and, 116
Lane, Robert, 27, 42–43
Lang, Martin, 79, 80, 82
Lasswell, Harold, 323, 324
Laws as theory, 64
Lead poisoning study, 292
Lee, Douglas B., 118, 119
Leendertse, Jan J., 78, 336–37
  Jamaica Bay simulation and, 79–84
Le Mat, Mary Frances, 115
Leontief, Wassily W., 90, 91, 92
Levels (system dynamics), 121, 192
Lewis, Anthony, 165
Limits to Growth, The, 2–3, 21, 120–21, 142, 144, 145, 160, 161, 164, 179
Limits to growth model
  classification of responses to
    confrontationists, 168–69
    economic-optimists, 167–68
    Malthusian-pessimists, 166–67
    technological-optimists, 167

Lindblom, Charles, 39
Lindsay, John, 83, 238, 239, 240, 241, 242, 287, 294
Linear economics
  defined, 87
  input-output analysis, 87–93
  linear programming, 93–96
  two-person zero-sum games, 96–98
Linear programming, 93–96
Linear programming models, 60
LINK project, 144
Linstone, Harold A., 174–75
Lowell, Massachusetts, 154–56, 157
Lowery, Robert, 251
Lowry, Ira, 78, 116, 117, 126
Lowry model, 116
LR model. *See* Laffer-Ransom model
Lusher, David, 202

Macro models, 58
Macroeconomic models, 234–35
Maddox, John, 165
Mahoney, Michael, 113, 114
Maisel, Sherman J., 211
Malthus, Thomas R., 143
Mankind at the Turning Point (Mesarovic et al.), 177, 178–80
Mansholt, Sicco, 167
Marron, Donald B., 217
Marschak, Jacob, 126–27, 199
Martin, William McChesney, Jr., 210
Maryland Bureau of Air Quality Control, 70
Maryland Power Plant Siting Law, 69
Mass, Nathaniel J., 152
Massachusetts Institute of Technology, 5
Mathematical models, 53–55
Mathematical programming, 102
McClung, Nelson, 113
McCormick, David, 274, 275
McCracken, Paul W., 12
Meadows, Dennis, 2, 6, 78, 120, 162, 181
Meadows, Donella, 2, 6

Index 349

Mediating institutions, 231–45
  forging appropriate connecting
    links, 234–35
  need for, 232–34
  Rand Institute, 235–47
  role of, 338
  role-defining function of, 316–17
Mental model, 47–48
Mesarovic, Mihajlo, 144, 177
Methodological theory, 67
Methodologies
  for policy modeling, 85–139
    algebraic methods of operations
      research, 102–104
    econometric modeling, 104–107
    history, 85–87
    input-output analysis, 87–93
    land-use analysis, 115–20
    linear programming and, 93–96
    microanalysis, 107–15
    probabilistic methods of operations
      research, 98–102
    system dynamics, 120–27
    two-person zero-sum games, 96–98
Michigan Quarterly Econometric
  Model, 203
Microeconometrics. *See* Microanalysis
Microanalysis, 74, 107–15, 128
  model of housing, 128–31
  policy modeling methodology,
    107–15
  TRIM model, 114–15
Micro models, 58
Millikan, Max, 314
Minneapolis-St. Paul Metro Council,
  77
Mishan, E. J., 164
Mistaken-identity test, 126
Mitchell, George, 211
Mitchell, Herbert, 90
M. I. T. *See* Massachusetts Institute of
  Technology
MKE Associates, 221
MMM model. *See* Monthly money
  market model
Model analyzer, 339–40

Modelers
  bridge between modelers of
    different persuasions or
    methodologies, 180
  Leendertse, Jan J. as, 79–84
  policy modelers vis-à-vis policy
    makers, 180
  professional standards and, 338
  role of the, 76–78
Modeling
  in cross section, 47–84
  as a form of policy research, 23–46
  lessons concerning, 19–22
  LR model, 14–19
  mediating institutions, need
    for, 232–34
  national economy, 7–19
  policy analysis and, 30
  policy makers and, 322–26
  as political instrument, 21–22
  political process and
    in debate, 333–35
    expert, role, 335–37
    explicitness and conflict, 332–33
    nature of the problem, 320–28
  politics in, 329–30
  in the public eye, 1–22
  surtax episode, 213–14
  tension between modeling and
    politics, 330–32
  unconditional forecasting, uses of
    in, 24
Modeling process, 63–76
  data and validation, 70–74
  hypotheses and, 64–66
  institutionalizing of, 326–28
  methodology, 74–76
  theory, 64–70
Model of the world, 1–7
Models
  analysis of, 180
  behind the scenes use of, 20–21
  dynamic, 56–58
  in education of policy makers, 25
  effect of political context on and
    their usability, 44–45

Models *(Continued)*
  formal, 48–59
  intuition and, 259–61
  mathematical, 53–55
  micro and macro, 58
  policy modelers vis à vis policy makers, 180
  physical, 51
  political uses of, 45–46, 336
  purposes of, 59–62
  role-playing, 59
  schematic, 49–50
  static, 56
  symbolic, 51–58
  uses of, 24–26, 62–63
    conditional forecasting, 24–25
    information-producing, 24
Moeller, John, 114
Monetarist doctrine, 12, 187, 224
Monetarist St. Louis model, 224–25
Money supply
  GNP and, 12
  LR model and, 15
Monte Carlo simulation, 58, 101–102, 109
Monthly money market model, 215–16
Moore, Geoffrey, 212
Morgan, James, 110
Morrison, Peter A., 151
Morse, Philip M., 98, 100, 102, 110
MOSTEK Corporation, 155
Moynihan, Daniel Patrick, 29, 38, 113
MPS model, 212
MQEM. *See* Michigan Quarterly Econometric Model
Myrdal, Gunnar, 340
Multimodeling, 69
  hazards of, 69–70
  political process and, 334
Mumford, Lewis, 68

National economy
  econometric modeling and, 189–90
  Forrester model and, 181
  GNP forecasts, 8–9
  LR model, 14–19
  modeling the, 7–19
  models of the, 195–230
    table and chart of, 197–98
National (Resources) Planning Board, 31
NEP. *See* New economic policy
Nerlove, Marc, 218
New economic policy, 186
New Jersey guaranteed annual income experiment, 37–38
New York City, 99, 235–47
  urban dynamics model of housing market in, 150
New York City-Rand Institute, 83, 235–317, 328, 338. *See also* Rand Institute
  beginning of, 240–42
  demise of, 246–47
  problem of constituencies, 242–45
  state plans and objectives, 236–38
New York State Housing Finance Agency, 298
Nixon, Richard M., 21, 52, 186
Nixon administration
  full employment and, 8–9
  GNP forecasts and, 8–9
Nordhaus, William D., 163, 164
Normative models, 59
NUS Corporation, 69

OBE model, 204
Office of Economic Opportunity, 37–38
Office of Health Systems Planning (HSA), 295
Office of Program Analysis (HSA), 295
Office of Research and Statistics model, 114, 115
O'Hagan, John T., 251, 255, 256, 257, 279, 282
Oil shortage, 88
Okner, Benjamin A., 112
Okun, Arthur M., 84, 227–28
One-Bank Holding Act, 222
Operations research
  algebraic methods of, 102–104

Index

Monte Carlo simulation, 58, 101–02, 109
  probabilistic methods of, 98–102
Operations Research Council (N.Y.C.), 256
Optimization models, 60
O/R. *See* Operation research
Orchard-Hays, William, 95
Orcutt, Guy H., 109–11, 113, 115
Organic growth, 178
ORS model. *See* Office of Research and Statistics model

Pack, Janet, 76, 151
Parameters (in models), 54, 55
Parametric programming, 96
Passell, Peter, 145
Passer, Harold, 16
Peccei, Aurelio, 3, 6, 164–65
Pechman, Joseph A., 112
Pestel, Eduard, 144, 177
Peterson, Peter G., 2
Physical models, 51
Pierce, James L., 16, 214–15
Pittsburgh Community Renewal Program, 116
PLUM. *See* Projective Land Use Model
Policy analysis
  PPBS and, 33, 36–37
  simulation and, 30
Policy evaluators, 29, 30
Policy makers
  models and, 335
  policy modelers and, 180
  responsibilities of, 324–26
  role of, 322–24
Policy making, models and, 320–21
Policy modeling
  methodologies for, 85–139
    algebraic methods, 102–104
    econometric modeling, 104–107
    input-output analysis, 87–93
    land use analysis, 115–20
    linear programming, 93–96
    microanalysis, 107–15

    probabilistic methods, 98–102
    system dynamics, 120–27
  use of, 336
Policy models, 63
Policy research
  big decisions and, 40–42
  decision making and domain of knowledge, 27–42
  forms of, 28–30
  historical antecedents, 31–32
  incremental decision making and, 39–40
  modeling as form of, 23–46
    disappointments of, 26–27
    uses of, 24–26
  political context of, 42–46
  PPBS movement, 32–33
  social experimentation and, 37–38
Political process
  adversary modeling and, 334
  counter modeling and, 334
  modeling and, 319–41
    in debate, 333–35
    expert, role, 335–37
    explicitness and conflict, 332–33
    nature of the problem, 320–28
Political uses of models, 45–46
Politics
  in modeling, 329–30
  tension between modeling and politics, 330–32
Pool, Ithiel de Sola, 111
POPSIM model, 115
PPBS. *See* Program Planning Budgeting System
Prescriptive models, 59, 60
President's Commission on Income Maintenance, 113
Pressman, William, 81–82
Pressure groups, 43
Price, Don K., 43
Principles as theory, 64
Principles of Systems (Forrester), 120, 121
Private consultants, New York City and, 243

Probabilistic methods of operations research, 98–102
Program Planning Budgeting System.
　civilian agencies and, 35–36
　inside and outside the Pentagon, 33–37
　Johnson, Lyndon, and, 28
　movement, 32–33
　New York City use of, 239
Projections, 62
Projective Land Use Model, 118
Projector, Dorothy, 114
Proxmire, William, 8, 13, 14
Pugh-Roberts Associates, 78

Quadratic programming, 103
Quarterly models, 203–204
Queueing theory, 302, 306, 307

Rademaker, O., 125, 175–76
Rand Corporation, 34, 239–40
Rand Institute, 83, 235–317, 328, 338
　Health and Hospitals Corp. and, 288–89
　health project team of, 289–90
　Health Services Administration and, 287–88
　　obstacles to comprehensiveness in research, 293–94
　　poorly defined research tasks of, 290–91
　　research problems, 312–14
　hospital bed utilization model
　　beginning problems, 299–301
　　conducting the study, 301–304
　　political setting and, 297–308
　　problems of implementation, 304–308
　New York City Fire Department and, 252
　　call on, 265–67
　　differentiated roles, 314–16
　　impact of research and, 276–79
　　impact of research setting, 280–85
　　research problem, 312–14
　　simulation model of, 267–70
　　testing proposed policies, 270–74
　　union participation, 274–76
　　workload issue, 266–67
　simulation, use of, 101
Random sampling, 101
Ranson, R. David, 14, 17, 18
Rates (system dynamics), 121, 192
Referential theory, 66–67
Rider, Kenneth L., 150, 153
Ridker, Ronald, 168
RIM model, 113–14
Rochberg, Richard, 148
Rockstroh, Jay, 76
Rockwell, Willard F., Jr., 320
Role-playing models, 59
Roosevelt, Franklin D., 31, 189
Rothenberg, Jerome, 158
Rothkopf, Michael H., 145
Routine models, 63
Rubin, Herman, 199

St. Louis model, 224–25
Samuelson, Paul, 9, 92, 142, 187, 195, 199
San Francisco Community Renewal Program model, 129–31
Sayre, Wallace, 280–81
Schematic models, 49–50
Schistosomiasis study, 292
Schroeder, Walter W., 150–51, 154, 155–56
Schulz, James H., 115
Scott, Peter, 164
Sector-by-sector analysis, 13
Shapiro, Harold, 203
Shell Laboratories in Amsterdam, 170–71
Shubik, Martin, 163
Shultz, George, 13, 14, 17, 52, 53, 236
Simon, William, 52–53
Simulation
　comparison of econometric models and system dynamics model techniques, 192–93
　Monte Carlo, 58, 101–102, 109
　policy analysis and, 30

Index

Simulation gaming, 25
Simulation models, 60, 61–62
   of Fire Department (N.Y.C.), 267–70
Sinai, Allen, 218
Slessor, Malcolm, 168
Smith, Howard K., 3, 168
Social experimentation, 37–38
Social science, increasing role of, 28
Social System Research Institute, 111
Socolow, Robert, 176
Solomon, Ezra, 203
Solow, Robert M., 67, 168, 202
South Bronx, 268
Specification of a model, 193–94
Spring Creek Water Pollution Control facility, 80
SSRC-Brookings model, 207–10
Starbuck, William, 73
Static models, 56
Statistical economics
   econometric modeling, 104–107
   microanalysis, 107–15
   See also Econometrics
Status variables, 55
Stein, Herbert, 10, 11, 52, 53
Sternlieb, George, 158
Stochastic models, 58
Stonebreaker, Michael J., 152–53
Structural equations, 192
Suits, Daniel B., 202
Suits' University of Michigan model, 202
Sullivan, James L., 154, 155, 156
Surtax episode, modeling and, 213–14
Survey Research Center, 110
Swersey, Arthur, 257–58, 259, 260, 261, 262, 279, 336
Symbolic models, 51–58
   computer, 55–58
   mathematical, 53–55
   verbal, 52–53
Synthesis, 49
Systems analysis, PPBS and, 33
System dynamics, 4, 5, 120–28, 141–82
   checking and analysis of models in, 180–81
   counter modeling of, 145–46
   data, role in, 187–88
   delay, role in, 124–25
   equilibrium and, 125–26
   feedbacks in, 122–24
   housing model and, 132–36
   legacy of controversy and, 141–46
   limits to growth model and, 164–70
   as methodology for policy modeling, 120–27
   methodology of, 75
   national economy model and, 181
   simulation technique compared to econometric modeling, 192–93
   simultaneous equations and, 191–92
   table functions in, 124
   urban dynamics model, 146–58
   world models and, 158–79
System dynamics model
   checking and analysis of, 180–81
   delay, role in, 124–25
   equilibrium and, 125–26
   feedbacks in, 122–24
   of housing, 132–36
   national economy model and, 181
   simulation technique compared to econometric model, 192–93
   table functions and, 124
Szanton, Peter, 240, 241, 242, 243, 244, 246, 257, 258

Table function, 124
Tactical control units, 276
Tax reform, microanalysis and, 111–12
Terenzio, Joseph, 296
Theory, 49
   methodological, 66–67
   modeling process and, 64–70
   referential, 66–67
Third-party model analysis, 339–40
Thurow, Lester C., 218
Tideman, Nicholas, 115
Time-Oriented Metropolitan model, 117, 118

Time series data, 187, 190–91
Time Series Processor, 217
Tinbergen, Jan, 106–107, 195, 196
Tinbergen's League of Nations model, 196–99
TLN model. *See* Tinbergen's League of Nations model
Tobin, James, 202
TOMM. *See* Time Oriented Metropolitan Model
TPZS. *See* Two-person zero-sum games
Train, Russell E., 169
TRIM, 114
TSP. *See* Time Series Processor
Tucker, A. W., 96
Turing test, 126
Two-person zero-sum games, 96–98
Two-platoon system, 277–78

UDM. *See* Urban Development model
UFOA. *See* Uniformed Fire Officers Association
Ulam, Stanislaw M., 101
Unconditional forecasting, 62
 model use for, 24, 25
Undifferentiated growth, 178
Uniformed Firefighters Association, 263, 275, 276, 278
Uniformed Fire Officers Association, 263, 275, 278
Universal constant, 54
Urban Development model, 119
Urban Dynamics (Forrester), 120, 122, 132, 142
Urban dynamics model, 132–36
 applications of, 153–57
  Anaheim, Calif. and, 156–57
  Lowell, Mass., 154–56
 conclusions of, 146–47
 counter modeling of, 150, 151–52
 nature of responses to, 157–58
 response to, 147–53
Urban Institute, 111, 233, 338
Urban models, 119

U.S. Army Corps of Engineers Jamaica Bay simulation, 80–81
U. S. economy, models of the, 195–230
 table and chart of, 197–98
Utsumi, Takeshi, 144

Validation, modeling process and, 70–74
Vancouver Regional Inter-institutional Policy Simulator, 119
Variables (in models), 54
Verbal models, 52–53
Verification, 70
Volkswagen Foundation, 3, 177
Von Neumann, John, 96, 97, 101, 196

Waddington, C. H., 164
WAI model. *See* Wharton Annual and Industry model
Wald, A., 96
Wallich, Henry C., 165
Warden, Charles B., Jr., 220
Washington, D.C., Council of Governments, 76
Watt, Kenneth, 144
WEFA. *See* Wharton Econometric Forecasting Associates
Welfare reform, 111–12, 113
Wharton Annual and Industry model, 206–207
Wharton Econometric Forecasting Associates, 207, 223
Wharton EFU model, 205–206
Wharton Mark III model, 206
Wharton merged model, 205–206
Wharton model, 184, 204
Whitehead, Alfred North, 48
W-III model. *See* Wharton Mark III model
Wilensky, Gail, 113
Wilensky, Harold, 41
Wilson, John, 222
WM model. *See* Wharton merged model
Wold, Abraham, 196
Wolfe, Philip, 103

Work load negotiations with Fire Department (N. Y. C.), 272–74, 281
World Dynamics (Forrester), 5, 6–7, 120, 124, 142, 159, 162
World models, 158–79, 181
 counter modeling of, 170–76
 system dynamics methodology application, 5–6
 World2, 5–6, 125, 159–60
 World3, 7, 19–21, 23, 25, 55, 158–61, 172–76
WO model. *See* Wharton model
World2 model, 5–6, 125
 backcasting and, 174
 Boyd, Robert, counter model, 171–72

GLOBE 5, 172
 response to, 161–64
 simulation of, 159–60
 Sussex analysis of, 172–73
World3 model, 3, 7, 19–21, 23, 25, 55, 158–61, 172–76
 initial reaction to, 20
 political issues and, 19, 20, 21
 response to, 6–7
 simulation of, 160–61
 Sussex analysis, 173–74
 use of, 25–26
World problematique, 3, 4–5
Wright, Richard D., 174

Zarnowitz, Victor, 68, 205